James C. Miller

James C. Miller

*A Pictographic History of
the Oglala Sioux*

A

Pictographic History

of the

Oglala Sioux

Drawings by Amos Bad Heart Bull
Text by Helen H. Blish
Introduction by Mari Sandoz

UNIVERSITY OF NEBRASKA PRESS · LINCOLN

Manufactured in the United States of America

To Jean M. and William H. Blish

Publisher's Preface

THE publication of *A Pictographic History of the Oglala Sioux*, termed by Mari Sandoz "the most important single publishing venture, by volume, of the Great Plains," would be a noteworthy event under any circumstances. The conditions surrounding the discovery, analysis, and ultimate publication of the Amos Bad Heart Bull picture history—an effort spanning some forty years and involving the efforts of many people—only add to its significance.

The pictographic record, a series of more than four hundred drawings and script notations made in an old ledger book by Amos Bad Heart Bull, an Oglala Sioux from the Pine Ridge Reservation, between 1890 and the time of his death in 1913, passed into the possession of the artist's sister, Dollie Pretty Cloud. In 1926, Helen Blish, a graduate student at the University of Nebraska, while looking for objects of Indian art learned of the existence of the picture history from W. O. Roberts, chief clerk at that time and later superintendent of the Pine Ridge Agency. She later described her first view of the ledger book:

> In a little one-room cabin, chinked with mud and having only a dirt floor, I met the present owner of the Bad Heart Bull manuscript, [Mrs. William Pretty Cloud] . . . . I made known my desire to see the book (through an interpreter, for she speaks no English); and without hesitation she lifted the lid of a small cheap trunk and drew out the manuscript. To her, too, it is a treasure, for it is the painstaking depiction of a critical time in the life of her people; but, more, it is a depiction done by the hand of her brother who is now dead. And there is no doubting the strong bond of affection that binds her loyally to him. A portrait sketch of him, done in pencil by Dollie's husband, hangs near the bureau . . . . Her pride in him, though she says but little, is at all times evident; and she has not yet been able to bring herself to part permanently with this manuscript, his handiwork.

It was only with great difficulty that Miss Blish was able to persuade Mrs. Pretty Cloud to allow her to use the book on a year-to-year basis for a modest annual fee between 1927 and 1940. Alternating between her teaching position in a Detroit high school and graduate work at the University, Miss Blish spent her vacations interviewing informants, chiefly He Dog and Short Bull on the Pine Ridge Reservation, often accompanied by John Colhoff, the official agency interpreter. Her major advisor at the University, Professor Hartley Burr Alexander, chairman of the Department of Philosophy and a noted student of Indian art and religion, took a keen interest in her project of analyzing and interpreting the pictographic history; and through his help she received two grants from the Carnegie Institution— one in 1927 and one the following year. She presented her master's thesis, "The Amos Bad Heart Bull Manuscript. A Native Pictographic Historical Record of the Oglala Dakota," in 1928, and in 1934 submitted to the Carnegie Institution a more comprehensive, three-volume report, which was later deposited in the American Museum of Natural History. Although publication of the report was strongly recommended by members of the archaeological and anthropological staffs of the Carnegie Institution and the American Museum, funds were unavailable then because of the Depression; and with Miss Blish's untimely death in 1941 the project lapsed.

When Mrs. Pretty Cloud died in 1947, the ledger book, a cherished personal possession, was buried with her, after the Sioux custom. In 1959 the University of Nebraska Press, having decided to publish the picture history, sought the permission of Mrs. Pretty Cloud's heirs to disinter the ledger long enough that all the drawings could be photographed in color and a permanent record made of them. All attempts were unsuccessful; one of Mrs. Pretty Cloud's descendants explained the family's position: "When that document was buried with my aunt, it was a treasured thing to her. . . . [It] is and was the belief on the part of my folks that when that was buried it was intended to be buried. The sacredness of the person, the respect for the deceased and her wish was such that a young person like me cannot sway or budge [them] one inch away from their conviction."

Fortunately, however, Professor Alexander had had the entire ledger book photographed page by page, at his own expense, when Helen Blish first rented it in 1927; two sets of prints were made at that time—one for Professor Alexander and one for Miss Blish. In the early 1930's Professor Alexander had some thirty enlargements made and colored by hand after the original drawings, and twenty-two of them were published in 1938 by a French firm, C. Szwedzicki, in a folio entitled *Sioux Indian Painting*, edited by Professor Alexander. None of the other drawings have previously been published.

The purpose of the University of Nebraska Press in publishing the Amos Bad Heart Bull pictographic history of the Oglala Sioux is to make available a major contribution to Indian art and ethnology, the text of which has previously been available only in manuscript form and the drawings, with the exceptions just noted, not at all. Although it is recognized that, after thirty years, advances in anthropology may have dated certain minor portions of the text, no attempt has been made to edit the research. Miss Blish's work stands on its own merits. The significance of this volume lies in the unparalleled combination of drawings and interpretation; time has not detracted from the achievement of the whole.

Publication of the Bad Heart Bull pictographic history has entailed the co-operative efforts of numerous individuals; we can mention here only those who made major contributions, although many others also gave valuable assistance. First and foremost, we owe a debt of gratitude beyond measure to Mrs. Nevill Joyner of Camden, South Carolina, and Mrs. Clyde J. Huston of Columbus, Ohio, Helen Blish's sisters, for providing a manuscript copy of Miss Blish's 1934 report and her set of photographs of the drawings, in addition to other manuscript materials used by Miss Blish in her work with the ledger book, and for giving so freely of their time in answering questions and filling in background details. We are likewise deeply indebted to Professor Hubert Alexander, who generously furnished his father's set of photographs of the Bad Heart Bull drawings, making it possible to fill in certain gaps that existed, as well as a complete set of his color prints. Mari Sandoz encouraged publication of this book in every way possible and took precious time from her own work during the last year of her life to write an introduction. Thanks are also due C. Szwedzicki of Nice, France, for permission to use the color plates published in Part II, "The Art of Amos Bad Heart Buffalo," of *Sioux Indian Painting*, edited by Hartley Burr Alexander (1938).

Among the persons who aided Helen Blish in her work on the Bad Heart Bull manuscript, Dollie Pretty Cloud and Professor H. B. Alexander were of special importance. Mrs. Pretty Cloud, in allowing Miss Blish to take the ledger book from the Reservation and use it over a period of years, made a great personal sacrifice without which the photographing of the drawings and Miss Blish's study of them would never have been possible. Through the years Professor Alexander provided encouragement, as well as material assistance in the form of efforts to obtain financial support and publication of Miss Blish's work. John Colhoff as interpreter and Short Bull, He Dog, and Samuel Charger, a Sans Arc Sioux from the Cheyenne River Reservation, as informants played central roles. W. O. Roberts, Mark Marston, the Reverend Dr. Nevill Joyner, and Father Eugene Buechel gave of their time and energy. The Carnegie Institution assisted with two grants; and the interest of Dr. A. V. Kidder, Chairman of the Division of Historical Research of the Carnegie Institution; Dr. John C. Merriam, President of the Carnegie Institution; Dr. Frederick P. Keppel, President of the Carnegie Corporation; and Dr. Clark Wissler, Curator-in-Chief of the Department of Anthropology, American Museum of Natural History, was gratifying.

Contents

List of Color Plates

Following page 10

List of Illustrations

LIST OF ILLUSTRATIONS

LIST OF ILLUSTRATIONS

LIST OF ILLUSTRATIONS

Introduction

THE old Teton Sioux had a saying, "A people without history is like wind on the buffalo grass." They were perhaps the most history-conscious of all the North American tribes; the Oglalas, one of the seven Teton council fires, probably the most concerned with their past; the work of Amos Bad Heart Bull surely the epitome of Oglala Sioux picture histories.

Many considered the Oglalas the most imaginative, temperamental and volatile, and quarrelsome of the Tetons. Far back in the pre-horse times, when the travois, the drags, were drawn by powerful dogs, small summer parties from the various Sioux villages around the headwaters of the Mississippi went out to the buffalo plains to make meat and hides for the winter. According to the old stories the first of these Teton hunters to remain on the Plains was a party of Oglalas sometime before 1640. Their division name is said to mean "scattered" or "scattered into small bands," perhaps over some internal dispute before that first group forded the Missouri at Old Crossing, near the present Verendrye National Monument in North Dakota, and never turned their faces east again.

Even after the Oglalas all moved west threats of rifts recurred, and became real with the whiskey killing of a chief, Bull Bear, by the young warrior Red Cloud from another band. This split of 1841 was not healed even superficially for approximately thirty years. Finally, at a Washington suggestion, Red Cloud, then the government chief, made Little Wound, called a grandson of Bull Bear, one of his subchiefs. The shaky solidarity of the Oglalas was threatened again when No Water's wife went away with Crazy Horse, the love of her girlhood. This was the privilege of every Sioux wife, particularly after she had dispatched her duties to the family by bringing a substantial and often older man to their ranks. But No Water lacked the poise expected of a Sioux husband. He followed his wife, wounded Crazy Horse, and set two factions against each other in fierce fraternal threat. Because Crazy Horse, as a

Shirtwearer, had vowed to put the good of his people first in all things, he had to give the woman back to avoid splitting the Oglalas as a rock is split by a powerful blow, but the rift was never really healed.

As might be expected of so volatile a people, the Oglalas produced three of the outstanding ten, twelve men of all the Tetons in the struggle against the encroaching white man. Each of the three was an inspired fighter against the army: Sitting Bull the Good, who used his gun only for the protection of the white man after he made peace in 1868; Red Cloud, whose war prowess and leadership forced the government to retreat from the Bozeman Trail forts in 1868; Crazy Horse, that intrepid cousin of Amos Bad Heart Bull, who led the Oglala hostiles through the Custer fight to the end of the buffaloes and the possibility of maintaining life off the reservations.

The talents of the Oglalas showed themselves in other ways besides genius in war, the hunt, and strength in the councils. They were outstanding in the preservation of band and tribal history and in art, conspicuously tied to the historical recordings in peoples without a written language. There were numerous and extensive winter counts among the Tetons, some covering well over three hundred years, in which each winter, each year, is identified by the picture representation of an outstanding event. More of these have apparently been kept by, and preserved from the Oglalas than from any other division of the Tetons. They show changes in the social outlook as well as in the art presentation after the coming of the horse, which was perhaps the most important single factor in both. The horse was the first readily negotiable property of universal value that the Sioux possessed, and made an Indian on the Plains not only a mobile warrior and hunter but a capitalist, changing much of his largely communal society.

Still, certain basic responsibilities, such as general defense and food for everyone, remained from the dog-travois days to the reservation period. The helpless ones must always be protected, and so long as anyone in the village had meat, everyone ate. The horse facilitated the discharge of both of these responsibilities and brought in a new occupation and pastime. Stealing horses became not only a joyous pursuit but was as respected an occupation as stealing customers from a business rival in white society. A youth got much of his standing in the community, his eligibility as a husband and member of his future wife's family, through his proficiency as a catcher of horses from among the wild mustangs and particularly from the herds of his enemies.

Actually, no aspect of Plains Indian life remained untouched by the horse. One important impact was increased protection and enlargement of buffalo grounds and the development of the great organized hunts for winter meat and robes. There was also the mobility brought to the women and the easing of the burdens they had always carried so that the men could have both hands free on the bow and the spear against any attacking animal or ambushing enemy, and for game that flushed within the short range of the weapons and the running moccasin. With the horse the distances fell back as the horizon retreated, extending not only the field of activities but the imagination and the artistic eye, both stimulated by the beauty of the animal itself, particularly in motion, as they were wherever the horse appeared, whether in the prehistoric, the antiquarian or the classical worlds.

The art of the Sioux served the double purpose of adornment and the recording of historical personages and events. To most of the Indians, except band historians and recorders like Amos Bad Heart Bull, art was largely concerned with costume, regalia, and heraldic ornamentation, the paint and feathers of the warrior and chieftain, the pattern and adornment of the pipe, the calumet. This ornamentation was always basically geometric, even the animals and man, for the full-blood Sioux. Floral and twining designs were for white blood—white men and mixed-bloods.

The designs and portrayals on lodge, pipe, arrows, shields, and regalia were owned by the man; the designs of moccasin, shirt, and dress, quilled, painted or in beads, the ornamentation of the parfleche and cradleboards were the property of the woman. These designs, man's and woman's, and the patterns for the things adorned with them, as well as the good name of the family, the stories of exploits and honors were all that was inherited. As the old Sioux liked to say,

"Only those things not made less by division are to be passed on." Other property, such as horses, bows, guns, powder, blankets, and robes, was distributed at the owner's death in the Giveaway dance, usually to the less fortunate and the needy. Amos Bad Heart Bull painted an excellent picture of a Giveaway.

Every Sioux child was an artist and learned not only to read the pictured instructions and directions left on buffalo skulls, in sand or mud, or on barked patches of trees, but to draw messages for others. In this way reports of moves, destinations, and happenings were left for later comers and passers along the trails. Often these were in great detail, as the accounts of the sun dance of 1876, left behind in the Rosebud River valley, told the story of Sitting Bull's vision of soldiers falling into his camp. These picture accounts were easily read by other bands, even other tribes, as easily as the crossed brush laid at a lodge door to tell that the owners were away.

In addition to the artistic development and ornamentation of the various accoutrements of Sioux life, there were the picture autobiographies, often valuable as art as well as history, the accounts called "brag skins" by the more humorous of the old Indians, rather like *Who's Who* entries of achievement, particularly the autobiographies on skins or cloth or paper drawn during the agency period when the Indians, technically at least, were prisoners of war and too often bound to please some white man of the military, agency, or ministry. Traditionally the exploit skins were to make heroes of the autobiographers, in the later period usually at the expense of other tribes, with no identifiable white men because that might bring avenging and retribution now that the Indians were helpless.

In addition to the utilitarian and artistic purposes of picture writing, and the strictly autobiographical, there are the historical records and accounts kept by the band historian of the Sioux, apparently developed to the highest degree among the Oglalas. The calling of band historian was as honorable as that of a great warrior, hunter, or holy and medicine man, and more select. There was only one at a time in the band, although the man was expected to develop a successor, either a son or nephew. If there was none of these, some other promising youth was selected, the historian and his wife his second parents, their lodge the youth's second home, easier and more casual than his own formal one, where, after he was seven years old, he could never address his mother or his sisters directly but must always speak through a third person.

The requirements of a band historian were largely two. First there must be objectivity, the ability to be in a fight or a ceremonial or hunt and yet view it beyond the purely personal involvement, observe what happened all around, see it with the eye of the people as well as an individual. The second requirement was the artistic ability to portray the event or the incident so others could grasp the action and the meaning, with something beyond the factual content, something broader, more, as the Sioux liked to say, of the sky and the great directions, a meaning more elevated, more profound.

The pictures were varied, showing the events of band life: ceremonials, hunts, moves, buffalo stampedes, floods, fires, all the happenings. The battle scenes must not only suggest the action and the outcome but depict the partisan combatants in the pertinent regalia so they could be recognized, not necessarily as they went into war, which was usually stripped to breechclout, moccasins, and paint. In the picture histories the warrior was usually shown with all the accoutrements of his warrior-society connections: the elaborate and expensive ceremonial tails, perhaps the special paintings, hair arrangement, and the official feather headdress of his rank in the society. His personal identification was shown by his shield and paintings and accoutrements, too, perhaps even with the long-tailed ceremonial warbonnet, because all these were as surely indicators of his name as "John Jones" identifies the white man, more, for the Indian's personal marks were never exactly duplicated.

These formal band histories had to have the approval of the headmen and be above the challenge of anyone involved. During ceremonials, particularly those honoring a group or a man (as the honoring of Amos Bad Heart Bull's uncle, He Dog) or when important visitors from other bands, divisions or tribes came visiting, the historian might be called upon to recite some appropriate deed or testing. He would unroll his picture skin or later, when paper became available, open his book and recount the event from his portrayal.

"The picture is the rope that ties memory solidly to the stake of truth," was the saying of the old band historians.

Sometimes there were unhappy events to record, not only storms and floods and stampedes and the

death of a great man, as Amos Bad Heart Bull's "Chief Crazy Horse," but stories of a man who had to be driven out, ostracized. In Sioux society of the buffalo days it was possible to become as free a man as has ever been known. A youth was expected to discharge his duties to his family, his band, and his tribe, largely the duties of the boy, the young warrior, the young hunter. When once they were honorably fulfilled he was free to be anything he could envision, anything he wished, with no one to say "No!"

But if the youth set his moccasins upon a bad road and became a troublemaker, he was first warned, then spoken to quietly by a group of the respected men, and finally he faced a vote of ostracism, a driving out for a varying length of time up to the usual four years for murder. A society without jails cannot tolerate a troublemaker; with no locks, no thief; with no paper to record a man's word, no liar.

In the picture histories of the North American Indian that reached white-man notice surely the most comprehensive, the finest, is the one by Amos Bad Heart Bull, and only the accident of a Helen H. Blish brought this to any attention before it reached the customary interment with the body of the last close relative.

Helen Blish, with her early familiarity with Indians and the Indian mind, her historical training, her inquiring mind, her even and humorous temperament, was the best person for the interpretation and study of this picture history. I recall the first time she showed me the ledger filled with the Amos Bad Heart Bull pictures. She opened the worn cover to the account of the Reno fight in the Battle of the Little Bighorn. I knew about Indian paintings and drawings from early childhood, had watched an old buffalo-hunting Sioux unroll a big skin and tell of his accomplishments, and had seen small children read the pictures left by their mothers in the dust, telling where they had gone, what was to be done. I was familiar with artistic Indian decorations of many kinds, and the winter counts, and historical portrayals, but I had never seen anything to equal the astonishing narrative content of the Bad Heart Bull pictures, nothing with the development of movement and suspense, or the sustained artistic qualities, particularly in the presentation of the horses and groups of people.

The Bad Heart Bull family belonged to the Hunkpatila band whose place was last in the Oglala camp circle, just north of the opening that was always to the east, always toward the rising sun.★ The family was related in some degree around most of the circle, into most of the other six bands, particularly to Red Cloud's Bad Faces, Old Smoke's people. They were warriors and council chiefs, with several members of the very select and honored Shirtwearers' Society, a small group of the Oglalas chosen from among their leaders for special honor and duties, and committed to very special vows: to walk in humility, walk as the poorest of the people, whose good must always come first, and to hold themselves invulnerable to all praise and blame and abuse.

"If a dog lifts his leg to my lodge I will not see it."

To have a Shirtwearer uncle, He Dog, a band historian father, old Bad Heart Bull, and a cousin, Crazy Horse, perhaps the greatest war leader of the entire Sioux nation, within one close-knit family suggests something of the potential of the Oglalas. Still, such connections can be a great handicap instead of a strong motivation to a youth who finds himself growing up in the humiliation of an Indian reservation from 1881 through the shocking butchery of Wounded Knee in 1890, when women and children were mowed down by Hotchkiss guns in the freezing cold of a late December day. To this son of the Bad Heart Bull family, the life that had made his people great was closed, and yet the past was a stimulus that showed its power early. Young Amos had the artistic gift of the Indian child to a high degree; and despite agency taboos, overt and subtle, against tribal rituals and ceremonials, even the recounting of tribal history, the youth sought out the stories of his people. He gathered all the white-man documents and books about the Sioux that he could locate. His father had died early but three of the man's brothers lived well into the 1930's, with clear memories. One of them, He Dog, was the brother chieftain of Crazy Horse, well informed and dedicated to the most honorable way of life of the old buffalo-hunting days. He and his brother Short Bull had held out with the hostiles to the last, and kept the knowledge of the old ways fresh in their minds.

Unmilitary, disinterested in warlike activities, young Amos became the contemplative artist who probed to the essence of whatever he portrayed. His horses run, his Indians posture, parade, and fight. Without the formal restrictions of the regular band historian, whose pictures had to win the approval of the band officers, Amos was free to follow his artistic eye, his own interests, in portraying his people objectively, with factual meaning and the larger implications beyond. Not that he failed to follow certain conventions of the band historian. In the fight pictures he shows the horses' tails tied up in the sign of war, the tails loose when the attack was sudden and unexpected. He makes no attempt at facial resemblances, showing little differentiation between individuals except in hair arrangement, in addition to the paint and accoutrements. The enemy is given the usual treatment—shown stripped to breechclout and moccasins without individual identification, the only tribal hint in the hair, such as the Crow roach.

In these usual things Amos Bad Heart Bull excells, but he has added a great deal generally omitted by the band historian. His fine understanding of the beauty of the horse permeates much of his art, as the horse influenced the society of the hunting Sioux. Even in the pictures of the Reno fight the horses are the dynamic element—the formal march of the soldier attack, the thrust of the charging Indians, and once more the formal march, but this time the Indians with their captured cavalry horses. The picture of the moving camp in all its conventional panoply and array, with the pipe bearers walking ahead, the warriors out in front and all around, the travois in the center, the women and girls in their finest adornments, the youths riding along outside, showing off, tells more than a whole book could of the orderly life of the Plains Sioux.

The artist includes much that is social history and social commentary, from the most ceremonial of dances and honorings through various warrior and honor societies, and the subsidiary ceremonies, such as the magnificent and humorous picture of the Grass Dance, with the dog looking out of the stew pot, down to the ordinary village activities, even work and the courtship customs, including the "standing in the blanket" as the Indians called it.

Without doubt the Amos Bad Heart Bull picture history is the most comprehensive, the finest statement as art and as report of the North American Indian so far discovered anywhere.

MARI SANDOZ

★[Miss Sandoz is in error here, for Miss Blish indicates later (p. 402) that the artist's family belonged to the Bad Face (Ite Sica) band of Oglalas, a statement which was reconfirmed in 1967 by a direct descendant of the artist in a telephone conversation with the editor.—ed. note]

*A Pictographic History of
the Oglala Sioux*

Foreword

A FEW very brief explanations are necessary. In the first place, there is the matter of abbreviations used in footnotes. Because of the frequent reference to certain source publications, I have resorted to the following denotations: *APAMNH* for *Anthropological Papers of the American Museum of Natural History*; *ARBAE* for *Annual Report of the Bureau of American Ethnology*; BAE in connection with bulletins of the Bureau of American Ethnology; and *Am. Anthrop.* for *American Anthropologist*.

Second, my use of the term *Lakota* may deserve a bit of explanation. Where reference is made to the tribe as a whole, I have used the general and better-known spelling *Dakota*. But where my reference is to the Oglala (Teton) division, I have used the former spelling in keeping with the literation peculiar to that dialect.

Third, in my page-by-page editing in Part Two, I have tended for the most part to mere allusion to already published material on the subject in hand and to discussion chiefly of new materials or to the pointing up of contrasts with the findings of older authorities. I have at no time intended or attempted a complete revamping of all of the available published material on any subject.

And finally, my chief Indian informants have been two old men, He Dog (*Sunka Bloka*) and Short Bull (*Tatanka Ptecela*), of the Pine Ridge Reservation, South Dakota.

HELEN H. BLISH

[N.B. Throughout her manuscript Miss Blish used the correct literal translation of the artist's family name, *Tatanta Cante Sica*: "Bad Heart Buffalo." The form "Bad Heart Bull" is used herein, however, because that is the translation carried on government rolls and consequently is the name by which the family is commonly known. "Short Buffalo" has likewise been changed to "Short Bull." —*ed. note*]

Part One

CHAPTER I

The Artist and His Work

THE discovery of the intimate record of the life of a people is at no time an insignificant event. If, however, such a record is found portrayed in a way which combines artistic manner of expression with seeming authenticity, the significance deepens; interest broadens; and students of the history of peoples must give heed lest something of value in the interpretation of a particular culture—and consequently all culture —be lost.

Of such import is the pictorial record created by the young Oglala Dakota Amos Bad Heart Bull, whose other and personal name was Eagle Lance. He lived during that period of Dakota history when the tribal life was fraught with danger and seething with restlessness, the period in which not only the traditional warfare with hereditary Indian enemies but also intense reaction against the encroachments of the white race occupied the western Sioux. The outline of the contents of the young Indian's record (Part Two, Chapter VI) indicates not only an extensive but also an intensive treatment of the history of the Oglalas during that time. The artist intends to give a thorough description of the life of the tribe over the period with which he himself came into closest contact and of which he consequently has clearest knowledge.

He was born in 1869 in what is now Wyoming and so was too young to take part in the fighting of the tribe during the last struggles against its enemies—red and white. He had ample opportunity, however, to become acquainted with those phases of the older tribal organizations that existed, or the tribal movements and wars which took place, before his own time. His father and uncles,[1] until comparatively late, took a decided stand against the whites and the government. They played an active part in more than one battle against the troops, as well as against their old-time enemies the Crows and Shoshonis; and they unquestionably told Amos, on many occasions and in great detail, of the battles and their results.

It was largely from them that he secured the material which made possible the several portrayals of the Battle of the Little Big Horn, which hold such a prominent place in his narrative. Young though he was at the time of the Custer fight, certain childish and vivid impressions of the battle were left upon the mind of the boy himself. This is true too of some of the Indian fights of this same year, but in the following years, he was consciously interested in the details of the Crow wars, in the clashes with government military forces, and in the beginning of the change from the old life to the new.

During the year 1890–1891, Amos was enlisted as a scout in the United States Army at Fort Robinson, Nebraska.[2] It was at this time that he purchased from a clothing dealer in Crawford, Nebraska, the large ledger which contains the record. His uncle, Short Bull (*Tatanka Ptecela*), was then serving his seventh year as United States scout at Fort Robinson, and the two men were much together. The younger man possessed artistic gifts and a strong interest in the history of his tribe; so, under the additional stimulus of his uncle's interest and firsthand knowledge of institutions and events, he began inscribing the detailed history which he had been planning even earlier.

---

[1] Bad Heart Bull the elder, He Dog, Only Man, Little Shield, and Short Bull; all but Bad Heart Bull and Only Man are still living (1934).

[2] In No. 324 of the manuscript the artist has portrayed a mounted figure in uniform, beside which—aside from a notation in Lakota—appears the legend "Fort Robinson: Neb. U.S. Scout. 1890. Amos Eagle Lance. B. H. Bull."

According to the uncle, the boy for some time had been interested in treaties and other official documents concerning Indian–federal government relations and had been collecting them; as a result, he possessed a considerable number of books and published reports, which, incidentally, he could not read himself. More important to us was Amos' great interest in the *native* histories—both recorded and unrecorded—of his own people. Before 1891 he himself had drawn a complete winter count (the typical form of tribal record among the Sioux)[3] of the Oglala Dakotas, which covered some three hundred years.[4] It was while working upon this, which in accordance with the pictographic method of winter counts could give but the barest sort of historical outline, that the boy realized the quantity of material that was being left untouched—the battles, rituals, ceremonies, and various activities and interests that were not being recorded and yet were vitally significant in the life of the people. Prompted by a real historical and sociological sense, he decided that it was most desirable to make a more complete record. The result is the manuscript with which this volume deals.

In spite of Amos' service as a scout, he was not essentially a fighting man. His age, of course, was one reason for the unmilitary tendency of his career, for he was barely twenty-one at the time of the Ghost Dance disturbance, which not only marked the end of Indian wars but also came several years after the real fighting days of the Sioux were past. The warrior life, moreover, would have been hardly consistent with his general character. His temperament was essentially artistic rather than combative, and much of his time was spent in the graphic depiction of the native life that he knew both through observation and through the teachings of his elders. The period treated in his manuscript covers the years of greatest activity in his own life and in the lives of his father and uncles; consequently, it is natural that the young man should know it well. Amos' life was relatively short, for he died in 1913; most of the drawings in the manuscript, therefore, were made during the last ten years of the last century and the first ten of the present one.

Since he belonged to a generation later than the great fighters and organizers of the period and since he was by nature more inclined toward peace than antagonism, perhaps he found it easier to view the tribal life and activity more objectively and with less bias than might otherwise have been possible. Be that as it may, he has portrayed a complete cross section of the life of his people in the greatest detail of tribal organization and administration, costumes, secular activities, religious ritual and ceremony, and methods of warfare; and—this is significant—he has done it to satisfy his *own* desire to have the record in documentary form, for the manuscript is not kept in the tribal archives and was not made in compliance with demands of tribal officers. As a result, the record is made freely, straightforwardly; furthermore, it is done strictly from the Indian point of view. In consequence of all this, and of the last fact in particular, the work is in a certain distinct way more valuable than it could otherwise have been.

According to Bad Heart Bull's relatives, the boy had no schooling. His education was almost entirely that which he received, after the manner of primitive tradition, from his father and uncles. In addition to this, however, he instructed himself in the art of drawing and that of writing in Lakota.[5] It was through the influence of one of the missionaries that he began to use the technique of writing. As Clark Wissler points out, a number of the Sioux, even the older men, learned to use the Riggs system of writing after the establishment of reservation life,[6] and their manuscripts have furnished some valuable details regarding ceremonies and legends. By the use of this system, Bad Heart Bull has entered practically all of his literal notations in the manuscript. The brief notations in English are the result of his contact with the whites during the period of his enlistment and his life on the Pine Ridge Reservation.

It is the development of his artistic style and the consideration of possible outside influences on that style that are of particular interest to us here. I can

---

[3] See Chapter II, "Dakota Histories and Historical Art."

[4] This has since been lost. In chronological extent, it was an exceptionally long winter count. It is unfortunate that it is missing, for—aside from the great reach of its record— one feels, after comparing Bad Heart Bull's drawings with those found in winter counts, that his was probably more

artistic in execution than other "calendars" of the same character.

[5] *Dakota* according to Oglala dialect.

[6] Clark Wissler, "Societies and Ceremonial Associations in the Oglala Division of the Teton Dakota," *APAMNH*, XI, Part 1 (1912), 21.

find no data that would indicate that he received any instruction in drawing from a source outside his own tribe. In fact, as I have said before, his relatives say that he taught himself, and I am convinced that this is the case. His artistic technique is built upon an entirely native manner of expression traditional among Plains Indians generally; it belongs to a distinctly Plains art genre which is exemplified in all narratives of exploit among all the tribes in this culture area. Whether the records be drawn on buckskin, buffalo or elk hide, cloth, or paper; whether they be found on tipi cover or curtain, pictographic robe, or on loose sheets of cloth or paper—they all belong to the same genre, the same artistic type.

Naturally, Bad Heart Bull's work varies in quality. But in general it maintains a fair standard of excellence. One cannot compare the record as a whole with any other record of similar artistic type, for it stands a thing unique in its scope and extent. Numerous brief records of personal exploits and ceremonials and similar themes there are, to be sure (to some of these I refer specifically and in detail in Chapter II, "Dakota Histories and Historical Art"), but no other manuscript or series of manuscripts, either by a single person or by a group of recorders, has been discovered which is as pretentious or as truly historic in its conception and plan. Without doubt there are among these lesser records specimens in which single compositions equal or perhaps surpass many of Bad Heart Bull's compositions drawn in large scale (which is the scale of the genre). But few, if any, specimens surpass certain of the large-scale compositions of Bad Heart Bull at his best. The young Oglala possesses a technique which makes practically all of his compositions dynamic in quality. His running horses move; his fighting Indians are instinct with action. There is a naturalism and realism about his treatment which—though it is based upon a crude and primitive technique and is naïve and primitive itself—puts life into the creatures of his pen and brush. He uses freely the widespread conventionalizations characteristic of his culture, but he makes figures that live. More than most of his fellow Indian artists he gives to his drawings a vital, dynamic quality. He uses the same basic technique as other Indian artists, but he adds something to it, something of his own—a something which comes from a greater technical skill, though this is not all; for it must come, too, from a certain genius for observation, from imagination, and beyond that from the individual and

peculiar attitude of mind and spirit which lies behind the initial conception of the work, namely, his great desire to portray the life of his people.

It is not, however, so much the more obvious technique of the actual drawing in the large-scale compositions that calls forth the special interest and enthusiasm of artists of our own race. Rather it is his feeling for mass, his ability to handle groups, that demands remark. This ability appears most strikingly in his miniature portrayals, and these are distinctly Bad Heart Bull's own and unique contribution.

After a little study of the manuscript it seems more and more certain that these miniature drawings, each of which contains a hundred or more figures, are a comparatively late development and that they have been introduced for the sake of supplementing the large-scale portrayals of certain episodes, for the sake of giving the action as a whole; they are panoramic in character and purpose and give the observer a glimpse of the episode from above and from one side. The large-scale drawing presents the closer, detailed view of a portion of the action; the miniature presents the picture of the action in its totality.

I shall discuss at greater length in another chapter the nature of Bad Heart Bull's technical achievement. Here I wish but to suggest the general intent of the work and the character of the man's accomplishment. The first fact that impresses one is the great number of the drawings, their wealth of detail, and the inescapable evidence of hours and hours of painstaking execution. Then comes the realization of the artistic ability of the recorder—his naïvely effective use of balance, color, rhythm, spotting, and perspective; his feeling for decoration; his varying uses of impressionism; and his development of conventionalizations. Finally, one is impressed by the thoughtfully critical attitude, the ingenious and far-reaching conception of the work, and especially the maturity of mind and breadth of vision which prompted the young Indian to undertake, of his own accord, the careful accumulation and preservation of data of such historic and cultural significance as this. He is one of the few who could stand aside and view the life of his people objectively, who could stand by in appraisal and with the poise of a critic. He possesses, more than do most of his fellows, a feeling for history. He plans to preserve, before it is too late, a complete picture of his tribe, not only records of individual exploit, but the record of the total tribal life, in which individual exploit is shown as it fits into the larger picture-as-a-whole. It is the life of a people that is being shadowed forth, and of a people caught in that period of its existence which was surely both its most heroic and its most tragic, so that, in effect, the pictorial series moves from beginning to end with an epic sweep which may properly qualify it to stand beside works of literature which in other races deal with analogous themes. In brief, the Bad Heart Bull manuscript is no mere collection of pictures; it is a moving and truly splendid composition.

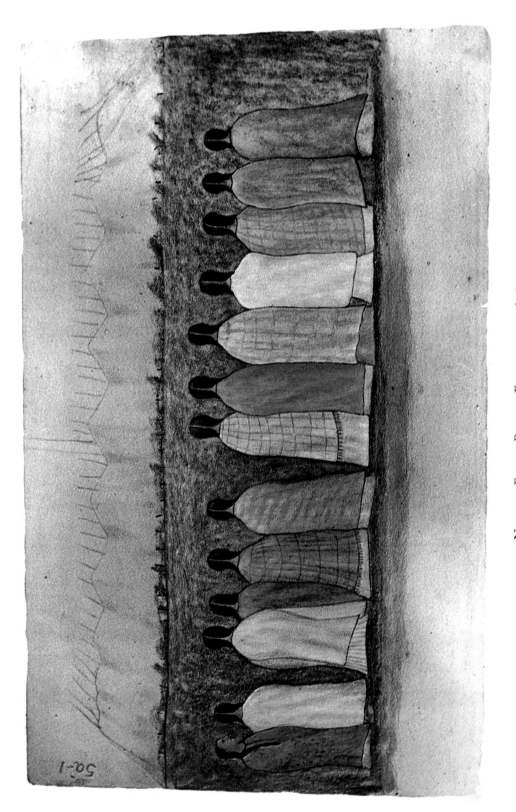

No. 10. Events Perhaps Earlier than 1856
(For a description of this drawing, see p. 92.)

No. 84. Sioux-Crow Fights

(see p. 168)

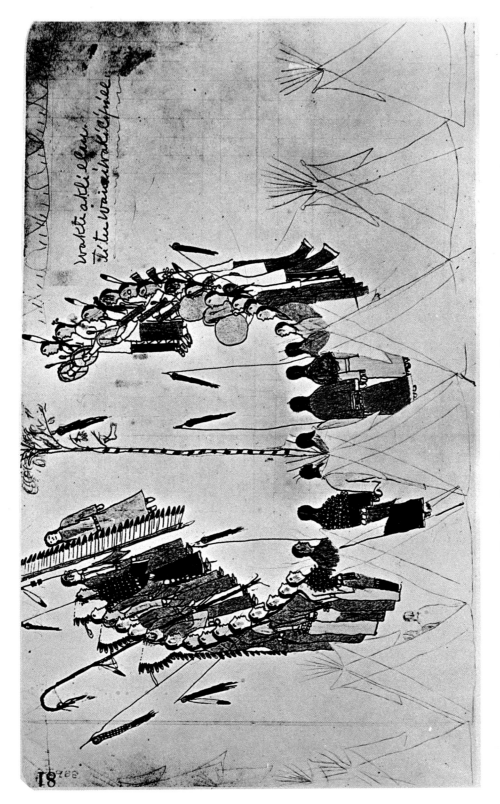

No. 85.   Early Social Life and Its Reorganization
(see p. 169)

No. 128.   The Battle of the Little Big Horn

(see p. 214)

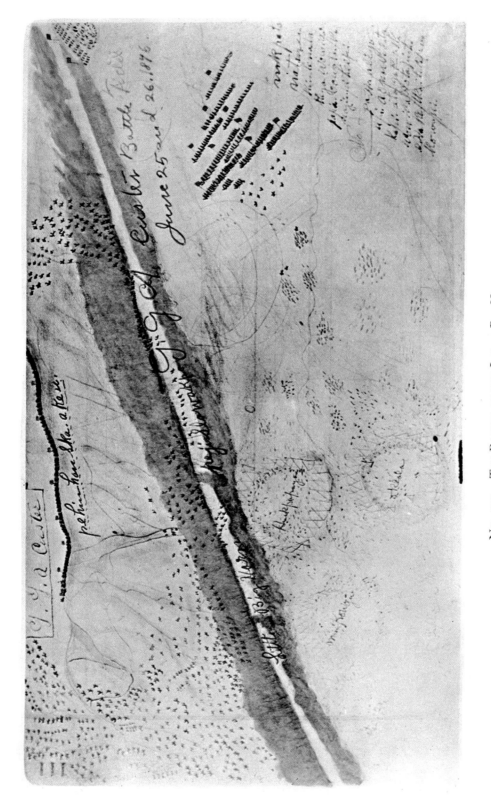

No. 129.   The Battle of the Little Big Horn

(see p. 215)

No. 130. THE BATTLE OF THE LITTLE BIG HORN
(see p. 216)

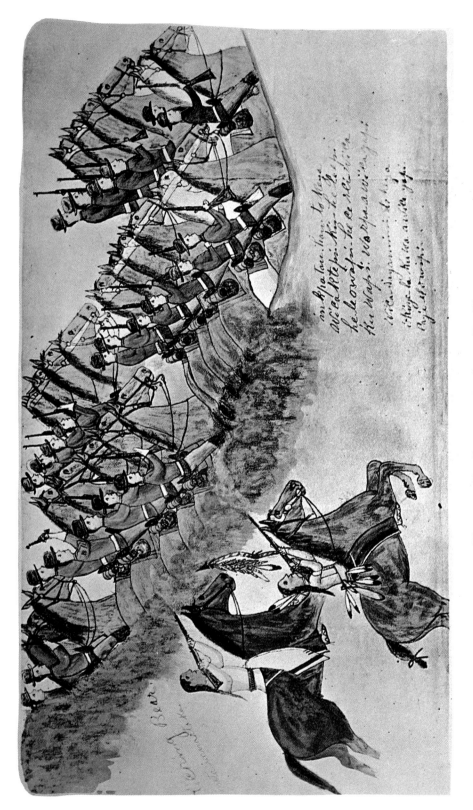

No. 131.   The Battle of the Little Big Horn

(see p. 217)

No. 137.   The Battle of the Little Big Horn

(see p. 223)

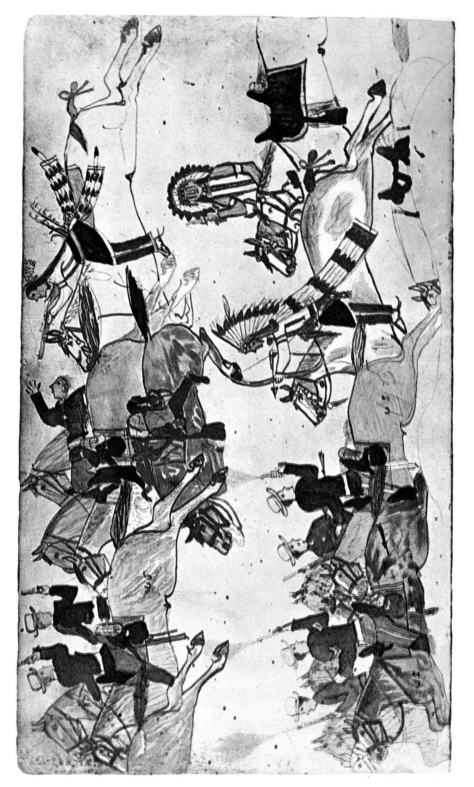

No. 140. The Battle of the Little Big Horn

(see p. 226)

No. 143.   The Battle of the Little Big Horn

(see p. 229)

No. 144. The Battle of the Little Big Horn
(see p. 230)

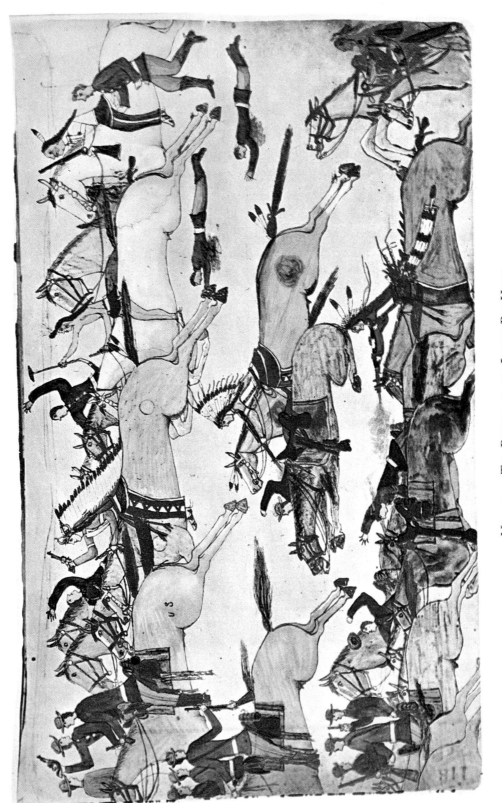

No. 145.   The Battle of the Little Big Horn
(see p. 231)

No. 146. The Battle of the Little Big Horn

(see p. 232)

No. 147.   The Battle of the Little Big Horn

(see p. 233)

No. 148. The Battle of the Little Big Horn
(see p. 234)

No. 149.   The Battle of the Little Big Horn

(see p. 235)

No. 151.   The Battle of the Little Big Horn.

(see p. 237)

No. 158. THE BATTLE OF THE LITTLE BIG HORN
(see p. 244)

No. 162.   THE BATTLE OF THE LITTLE BIG HORN
(see p. 248)

No. 166.   The Battle of the Little Big Horn

(see p. 252)

No. 182.   The Battle of the Little Big Horn

(see p. 268)

No. 202. Early Social Life and Its Reorganization
(*see p. 294*)

No. 204. Early Social Life and Its Reorganization

(see p. 296)

No. 304. Early Social Life and Its Reorganization

(see p. 401)

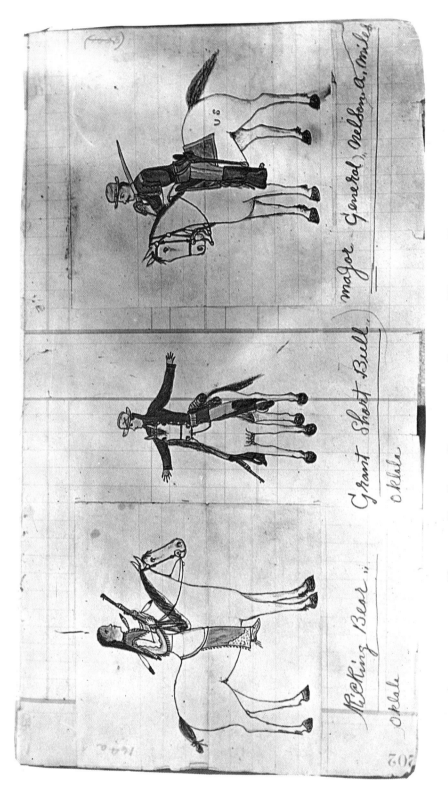

No. 315.   The Ghost Dance and the Battle of Wounded Knee
(see p. 412)

No. 337. "Greater Indian Shows"

(see p. 432)

No. 383. "Greater Indian Shows"

(see p. 474)

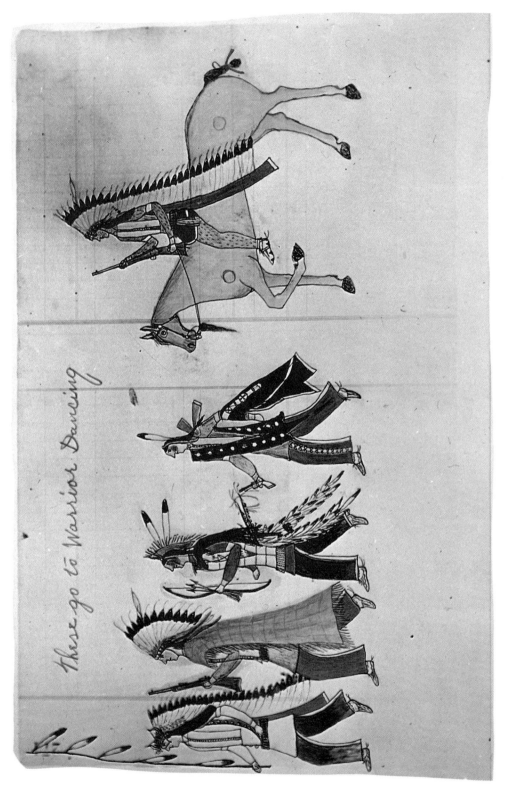

These go to Warrior Dancing

No. 385. "Greater Indian Shows"
(see p. 476)

No. 406.   "Greater Indian Shows"

(see p. 492)

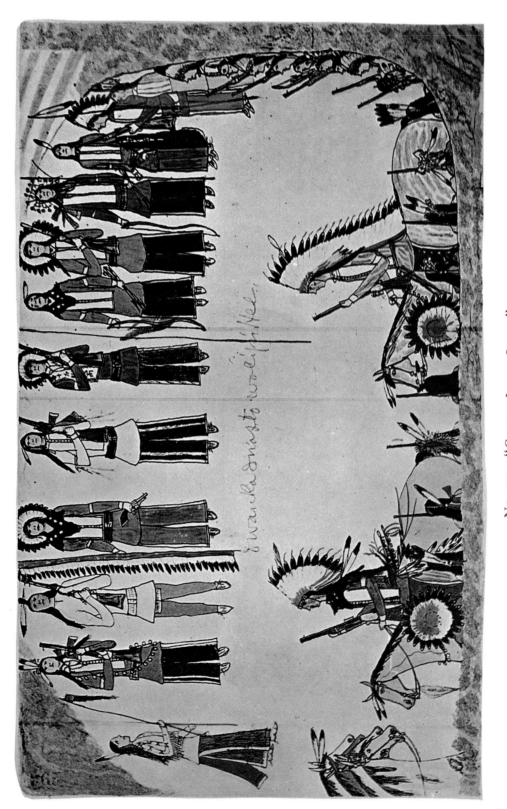

No. 407. "Greater Indian Shows"

(see p. 493)

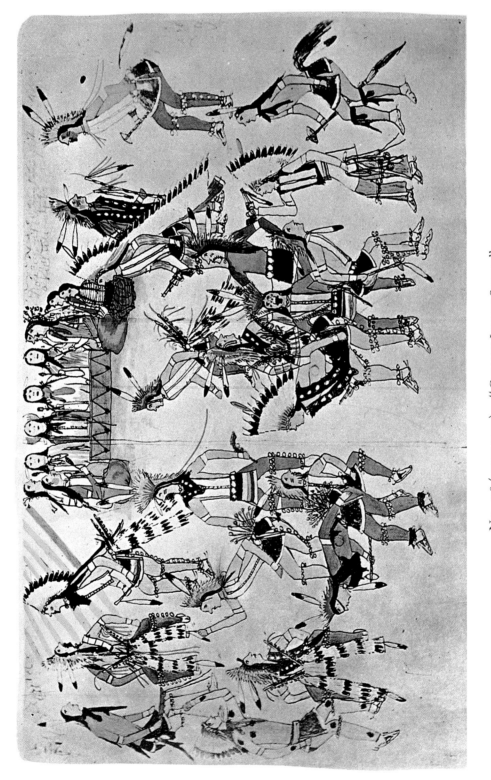

No. 408 (upper half). "Greater Indian Shows"

(see p. 494)

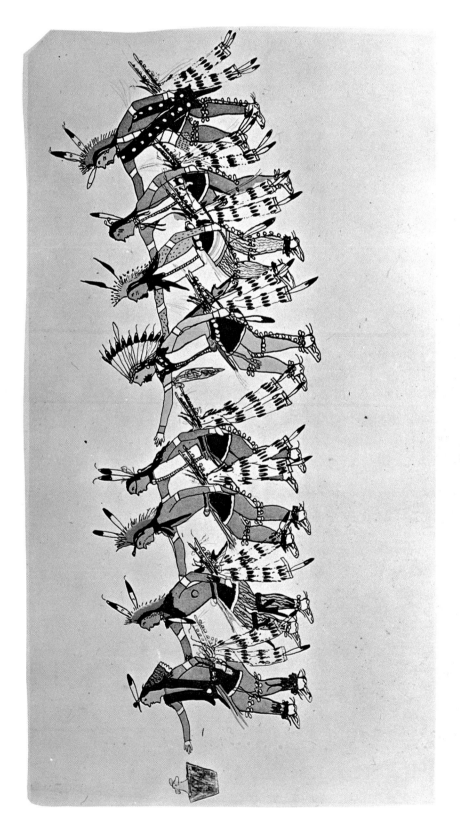

No. 410. "GREATER INDIAN SHOWS"

(see p. 496)

CHAPTER II

Dakota Histories and Historical Art

THE number of native North American Indian records of a historical nature, published with commentaries, is small; and any additions to the number possess real interest from their intrinsic value both as primitive art and as historical material per se. Garrick Mallery has reviewed, rather exhaustively up to a certain point, the material of this sort in the fourth and tenth reports of the Bureau of American Ethnology in connection with his articles on Sioux Winter Counts. I shall simply sketch briefly main sources of this type, including and supplementing Mallery's, before entering upon any discussion of the new material in hand.

TYPES OF INDIAN PICTORIAL ART

DIGHTON ROCK

One may well begin a general survey of published discussion of North American pictography with mention of the famous Dighton Rock, which has received so much attention among antiquarians and ethnologists. Henry R. Schoolcraft, in the first volume of his work on the American Indian,[1] and Mallery, in the *Tenth Annual Report of the Bureau of American Ethnology*,[2] both treat fairly fully of this record. From the standpoint of chronological age, it probably should be placed near the head of the list of records that are discussed by commentators. The inscription is cut into the face of a rock cliff which rises from the Taunton, or Assonet, River on the Massachusetts side about ten miles from the river's mouth. Students of various cultures and peoples have identified this rock record as Scandinavian, Oriental, Phoenician, Scythian. But the Algonquian origin is now generally granted, although Charles Christian Rafn, in 1830, in what is probably the best description of the inscription itself, questioned its Indian character.[3] Securing copies of the record was difficult for natural and other reasons, including changing light and shifting tides and the complexity of the inscription; but several have been made. No two of these, however, are exactly alike in detail, though all without any doubt represent the same inscription. Plate LIV in Mallery's discussion in the tenth report is a copy of the reproduction in Rafn's article and shows the nine drawings, from Dr. Danforth's in 1680 to the official one of the Rhode Island Historical Society in 1830.[4]

LA CROSSE VALLEY CAVE DRAWINGS

Another type of wall record, probably of some antiquity, is that found in a cave in La Crosse Valley, Wisconsin. According to the Reverend Mr. Edward

[1] Henry R. Schoolcraft, *Historical and Statistical Information Respecting the History, Condition, and Prospects of the Indian Tribes of the United States* (6 vols.; Philadelphia, 1851–1857), I, 108–120, Plate 36.
[2] Garrick Mallery, "Picture-Writing of the American Indians," *ARBAE*, X (1888–1889), 86–87, 762–764.
[3] C. C. Rafn, *Antiquitates Americanae* (Copenhagen,

1845), p. 357. Quoted by Mallery in "Picture-Writing," p. 763.
[4] Mallery, "Picture-Writing." The other drawings: 1712—Cotton Mather's; 1730—Dr. Isaac Greenwood's; 1768—Stephen Sewell's; 1788—James Winthrop's; 1807— Mr. E. A. Kendall's; 1812—Job Gardner's; 1790—Dr. Baylies' and Mr. Goodwin's.

Brown,[5] the drawings engraved and charcoal-painted on the walls of this cave had been buried for at least 150 years when he discovered them in 1887.[6] The walls bearing the inscriptions had originally been those of an open cavern facing a swamp or lake. Then a landslide covered the site, and it was only by accident that the existence of the cave was rediscovered. Year rings on trees involved indicate an age of at least 150 years. Geological data point to the fact that there were four periods of occupancy of the cave; to which period the pictographs belong, one cannot say, but John A. Rice estimates that the pictures probably date back from 300 to 800 years.[7] Their crudeness would seem to corroborate this chronological placing, indefinite though it is.

In all there are seventeen drawings. Most of these are of animals; but in two drawings, both of which portray the hunt, representations of human figures appear. Lyman C. Draper, secretary of the Wisconsin Historical Society at the time of the discovery of the cave, feels that the rude representations were "doubtless made by the Sioux."[8] At any rate, they represent clearly an early stage in primitive art; and, though the interpretation of them can be only conjectural, they are significant for their intrinsic artistic value and for the light that they may throw upon the existence and movements of probably prehistoric inhabitants of the region.

BUFFALO ROCK

There are, however, published discussions of several other rock records which are without doubt more significant to the student of native American pictography and to ethnologists generally, since there is by no means the same degree of indefiniteness regarding their origin. One of these, known appropriately by the name Buffalo Rock, has been drawn on the open faces of a large boulder standing by itself on the east bank of the Snake River at the mouth of a lateral canyon about eighteen miles above Lewiston, Idaho.[9] The figures inscribed on the faces of the stone are crude but, for the most part, identifiable. Three

methods of inscription have been used: (1) painting with red and yellow ocher and with black; (2) pecking with a pointed instrument; and (3) a combination of the two—the surface painted, then the figures brought into tone relief by pecking the paint away. On the upriver face are two crude figures of buffalo painted in red (hence the name Buffalo Rock); near them, in black and white, are two apparently conventionalized signs composed of a perpendicular mark flanked by a series of short, lighter straight marks, one above the other at the right. On the downriver side are figures that appear gray because they are pecked out of the painted surface. These seem to represent men, some with horns (which may very likely represent buffalo headdresses) and some with bows or wands in their hands. From the shoulders down, the crudely shaped bodies resemble the tails of fish, H. T. Spinden points out. Above one man's figure is that of a mountain sheep or goat with elongated horns.

Near Buffalo Rock is a second boulder, inscribed by pecking alone. On it are a mountain-goat figure, what may represent a snake, and geometric designs.

The exact meaning of the series of symbols is not known and probably cannot be discovered. Without doubt, the inscription dates back a great many years. But the general character—of both method and matter—is of great interest to students of native North American cultures. Spinden states positively that there is no reason to doubt the Nez Percé origin of the inscriptions. They are all characteristic of Great Basin petroglyphs generally—"petroglyphs which served the double purpose of decoration and aids to memory."

RECORDS OF THE COLUMBIA RIVER REGION

Still farther west are the rock records of the Columbia River region. The ethnologists making special report on these use the term "petrography" to designate all records made on rock; then they make a careful, technical distinction between the terms

[5] Edward Brown, "The Pictured Cave of La Crosse Valley, near West Salem, Wisconsin," *Wisconsin Historical Collections*, VIII (1877–1879), 174–183; John A. Rice, "Additional Notes on the Pictured Cave," *Wisconsin Historical Collections*, VIII (1877–1879), 183–187.

[6] W. J. Hoffman, Bureau of American Ethnology, also visited this cave later. See *ARBAE*, X (1888–1889), xiv (Introduction).

[7] Rice, "Additional Notes," pp. 186–187.

[8] Lyman C. Draper, prefatory note to Brown, "Pictured Cave," p. 174.

[9] H. T. Spinden, "Petroglyphs and Pictographs of the Nez Percé," *Memoirs of the American Anthropological Association*, II (1907–1915), Part 3 (1908), 231–233.

"pictogaph" and "petroglyph."[10] A pictograph is a picture made by painting upon the rock in various colors, chiefly dull red; a petroglyph is a picture formed probably by pecking or by abrasion. The first type is found generally near the base of the rimrock; the second, commonly near the river, frequently on rocks "periodically submerged."

Both types are found in Oregon and Washington and on some of the islands of the Columbia, but appear especially abundant on the north side of the river east of the Dalles to the Snake River and "at least as far north as Central Washington." Both types, likewise, show a blending of the realism of coast art and the geometric style of the plateau area. In those pictographic drawings of naturalistic style, human, animal, and—very rarely—mythical figures appear; while in the petroglyphic manner are found the same human and animal figures as in pictography and in addition very commonly many other identifiable animals, anthropomorphic forms, and mythical creatures. In both types the same geometric elements —"sundisks," "fences," "rakes," "circles" (single and concentric), "spoked wheels," etc.—appear, with certain ones rather more frequent in the petroglyphs. Generally it would seem that the realistic forms are found more commonly in the petroglyphs; the geometric, mainly in the pictographs.

The purpose of both pictographs and petroglyphs is a matter for conjecture. Very likely more than one motive is responsible for their creation. The suggestions have been varied. Do they mark burial sites; commemorate visions, puberty ceremonies, etc.; aim to increase game? These and others are reasonable possibilities. Justly do the authors of the report, however, urge consideration of the logical probability— often overlooked—that many a pictograph may be the result of idle artistic amusement.

In the same region is a group of rock records unique in the area. This series is treated in a second report by two of the same ethnologists.[11] The pictures are found on the north bank of the river, opposite the town of The Dalles, Oregon. Here, above the high-water channel, the petroglyphs run "like an aboriginal natural history gallery."

A basaltic escarpment at this point on the river bank forms a small canyon. It is aptly designated as "Petroglyph Canyon," for the west wall is entirely decorated with carvings, except for one pictograph.

The location is by its very nature quite isolated, a fact which adds to the interest of the find, for petroglyphs are not common to the Dalles region generally, though pictographs in color are. The petroglyphs, however, are stylistically quite different from others in the same general area, though, as in the petroglyphic records discussed in the first report on the Columbia River region, they are characterized by realism. There is an abundant array of anthropomorphic or distinctly human figures, animal forms, and "water animals" (so designated by the local Wishram Indians)—some perhaps mythological— and in addition there appear conventional designs, such as stars, comets, and turtle-like figures. The identifiable animal figures include the buffalo, the deer, the elk, the horse, the mountain goat, the mountain sheep, the rattlesnake, and the wolf or coyote—a list which, generally speaking, distinctly suggests a more eastern territory.

The one pictograph is a drawing of an American buffalo, painted a dull, rusty red, on the highest rock of the wall and done in the same style as the petroglyphs. This picture, with its concentration on the buffalo, seems especially to point to a more eastern tribe for origin, the reporters think, since buffalo— even strays—almost never entered the Columbia River region. Pictographs are abundant in this general vicinity, but, unlike the one in Petroglyph Canyon, they are devoted chiefly to conventionalized designs and not one of them contains an animal figure of this type.

The pictograph *and* the petroglyphs, however, in theme, style, and spirit, bear considerable resemblance to the Buffalo Rock record. The closest analogy seems to be a series of pictographs in Shinume Canyon, Utah.[12] Certainly the Dalles petroglyphs appear to be most nearly related to the petrography of the Great Basin area. The reporting ethnologists think it quite likely that they were made by the Snakes, a branch of the Shoshonis. Lewis and Clark report finding the

---

[10] W. D. Strong, W. E. Schenck, and J. H. Steward, "Archaeology of the Dalles-Deschutes Region," *University of California Publications in American Archaeology and Ethnology*, XXIX, 1 (1930), vii, 1–154.

[11] W. D. Strong and W. E. Schenck, "Petroglyphs near

the Dalles of the Columbia River," *Am. Anthrop.*, XXVII (NS), 1 (January–March 1925), 76–90.

[12] *Ibid.*, p. 89. See also Mallery, "Picture-Writing," p. 121, figure 89.

immediate southern bank of the Columbia largely inhabited (by Indians, of course) from near the mouth of the Walla Walla to the Dalles *because of fear of the Snakes*. These Shoshoni Indians may have made the petroglyphs for one reason or another during a period of peace, or to mark their entrance into enemy territory.[13]

CANADIAN ROCK DRAWINGS

To complete my summary of rock records of North America treated in published discussions, I turn to a group of pictures found in Canada.

Harlan I. Smith, in his paper on prehistoric Canadian art, records an interesting collection of petroglyphs of various types found in different culture areas.[14] They come from British Columbia (both coastal and interior regions), Alberta, Saskatchewan, and Ontario; and they exemplify all three techniques of petroglyphs: pecking, painting, and incising.

First are three apparently pecked pictures from the Northwest Coast area (Plates XXXII and XXXIII, figures 3 and 4; all textual citations of plates and figures in this section refer to Smith's paper). The figures seem to be, for the most part, conventionalizations of sea creatures, and belong to an art type peculiar to southern Vancouver Island.

A second coast type, also from British Columbia, is that found on the beach at Fort Rupert, *northern* Vancouver Island. One picture (Plate XXXIII, figure 1) represents the sea monster Ia'kin and a number of faces battered (as Smith has it) in the rock. The second (Plate XXXIII, figure 2) shows a group of crude faces *pecked* in the rock. Both, Smith says, *may* be modern. The Indians, however, describe them as made "before animals were turned into men."

The third type (Plate XXXIX) is characteristic of the plateaus of interior British Columbia but is quite distinct from the coast types. It is much given to fine straight lines and considerable (but rather simple) conventionalization. The example given is that found painted upon a rock on the Thompson River[15] near Spence Bridge. The symbols seem to be, in a number of cases (perhaps in all), marks of direction: trail crossings, indications of placing of sacrifices (especially at trail crossings), "girl's lodge with fir branches hanging down." Among those not necessarily connected with direction are simple conventionalizations of fir branches (sometimes by themselves, sometimes in connection with other symbols), an unadorned line of several curves representing a snake, and two not at all obvious conventional portrayals of dogs made almost entirely of straight lines.

Another group of figures (Plate XL) exemplifies a second type characteristic of the British Columbia plateau region. This one, found in the West Kootenay country, is quite distinct, however, from the preceding. Smith points out that the pictures shown are but a few from among many painted in red, black, and green on granite surface. The general character and effect of these drawings are decidedly different from those of the Thompson River picture. Straight lines do not predominate; lines are heavier; and, while there is considerable conventionalization— which I cannot explain—the animal figures, though crude and unidentifiable, are much more realistic than those in the former pictograph. One mark of possible similarity, however, is found in figure 2, which seems to resemble somewhat the "unfinished basketry" symbol of the other drawing.

The fifth type of inscription is found painted in red on a cliff at the foot of Seaton Lake, British Columbia. The figures shown by Smith (Plate XXXVIII) are selected from among the most distinct—"about one-third to one-half"—that appear on the cliff.[16] They include not only the simple conventionalizations of trail crossings, fir boughs, and unfinished basketry, but also the thunderbird (figures 27 and 50) and other animals and things (e.g., figures 19, 38, 15, 32, 35) and, in addition, quite *realistic* figures (these always painted solid) of various animals—several of them horned, some of them quite apparently mountain sheep or goats (e.g., figures 13, 16, 48). Further, they include a number of more complex images consisting of single figures symbolically grouped to form a larger unit (e.g., figures 46, 51, 52).

---

[13] Strong and Schenck, "Petroglyphs," p. 90.

[14] Harlan I. Smith, "An Album of Prehistoric Canadian Art," *Anthropological Series*, No. 8 (June 1923), Bulletin 37, Victoria Memorial Museum. Many of these petroglyphs have been discussed to one extent or another earlier than Smith's article. For his bibliography, see pp. 9–18 of his paper.

[15] See also James Teit, "A Rock Painting of the Thompson River Indians, British Columbia," *Bulletin of the American Museum of Natural History*, VIII, 12 (1896), 227–230.

[16] See also, for discussion of detail, James Teit, "The Lillooet Indians," *Memoirs of the American Museum of Natural History*, IV, 5 (1906), 193–300, figures 61–100, Plates VIII–IX, especially Plate IX.

Sixth is a type exemplified by two pictures (Plates XLI and XLII) found in Alberta on Milk River across from "Writing-on-stone police barracks." The art form is one appearing "as far south as Wyoming, but not on the Pacific Coast or east of the Plains." The method of inscription is incising. The drawings are crude. In addition to conventionalized forms which I cannot explain, there are men figures and horse figures, the latter calling forth Smith's comment that they "at least must have been made since Europeans came to North America."

The next pictures come from this same general Plateau culture area and represent two varying techniques, both of which differ from that immediately preceding.

First there are four paintings. The first shows two grotesque faces painted in white "on concretions" near Grand Rapids, Alberta (Plate XLIII, figure 1). The second, third, and fourth (Plate XLIII, figures 2, 3, and 4) are done in red pigment on low cliffs of gneiss at various places on Churchill River, Saskatchewan. Men, animal, and bird figures of more or less realistic portrayal predominate, but they are accompanied by several conventionalizations that I cannot identify definitely. In general there seems to be a certain kinship between these latter pictures and those of the interior British Columbia inscription found at Seaton Lake (Plate XXXVIII).

The pictures of the other type (Plate XLIII, figures 5 and 6) are both pecked. One is a drawing of the "seven-armed-sun" on a stone tablet that was found "near a large 'graded pyramidal mound' on Bow River, Alberta." The other is a strange, conventional portrayal on a "Sesoators, or ancient sacrificial stone" found on Red Deer River near Bow River, Alberta.

The last pictographs of the series fall into groups of pictures found at various points in Ontario; all are Algonquian in type and therefore belong to the Eastern Woodlands culture. The first two groups (Plates LXXIX and LXXX) consist of nine pictures, all painted with red pigment and all apparently of one type. Realistic images of men and animals predominate. One of the latter obviously represents a bear (figure 2, Plate LXXIX), another (figure 2 [extreme right], Plate LXXX) a moose being shot by a man with a bow and arrow, and two others (figure 6 [right center], Plate LXXX) apparently water animals of some sort which bear a certain similarity to some figures in the plateau-area drawings at Seaton Lake, British Columbia (cf., e.g., figures 1, 4, and 11, Plate

XXXVIII). One picture (figures 2 and 3, Plate LXXX) contains two fairly realistic representations of men in a canoe; in one case, one of the men has his arm raised to throw a spearlike weapon (figure 2 [lower left], Plate LXXX). Several include what seem to be conventional portrayals of the same subject: a crescent-shaped line for the boat, short straight lines rising perpendicularly from it for the men (figures 1 and 3, Plate LXXIX; figures 1 and 2, Plate LXXX). There are numerous other conventionalizations (in fact, they predominate in one picture, figure 1, Plate LXXX), but I shall not try here to identify them. I do, however, wish to remark two rather complex conventionalizations, both found in figure 2 of Plate LXXIX. What seem to represent human figures appear in both, and in one there is an animal form (perhaps more); but quite obviously these individual figures are all definitely related in some larger, more complex image. Each larger conventionalization without doubt represents an episode, ceremonial in nature perhaps. Because of their greater complexity and seemingly episodic nature, these last two symbols are especially intriguing.

The third group consists of selected typical pictures pecked "in the top of a low, glaciated point of very soft, foliated, green chloritic schist rock" on the north side of the "peninsula forming the south shore of the northern half of Lake of the Woods" (figures 1–13, Plate LXXXI). All of these figures are decided conventionalizations.

Group four (figures 14–19, Plate LXXXI) bears some relation to the preceding in that all the pictures, with one exception (figure 15, Plate LXXXI), are extremely conventionalized and in that the modern Indians of the vicinity place the origin of both in some distant past. This latter group, instead of being pecked, however, is painted in ocher "on an overhanging wall of a hard greenstone" on the south side of Crow Rock Island (Ka-ka-ki-wa-bic Min-nis), which is not far out from the south shore of the northern half of Lake of the Woods.[17] The inscription was at one time more extensive, but has been "cut off [at figure 19] by falling of rock."

The last group is found at Lake Massanog, Frontenac County. These pictures also are painted, but in red; and they are closely related to both of the preceding groups in that they are entirely conventionalized. One figure (figure 20, Plate LXXXI)

[17] Cf. location of preceding picture.

doubtless represents a man. Some others are perhaps variants of figures found in the pecked group (cf. figures 21, 23, and 23a with 12, 1, and 4, respectively [Plate LXXXI]), but what the exact significance is, I cannot say. Several of these latter symbols *seem* definitely to approach the ideograph in character.

So we have in these Canadian petroglyphs types that represent the North Pacific Coast, Plateau and Mackenzie Basin, and Eastern Woodlands culture areas; that exhibit in technique pecking, incising, and painting; and that range in character from the relatively realistic to the rather highly conventionalized.

GRAPHIC ART OF THE ESKIMO

To the far north is the most remote of the native North American art expressions pertinent to this discussion—the Eskimo carvings on bone and ivory, treated by W. J. Hoffman in a detailed and rather lengthy report[18] which is made highly interesting by the numerous and excellent illustrations.

The art under discussion is prehistoric, and in many respects bears striking resemblance to the cave drawings of Dordogne, France. As a matter of fact, certain of the early ethnologists presented with some emphasis the thesis that the Eskimos were direct descendants of the cave men of France.[19]

Be that as it may, the drawings are made either by carving or by incising; they appear as decoration of utensils, weapons, and various other objects of common use; and they portray all the creatures and activities significant to the people.

The purpose, it would seem, is decidedly that of record—the recording of domestic activities, types of habitations and manners of conveyance, forms and uses of utensils and weapons, manners of preparation of food, games and pastimes.

Some go a step further and become episodic, recording individual exploit, combat, hunting and fishing, travel and geographic feature, and shamanistic ceremony. So the record takes on the quality of narrative. The great majority of the pictographs, however, are concerned with recording common,

daily activities. So the whole group gives a significant and interesting cross section of the everyday life of a people.

The art itself, excepting certain ideographic conventionalizations for gesture signs and signals, is characterized by a distinct realism that is at times amazingly naturalistic and by a technique that is highly developed. In the scenes of hunting or combat, for instance, though the work is done by carving and cutting, and that in a very hard material, men and animals *move*; they are not mere still portraits made by a careful observer and clever painter, but possess *vitality*.

THE WALAM OLUM

Daniel G. Brinton's account of the Lenape Walam Olum, however, is probably the most complete treatment of a North American Indian record up to the time of Mallery's discussions.[20] The record is very old and represents the art, history, and mythology of the eastern Indians of Algonquian stock in eastern Pennsylvania, New Jersey, and Maryland. Wooden tally sticks were used; and as Brinton's explanation of the derivation of the name shows, the record was painted:

> I have shown that *walam* means "painted," especially "painted red." This is a secondary meaning, as the root *wuli* conveys the idea of something pleasant, in this connection, pleasant to the eye, fine, pretty.
> *Olum* was the name of the scores, marks, or figures in use on the tally-sticks or records.[21]

We learn further that the records were not only painted but also incised, for in C. S. Rafinesque's title to Part I of his manuscript[22] of the Walam Olum he says: "First part of the painted-engraved traditions of the Linni linapi, &c.," and again, "First and Second Parts of the painted and *engraved* traditions of the Linni linapi."[23]

The record embodies the ancient cosmological myths of the Algonquian stocks and historical chronicles of the Lenapes after the legendary arrival on the American continent. The titles to the two parts of

[18] W. J. Hoffman, "Graphic Art of the Eskimos," *Report of the United States National Museum, 1895*, pp. 739–968.

[19] William Boyd Dawkins, *Early Man in Britain and His Place in the Tertiary Period* (London: Macmillan Co., 1880), p. 233.

[20] Daniel G. Brinton, *The Lenape and Their Legends* (Philadelphia: D. G. Brinton, 1885).

[21] *Ibid.*, p. 161.

[22] It is from the manuscript of C. S. Rafinesque (1833) that Brinton has reproduced the Walam Olum as it appears in *The Lenape and Their Legends*.

[23] Brinton, *The Lenape*, p. 162. The italics are mine.

the manuscript as given by Rafinesque are enlightening concerning the record's content and purpose. The first title reads:

Wallamolum
First part of the painted-engraved traditions of the Linni linape, &c., containing the three original traditional poems. 1. on the Creation and Ontogeny, 24 verses. 2. on the Deluge, &c., 16 verses. 3. on the passage to America, 20 verses. Signs and verses, 60, with the original glyphs or signs for each verse of the poems or songs translated word for word by C. S. Rafinesque 1833.[24]

The second is:

Wallamolum
First and Second Parts of the painted and engraved traditions of the Linni linapi.

II. Part
Historical Chronicles or Annals in two Chronicles.
1. From arrival in America to settlement in Ohio, &c. 4 chapters each of 6 verses, each of 4 words, 64 signs.
2. From Ohio to Atlantic States and back to Missouri, a mere succession of names in 3 chapters of 20 verses, 60 signs. Translated word for word by means of Zeisberger and Linapi Dictionary. With explanations, &c. By C. S. Rafinesque, 1833.[25]

OJIBWAY BARK RECORDS

From still another source and locality and a different period come the Ojibway birch-bark records, treated by Hoffman in his paper on the Mide-wiwin in the *Seventh Annual Report of the Bureau of American Ethnology*[26] and in his "Pictography and Shamanistic Rites of the Ojibway."[27] The records are of various sorts, but for the most part relate to the Mide, or "Grand Medicine Society," of this people.

It was in 1887 among the Ojibways of Red Lake, Minnesota, that Hoffman gathered data for the first paper. At that time, these people were "still practicing its [the Mide-wiwin] rites and ceremonies in language much of which is no longer spoken in ordinary conversation and [were] using a *pictorial method for the record of events or the transmission of ideas*."[28]

W. W. Warren, a member of the tribe, says in his work on the Ojibways: "... in the Medawe rite is incorporated most that is ancient among them, songs and traditions that have descended, *not orally, but in hieroglyphics*, for ... a long line of generations."[29] The central material element in the Mide rite in this band is what may well be called a cosmogony chart. It is fifteen feet long and twenty inches wide, and is made of several pieces of birch bark stitched together with thongs of lancewood bark. The two extreme ends are bound and reinforced by thin strips of hardwood secured by lacing and stitching to prevent fraying.[30] Hoffman points out that this chart is very ancient and, previous to his seeing it, had never been shown to any white man or to any other person not entitled by proper preparation such as fasting.

The priest, it seems, uses the cosmogony chart in preparing candidates for the rites of the Mide-wiwin, the purpose being to give a "*pictorial résumé*" of the traditions and history of the Ojibway cosmogony.[31] The main themes and figures of Ojibway mythology occupy the central portions of the chart.[32] But in addition, there are in the spaces between these figures and the outer margin numerous other figures representing "spirits," tutelary beings, and sacred animals, whose presence may be invoked by the Mide priests,[33] and concerning each of these the candidate must be instructed. It is these figures which form the subjects of the Mide songs. The chants themselves are committed to memory; but a record, simply a mnemonic chart, of each one is kept in the form of pictographs cut into birch bark.[34] The songs and records are interpretations of the marginal notations on the cosmogony chart, and each candidate must learn in detail the complete explanation of the figures of each song record.

---

[24] *Ibid.*

[25] *Ibid.*

[26] W. J. Hoffman, "The Mide-wiwin or 'Grand Medicine Society' of the Ojibway," *ARBAE*, VII (1885–1886), 143–300.

[27] W. J. Hoffman, "Pictography and Shamanistic Rites of the Ojibway," *Am. Anthrop.*, I–II (1888–1889), 209–229.

[28] *Ibid.*, p. 210. The italics are mine.

[29] W. W. Warren, "A Memoir of W. W. Warren: A History of the Ojibway," *Collections of the Minnesota State Historical Society*, V (1885), 67. The italics are mine.

[30] Hoffman, "Pictography," p. 217, and "The Mide-wiwin," p. 165, Plate IIIA. There is some discrepancy in the actual measurement of the chart. The first report says it is fifteen feet long and twenty inches wide; the second, that it is seven and one-half feet long by eighteen inches wide. But this fact is not important here.

[31] Hoffman, "Pictography," p. 218. The italics are mine.

[32] Hoffman gives complete explanations of the significance of this chart and several variants of it with illustrative plates in "The Mide-wiwin," pp. 168–187.

[33] Hoffman, "Pictography," p. 218.

[34] *Ibid.*, p. 219.

In addition to these ceremonial records, there are other Mide-wiwin records of a more personal nature. Records of individual members of the society are also kept. "Marked achievements and important events pertaining to the profession [of the newly elected member of Mide] are recorded from time to time, and as each successful act of sorcery or prophecy is an additional proof of ability it is recorded as a mark of honor."[35] Hoffman reports the appearance of such a personal record (of the original Mide owner) upon the back of one of the official charts of the Red Lake Ojibways.[36]

Aside from those of the Mide, however, the Ojibways keep pictographic records and notices of a few other types. There are geographic charts and characters indicating directions on the hunt or during other moves, and there are records of hunts, battles, treaties, and love letters.[37]

THE ROBE OF MAH-TO-TOH-PA

In the pictographic robe of the Mandan chief Mah-to-toh-pa (The Four Bears), discussed by George Catlin,[38] we have still another type of portrayal which in age, character, and source more nearly approaches the Sioux records with which we are chiefly concerned. The robe was made of the skin of a young buffalo bull and was finely dressed on the inner face. Upon this dressed surface, Mah-to-toh-pa has portrayed in picture writing the whole history of his wartime career.[39] The pictures give in detail the record of all the battles fought by this prominent warrior; it is purely a personal record, and a record of warfare.

Similar in spirit and character is the Crow robe obtained in 1925 by William Wildschut for the Heye Foundation, Museum of the American Indian.[40] The robe is of elk skin and bears the story of ten episodes of Crow warriors. It is quite significant and not at all surprising that in all these episodes the Crows' adversaries are Sioux.

These two robes are not unique in either purpose or execution. They are specimens of an art widely practiced among the Plains Indians; countless specimens have been discovered and bought by travelers and students of Indian culture, and every museum which deals at all with Indian ethnology has at least one. But for the majority of these, exact data are lacking, and thus much of the significance to the student is lost. Mah-to-toh-pa's Mandan robe and Wildschut's Crow robe are particularly significant for the simple reason that complete data are published and available.

DAKOTA OFFICIAL TALLIES AND WINTER COUNTS

Mallery's discussions of North American Indian pictography in the reports of the Geological Survey and the Bureau of American Ethnology make up what is in reality the most comprehensive published treatment of the subject.[41] His chief interest in these discussions is the Dakota winter counts, or calendars, which are ideographic and purely chronological in character. They are more extensive than any other kind of North American historical record known, in point of historical time covered, and are quite different in purport.

In connection with these discussions, Mallery also gives in the fourth and tenth reports of the Bureau of American Ethnology two Oglala Dakota ideographic tabulatory records, or tallies, of individual members of bands or tribes. I shall treat both the winter counts and tallies in greater detail in a later section.

CALENDAR HISTORIES OF THE KIOWAS

In the *Seventeenth Annual Report of the Bureau of American Ethnology*, James Mooney discusses three yearly calendars and one monthly count of the Kiowas. These correspond quite definitely to the Dakota winter counts. There are a few distinctions, however. In the first place, the Kiowa records could

---

[35] *Ibid.*, p. 220 (bottom).

[36] Hoffman, "The Mide-wiwin," p. 171 (middle).

[37] Hoffman, "Pictography," p. 224, figure 10; p. 225, figure 11 (hunts); p. 226, figure 12 (battles); p. 227, figure 13 (treaties); p. 223, figure 9 (love letters).

[38] George Catlin, *The North American Indians* (2 vols.; London, 1841), I, 147–154.

[39] *Ibid.*; reproduction of the whole robe, Plate 65; enlarged detail reproductions, the three following plates; literal exposition, pp. 148–154.

[40] William Wildschut, "A Crow Pictographic Robe," *Indian Notes*, III, 1 (January 1926), 28–32, Plate 1.

[41] Garrick Mallery, "A Calendar of the Dakota Nation," United States Geological and Geographical Survey, Bulletin III, No. 1 (April 1877); "Pictographs of the North American Indians: A Preliminary Paper," *ARBAE*, IV (1882–1883); and "Picture-Writing of the American Indians," *ARBAE*, X (1888–1889).

not be called winter counts. The seasons are more clearly discriminated by the southern tribe; summer and winter are definitely differentiated. A heavy vertical bar, indicating that vegetation is dead, marks the winter entry. Most of the summer events are attached to a figure representing the medicine lodge, for the great medicine dance took place in the summer months; in some cases, however, for years when the dance was omitted, summer is indicated by simply placing the entry between the two winter records; and in some of the last years, after the medicine dance had been practically abolished, the figure of a tree in foliage was used.

The Indians counted by lunar months entirely, calling the month a "moon," so it is quite natural and appropriate that the month entry is indicated by the sign of the crescent.

CHEYENNE CEREMONIAL ORGANIZATION

George A. Dorsey, in his paper on the ceremonial organization of the Cheyennes, presents still other Plains Indian records with native drawings, this time of a nature somewhat different from those immediately preceding.[42] In connection with his discussion of the myths of origin of the Cheyennes, the Medicine Arrows, and the Sun Dance, he presents five drawings done in crayon and lead pencil and one diagram in ink (Plates XII–XVII). These are all the work of Richard Davis, a fullblood Cheyenne. Two of the drawings are particularly noteworthy in connection with the study of the Bad Heart Bull manuscript: Plate XVII is a portrayal of a Cheyenne migration, not unlike the Lakota migration in No. 5, and Plate XIII shows the Cheyenne leaders seated in a semicircle for purposes of consultation and judgment, rather in the manner of the Lakota *wakicunza* in No. 1.

Aside from these, there is also a group of colored drawings (six in all) representing the five ancient warrior societies established by the great Medicine Arrow Prophet,[43] and one, the Wolf Society (Plate XI, figures 1 and 2), which was not organized till after the coming of the white man. This group, with Plates VI and VII showing warrior shirts and war-

bonnets, corresponds in a definite sense—though not in completeness of detail or suggestion—to the warrior-societies group (Nos. 22 to 31) in the Oglala record.

WHITE BIRD DRAWINGS OF THE BATTLE OF THE LITTLE BIG HORN

I have photographs of three drawings of the Battle of the Little Big Horn which were made for Captain Richard L. Livermore and are now in the museum of the United States Military Academy at West Point. All three pictures are painted on muslin. The first is called "Custer's Fight" and measures $27\frac{3}{4}$ by $35\frac{3}{4}$ inches; the second one, "The Battle of the Little Big Horn," is the largest, measuring $67\frac{1}{2}$ by 98 inches; the third, "Reno's Retreat," is the smallest, being 25 by 30 inches.[44] For details regarding these drawings, I quote in full from Memorandum 6-370A of C. S. Schopper in the West Point Museum:

The three pictures of the Battle of the Little Big Horn, of June 25, 1876, were painted by White Bird, a Northern Cheyenne Indian, in 1894 and 1895. White Bird took part in the battle as a boy of about fifteen, but the pictures probably represent the tribal account of the battle as well as his own recollections.

The largest picture shows two actions, the intermediate one the attack on General Custer, and the smallest one may show the repulse of Major Reno's battalion or an incident of the attack on General Custer, a question that can be decided by contemporary accounts stating where the one negro accompanying the command was killed. This negro was well remembered by the Cheyennes who had seen few of that race. The wounded Indians represent individuals known or remembered by the Cheyennes, but no officers nor soldiers are remembered by the Cheyennes with the exception of General Custer, painted in a fringed buckskin coat, and one officer near him, whom they noted without being able to identify him.

The notes accompanying the pictures have been lost, but the pictures themselves bear many indications of accuracy of detail, the burning of tepees is corroborated by a Sioux on p. 565, 10th Annual Report of the Bureau of Ethnology, 1888–89.

Delivered at the Museum by Captain Livermore, June 12, 1914, with instructions to mark the largest picture "The Battle of the Little Big Horn," the

---

[42] George A. Dorsey, "The Cheyenne. I. Ceremonial Organization," *Field Columbian Museum Publication* 99, *Anthropological Series*, IX, 1 (March 1905), Plate I.

[43] *Ibid.*, Plate VIII, figure 1, Red-Shield warrior, figure 2, Hoof-Rattle warrior; Plate IX, figure 1, Coyote warrior,

figure 2, Dog-Men warrior; Plate X, figures 1 and 2, Inverted or Bow-String warrior.

[44] West Point Museum file numbers 1207, 1208, and 1209, respectively.

second largest one "Custer's Fight," and the smallest one "Reno's Retreat."

(Signed) C. S. Schopper

RED HORSE DRAWINGS OF THE BATTLE OF THE LITTLE BIG HORN

Mallery includes in his discussion of Sioux records in the tenth report of the Bureau of American Ethnology another portrayal of the Custer defeat. This series was done by Red Horse, a Sioux, at Cheyenne River Agency in South Dakota in 1881

and was submitted by Dr. Charles E. McChesney, acting assistant surgeon in the United States Army. There are ten plates in the group of reproductions,[45] three of which are colored (Plates XLV, XLVI, and XLVIII). Red Horse was a Sioux chief, and he, too, took part in the Battle of the Little Big Horn.

For matters of comparison, not only from the point of view of art but also from the point of view of historical record as such, the interpretations of White Bird and Red Horse, with those of Bad Heart Bull, form a source group that should possess some real value.

CLASSIFICATION

As is evident from the foregoing summary, the purposes and characteristics of pictographic documents are varied. Mnemonic charts, geographical charts, personal communications, traditions, biographical records, tabulatory records, chronologies, and records of historic episodes—these are the main heads under which most pictographic writings may be classed and treated.

MNEMONIC CHARTS

Of the first, the most prominent examples are the Mide song records discussed by Hoffman and Mallery. A. B. Skinner also gives some Dakota examples in his discussion of the medicine ceremony of the Wahpeton Dakotas.[46] He describes and gives the purpose of three song records incised on thin strips of wood, both flat faces being inscribed. "These are," he says, "identical with those collected from the Menomini, Ojibway, and other Central Algonquin tribes."[47] They are purely mnemonic in purpose and character. Many of the songs are now forgotten, Skinner points out—a fact which indicates still more the essential character and original purpose of the records.

GEOGRAPHICAL CHARTS AND PERSONAL COMMUNICATIONS

I do not wish to do more than mention geographical charts and personal communications of various

kinds, since they are not particularly characteristic of the Dakotas. I have spoken of the former and of love letters, which form a type of the latter, in the preceding section in connection with Ojibway records. Hoffman discusses those in both of his papers on the Ojibways. Mallery shows, also, pictographic notices of departure and direction, particularly as found among the Alaskan Indians.[48] Then he gives in detail the letter sent by Turtle-following-Wife, a Southern Cheyenne, to his son Little Man, who was visiting at the time at Pine Ridge Reservation in South Dakota.[49] The form of communication was not unusual and was perfectly understood by the recipient; this latter fact indicates that there was a definite practice and method of pictorial communication. In all cases of this sort, as in others, however, there is the need of familiarity with the practice and methods of such communications in order to be able to interpret them. This points to the further fact that the practices were widespread and that the methods were organized, to some extent at least.

TRADITIONS

One of the large classes of native documents of this sort is that dealing with traditions. Outstanding examples of this type of record, already published, are the Walam Olum of the Lenapes and the Mide cosmogony chart, already mentioned. The Cheyenne ceremonial drawings accompanying Dorsey's paper

[45] Mallery, "Picture-Writing," Plates XXXIX–XLVIII inclusive, pp. 563–566.

[46] A. B. Skinner, "The Medicine Ceremony of the Menomini, Iowa, and Wahpeton Dakota," *Indian Notes and Monographs*, IV (1920), 267–273, figures 10 and 11, Plate XXIII.

[47] *Ibid.*, pp. 267–268.

[48] Mallery, "Pictographs," pp. 147–151, figures 47–52; "Picture-Writing," pp. 332–334, figures 439–444.

[49] Mallery, "Pictographs," pp. 160–161, figure 61.

on the ceremonial organization of the Cheyennes also belong here. And the Dighton Rock inscription, if Schoolcraft's explanation is correct,[50] is a significant example. Most Plains and Forest tribes have some records of this type; they are concerned with ceremonials and rituals and consequently are usually more or less mythological in character and subject matter.

PERSONAL RECORDS

Personal records, depictions of an individual's exploits, such as the robe of Mah-to-toh-pa (treated earlier in this chapter), are quite common, especially among Plains Indians. In fact, these are perhaps the most frequently found pictographic records. Every museum has its quota of painted skins or cloth or of incised bark or wood bearing the record of a chief's or warrior's or priest's achievements, and it is not unusual even yet for hitherto undiscovered specimens to appear. These records are likely to be biased, since usually they are made by the person whose deeds are being celebrated, so that they cannot be accepted unquestionably as historically accurate; as Mallery remarks, they are likely to be "bragging biographies" and "partisan histories." But when carefully examined and reliably translated, explained, and checked, they can frequently serve a real corroboratory and comparative purpose.

TABULATORY RECORDS

Serving a more official, practical purpose—an economic or civil purpose, perhaps—are tabulatory records, such as the Oglala Dakota Roster and Red Cloud's Census, treated by Mallery in the fourth report of the Bureau of American Ethnology.[51] The first is done in color, for the most part with colored pencils, on a sheet of heavy foolscap. It is the record of the heads of the eighty-four families of the Northern Oglalas of Chief Big Road's band at the time when that band was called in to the agency on Standing Rock Reservation, Dakota Territory, in 1883 following the joint hostilities, with Sitting Bull's adherents, against the whites. When called upon to give an account of his followers, the chief made or

caused to be prepared, and himself delivered, this record, or tally, to Major James McLaughlin, at that time agent in charge of the reservation. The document represents the heads of all the families of the band, with indications of subband divisions also. The symbol in each case is a totemic ideograph of the head of the individual, and indicates the identity of the person represented by means of personal designations of insignia or tokens of authority, the personal name, the status of the individual, and signs of particular achievement.[52] For instance, the five main chiefs are indicated by the pipe and pouch, emblems of chieftaincy, and each bears three horizontal bands across the cheek; the personal name is indicated—in the usual way—by the individual totem placed above the head. It is to be noticed, too, that the arrangement of the transverse face bands and the designs on the pouches vary with the individual.[53]

The twelve subchiefs are indicated, first of all, by the war club held vertically before the face, an arrangement which signifies that each has led a war party. The three transverse marks on the cheek indicate that these men are *akicita-itacampi*, or marshals in the civic organization. And finally, the individual totem appears above the head to indicate the exact identity of each man.

For the rest of the persons included in the count, the personal-name symbol alone is used, except that a round cheek mark serves to distinguish the four women from the men, who wear a single transverse stripe.

Red Cloud's Census[54] is another document of the same general character as Big Road's Roster, but is longer. It was prepared under the direction of Chief Red Cloud on the Pine Ridge Reservation in Dakota Territory about 1880. It was made on seven sheets of manila paper and bears the names of the faithful adherents of Red Cloud at the time when the agent, following some difficulty with the chief, had named another person official chief of the Indians at the agency. This list contains 289 names. All of the ideographs are in black and white; evidently, though, the various sheets, as Mallery points out, were prepared by different persons, for the ideographs of the

---

[50] Schoolcraft, *Historical and Statistical Information*, I, 112–114.

[51] Mallery, "Pictographs," p. 174, Plates LII–LVIII (Oglala Dakota Roster), and pp. 176–181, Plates LIX–LXXIX (Red Cloud's Census).

[52] *Ibid.*, pp. 168–187.

[53] For comparison of the ideographs for these five men, Plate XXVI in Mallery, "Picture-Writing," is especially good.

[54] Mallery, "Pictographs," pp. 176–181, Plates LIX–LXXIX.

different groups show technical peculiarities of execution.[55]

A comparison of the ideographs of names found in both lists—the Roster and the Census—brings out the fact that there is a considerable degree of latitude in the matter of individual ideographic writing; the general character of the designation is the same, but the different representations are very likely to show decided individuality in execution on the part of the various "writers." Mallery calls attention particularly to the varying symbols for Chief Big Road in the two enumerations and remarks, "... it is obvious that the ideographic device was not fixed but elastic and subject to variation, the intention being solely to preserve the idea."[56]

WINTER COUNTS

This same fact is to be noticed in connection with the Dakota winter counts, or calendars, which make up the principal form of chronological record among these people. The Honorable John A. Rice of Wisconsin is, I believe, one of the first persons to describe in print this sort of document. In a short note on the La Crosse Cave he incidentally remarks:

> I have an interesting *fac-simile* of an attempt at history-writing by the Sioux, with its interpretation. *It is a rough representation of some event in each year,* occurring during the period from 1860 to 1870.[57]

Quite evidently he refers to a specimen of the characteristic Dakota chronological record which Mallery treats exhaustively in the fourth and tenth reports of the Bureau of American Ethnology and which I shall discuss later. The point I made in the preceding paragraph regarding personal designations—the elasticity and latitude in the matter of ideographic device—is in part included in Rice's expression "rough representation," I am sure; Mallery speaks of it also in direct connection with the winter counts. Rice, in that short sentence, further puts his finger upon the central distinguishing feature of the Dakota counts: the representations are of some *one* event *in each year*; they are year markers, and so serve as calendars. But I shall treat of them in more detail later.

HISTORIC EPISODES

In addition to all these forms of pictographic record, I have considered in one group historic episodes as such. In this class I include such documents as the Cheyenne drawings of the Battle of the Little Big Horn, the Red Horse drawings of the same event, and numerous portions of the Bad Heart Bull narrative. Particularly outstanding in the latter manuscript would be the two series representing the Custer affair (Nos. 126–169 and 170–185), various Sioux-Crow battles (e.g. Nos. 245 and 220–235), and the Wounded Knee disturbance of 1890 (e.g., Nos. 314, 316, and 317).

All specimens in the last class, however, are of a rather different character in technical device. They are not ideographic in the sense in which the winter counts or the Roster and Census are. They are, rather, completely illustrative in style; they are detailed and realistic, a tendency which is characteristic of the whole Bad Heart Bull record.

WINTER COUNTS

One authority on Indian pictography remarks that "probably more distinctive examples of evolution in ideography and in other details of picture-writing are found still extant among the Dakota than among any other North American tribe."[58] Its purpose among these people was chiefly the representation and recording of biographical data, historic episodes, and chronology, especially the last. In the old days of the free life in the open, skins made up the most common record-bearing material. To be sure, practically all weapons, ceremonial articles, and garments bore significant inscriptions and decorations, and, in addition, records were sometimes carved or painted on cave and cliff walls; but historical art and records were usually made on skins—painted or drawn with brushes made of wood or bone and in colors made from native clays and the juices of plants mixed with water. Later, when the coming of the whites and the passing of the great herds of buffalo, deer, and elk seriously affected the leather supply,

---

[55] *Ibid.*, p. 176.

[56] Mallery, "Picture-Writing," p. 421. Cf. figure 540 on p. 421 and *a* of Plate XXVI opposite p. 420.

[57] Rice, "Additional Notes." The italics in the last sentence are mine.

[58] Mallery, "Pictographs," pp. 93–94.

cloth and paper were used. So one finds the Sioux winter counts on skins, cloth, and paper; often a cloth record represents a copy of an original done on skin, as in the case of the winter count of The Swan used by Mallery.[59] Among the records done on paper are the Short Man copy of the Oglala winter count and the report of Bad Heart Bull with which this book is chiefly concerned.

I have said that among the Sioux the principal purpose of pictography was the representation of chronology and that their most unique and characteristic chronological record is the winter count. Mallery, in his discussion of pictorially presented Indian chronology, makes the observation that "the Mexican system, much more scientific and more elaborate than that employed by the northern tribes, resembled it in graphic record or detail of exhibit, and is highly interesting as compared with the Dakota Winter Count."[60] That statement as it is structurally arranged rather shifts the emphasis from the Dakota to the Mexican; I could wish, since the Dakotas are my main concern and his also, that Mallery, even for the sake of his own theme, had made his remark otherwise. But even as it stands, it makes a point: the Dakotas can, in one respect at least, be likened to the ancient Mayas. To be sure, the Mayas of the Old Empire, with their extensive knowledge of astronomy and mathematics and their consequently elaborate calendar and chronology systems, were vastly more advanced than the nomadic and warlike Indians of our western plains; for that reason the fact that the Sioux have in their chronological methods anything at all comparable to those of the older civilization is significant. The point of similarity is the method of designating the years, the graphic representation of event or fact; both systems are ideographic in character.

There is this difference between the Mayan and Dakotan chronologies, however, a difference which in its way shadows an inherent difference in the two peoples' psychologies: the Maya period markers, as we may call them, were erected and prepared before the actual date of their dedication; there was a certain prophetic, forward-looking tendency in the Mayan manner of conceiving time and its passage that kept their eyes always to the future event.[61] The Dakota

year markers, on the other hand, deal with past events, and are prepared after the events have occurred (in fact, one term which is used to designate them, hekta yawapi, means "counts back");[62] they are strictly memoranda of past happenings. The two peoples simply assume diagonally opposed angles of chronological vision.

In his several papers, Mallery has capably treated the subject of Indian picture writing, particularly the so-called winter counts of the Sioux. I shall simply recapitulate the outstanding characteristics of the winter counts of the Dakotas before proceeding to detailed discussion of some individual records. As Mallery points out, these year counts were the outline-like representation of successive events, year by year, "the device by which was accomplished the continuous designation of years." As Good Wood, a Blackfoot Dakota enlisted at Fort Rice expressed it, they contain "something put down for every year about their nation"; they are in reality calendric.

The term "winter count," to a degree, speaks for itself. The winter season in the northerly section of the Middle West is the one of commanding significance, for it covers an extended period of time and is intense in its characteristics. The Dakotas, then, count by winters, their "year" covering parts of two of our calendar years; as a result, there is sometimes some question as to the exact time of occurrence of a given event, since the Indian graphic system does not designate day, week, or even month directly. The winter count is simply a calendrical framework of events or facts which are significant to the tribe or band as a unit. In fact, the points noted seem frequently of scant *general* interest or concern; but that indicates one of the essential characteristics of the winter counts as such: they are not bodies of general history but are, rather, individual records of an individual group; and the choice of the representative event is directed by the question of significance to the band. If the point chosen happens to coincide in the counts of several different bands or tribes, an event of widespread importance or significance has occurred, or perhaps several bands have spent the winter in close proximity and combined activity. When several happenings of signal importance have taken place, the choice among them represents the

[59] Ibid.
[60] Mallery, "Picture-Writing," p. 265.
[61] Sylvanus G. Morley, "Inscriptions at Copan,"

Carnegie Institution Publication 219 (Washington, 1920), p. 397.
[62] Mallery, "Pictographs," p. 128.

individual and strongly felt reaction of the band as a whole or perhaps occasionally of the recorder personally; the choice will reflect usually that incident or circumstance which has made the deepest impression on the band or tribe consciousness. The incoherent character of all the winter counts points to the fact that in no sense do they aim at narrative; their chief concern is the erection of effective calendric milestones.

Up to the time of Mallery's account of the so-called Lone Dog winter count, published in 1877,[63] ethnologists generally seemed unaware of the existence of such documents.[64] "Bragging biographies of chiefs and partisan histories of particular wars delineated in picture-writing on hides or bark are common," says Mallery;[65] but an organized document of this sort was something new. Its discovery and publication, however, aroused interest in native records, and a number of specimens of the same genre came to light in consequence. The result was Mallery's "preliminary" paper in the Bureau of American Ethnology report for 1882–1883 and his final paper in 1888–1889.

The Lone Dog count, to which I have referred, was done by Lone Dog, a Yanktonai Dakota, who is said to have been among the hostiles under Sitting Bull in 1876 and who was located near Fort Peck in the fall of that year. Mallery, however, worked from a copy of a duplicate[66] of the original,[67] a copy made on cotton cloth.[68] That the record was well known, there can be no doubt for Mallery received interpretations from numerous Indians from various localities, all of which agree in essential character.[69]

Plates VI in the fourth report and XX in the tenth are reproductions in color of the copy from which Mallery worked.[70] The original was kept on a buffalo skin, and the copy has been painted to indicate this. The year symbols begin at the center and move out and around in a counterclockwise spiral. The period covered is that from 1800–1801 to 1869–1870.

The Flame's winter count[71] covers a longer period, beginning with 1786–1787 and ending with 1876–1877. The facsimile from which the author worked was a copy about a yard square, also done on cotton cloth.[72] The arrangement of the pictographs is different, however. The record begins in the lower left corner, moves horizontally across to the lower right corner, then turns back in a straight parallel line to the left, and so on—in so-called boustrophedon style.[73] The interpretation of this count was secured from the Indian artist himself at Fort Sully in April, 1877. Although The Flame is reported to be a Two Kettle Dakota by birth, he generally lived with the Sans Arcs and so is really representative of them.

A third count is that of The Swan, a Miniconjou chief at Cheyenne River Agency.[74] The original (called in translation a "History of the Miniconjou Dakotas") was done on dressed antelope or deer skin, but Mallery worked from a facsimile made on cloth by a Two Kettle Sioux. The record covers the years 1800–1801 to 1870–1871.[75] Like the Lone Dog count, The Swan's also is arranged in a spiral, but its movement is clockwise.

Major Joseph Bush in 1870 secured from a trader, James Robb, at Cheyenne River Agency, a fourth record, which is about the same size as Lone Dog's and is similar to it in general character. This one, however, ends in 1869–1870 and in some respects differs in interpretation.[76]

In 1868 and 1869, *Mato Sapo* (Black Bear), a Miniconjou warrior on the Cheyenne River Agency Reservation, near Fort Sully, made or copied on cloth what he called a "History of the Miniconjous." This record is smaller than the Lone Dog count, is arranged in an elliptical spiral, and ends with 1868–1869.[77]

All of these, because of striking resemblances to the Lone Dog count and because Lone Dog's was the first published, Mallery calls the Lone Dog system of winter counts. For the sake of comparison, the

[63] Mallery, "Calendar."

[64] Mallery, "Pictographs," pp. 89–90. In the same year, however, Rice made note of such a record in his possession. See Rice, "Additional Notes."

[65] Mallery, "Pictographs," p. 90.

[66] Duplicate possessed by Basil Clement, a half-breed living at Fort Sully.

[67] Mallery, "Pictographs," p. 90.

[68] Copy made by Lieutenant H. T. Reed, First U.S. Infantry.

[69] Mallery, "Pictographs," pp. 103–126, Plates IX–

XXXII; "Picture-Writing," pp. 273–287, figures accompanying text.

[70] Mallery, "Picture-Writing," p. 266 (middle).

[71] Mallery, "Pictographs," pp. 100–127, Plates VII–XXXIII.

[72] By Lieutenant Reed.

[73] Mallery, "Pictographs," p. 93.

[74] *Ibid.*, pp. 103–126, Plates IX–XXXII.

[75] The years correspond to those mentioned by Rice.

[76] Mallery, "Pictographs," p. 94.

[77] *Ibid.*, pp. 94–95.

commentator in the fourth report has arranged a series of plates showing the ideograms of the Lone Dog, The Flame, and The Swan winter counts in parallel and has accompanied them with literal translations.[78] The similarities for the years common to all three (1800–1801 to 1870–1871) are striking. The only difference, except for slight mechanical individualities of the recorders, is in The Flame's event for 1870–1871; he records the death of his son rather than the tribal episode, a battle between Hunkpapas and Crows, which the other recorders represent.

From the more western Brulé and Oglala Dakotas comes a second group, which Mallery calls the Corbusier winter counts, since they were secured and submitted to him by Dr. W. H. Corbusier, assistant surgeon in the United States Army stationed at Camp Sheridan, Nebraska, not far from the Pine Ridge Agency, South Dakota.[79] There are at least five of these extant Corbusier reports,[80] but Mallery secured only three.[81] He reproduces in parallel the less extensive of these, namely, Cloud Shield's and American Horse's, in the fourth report.[82] In the tenth[83] he gives Battiste Good's, which is the most extensive and in some respects the most significant of all. In both he inserts occasional comparative references to a fourth count (White Cow Killer's) to which he had access. These show somewhat more variation than the Lone Dog series, but they also show a closer relationship. There is decidedly more variation in the ideograms. Even when the subject matter is the same for the different counts, the individuality of the recorder is more evident than in the Lone Dog system.

The translation of still another Oglala winter count, showing noticeable relationship with the Corbusier group, has been used and still is used in semiofficial calendrical capacity in the government Indian office at the Pine Ridge Agency. The fact that it is so used speaks for its acceptance as, at least relatively, authentic. This count begins with the year 1759 and is continued to date. It partakes, in the matter of choice of events and general nature of

information, of the winter count characteristics of which I have spoken. Further, it shows enough marked similarities to the Corbusier counts to speak for its authenticity and enough differences to indicate the originality and individuality of the recorder or his band.

I have in my possession a pictographic representation of a portion of this winter count. The document was done by an Oglala Dakota by the name of Short Man and covers the period from 1821 to 1923. The technique of the artist is not remarkable, although the record is quite similar in manner of portrayal to the Big Road Roster and Red Cloud's Census. I am of the opinion that it is a rather poor copy of an original and official record of the band. It is, however, a true winter count and is of value because it is an example of this type of document and because it brings out several characteristics of the genre.

The manuscript itself is an old paper-covered "composition book" whose binding has been reinforced with heavy linen thread. Much handling has worn the book so badly that parts of the cover are in shreds; there is hardly a page that is not torn and badly dog-eared. The record begins on the last page —Chinese fashion. In some cases a whole page is given over to the ideograph for one year, in others two years are portrayed, and in a few, three. And the book is full.

A comparison of this count with those of Battiste Good, Lone Dog, American Horse, The Swan, and The Flame brings out a number of coinciding entries and a great many contrasts, all of which simply bear witness to the general character of winter counts—the tribal interest and band interest. There is enough similarity to bespeak tribal authenticity and enough dissimilarity to indicate experiences unique to the particular band and to show the assertion of the individuality of that band and possibly particularly of the recorder. There is one error in the Short Man record which throws all the subsequent events one year late. The first issue of annuities is given by Short Man as occurring in 1852. The Corbusier counts given by Mallery[84] agree in placing this in the year

---

[78] *Ibid.*, pp. 100–127, Plates VII–XXXIII.

[79] *Ibid.*, pp. 127–146, including Plates XXXIV–LI.

[80] *Ibid.*, p. 129.

[81] Cloud Shield's (Oglala), American Horse's (Oglala but different band), and Battiste Good's (Brulé).

[82] Mallery, "Pictographs," pp. 130–146, Plates XXXIV–LI.

[83] Mallery, "Picture-Writing," pp. 287–328, figures accompanying text. Plates XXI–XXIII are in color (prehistoric cycles).

[84] American Horse's and Cloud Shield's, I and II respectively, Plate XLVI and p. 142 in Mallery, "Pictographs"; Battiste Good's, p. 323 in Mallery, "Picture-Writing."

1851, however. The Lone Dog series do not mention it at all. The chronology of the Short Man record seems to tally with the official translated "calendar" and with the other Corbusier counts when the adjustment for this error has been made.

All the records except American Horse's designate the year 1821–1822 by ideographs representing falling stars. American Horse points out, rather, the fact of the introduction of whiskey in this year, a point which Battiste Good also mentions secondarily. The year 1823–1824 shows some variation, however. The Lone Dog counts all emphasize the combined attack of United States troops and Dakotas upon the Arikaras.[85] Battiste Good mentions both this and the plentiful supply of corn.[86] Cloud Shield mentions only the joint expedition against the Arikaras. American Horse shows only the ideograph to indicate the abundance of corn, but the translation adds "which they got at the Ree [Arikara] villages." The possibility of some connection between the great supply of corn and the conquest of the Arikara villages is not at all inconceivable, and from translation of American Horse's count would seem really probable. The year 1828–1829 is characterized in the Lone Dog system by the establishment of a trading post;[87] Battiste Good designates it "Killed-two-hundred-Gros Ventres [Hidatsas][88] winter";[89] American Horse and Cloud Shield emphasize the capture of many antelope; White Cow Killer says "Many-Rees-Killed Winter";[90] and Short Man records "Many Mandans Killed." Evidently the fight referred to by Good, White Cow Killer, and Short Man was of considerable significance to the western Dakotas. The seeming

discrepancy in the matter of the tribe is not in reality a discrepancy, for, according to Bulletin 30 of the Bureau of American Ethnology, Part 1,[91] the Hidatsas (known also as Gros Ventres), Mandans, and Arikaras were closely allied after the beginning of the nineteenth century. The year 1855–1856 shows a fine variety of notations: the Lone Dog series consistently record General William S. Harney's council with the nine Sioux bands at Fort Pierre on March 1, 1856;[92] American Horse records the killing of a Pawnee by a band of Oglalas; Cloud Shield records the murder of two tribesmen by their own people; White Cow Killer records "A-Medicine-Man-Made-Buffalo-Medicine-Winter";[93] Good records the taking of Dakota prisoners, the killing of Dakotas by white soldiers, and the Harney event;[94] and Short Man simply records "Meeting Crows in Peace."

The presence of variety in unity, as one might say, is unquestionable in the winter counts. The event chosen, the ideographic character, the arrangement of the characters, all vary to one degree or another. The main object is a plan which will accomplish a certain historical continuity by a mere regular addition—forward or backward—of historic occurrences in order to form a trustworthy supplement to the memory. And the number and variety of these Dakota records have added a significant and valuable chapter to the annals of native American Indian lore; covering as they do periods of varying extent and—in the case of Battiste Good's—reaching back into the realms of legend, they build up a historical skeleton of no mean structure.

BAD HEART BULL'S MANUSCRIPT

There is another statement in Mallery's discussion of the Dakota winter counts which is particularly significant in connection with the study of the Bad Heart Bull manuscript. "If they [the winter counts]

had exhibited a complete national or tribal history for the years embraced in them," he says, "their discovery would have been in some respects more valuable."[95] The record of Amos Bad Heart Bull is

[85] Mallery, "Pictographs," pp. 111–113, Plate XVI.
[86] *Ibid.*, p. 112 (bottom), and "Picture-Writing," figure 380 and p. 318.
[87] Mallery, "Pictographs," Plate XVIII and p. 114.
[88] The reference is to the so-called Gros Ventres of the Missouri, not to the Gros Ventres of the Prairies, a detached branch of the Arapahos. The use of the same general name, Gros Ventres, for two distinct tribes may easily cause confusion. See Frederick W. Hodge, ed., *Handbook of American Indians North of Mexico* (Washington, 1907), BAE Bulletin 30, Part 1, p. 508.

[89] Mallery, "Picture-Writing," figure 385 and p. 319.
[90] Mallery, "Pictographs," Plate XLIII and p. 138.
[91] Alice C. Fletcher, "Arikara," BAE Bulletin 30, Part 1, p. 84; J. O. Dorsey and Cyrus Thomas, "Mandan," BAE Bulletin 30, Part 1, pp. 796–798.
[92] Mallery, "Pictographs," Plate XXVII and pp. 121–122.
[93] *Ibid.*, Plate XLVII and p. 143.
[94] Mallery, "Picture-Writing," figure 412 and p. 324.
[95] *Ibid.*, p. 271 (middle).

that "discovery . . . in some respects more valuable"; it does give, as I have indicated elsewhere, the complete history of the Oglala Dakotas for the last half at least of the nineteenth century and the beginning of the twentieth.

In purpose and character, the Bad Heart Bull document is quite different from the winter counts. In the first place, it gives full historical and cultural detail; and in the second place, that detail is given in generally chronological and coherent sequence, with interruptions only to allow for a complete "discussion" of some phase of tribal life or organization—social, religious, political—and then only as that "discussion" belongs integrally to the action. The design, as will subsequently be evident to a degree, is narrative rather than calendric. The record is intended to give a full and authentic account of the tribal life of the Oglala Dakotas during that period of stress and strife and rebellious readjustment which falls within the sixty or seventy years covered by the record.

The distinctive difference in general technique in this manuscript and the calendars is indicative of the contrasting and supplementary purpose of the Bad Heart Bull record. Generally speaking, I may say that the winter counts are ideographic in character, while this new record is iconographic. The year symbols of the winter counts are relatively simple in their construction and extent, but they represent a whole thought. A whole idea or phase of meaning usually is portrayed by a single image—an image of a single element or an image of one element added to another in the case of complex ideas or descriptions. The symbols are built up more or less as the Chinese symbols are, except that they have not become so set, so solidly conventionalized; the recorder is free to follow the dictates of his own mind in the arrangement of the elements, and in fact is free to use elements or symbols of his own origination, tempered somewhat, of course, by the general practices of his people. The account of Bad Heart Bull, on the contrary, is made up of pictures that give the full action of the story in illustrative style. For example, compare Battiste Good's ideograph from 1877–1878,[96] representing the death of Crazy Horse, and Bad Heart Bull's depiction of the same event in No. 304. Battiste Good's explanation is: "Crazy-Horse-came-to-make-peace-and-was-killed-with-his-hands-

stretched-out-winter." The symbol consists of three connected elements: the figure of a man with outstretched hands, the name device—an odd representation of a horse—above the man's head and connected with it in the usual way by a line from the mouth, and a second, smaller human figure represented as running a bayonet into the body of the first figure. The whole is quite compact. Bad Heart Bull's description of the event is entirely different in character. This particular drawing covers all of one page and part of another and is a strange combination of two widely divergent angles of vision: the guardhouse and the main actors in the scene appear in close-up in the center of the scene; surrounding that center are the buildings of Fort Robinson and a highly conventionalized representation of soldiers drawn up in review formation, all in miniature, while outside the barracks in the foreground is a miniature and impressionistic portrayal of horses and human beings, perhaps Crazy Horse's people. The whole scene is suggested; action is portrayed in the central group and in the group outside the barracks; something is actually *taking place*.

Further, in a number of cases, the artist, in his desire to present the complete and detailed story, has given more than one portrayal of a particular event or phase of an event in order that the episode may be seen from various angles of vision and so may be more completely understood; this he does especially in some of his battle scenes. The most prominent example of this is, of course, the double portrayal of the Custer fight—one series close view, the other distant. Among the Sioux-Crow encounters, there is a double picturing in Nos. 101 and 102. The composition No. 102 is a close-view representation of a fight in which a party of Crows has been trapped on top of a butte and is being annihilated by the much larger band of attacking Sioux. On the page opposite (No. 101), Bad Heart Bull has inserted a miniature, impressionistic portrayal of the same event. The latter suggests more adequately the hopeless position of the Crows—the great number of oncoming Dakotas and the utter impossibility of escape from the butte; the larger-scale drawing emphasizes the gruesome detail of the slaughter on top of the butte. The recorder has simply made his report more complete and comprehensive in scope and suggestion by means of this serial manner of portrayal.

This technique is one of the features which probably will make Bad Heart Bull's record a work of

---

[96] *Ibid.*, p. 327 and figure 434.

some significance to North American ethnology, a work of perhaps considerable significance to the study of the history, art, religion, and ceremonial and civil organization of the Indian. In particular it will be valuable to the study of the historical art of the Dakotas and consequently of similar art of all Plains Indians and so, in turn, of all Indian art.

That the record is fairly accurate historically, there is no doubt. Bad Heart Bull's portrayals of warrior societies, the Battle of the Little Big Horn, the death of Crazy Horse, and the Ghost Dance trouble of 1890 and 1891—all outstanding subjects—corroborate rather consistently the generally accepted reports of these organizations and events in the main points and in general spirit. Whether or not a close checking showed fidelity to historic episode, however, this significant fact would remain: the record throws much light upon methods of Indian warfare; upon the details of manners of fighting, of costume, weapon, and maneuver; and—perhaps this is even more significant—upon the Plains Indian attitude toward war as a perfectly normal activity and accompaniment of life, as in fact an integral part of life.

CHAPTER III

The Bad Heart Bull Manuscript as History

THOUGH Bad Heart Bull, of course, knew nothing of Herodotus, his purpose in making a record was obviously and expressly the same as that of the "Father of History." The Greek avowedly wrote his renowned chronicle "in order that the things men have done might not in time be forgotten, and that the great and wonderful deeds of both Greeks and barbarians might not become unheard of, this, and why they fought with one another."[1] So far at least the young Oglala can claim kinship with Herodotus and consequently earns the name historian—he is attempting to preserve the record of the life of a people. Analysis of the Dakota and the Greek records shows further similarities. Bad Heart Bull, like Herodotus, does not preserve *merely* the record of exploits of arms—though in both the note of exploit and warlike feat is the dominant one—but sets forth the record of manners, customs, traditions, institutions. He, also, is giving a complete cross section of the life of his people—social, economic, ritualistic, political, and military—*as he knew it*. He reflects the inherently pluralistic nature of history as such and suggests the closely interwoven character of the plural phases of life, an integration which is more marked, or at least more obvious, in a primitive society such as he describes than in most higher civilizations.

Once it becomes evident that the record is historical in nature, the important question is, "Is the record a true one?" The question is twofold in its implication, for truth in the portrayal of history is of two kinds: truth to detail, accuracy in point of facts enumerated; and faithfulness to the spirit and atmosphere of the times, truth in the bodying forth of the character of a people and its life as a whole. Both types of truth are

of extreme importance, but for the moment the second will interest us more, for a worthy and dependable physical and spiritual panorama is more significant to sympathetic understanding than the detailed description of episode, institution, and object.

In itself the recorder's interest in the activity and practices of his people, to the extent of studying and preserving them "in order that the things men have done might not in time be forgotten," bespeaks a decided maturity of mind and thought, a maturity which, however, does not exclude a distinct, almost youthful eagerness in the study and presentation of the life to be portrayed. The steadiness of maturity may conceivably be accompanied by a youthful spirit of eager adventure; disciplined observation and thought may combine with keen imagination for a more complete understanding of that which is to be set forth. This rather paradoxical combination we find in Amos Bad Heart Bull.

I have already discussed at some length in the preceding chapter the various types of Dakota historical documents. Those here significant are the winter counts, for purposes of comparison and corroboration; records of ceremonial organization and performance; personal records; and records of historic episodes. The last of these types is the one most closely akin to this particular manuscript.

In Part Two, Chapter VI, I have briefly outlined the whole record, according to episodes, under six headings: Events Perhaps Earlier than 1856; Sioux-Crow Fights; The Custer Affair on the Little Big Horn; Early Social Life and Its Reorganization; The Ghost Dance and the Battle of Wounded Knee; and "Greater Indian Shows." These headings cover the whole record and indicate fairly closely in their arrangement the sequence of the record and the sequence according to chronology. It is appropriate

[1] F. J. E. Woodbridge, *The Purpose of History* (New York: Columbia University Press, 1916), p. 5.

to place "Sioux-Crow Fights" immediately after the introductory section on the earliest events, for these battles begin at once and continue, with brief interruptions, through the record until the time of the Ghost Dance trouble and the Battle of Wounded Knee. The Custer fight is treated in the natural chronological order. "Early Social Life and Its Reorganization" is taken up next, for, although drawings on this subject are scattered throughout the narrative, a goodly number on various specific aspects of this phase of the tribal life are found following the Little Big Horn series. As for the rest, they follow the natural, chronological order and the order of the record. The second chapter of Part Two (Chapter VII) includes a detailed, page-by-page discussion of the whole record. Here I wish to treat the divisions of the record in their larger, unified aspects, that is, as expositions of single themes.

EVENTS PERHAPS EARLIER THAN 1856

Whether or not the first section portrays some specific council, tribal move, Sun Dance performance, and buffalo hunt is a question, but a question of relative unimportance. The drawings in these various groups *may* represent particular events. On the other hand, they may merely form a background for better understanding of the life and activity which is to be described in subsequent pages. In either case, the section is an introduction to the whole narrative; the significance to the record as a whole is the same from both points of view. Whether one assumes one view or the other, 1856 is a date subsequent to these first events, and the fights and other activities enumerated also follow this date.

No dates whatever are given in the introductory section. This fact and the fact that the warrior societies and various ritualistic symbols and distinctive Teton costume are treated in purely subjective fashion may well indicate that the artist looks upon these pages as introduction, and I shall assume this in my discussion.

THE COUNCIL

The relationship of the various elements in this section is a vital one. The council scene suggests the close civic organization and administration of the tribe. Four councilors (*wakicunza*, i.e., "thinkers"),[2] men of wisdom and high standing, hold in their hands the regulation of the civic and economic life of the people.[3] Their official lodge stands in a prominent place in the great central area within the camp circle (see No. 1). After due deliberation within it, they move out into the center of the area, where they sit in a solemn group and issue their orders to the attendant *akicita*, or marshals, of the camp (see No. 1), who are the actual executives and in one sense also the judiciary.[4]

Taken in connection with the pictures of the tribal move, the warrior-society regalia, and the buffalo hunt which follow, it seems evident that the council portrayed is one concerned with the annual spring reorganization of camp.[5] For each of these three significant elements and activities in the tribal life, spring was an all-important season; then the bands drew together, the camp circle in its civil and social aspects was reorganized, new officers were appointed, and plans were made for future activities; then the warrior societies underwent an annual revitalization, new members and officers were elected, and new paraphernalia were made; and then very frequently a

---

[2] According to Clark Wissler, "Societies and Ceremonial Associations in the Oglala Division of the Teton Dakota," *APAMNH*, XI, Part 1 (1912), 14.

[3] These four are elected "to organize and control the camp," and they "serve for about one year. It seems to have been the custom to re-elect two or three of them so as to have experienced men in office." *Ibid.*, p. 8. "It is clear that all the civil and economic affairs of the camp are in the hands of the wakicun. On all these matters, they are free to instruct and can enforce their orders through the akicita. They decide when to break camp, where to go and again select the new site. Hunting must be carried on when and as they direct. They also see that every person receives a fair share of the meat and is provided with enough robes to make the winter endurable. They settle disputes, judge and compound crimes, and make rules to ensure proper decorum in camp. However, our informants all felt their chief function to have been the regulation of the hunt, or the conservation of the food supply." *Ibid.*, p. 11.

[4] The *akicita* had the power to arrest and punish *on the spot* offenders against the law of the tribe.

[5] "In former times, the tendency was for the people to scatter out in winter, but early in the spring the camp circle was formed and its government organized. This was initiated by the selection of the wakicun [should be wakicunza or wakiconze]." Wissler, "Societies," p. 8.

great buffalo hunt took place, a hunt which had been planned in the council and which formed the initial step in the reviving and rehabilitating of tribal life.

TRIBAL MOVE AND BUFFALO HUNT

The drawings of the tribal move (Nos. 5 to 7) portray the traveling of the band en masse according to the plans made by the *wakicunza* in council assembled (see No. 1). The close sequential relationship between the council, the move, and the buffalo hunt (Nos. 16, 17, and 19) clearly bears out the fact that the chief function of the *wakicunza* was economic (and consequently civil); that is, that it concerned the regulation of the hunt and the conservation of the food supply.[6] It but emphasizes the supreme importance of the buffalo in the life of the Dakota, first economically and subsequently and consequently civically, religiously, and artistically.

SUN DANCE

The place and significance of the Sun Dance in the opening section is an equally integral part of the background which the artist is building; it is, in a measure, the religious expression of the importance of the buffalo, to which I have just alluded; it is inherently linked up with all the rest. In the matter of sequence, the Sun Dance series precedes the societies series and the pictures of the buffalo hunt. This would further bear out the impression of a subjective attitude on the part of the artist so far as this introductory section is concerned, for the Sun Dance was performed later in the season, usually at midsummer, occasionally about "the time when chokecherries were ripe" (about August), before the fall hunt. The significant fact here is that it is being enumerated as one of the vital elements in the life of the tribe and as an element bearing extremely close relationship to the hunting of buffalo, the great staple of life. It is a prayer for the preservation and continuation of the life of the people as a people. Certainly the success of the hunt was of prime importance to that life.

SOCIETIES AND THEIR REGALIA

The placing of the warrior societies and their regalia at the end of the introduction seems quite arbitrary—further evidence, perhaps, that the parts of this section are treated in a general, subjective manner. The societies would have been reorganized and refurnished before the Sun Dance and before the buffalo hunt in the ordinary sequence of events. In fact, they would have become quite active early in the process of the spring rejuvenation because they enter extensively and significantly into the civil and ceremonial peacetime regulation of the camp, as well as into the fighting.

It was from among six of the eight warrior societies that the marshals, or *akicita*, of the band were traditionally chosen.[7] The other two were not *akicita* societies among the Oglalas, that is, they did not take official part in the policing of the camp; they corresponded to them in other respects, however.[8] In general, the membership of these two seems to have been composed of men somewhat older than those in the others, although among the Oglalas there were no specific age limits in the societies.[9] The two organizations seem to have been exponents of certain significant social elements; they took *unofficial* part in regulating the camp life. The Omaha Society had a special healing ceremony that assumed some prominence in the tribe,[10] and members of the Miwatani Society were looked upon as special advocates of peace within the camp circle, their official pipe being frequently used as a peace pipe in the re-establishment of tranquillity after disturbance.[11] In all cases, though, the chief emphasis in the societies is the same: they are primarily *warrior* societies, no matter what the incidental characteristics may be.[12] The requirements for entrance into the societies and the stipulations to be met by officers and members thereafter leave no doubt as to the driving purpose of the organizations. Bravery and integrity in war are the watchwords of all of them.

The emphasizing of this aspect of the societies, however, should not overshadow the other and very

---

[6] Cf. Wissler, "Societies."

[7] Tokala, Kangi Yuha, Cante Tinza, Iroka, Sotka Yuha, and Wiciska; cf. Wissler, "Societies," pp. 13 ff.

[8] The Miwatani probably comes from the Mandan tribe, since the word *Miwatani* is the term used by the Lakotas to designate that tribe; the Omaha comes from the Omaha tribe.

[9] Wissler, "Societies," pp. 41–42.

[10] Unpublished notes.

[11] Wissler, "Societies," p. 47.

[12] Cf. my paper, "Ethical Conceptions of the Dakota," *University of Nebraska Studies*, XXVI, 3–4 (July–October 1926).

significant phase of their nature; civil, social, and fraternal obligations are held constantly before the members, some of the societies stressing certain of these elements, some of them others. Always, however, there is the demand for loyalty to fellow members, regard for the poor and needy, and the observance of strict morality according to tribal and fraternal codes.

SIOUX-CROW FIGHTS

Of the compositions in the record, the great majority belong to the second division, "Sioux-Crow Fights." This fact shows the record to be decidedly true in spirit and atmosphere, for the struggles of these hereditary enemies formed the running accompaniment of their lives over a period of many years. The truth of the recording, from the standpoint of accuracy of detail, is another question and one which will have to be met chiefly with material from winter counts. Many of the incidents can be identified, and, particularly in Part Two, I do identify them. But here, as I have intimated elsewhere, the truth of the picture-as-a-whole, faithfulness to the spirit of the fabric of the life portrayed, is of primary importance. I simply wish to emphasize chiefly the total effect, and to call attention to the bodying forth of the type of existence of this people.

Plains Indian warfare was of such scattered and, on occasion, trivial nature that it would be pointless in a discussion of this sort to reproduce each fight in detail. Many of the skirmishes were purely accidental affairs—the unpremeditated meeting of two enemy warriors or of groups of two or three, the pursuit of one or two by a single enemy, and so on. Their portrayal is necessary to such a record as Bad Heart Bull's in order to make the picture complete; they are distinctly characteristic of the life of the Plains peoples. So we see Young Man Afraid of His Horses killing the Crow-with-his-face-painted-black-in-sign-of-previous-victory (No. 47); the killing of four Crows by Dakotas in 1864 (Nos. 49 to 52); the killing of White Tail Feathers after his spectacular act of counting coup on a live enemy (Nos. 55 and 56); the killing of two Crow women and a baby on the way from one camp to another (No. 57). All these, and others of similar nature, are characteristic of the record and of the life of the Dakotas.

For episodes occupying a larger place in the tribal life and annals, the earliest date given in the record is 1856. This accompanies the portrayal of what is called the Captive Hill fight (No. 32). A party of Miniconjou, Oglala, and Sans Arc Sioux trapped a small body of Crows in a cave on Captive Hill (or Butte), near the head of Owl Creek (Moreau River) northwest of the Black Hills, and killed ten. The fight was so important in the Oglala mind that it was used to identify the year 1856 in their winter count.

There are, however, two portrayals of battles appearing before this, both of which seem to be accidentally inserted in the introductory section. One (No. 18) is a miniature depiction of one of the interesting and typical single combats fought between the lines of opposing forces. There is nothing to identify the particular episode except the name of the Little Big Horn River. The other (No. 20) is a description of a famous fight which took place somewhere between Tongue River and the Big Powder River in Montana at a butte called, as a result of this fight, "They-Flee-Around-It." The Sioux surprised a Crow village at the foot of the butte. In panic the Crows fled around it, closely pursued by the Dakotas, who took many captives. I cannot indicate the chronological place of the occurrence more definitely than to say that it happened before He Dog's time and that he is now over ninety years of age.[13]

From the time of the first dated fight, one Sioux-Crow encounter follows another consistently. To be sure, there are interruptions for the picturing of the Custer fight on the Little Big Horn and for dance ceremonies and other social, ceremonial, and semi-ceremonial activities. But even in these the undertone of the struggles with the Crows is felt, for usually there is *some* relationship—direct or indirect—between the picture of activity and the enmity of the Crows.

The first of the more imposing engagements begins in No. 41 and bears the initial notation: "All tipis were erected in a circle with all horses in the center." This is the first of two famous fights on Arrow Creek in Montana, each of which is known as "Arrow Creek fight"; it took place in the winter of 1863.

---

[13] Field note made in July, 1929.

Many an event is *placed* by the Dakotas according to its chronological relation to this first Arrow Creek fight. In order to meet the attack of a large party of Cheyennes and Dakotas (chiefly Oglalas), a band of Crows barricaded themselves in a naturally sheltered spot by placing their lodges in a close circle, with the women, horses, and impedimenta in the center. The engagement is consequently known also by the name "Defending the Tent." The series depicting the fight is made up of the drawings from No. 41 to No. 48. The first is a miniature, in very small scale, showing the barricaded camp, the lines of the Dakotas, and a small skirmish line of Crows. The next three are large-scale drawings showing particular heroes in action. No. 43, for instance, portrays Brave Wolf, a Cheyenne, "brought in pierced with arrows." Exhibiting the type of courage so dear to the American Indian of the Plains, he had charged alone into the midst of the Crows and circled back. A hundred enemy warriors followed him out, shooting at him. In midstream, halfway back, he fell; his comrades[14] rescued him, but he was dead.

This battle was a strenuous one. The opposing forces charged back and forth. The Crows tried to drive the Sioux back across the creek. Then the Sioux forced the Crows to the very doors of their lodges; but they could not overcome them, for the land was too open and their numbers were too limited (see Nos. 45 and 46), and they finally had to give up and leave with a loss of ten men.

Then follows what is sometimes—and very fittingly—called the "Battle of the Big Dust." The fight occurred in Montana in the vicinity of the present Assiniboin Reservation. According to Left Heron (*Hoka Cakta*, literally "Left-Hand Heron"), tribal historian, the battle took place in 1861, "before either Arrow Creek fight." It is therefore slightly out of chronological order here.

The series devoted to its depiction is a long one, extending from No. 61 to No. 78. A large party of Dakotas was out on a horse-stealing expedition. Northern Sioux predominated, but by sheer accident four Oglalas were with them. Approaching the Crow camp, the Sioux discovered a lone "horse wrangler" in charge of the herd. Red Shirt, an Oglala, attacked and killed him, while the main body of Sioux began to run off the horses.[15] The Crows soon discovered what was happening, and a furious battle ensued. So many horses were stampeded and so many men were soon engaged in the struggle that the dust rose in thick clouds that seemed "almost like smoke from a prairie fire." Before the onslaughts of the thoroughly aroused Crows, the Dakotas scattered along the ridges and valleys.[16] Consequently the whole was a series of running fights, and the battle covered a long stretch from the Upper Missouri River to Dry Creek. The engagement was rather a hapless one for the Dakotas, for they lost heavily. Several chiefs were killed, two being shot from their horses. Once more the Dakotas could hardly claim a victory.

The successive pages in the series present various scattered single episodes in the whole action, frequently for the sake of recording the exploits of individual heroes. In No. 64, Buffalo Walks in Sight and then Brave Bear (familarly known as Sells His Gun) count coup on a Crow. Here also Red Thunder, a Miniconjou chief, meets his death. No. 62 seems to portray the activities of three of the four Oglalas who became involved in the engagement. But for the most part, drawing follows drawing for the simple purpose of creating the general effect of the whole encounter; of suggesting the general type and particular details of fighting; of exhibiting types of fighting equipment and individual, personal designations and manners in which they were worn. Every page bears examples of the special symbol of rank of some office in one of the several warrior societies[17] or the personal emblem or charm of some special warrior; and always there is the consistent suggestion of tense activity, excitement, and motion.

The next engagement of any magnitude (Nos. 100 to 102) was precipitated quite accidentally, probably in 1867. Two Hunkpapa Dakotas had discovered and killed a lone buffalo bull. As they were butchering it, they were surprised and surrounded by a large party of Crows who were out on a war expedition (see No.

---

[14] He Dog and Short Bull.

[15] See No. 61: Red Shirt and wrangler in foreground; camp and larger forces in small miniature in background.

[16] Bad Heart Bull uniquely indicates the valley and ridge divisions by wavy lines drawn across the page. See No. 68, for example.

[17] Notice, for instance, the Sotka Yuha lance, lower left, No. 63; the Miwatani headdress and "stake robe," lower left, No. 65; the characteristic Crow manner of painting the face for battle, Crow at top right, No. 76; the Chiefs Society shirt, upper left, No. 78; and bird headgear, lower right, No. 62.

100). One of the Dakotas was killed at once. The other, however, possessed a repeating rifle, which he used to such good effect that he escaped from the attacking Crows and was able to make his way back to the main band of his people. His recital was all that was needed to set in motion a Dakota war expedition. For two nights and a day, the Hunkpapas trailed the guilty Crows. The second morning they overtook them, drove them to the top of Mountain Sheep Butte at the mouth of Tongue River, and there laid siege. Thirty Crows and one Dakota by the name of Fast Horse, who had some time before deserted his own people and allied himself with the enemy, made up the marooned party. Every one of them was killed—every man and the horse of the traitor Dakota, the only horse which reached the top of the butte with the doomed warriors.[18]

The chronology of the record is here interrupted by the insertion of the two encounters with troops, Crook's fight on the Rosebud and the Little Big Horn fight which followed a few days later.

The next Indian episode, however, follows in the proper Sioux-Crow sequence. This is one of the most exciting of the fights between Dakotas and Crows, and its presentation is the longest, for any single engagement, in the record (Nos. 219 to 284). The time was "the year that a tree fell on an old woman and killed her," that is, 1869–1870.[19] The battle is known as "When They Retreated into Camp" or the "Battle Where They Drove Them Back to Camp," and it took place in Montana near the head of Rosebud Creek. As in the case of the "Battle of the Big Dust," the Dakotas were stealing horses, the Crows discovered them and gave chase, and the Dakotas scattered on both sides of the ridges; and again the encounter was characterized by scattered and running fighting. The number of Crows was overwhelming, and as a result, the Dakota flight was precipitate. Relentlessly the Crows drove them in speedy retreat to the very ring of their own camp circle (thus the battle receives its name); it seemed that the whole Dakota camp was doomed. But at that auspicious moment a second party of Dakota warriors, returning from another expedition, put in an appearance. At the very moment of their triumph,

the Crows were halted. Wearied from the previous struggle, their horses worn out by the long running fight, the Crows were no match for the fresh Sioux party; and they, in turn, were borne back in full retreat—even to *their* own camp. So the Dakotas avenged themselves for their defeat at the "Battle of the Big Dust."[20]

The second Arrow Creek fight is the next battle of moment (Nos. 288 to 296). The time of the event, according to He Dog, Short Bull, and Left Heron, was about 1872. In this engagement, which is sometimes referred to as the "Battle of Many Hidings," the Crows maintained an advantage.[21] As He Dog shrewdly yet naïvely explains, there were too many leaders among the Sioux. Hunkpapas, Miniconjous, Oglalas, and Sans Arc were involved, and each band boasted a generous supply of leaders. The result was obvious. The prominent features, however—from the Dakota point of view at least—were the astounding and courageous feats of the young warrior Runs Fearless. As the Dakotas were retreating, this warrior turned and, singlehanded, charged the enemy. Then occurred another of those interesting and characteristic examples of single combats between the lines (cf. Nos. 18 and 34). Bad Heart Bull shows this in miniature in No. 289. Four Crow warriors advanced singly to meet Runs Fearless; all four counted coup on him, but only one of the four escaped alive; Runs Fearless, however, came through unharmed.

One of the few truly decisive battles and the last of the prominent Sioux-Crow fights is pictured in Nos. 301 and 302—the first in panoramic miniature, the second in close-up scale. The date is 1875. Bent on avenging the death of a comrade killed a few days before, a large party of Crows surprised a scouting party of seven young Oglalas in their camp in a ravine among the mountains. After some desperate fighting, they killed all seven. The event naturally made a deep impression on the Oglala tribe; in fact, their official winter count bears the entry "1875. Killing of seven Loafer Indians" (i.e., members of the Loafer band of the Oglala Dakotas).

With this tragic event and another brief skirmish pictured in No. 303, the recording of Sioux-Crow fights ends. It is interestingly noticeable that the

---

[18] No. 101 is a miniature portrayal of the besieging of the butte, and No. 102 is a close-up of the top of the butte; the horse of Fast Horse is prominent in both.

[19] Short Man winter count.

[20] For details of fights and fighters, see the drawings in Part Two.

[21] Very few Indian fights could be termed *decisive*!

young Dakota records with equal candor Sioux victory and defeat; he seems to be inhibited by no false sense of loyalty. The Crows, too, won on occasion, and he portrays their victories with no less vigor than their defeats.

THE CUSTER AFFAIR ON THE LITTLE BIG HORN

The fight of greatest general interest, however, is the defeat of Custer on the Little Big Horn River in Montana.

I summarize this famous fight but briefly. The literature on the subject is so varied and contradictory in many of the details that in large part it must be considered conjectural. I do not wish here to enter into any controversial discussion, but simply to outline those main movements which seem to stand the test of checking and counterchecking the reports of various informants. Chiefly I follow the report of Captain Edward S. Godfrey, published in the *Century Magazine* for January, 1892,[22] and still considered one of the most dependable discussions of the fight.

On June 19, 1876, Major Marcus A. Reno, in charge of the right wing of the Seventh Cavalry, reported to Brigadier General Alfred H. Terry, commander of the Yellowstone Expedition, the discovery of a large Indian trail that led up the Rosebud River. It was decided by Generals Terry and Custer and Colonel John Gibbon, in conference on board the steamer *Far West*, that General Custer, in command of the Seventh Cavalry, should follow the trail discovered by Reno. No apprehension concerning the outcome of a meeting with the Indians seems to have been felt by the officers at this time; their great concern was only that the Indians, aided by the rugged nature of the country, might evade them.

Each man of the command was provided with a hundred rounds of carbine and twenty-four rounds of pistol ammunition which was to be carried upon his person and in his saddlebags. Fifty more rounds of carbine ammunition per man was to be carried on the pack mules.

The written instructions to Custer, as commander, suggested that he follow the trail up the Rosebud; that, should the trail turn toward the Little Big Horn, he still follow southward, perhaps even as far as the headwaters of the Tongue River, and then turn toward the Little Big Horn, "feeling constantly, however, to [the] left so as to preclude the possibility of the escape of the Indians to the south or southwest by passing around your left flank."[23] These suggestions were followed.

On the march of June 23 and 24, numerous campsites were discovered, *all* of which indicated the camping of not one band but several. *One* of them was extremely large and included a Sun Dance lodge and dance site, indicating significantly that the various groups had gathered and halted for the great midsummer sacrificial and propitiatory ceremony of the Plains Indians. During the morning of June 25, it was discovered that the troops were being observed by individual Indians or by small groups. Immediate action was necessary.

The village was located on the banks of the Little Big Horn. Custer ordered Major Reno with his battalion to march down a small valley toward the Little Big Horn and the upper end of the Indian camp, and Captain Frederick W. Benteen with his battalion to the front and left along a line of high bluffs, a line of advance which proved most difficult because of the rough and forbidding nature of the country, which threw the troops by degrees back toward the path of the command as a whole. Custer himself led his battalion somewhat to the right along a high ridge, with the intention of skirting the camp and then approaching from the lower end in order that the village might be charged from opposite ends at the same time—by Reno's forces from the upper and Custer's own from the lower end. It was good strategy and might have brought about a somewhat different result had it been carried out.

There is no doubt that Custer had little conception of the actual number of fighting Indians with whom he had to deal. But it seems evident, too, from reports by both whites and Indians, that had Reno's attack been more fearless and aggressive, the outcome might not have been so completely tragic for Custer. Had a vigorous attack on the upper end of the village occupied the warriors even for a brief period, Custer

---

[22] Edward S. Godfrey, "Custer's Last Battle," *Century Magazine*, XLIII, 3 (January 1892), 358–384.

[23] *Ibid.*, p. 364.

might well have reached the opposite end with an attack more or less surprising to the Indians, for his approach was not suspected by the main body of fighting warriors until after Reno's retreat to the bluffs.

Reno's attack, however, was most conservative. He led the battalion in a brisk advance on the village; but instead of charging as ordered, he commanded the battalion to dismount and fight on foot. Then, at the first heavy rush from the Indians, he ordered a retreat; almost immediately he countermanded that order; and then, before the second command could be executed, he again ordered a retreat. The result was confusion. Many of the men did not hear the third order and were left in a most precarious position, unmounted. The battalion was completely demoralized. The retreat developed into a mad riot of fleeing men and riderless horses. The main remnant of the command retreated in full rout across the Little Big Horn to the high bluffs beyond, where they, with Benteen's command, later entrenched themselves. Some of the soldiers, most of them without horses, managed to reach a small wood near the river where they could fight from cover and whence some made their escape, after nightfall, to the ridges and their entrenched comrades. But many of the men, mounted and otherwise, lost their lives in that mad flight from the Indians.

No one can know, of course, the details of what happened to Custer and his battalion after they left the rest of the force. Once or twice Benteen's men had a brief glimpse of them as they moved along the ridge at the beginning of their march. Considerably later, the Indians under the leadership of Gall, the Hunkpapa war chief, halted in their attack on Reno's men on the bluffs, turned suddenly, and nearly all rode down the valley and out of sight. Then firing was heard. Quite evidently the unexpected news of Custer's approach had changed the Indian center of interest; Custer's command had become the point of attack. Gall himself says that Reno was not utterly annihilated because the great mass of warriors hurried to the attack on Custer's approaching column.

The outcome as far as Custer's battalion is concerned is well known. No soldier of the command lived to tell the story. But no one questions the soldierliness of those men. "It was hard fighting,"

says Brave Wolf, fighting chief of the Cheyennes, "hard all the time. I have been in many hard fights, but I never saw such brave men."[24]

That night and the next day, the combined forces of Reno and Benteen and the pack train, entrenched at the top of the bluffs, withstood the intermittent attacks of the Indians. About noon of the second day, the long strain was ended. At the approach of General Terry with his command, the Indians all withdrew. "They saw infantry," says a Dakota, "and they don't seem to like them—they bury themselves in the ground like badgers and it's too slow fighting."[25] Terry had come to the rescue. The Battle of the Little Big Horn was over.

The Indian recorder gives three series portraying the fight—two completely coherent and effective and a third much less forceful and artistic. Sixty-seven pages are given to the presentation of this one great episode: fifty-six (Nos. 126 to 176), which include the first two series, are devoted to the approach, attack, retreat, and entrenched defense of Reno's command and eleven (Nos. 177 to 185), to the destruction of Custer and his troopers. The first series (Nos. 126 to 169) is the earliest account and by far the longest; it presents, in large-scale drawings and in great detail, various views of the fight. Not only does it contain numerous portrayals of personal exploit, such as those of the elder Bad Heart Bull, Kicking Bear, and Hard to Hit meeting Reno's force in the first attack (No. 131) and Bad Heart Bull killing a Ree scout (No. 165); but also it gives countless details of costume and manner of fighting and suggests an atmosphere of fierce struggle, confusion, and riot. The second series (Nos. 170 to 176), done in unique miniature, is concerned with panoramic effects; episodes are presented as whole units seen from above and at an angle. Here again the atmosphere of intense action and confusion is secured. The third series (Nos. 177 to 185) is by no means as convincing or artistic as the other two. The scales are mixed and the technique, for the most part, is less finished. It would appear that the artist was much less interested in the portrayal of the annihilation of Custer's command than in the Reno engagement.

The large-scale series faithfully reflects the movements and atmosphere of the Reno action. The early drawings portray the troops, in regular formation,

[24] George Bird Grinnell, *The Fighting Cheyennes* (New York: Charles Scribner's Sons, 1915), p. 340.

[25] John Colhoff, letter of April 7, 1929.

being met by scattered warriors. A new spirit soon shows itself, however; in increasing numbers Indian figures are seen among those of the soldiers. The effect of growing activity is evident, and early in the series the demoralization of the troops begins to show itself. Across page after page the red warriors pursue blue-coated troopers; the Indians are the aggressors, the soldiers are concerned only with defense and flight. According to numerous Indian reports, the soldiers in this engagement seemed to make little attempt to defend themselves; their one thought was to get away safely. "It was like chasing buffalo—a great chase," the Northern Cheyennes told George Bird Grinnell.[26] Bad Heart Bull's portrayal bears out this report. Fleeing soldiers, without pausing, turn in their saddles to fire at the fast-following Sioux and Cheyennes, or even fire into the air or back at the foe without looking to take aim; consternation grips them. The Indians were fired by an intense fighting spirit at the moment and were quick to sense their advantage; the troops seem to have been gripped by an equally intense spirit of apprehension and terror. As the series progresses, the increasing demoralization is evident, quite in keeping with the actual situation. Indian warriors ride up beside fleeing soldiers and, unopposed, strike them with sword or war club, shoot them with rifle or revolver, or try to drag them from their horses; soldiers fall from their horses, some helpless, some able to attempt escape on foot. As the end of the series is neared more and more bodies of fallen soldiers bestrew the field, while some Indian warriors continue the pursuit to the river and others catch and hold the riderless cavalry horses. The last page shows the bodies of a number of dead or fatally wounded soldiers lying, almost stripped, upon the ground, while several warriors ride back in leisurely fashion, leading captured army horses. Throughout, the prevailing impression is that of riotous confusion and the relentlessly overwhelming force of numbers and fury of attack.

The shorter series, done in miniature, covers the same period and secures the same impression, but from a different angle. As I have said before, in this series the effect is panoramic; one sees the action as a whole, viewed from some distance above and at an angle. The *increasing* confusion can be seen at a single glance (Nos. 173 and 174) as a large portion of the action is pictured in a single composition. The miniature series is more complete in one way, however, for it includes not only the retreat of Reno but, as well, the final entrenched position on the bluffs (No. 176) —the pack train and a small detachment of cavalry occupying the center of the barricaded position, most of the men dismounted and, from the little cover securable, meeting the charges of the Indians, who completely surround the entrenchments. The disorganized flight has given way to dogged resistance.

There is little to be added to what I have already said regarding the third series, with its mixed scales and its concern with the Custer episode proper. It opens with a very rough, incomplete sketch (No. 177) showing Custer's approach being watched by the Indians, who are themselves invisible to the troopers. The outstanding feature of this composition is the effective, impressionistic portrayal, in tiny miniature, of the advance of Custer's column in formation along the high ridge. The other two most prominent compositions in this group are in intermediate and large scale, respectively. The first (No. 183) shows the last stand of the remnant of Custer's command and indicates intensely vigorous fighting; it shows, at the center, Crazy Horse, the Oglala war chief, killing Custer with a club and, at the bottom, one mounted trooper making his escape, hotly pursued by three warriors. The second (No. 184) shows the same escaping trooper, "Custer's last man," his revolver at his temple, taking his own life. For the rest, the same prevailing impression of confusion found in the first two series persists.

The story as a whole, as given in the three series, carries faithfully effective suggestion of the hopelessly desperate situation of the troops, the relentless and continued onslaughts of the Indians, and the utter desolation of overwhelming defeat.

EARLY SOCIAL LIFE AND ITS REORGANIZATION

In his depiction of the social and economic life, Bad Heart Bull touches upon both the old and the new

[26] Grinnell, *The Fighting Cheyennes*, p. 337.

tribal activities; he marks the transition from the old wandering, hunting, and fighting days to agricultural activities and a more settled form of existence. In this section, I call attention briefly to the outstanding points not mentioned in the first section. I have roughly divided this fourth section into four lesser divisions for the sake of clearness: ceremonies, other than the Sun Dance of the introductory section and the *Hunka*, Omaha Dance, and Grass Dance of the last section; the more strictly social aspects of life; cases of serious friction between whites and Indians; and activities of livelihood.

CEREMONIES

Among the Lakota ceremonies not yet discussed, there are three general types: those "danced" in appeal to the spirits for aid in war; dream-cult ceremonies, which are performed in accordance with dreams; and ceremonies performed in fulfillment of a vow. It may well be said, of course, that all ceremonies of the old Lakotas were in some degree or other related to war and the chase, that they were all based primarily upon economic needs. This is true enough. Yet the practical, economic aspect obtrudes in varying degrees, and in some ceremonies, particularly some found in the last class, the spiritual element predominates overwhelmingly. Bad Heart Bull represents all these types, giving either all the ceremonies of the class or those that are most significant.

War. The first type I shall pass rapidly. The ceremony of the Sacred Bow (Nos. 98 and 99) and the Victory Dance (No. 85) are both concerned entirely with war. The first of these might be said to belong to the ceremonies performed to fulfill a vow, for on occasion it was danced to fulfill a promise made to the Great Spirit for help in time of extreme danger in battle; but in most cases it was performed before an important warlike undertaking. It was primarily *war* "medicine,"[27] and its symbolism—as He Dog points out—is entirely that of destructive forces. So I place it here. The performance portrayed by Bad Heart Bull was staged as war medicine. It was after the battle "When They Drove Them Back to Camp," which I have already described, that the Dakotas made this appeal to the Great Spirit. Although, by a freakish turn of fate, the Crows had finally been routed in this battle, the Dakotas felt deeply humiliated by their near-defeat and sought

further revenge. The Sacred Bow "race" was run in preparation for the later undertaking of vengeance.

The Victory Dance was a Plains-wide institution and needs little explanation.[28] In my brief summary I shall follow chiefly He Dog and Short Bull. Obviously the Victory, or Scalp, Dance was related to war. The ceremony was known among the Dakotas by two names, *iwakicipi*, "they dance for it," and *wikte akli ecan*, "kills and comes back"; and, as would seem appropriate, was danced only on the warriors' return from a successful war expedition of some moment.

The dance was a circular one, performed around a central pole which was spirally striped with black and was decorated near the top with hands, feet, and scalps of enemies. The movement was from right to left, the women forming one part of the circle, the men the other. Enemy scalps, borne on long scalp sticks, formed a prominent feature of the ceremony. The women dancers, however, not the warriors, carried them. The women had lost relatives in the fight. To them, other warriors brought scalps in sign that vengeance had been accomplished; so, bearing the scalps, they danced in honor of their dead. The men in the dance were successful warriors, who in the ceremony carried small hand drums and acted as the singers and drummers of the occasion. The songs used were really recitals of news and were sung in praise of warriors, both living and dead, who had distinguished themselves in the battle being celebrated; the occasion was veritably a song of glory to the heroes.

According to He Dog and Short Bull, the performance pictured here commemorated a famous battle—almost the last—between the Dakotas and the Gros Ventre Blackfeet, a fight not portrayed in Bad Heart Bull's record, and was an especially large one, enjoyed by everyone.

Cult. Of the three types, the cultic performances occupy the largest place in the record. In camp, this type of ceremony aroused a general excitement and interest peculiar to itself. Primarily it was given in accordance with an individual dream[29] in which the dreamer received instruction concerning the identity of his guardian spirit and the nature of his personal medicine; the performance itself served as a test of

---

[27] Clark Wissler, "Some Protective Designs of the Dakota," *APAMNH*, I, Part 2 (1907), 50–52, and my own paper, "Ethical Conceptions of the Dakota."

[28] See, for example, Frances Densmore, "Teton Sioux

Music," BAE Bulletin 61, p. 361; Luther Standing Bear, *My People, the Sioux* (Boston: Houghton Mifflin Co., 1928), p. 57; and Wissler, "Societies," pp. 27, 44, 80.

[29] Wissler, "Societies," pp. 81–99.

the efficacy of that medicine. Frequently a particular day, known as "Medicine Day," was set aside for these cultic ceremonies, and usually several different groups were represented on that day, a group being formed by different persons who had dreamed of the same spirit creature. The activities of the dream dancers were not confined to one spot; the whole camp circle was legitimate territory for their performances. Not infrequently the occasion took on an air of entertainment, and much merriment was aroused by the competitive and antagonistic antics of members of the various groups, as, for instance, on the day when the "wasp men" suddenly appeared and put to flight the "bear men," who had been harrassing the camp. This aspect of the ceremonies must not be allowed entirely to overshadow the primary seriousness of their nature, however.

The first dream-cult ceremony pictured is the black-tailed deer performance shown in No. 115. He Dog recalls that immediately before the fight on Rosebud Creek—June 17, 1876—there was a ceremony "imitating the black-tailed deer, long-tailed deer, elk, and bear"; drawing No. 115 portrays the black-tailed deer portion of the festivities. The cultic identity of the dancers is indicated by the fact that they are painted either blue or black and are equipped with other symbols peculiar to the black-tailed deer dreamers. The fact that this is a dream-cult dance and the cult is that of the black-tailed deer is further indicated by the two preceding drawings (Nos. 113 and 114), which are strictly symbolic in character and portray the "dream" or "spirit" deer. This is the only case in which the dream is indicated in this way by Bad Heart Bull.

There are, however, other drawings which show dreamers of various other animals. Nos. 186 and 187 present long-tailed deer, elk, bear, and buffalo in addition to the black-tailed deer; and No. 190 shows coyote or wolf dancers and *heyoka* (clowns) with a buffalo.

The costuming, body painting, and ceremonial equipment in all cases distinguish one cult from another. It is noticeable, too, that among the several members of the same cult there are slight variations in decoration and equipment. These differences depend upon the spirit instructions received in the individual dreams and serve to aid fellow tribesmen in identifying their fellows; they bespeak the inherent individualism evident in Dakota psychology. Several

times He Dog and Short Bull have identified in this way different men portrayed in the drawings.

The cultic performances thus far referred to were all characterized by the participation of the so-called "magic shooter." This character was an institution peculiar to the performances of the organizations mentioned; its purpose was to attempt to disprove the dancers' medicine. A medicine man played the part of the "magic shooter," and might be said to be the evil-spirit element in the ceremonies. He was the one who officially tried to injure the dream dancer by shooting at him—small stones, claws, grasshoppers, fingernails, even arrows, and on one occasion at least, a bullet. Crouching, he hid behind bush, tipi, or tree and attempted to come upon the dancer by stealth. If the dreamer's medicine were truly potent, he would be enabled to evade the missiles or, if they struck him, to throw them off or cough them up, while in reality he proceeded unscathed. And according to the magic law, the "magic shooter" needed to be extremely cautious lest his magic shooting return upon him like a boomerang; the small circle often seen painted upon a dancer's body (as with the elk dancers, No. 187) was called *onte*, which means "causes death" (i.e., *to the person who tried to hit it*). Thus the dancers were not entirely at the mercy of the "magic shooter" or of each other.

The one other cultic dance given by the young Oglala differs from the preceding chiefly in the fact that in it there is no "magic shooter." The Horse Dance[30] (No. 318), like the others, was performed in fulfillment of a dream message; but it was not danced as a test of the dreamer's medicine except that through it the dreamer sought a further vision—sometimes, in the case of a shaman, to receive guidance in case of emergency.[31] The performance itself was in certain respects more pretentious and impressive than the others and was usually not given on the same day. It was rather a spectacular affair, for—as Bad Heart Bull's drawing shows—the horse dreamers, wearing masks which left no openings for the eyes, charged back and forth in a body on horses that were bare of any equipment other than symbolic painting. He Dog remarks that he never knew of an accident in one of these dances although he has witnessed and even participated in performances when many horses were present; and he adds naïvely that the horses seemed to realize that they were playing an important and responsible role.

[30] *Ibid.*, pp. 95–98.

[31] Field notes, 1929.

Vows. In the third class (to which the Sun Dance belongs), we find one type of ceremony where the material, economic interest predominates and another in which the spiritual element is foremost. The rite of "the one that carries the buffalo skulls slipped through the pierced flesh of the back" (No. 189) belongs to the former. The man is "dancing" to propitiate the buffalo. He has vowed that if the buffalo spirits will help him in stealing horses and otherwise providing for economic needs, he will perform this ceremony. So, ritualistically prepared by a medicine man, he comes into camp from a medicine lodge in the hills, dragging buffalo skulls tied to thongs that are slipped through the pierced flesh of his shoulders, and the buffalo spirits are appeased.[32]

The most common and in some senses the most poignant ritual of this type is the *hanble ceyapi*, or "cry to God." It is the ceremony of vigil, the "retreat," of the American Indian. The devotee, boy or man, with fasting and prayer, casts himself in humble appeal before his god. Sometimes he seeks a vision for himself in which his guardian spirit will appear to him; usually he has promised in an hour of great distress, ordinarily in the case of serious illness of a relative or dear friend, to sacrifice himself thus if the Great Spirit will but answer his prayer. Thus does Old Buffalo indicate the nature of the rite and so imply the unselfishness of the act:

> I had heard that when men came to helplessness in sickness they did this.
>
> I go on a high hill and make a vow, saying "Wakan-tanka, I call upon you. Have pity on me. My niece is on her deathbed. Have pity on her, so she can live on earth and know you. Give me strength to do what is right and honest. I will give four sacrifices. I will smoke a fine pipe. It is a Chief pipe, so you can bless it. I will do this in your honor if you will spare her life."[33]
>
> The girl gets better. . . .[34]

So for four days during the heat of July, Old Buffalo remained alone and without food or water upon the top of a high hill, performing, with ceremonial precision and in deep humility, the rite which was the fulfillment of his vow. Thus he sought the vision which should show that his offering was accepted.

Hanble ceyapi, says He Dog, is one of the extreme sacrifices.

SOCIAL LIFE

The ceremonial aspect of Lakota society is one of that society's outstanding features, but it is supplemented by a more strictly social phase. Bad Heart Bull reflects this particularly in the drawings in which the main object is the presentation of costumes and tipi furnishings and those showing courting scenes and games. No. 8 portrays winter costumes of men; No. 207, courting costumes of young men and the arrangement of the bed, wall curtains, and parfleche cases in a typical lodge; and No. 214, typical costumes of women.

Eight compositions depict courting scenes (Nos. 86, 87, 112, 210, 342, 355, 356, and 361). The first two and the fourth are expressly meant to show "how courting was done long ago." The rest are all incident to some special occasion or activity. No. 112 is presented as proof of the time of a change of camp; the bridegroom knew that the bands had been camped on the Little Big Horn *two* nights before Custer appeared, because the *first* night he courted his lady and the *second* she consented and they eloped! The others are all incident to the roundup and to Fourth of July celebrations of the later, more settled life.

Especially interesting among these drawings of social life is the series of eight pages showing ten games—games of men, women, and children (Nos. 206, 208, 209, 211, 213, 215, 216, and 217). These drawings serve as excellent illustrations for Stewart Culin's, J. O. Dorsey's, Luther Standing Bear's, and J. R. Walker's discussions of the same games.[35] One is impressed by three facts: practically all of the games are those of chance where betting flourishes; they have come down from a dim antiquity; and in at least one case—*ba inyankapi* (No. 208)—the game has

---

[32] The ceremony resembled somewhat the first form of the Sun Gaze Dance (No. 13), but in that case the skulls did not touch the ground (see Nos. 13 and 189).

[33] All of these things symbolize the *hanble ceyapi*.

[34] Densmore, "Teton Sioux Music," pp. 274-275.

[35] Stewart Culin, "Games of the North American Indians," *ARBAE*, XXIV (1902-1903), 392, 415-418, 503-509, 514, 745-746; J. O. Dorsey, "Games of Teton Dakota Children," *Am. Anthrop.*, IV, 4 (1891), 329-345; Standing Bear, *My People*, pp. 28-48; J. R. Walker, "Sioux Games. I," *Journal of American Folk-Lore*, XVIII, 61 (1905), 277-290, and "Sioux Games. II," *Journal of American Folk-Lore*, XIX, 75 (1906), 29-36.

at some remote time been an important part of a ceremony for the securing of protection against want.

The third point is especially interesting, and one which is more likely to be missed than the others, so I elaborate it slightly. The myth of origin given by Wissler[36] and included by Walker in his paper on Sioux games[37] indicates an ancient ceremonial significance and a close association with the Sacred Hoop of the Dakotas.[38] A band of Sioux traveling in the lake country of Minnesota came upon evil days. The food supply was exhausted. The whole band faced starvation. One of the young men asked permission to fast. Ceremonially prepared by a medicine man, the young warrior withdrew to the peak of an isolated, bare-topped hill to hold his lonely vigil, fasting and "praying" in an appeal to the Great Spirit in behalf of his people. Two days and two nights passed. Then the watchers in camp saw a buffalo approach the young man on the hill, circle him, and disappear on the other side. At midday the boy returned to the camp, following the ceremonial procedure prescribed for dreamers or fasters. After purification at the hands of the medicine man, he proceeded to a lodge especially erected for him at the center of the village. There, with the help of several young men whom he had chosen, and according to his vision, he prepared the hoop and wands necessary for playing the "game" of which he had dreamed. The "dream buffalo" had presented the dreamer with a sacred pipe, sage, sweet grass, special songs, and a definite ceremony necessary to make the playing of the game efficacious. With all of this the dreamer acquainted his assistants and with due reverence taught them the ritual and the game. It was noticed that the hoop left buffalo marks in the dirt as it rolled. After the proper preparation and the performance of the ceremony, the young leader prophesied that on the fourth day from that time there would be many buffalo. He then had it announced that the next morning four buffalo would approach the camp from the west and that they were to be allowed to pass through unmolested. It says much for the people's respect for spiritual powers that no person in the camp disturbed the four buffalo when they appeared and made their way through the village as predicted. The young prophet and his assistants played the hoop game continuously during these days. Early on the morning of the fourth day,

the chief dispatched a sentinel to watch from the top of a hill. From that vantage point the sentinel discovered a huge herd of buffalo very near and signaled the news to the tense crowd at camp. A great hunt followed, and the band was saved from destruction by starvation. Thereafter the hoop and wands were cared for by a particular officer; a special tent was maintained for the game and its paraphernalia and for the prophet and his assistants, and the game was used ceremonially in times of emergency for calling buffalo. After the prophet's death, however, the game degenerated into a gambling sport played by the people. So one may catch brief intimate glimpses into the fabric of a people's life.

DIFFICULTIES OF ADJUSTMENT

Opposed to this social aspect of tribal life is the antisocial element of friction between the whites and the Indians. Besides the Custer disaster, there are recorded three other engagements between the government forces and those of the Indians. I shall merely mention them, and I do so here because they were a distinct part of the Indian struggle against the change of the social order. The first of the three episodes is accidentally placed last in Bad Heart Bull's record (No. 297), not, however, because he did not know its correct chronological order. This is the famous occasion when a part of General George Crook's command, under Colonel J. J. Reynolds, attacked and destroyed a Sioux and Cheyenne camp on Powder River—March 17, 1876. The second is the no less famous occasion of the engagement between Crook's command and the Sioux forces on Rosebud Creek eight days before Custer's attack Nos. 103 to 111). Neither episode reflected any glory to the troops, nor did either bring them any benefits. The last incident in this section (Nos. 305 and 306) is a skirmish between General Nelson A. Miles's command and Red Shirt's band in Montana. The date suggested by my informants (Bad Heart Bull gives no date) is "about 1880." This is late, however, for Miles's final campaign—in which this is an episode— took place in 1877. In these engagements, the difficulty bespeaks the Indian's resentment of white encroachment, and his defiant resistance to domination by another race and a forced change in the whole order of living. So it bespeaks also the assertion of a deep and inherent self-respect.

[36] Wissler, "Protective Designs," pp. 50–51.
[37] Walker, "Sioux Games. I," pp. 281–283.

[38] Wissler, "Protective Designs," pp. 40–41.

ACTIVITIES OF LIVELIHOOD

Last in the portrayal of the social life and its reorganization come the descriptions of activities of livelihood. It is strikingly noticeable that in all these activities there is a common element—the stock animal, first buffalo and then cattle. Going back to the earliest part of the record (and so, of course, to the earlier life of the tribe), one finds the killing and butchering of buffalo (Nos. 16 and 17); then one sees the processes and results of tanning (No. 212); and

last one is shown the beginning of stock raising after the inauguration of government control and reservation life. Incident to the last is a suggestion of agricultural activity (Nos. 359 and 362), the chief concern of which is the preparation of wild hay for the feeding of stock. The importance of stock raising is symbolized by the series of drawings depicting the roundup (Nos. 357 to 372). It is evident that in these later days, no less than in the earlier, the horse is the great friend of the Indian.

THE GHOST DANCE AND THE BATTLE OF WOUNDED KNEE

The story of the tragic episode of the Ghost Dance disturbance and the resultant fighting on Wounded Knee Creek in 1890 is sketched in six drawings (Nos. 312 to 317). The series begins with the picturing of three typical Ghost Dance costumes; the drawing is entirely diagrammatic. No. 315 is a rather symbolic, large-scale drawing showing three mounted men; at the center (the horse seen full front) is Grant Short Bull (my informant, Short Bull) with an arm outstretched to each of the other two—Major General Nelson A. Miles at his left, Kicking Bear at his right. General Miles was the leader of the government military forces in this campaign; Kicking Bear, the Oglala leader of the armed Indians in the Bad Lands, the active leader of the hostile element at that time. Short Bull represents the conciliatory spirit (therefore the arrangement in the drawing), for he carried dispatches between these two men.

No. 314 is a portrayal of an actual dance scene. The symbolic tree, the ceremonial pipes, the sacrifice banners, the costumes of the dancers, and the men lying in trance within the dance circle all bear witness to the nature and solemnity of the occasion; the last two would identify it as the Ghost Dance even if the

words of the Ghost Dance song had not been written upon the page.

Drawing No. 313 gives evidence of the Indian notion of Sitting Bull's significant relation to this activity, for, as the real introduction to the disturbance itself, it shows the arrest and killing of the Hunkpapa chief by the Standing Rock Indian police.[39]

The last two drawings (Nos. 316 and 317) picture in miniature "the killing of Big Foot," the northern chief, and the fighting on Wounded Knee Creek. The first portrays the chief warriors surrounded by soldiers just before the fatal signal for the sudden attack on the soldiers. The second portrays the scene just after the unexpected Indian attack had precipitated the fighting. The drawings are highly impressionistic but are less effective artistically than many of Bad Heart Bull's miniatures; the second one does, however, carry well the suggestion of intense confusion, the utter demoralization of the Indian throng, and the furious activity of the troopers.[40] The Indian attitude regarding the fighting is reflected in the artist's notation in Lakota on the first of these drawings: "This was worse than the Custer battle. They even killed a great many children."

"GREATER INDIAN SHOWS"

The latter portion of the record is given over largely to the depiction of two typical Indian celebrations of the Fourth of July, those of 1898 (Nos. 326 to 354) and 1903 (Nos. 373 to 411). A note on No. 327 indicates that the celebration of 1898 was the

first ever given on the Pine Ridge Reservation. The artist's portrayal is particularly interesting when studied in connection with the present-day celebrations of the Indians; for, although year by year they have lost some of their color and truly Indian

[39] Cf. James McLaughlin, *My Friend the Indian* (New York and Boston: Houghton Mifflin Co., 1910), pp. 194–222.

[40] Cf. James Mooney, "The Ghost Dance Religion and the Sioux Outbreak of 1890," *ARBAE*, XIV (1892–1893), Part 2, 867–879.

character, they still contain the elements and some of the forms of the old days.

Bad Heart Bull shows himself to be the truly critical historian in his long note on No. 327. His special reference is to the traditional give-away of the Dakotas, the practice according to which certain specified persons gave practically all that they possessed to others of the tribe—presumably the poor and needy. The lack of organization, careful direction and discreet restraint evident in this practice impressed the young tribesman deeply and brought forth a regretful prediction of resultant poverty for the tribe and an expression of hopeless desire that the Oglalas might be blessed with a true understanding of the situation and a real discrimination in meeting it.[41]

Specifically, the two pictured celebrations are those of the two Oglala bands located on White River, the *Ite Sica* and the *Canku ran*. They are, however, quite typical of the whole tribe and so can throw considerable light upon tribal manners of celebration, costumes, and social life. The celebrations cover several days and are in a sense a return to the old life. The give-away (to which I have already referred), the processionals, certain ceremonies, feasting, and courting appear as integral parts of the life of the season. The processionals include horses—ridden and led, which, with their trappings, are to be presented in the give-away—a few women in holiday finery, and dancers, appareled in full warrior regalia, on their way to the dance. Of the ceremonies indicated as particularly a part of these celebrations, there are three: the *Hunka* (No. 328), which—in its social and ethical implications—is one of the finest of Dakota rituals[42] and is frequently performed in connection with the give-away; the *Heyoka* (No. 338), the performance of the clown cult, whose members are called out to dance in propitiatory appeal to the sky spirits in case of threatening weather; and the two parts of the Omaha ceremony, the rather social so-called Omaha Dance (No. 408), and the more ritualistic Grass Dance (Nos. 409 and 410). Two examples of courting appear in the first celebration series. The first one (No. 342) is quite evidently a case in which the young man is forcing his attentions at an inauspicious moment, for—as the note indicates

—the young woman is making a hurried trip for water to be used in preparation of an important feast and demands that she be released till a later time; the second (No. 356) is a traditionally typical scene of courting in camp, several young couples occupying the foreground while others may be seen in the distant background. The first of these two courting pictures gives some evidence, too, of the importance of the feast in the celebration. Feasts were by no means minor affairs, either in size or in social significance. In fact, the dog-stew feast indicated in the second celebration series (see the pot and dog, Nos. 409 and 410) takes on a somewhat ceremonial character; it is given as a part of the Grass Dance of the ceremony of the Omaha Society.

These celebration series—"Greater Indian Shows," as Bad Heart Bull calls them—suggest a certain poignant wistfulness. They are distinctly a part of the later reservation life; yet they express a desire for the old-time native manner of living, for they are a temporary return to the older habits of life.

That point which stands out in greatest relief when one considers Bad Heart Bull's record as history is the artist's astonishing conception of the work as a whole, his far-reaching and comprehensive plan of the work. It differs from any other native North American historical record not only in its artistic accomplishment but—what is more important in the present discussion—to no less a degree in its historic scope and extent. The winter counts give only a skeleton-like framework of unrelated events as a calendar of the years; drawings of ceremonials, such as the Mide-wiwin bark records, merely outline in mnemonic symbols the steps in important rituals; and the great number of picture records simply tell tales of personal exploit, relate narratives of particular events in the lives of individual men. Here is a chronological narrative giving in intimate detail the story of the life of a people in all of its numerous ramifications. Bad Heart Bull, to a degree not attained by any other native North American recorder known, was possessed of the truly historical point of view; he could see events and institutions in their panoramic significance.

---

[41] For full quotation of the note, see the text accompanying drawing No. 327.

[42] Cf. J. R. Walker, "The Sun Dance and Other Ceremonies of the Oglala Division of the Teton Dakota," *APAMNH*, XVI, Part 2 (1917), 122–140, and my paper, "Ethical Conceptions of the Dakota."

CHAPTER IV

Bad Heart Bull as an Artist

BAD Heart Bull's work as an artist will have to be judged first of all according to standards of primitive art and then, if its quality demands it, according to some of the criteria of the art of more advanced civilizations. The fact that his work shows characteristics of both stages of development will become evident after very little study of his manuscript.

One must remember always that this work is essentially and primarily historical record, and that it was done in illustrative style at the natural prompting of a loyal Dakota's desire to preserve at least a portion of the life story of his people. Further, one must realize that for the most part he was using material with which he was familiar at first hand; he was describing a manner of life and its physical, mental, and spiritual accompaniments, in the midst of which he had lived or was living.

MATERIALS AND DATES

As I suggested in Chapter I, the actual drawing probably was done over a period of at least fifteen or twenty years. One looks to a number of aspects of the work, consequently, as possible indications of the relative age of various parts of the record. There is the question of different styles of technique as, in part at least, indicative of different stages in the development of workmanship; and there is the question of other internal evidence or factors in the development and revision of the narrative, such as the numerous insert pages and the many patches on drawings throughout the book.

In the matter of technique, the first fact that presents itself is that Bad Heart Bull is employing as the foundation of his work a type of pictographic expression common to his own tribe and to Plains tribes in general. The illustrative manner of portraying battle, hunt, ceremony, and ritualistic activity and symbol makes up a definite art genre of Plains Indian culture; and it is upon this as a basis that Bad Heart Bull builds and from which he develops a technique of his own.

The ordinary visual perspectives of this genre are those which I have called the third and fourth in my classification in Part Two, Chapter VI[1] (near views which contain twenty or thirty figures, and close-ups); and as the numbers in my previous discussion show, these two perspectives predominate by far in the record of Bad Heart Bull. In fact, all the drawings on the original pages of the ledger, except two at the end of the narrative,[2] belong to one or the other of these two classes. It is noticeable, too, that, with the exception of five compositions,[3] all the drawings on the original ledger pages exhibit a single type of technique and a fairly consistent quality of workmanship. Those five compositions are all topographic in character—two are the maps introducing the two Little Big Horn series, one is a map of another Montana location concerned with Sioux-Crow troubles, and two are diagrams of the camp circles and dance areas of the Fourth of July celebrations of 1898 and 1903—and they all display a certain native technical quality in conception and execution that the artist exhibits throughout the work.

[1] Pp. 76–77.

[2] Nos. 360 and 365. There was also one opposite No. 376, but this has been covered by a large patch.

[3] Nos. 129 (ledger page 111), 170 (ledger pages 142–143), 218 (ledger page 178), 327 (ledger page 209), and 375 (ledger page 261).

This consistency in technique and workmanship, coupled with the fact that the quality of both is peculiar to these pages, is significant, especially in view of the type and quality and placing of inserts. It seems to me altogether probable that the artist began his history on the first blank page of the ledger and continued it in order. In the first place, the distinctive technique and workmanship, of which I have just spoken, would indicate this. Not only, however, is the quality of both consistently unified, but the arrangement and treatment of subjects is orderly and coherently sequential; Bad Heart Bull is dealing with historical narrative, and that is necessarily chronological. So the drawings on these ledger pages portray in proper consecutive fashion the chronological order of events and in due relationship the social or ceremonial activities.

In the second place, the fact, arrangement, subject matter, and technical character of the drawings on the inserts seem to bear out the conclusion that the compositions on the original ledger pages are the earlier ones and that the inserts and their contents were added later. There are in all twenty-nine groups of insert pages, groups varying in extent from one or two to more than twenty pages and differing widely in quality of paper and size of pages, as I have indicated in the opening chapter of Part Two.

In the same chapter I have pointed out that the first sixty pages of the ledger are lacking. These evidently had been used for business entries by the merchant from whom Bad Heart Bull secured the book; they were probably removed when the Indian's period of ownership began. This space, however, has been filled with sixty-nine insert pages, the first and largest group of inserts. Of this number, fifty-four bear drawings and two bear script, leaving thirteen blank pages—seven full size and six small. Thirty of the drawings and both script notations comprise group I, "Events Perhaps Earlier than 1856," of my second classification of the contents of the record.[4] The other twenty-four are concerned with Dakota-Crow fighting. Practically all of these drawings are different from the others of which I have been speaking, either in quality of workmanship or type of technique or both, and the same differences are common to all the groups of inserts.

Inconsistent as the conclusion may seem, it is, on the one hand, the evidence among these inserts of an inferiority in workmanship in one type of technique, and, on the other hand, the appearance of another, superior and unique type of technique that makes me consider these insert pages later in execution. The near-view and close-up portrayals of action and fighting on these pages are for the most part inferior in technical quality to those of corresponding nature in the other series. Compare, for instance, the insert series from No. 131 to No. 136 (which I shall designate as insert series No. 2) with the following series, represented by Nos. 141 to 150 on the original ledger paper. The second group exhibits a vigor, a vitality and movement, a realism that is by no means attained in the first. There is greater variety among the figures; there is more individuality, more personality, in the portrayal of both men and horses. At the same time, there is not less unity and effectiveness of composition.

For the sake of detailed comparison, I call attention to No. 133, which is one of the better drawings in the second insert group, and to No. 146, which is taken at random from the other group. The total impression received from the second composition is one of greater vitality and motion; the first is fairly effective, but it exhibits a decided rigidity that the second does not show. Particularly do the positions of the bodies of the soldiers and the similarity of position of the horses' heads cause this effect of stiffness and comparative lack of realism. In No. 146 there are horses and men in several different positions, some quite gruesome, but all naturalistic in effect. In addition, there is a greater freedom and a truer artistic balance in the composition of the whole.

Further, there is a very definite and noticeable difference in the pure mechanics of the drawing—a difference in the handling of materials used, in certain conventional tendencies, and in type of figure (particularly the horse figure). The whole effect is quite different. In the first place, the drawing in No. 133 is comparatively sketchy; the lines are thin, evidently drawn in with a fine pen; the figures lack the suggestion of body and weight that the other drawings bear. In the second place, ink and paint are used less in this series; crayon coloring has been used predominantly. This fact alone would not necessarily be deeply significant, but since the elements of contrast and spotting have been almost wholly disregarded, it does have some weight. The kind of coloring and its manner of use are in large part responsible for the lack of body and weight; colors are simply put on

4 See Part Two, Chapter VI, p. 77.

plain and solid. In the matter of conventionalizations, one of the most noticeable affectations is the eye given to the horses; a curved line, a half-circle, bisected by a perpendicular line, represents the eye. This is not radically different from the representation of the human eye found commonly throughout the record, but for the most part, except for the insert drawings of this type, the *round* eye has been used for the horses. Another noticeable feature in this series of insert drawings is the omission of the lower portion of the hind legs of running horses. This may be rather significant in a later consideration. The most outstandingly characteristic element in these drawings, however, is the form of the horse, its proportions, outline, and general position. Whereas most of the horses in the record are long-bodied, small-headed animals, with a suggestion of sinuous litheness about them (see No. 150), the horses of the other insert series have a decidedly shorter body, a short, thick neck, and a large head. Whether the animal is running or standing still, it usually has the neck arched more or less and the ears cocked forward; and the animal is markedly larger in proportion to the size of the page than are the others. There is a suggestion of formal stiffness about all the figures.

If all the action drawings on insert pages were of this type, which contrasts so decidedly with the type characteristic of the whole book, it would be less difficult to generalize concerning their significance in the question of the relative time or period of their execution. But there are among the inserts a few[5] that exhibit characteristics so strikingly like those of the record as a whole—particularly those of the later portion—that drawing conclusions is somewhat complicated. A little study, however, makes possible what seems to me a feasible explanation. Especially pertinent examples of this other type of insert drawings (which for convenience I shall call series No. 1, since I consider them earlier) are Nos. 137 to 140 of the first Custer series. These came, as will be noticed, between the two groups which I have just discussed comparatively, insert group No. 2 and the group on the original ledger pages.

The drawings of group No. 1 are much more closely akin to the battle drawings as a whole, both in spirit and technique. But they are somewhat inferior, I think, in certain respects, although in a few instances

[5] Markedly Nos. 137, 138, 139, 140, 256, 257, 278, 282, and 283.

and in the matter of certain details, particularly horses' heads, they exhibit an unusually effective bit of portrayal. Consider No. 140, which is perhaps the finest piece of work in this insert series. This drawing is far superior to No. 133. There is much more realism here. The whole of the falling horse—especially the head—is particularly well done, and the heads of the three horses at the extreme right are exceptionally effective. But still, some of the life and fire of the earliest portrayals (as in No. 146) is lacking. There is a little tendency toward stiffness, especially in the position and attitude of the soldiers; there is, too, a little tendency toward a more formal symmetry which of necessity detracts from the realistic effect.

The most evident note of this symmetry is found in the parallel rows of fighters; the lines are too rigid. This arrangement, I believe, is a result of the artist's having been engaged just previously in making the long series of drawings of processionals in the Fourth of July celebrations at the end of the record. There are some striking resemblances between parts of some of the processional drawings and of the insert battle pictures. Compare, for example, the horses in No. 140 with those in Nos. 354 and 398. The whole general character is the same in all three cases. The shape of the horses' heads, the heavier outlines (as if a small brush or a stub pen had been used), the longer body, the more realistic effect of the whole—all these points help to mark what would seem to be a close relationship between this insert series and the original narrative.

There is, however, another and significant bit of evidence to indicate that what I have called the second insert series (of the near-view and close-up pictures) is the later one. There are plainly evident, on a great many pages of both original ledger-page drawings and the insert drawings which resemble them, horse heads of the type so characteristic of insert series No. 2. These have obviously been put in later, in the manner of a revision or re-editing. Usually the head and neck alone show, for the figures have been sketched in to fill some small space left vacant; and usually the result is not an improvement, at least so far as artistic composition and balance are concerned. It would seem that the artist, for the moment, lost his finer sense of discrimination and restraint in a meddling desire for added details.

There are over thirty drawings which bear these

additions, and they are of both kinds: those on original ledger pages and the related inserts which I have called series No. 1. Of the first type, No. 71 (ledger page 72) is a fair example; compare the two horses in the upper corners with those on the rest of the page. No. 265 (ledger page 194) shows even more clearly the detracting effect of the additions. Here there are seven added figures (two at the top left, three near the center below the Crow ambush, and two near the bottom); the result is that the composition seems rather cluttered, and those figures give besides an effect of lack of proportion. Among the drawings of insert series No. 1, the re-editing tendency shows plainly in No. 138, where there are two horses added on the left side of the page, and in Nos. 139 and 140, where numerous horse heads have been added so that they show just above the animals of the original composition. The decided difference in technique and character between these two types of animals makes the additions easily distinguishable.

There are three compositions of the late type appearing on pages of the original ledger.[6] This fact might seem to detract from the force of my arguments concerning the time of their execution were it not for the further fact that Bad Heart Bull left a number of ledger pages blank, probably in most cases because he thought he would wish to make later additions. As it happens, there are a few pages of the original ledger still vacant.[7]

Perhaps the most truly significant elements in these insert groups, however, are the miniature drawings, compositions which contain a hundred or more figures done in a minute scale and distinctly stylized. I have spoken of these as elements in the insert groups, for all of them (thirty-two in number), except two at the end of the narrative,[8] are on insert pages. This fact alone might well indicate that they are later in execution. But even more, the character and quality

of the drawings themselves show that they are a later, maturer development.

In the first place, this type of technique is peculiar to the work of Bad Heart Bull. I have said that his drawings as a whole belong to a widespread and distinct genre of Plains Indian art. The miniature type, too, is based primarily on that genre: it is very closely related to the large-scale type in general purpose and character; the subject and the spirit of treatment are the same; both types are illustrative; and the second grew up as a result of much work in the first type of technique, really as a distinct supplement to the first. I shall point out this supplementary nature of the miniature drawings at greater length a little later when I discuss the scales, variation of technique, and the relation of scales to convention; I have mentioned it briefly before.

In the second place, the drawings show—paradoxically—a naïvely sophisticated finish that puts them in a class by themselves. It is these minute group portrayals, with their unique conventionalizations and impressionism and an evident appreciation of composition, mass, balance, rhythm, and contrast, that cause modern artists to comment particularly; the drawings exhibit a *developed* technique of a sort which is not found in most primitive art or in the *first* work of any artist. It is this apparently advanced technique that makes me place these drawings among the comparatively late additions to the narrative, a conclusion which is supported, too, by the evidence of Short Bull.

In all cases the drawings on insert pages—of whatever type they be—merely supplement the main narrative; at no time do they change the theme or the center of interest. They give additional information and examples, or throw light on the action from another point of view. They are all unquestionably revisions resulting from late re-editings.

TECHNICAL THEMES

As one might judge from the general nature of the record, the most common technical themes of the artist are the human and the horse figures. In connection with the human figures, costumes also form a prominent theme, especially in ceremonial and

ritualistic drawings; and in those which make up the Independence Day series near the end of the narrative, costume is emphasized for its own sake and with conscientious concern for detail. The other main themes, much less frequent, include animals other

[6] Nos. 63 (ledger page 68), 67 (ledger page 70), and 81 (ledger page 76).

[7] Ledger pages 80 (opposite No. 85), 110 (opposite No. 129), and 152 (opposite No. 185) are *blank*.

[8] Nos. 360 and 365. There was also one opposite 376 on 377, but this has been covered by a large patch.

than the horse, ceremonial and ritualistic articles, and weapons.

The outstanding feature in the portrayal of all these themes is the note of realism, of naturalism. Contrary to tendencies among peoples of our own race and some others, the American Indian is sensual or perceptual rather than conceptual in his attitude and point of view; the Indian is not linguistically minded. What Roger Fry says of Paleolithic and Bushman drawings is true also, to a great extent, of this art genre of the Plains:

> Indeed, the preference for the profile view of animals —though as we have seen, other aspects are frequent— would alone indicate [the influence of "concepts which even the most primitive people must form"], but they appear to have been at a stage of intellectual development where the concepts were not so clearly grasped as to have begun to interfere with perception, and where therefore the retinal image passed into a clear memory picture with scarcely an intervening mental process.[9]

Herein lies the reason for that characteristic naturalism in the work of Bad Heart Bull.

HUMAN FIGURES

In the portrayal of men, and of all animals, the profile view predominates, as one would expect in primitive art or in almost any art in which the general purpose and subject matter are similar to those of this Indian artist. Like the Bushmen, however, Bad Heart Bull does not hesitate to attempt other and very complex attitudes, which he frequently renders with a certain degree of ease and success. In No. 256 at the left side of the composition there is a full-rear representation of a Crow warrior on foot in the act of shooting a mounted Dakota. It goes without saying that the attitude is a difficult one to achieve, but the artist does it quite convincingly. The Dakota opposing the Crow in this drawing is shown full front from the waist up, for he is turned toward the Crow with sabre raised to strike. The face is much less effective than either body portrayal, but of course it is less significant to the ultimate and total effect. In these full-front face depictions, in the closer-view drawings, Bad Heart Bull uses simply two short curves with a dot below each for eyes, two dots for nostrils, and a larger curve—which sometimes

becomes almost a straight line—for the mouth. His feeling that the facial features are relatively unimportant is further evidenced by the fact that in his miniatures he makes no attempt to distinguish features except to indicate the nose in profile by a very slight point in the outline. In picturing the human figure, next to the profile Bad Heart Bull uses the full face most frequently; there are very few rear views of the full figure, aside from those representing the dead lying upon the ground in a few of the smaller-scale drawings where one views the field from above and at an angle (see No. 183). One of the most noticeable representations of the rear view of both men and horses is found in No. 130, where a whole row of mounted and armed warriors is seen from the back. On the same page there is (at the right) an example of foreshortening in the portrayal of a rearing horse turned away from the observer. There are several drawings of this sort showing rearing horses and their riders, all of which are fairly convincing.[10] Nos. 202 and 204 show rather effective examples of foreshortening in the depiction of trotting and galloping horses; No. 290 represents horses falling in combat; and No. 227 is a fairly telling portrayal of a wounded Indian falling from his horse. There are a number of examples of the rear view of a galloping horse, a very difficult attitude to portray; perhaps the best of these is found in No. 303. A fairly good example of the opposite and hardly less difficult view, a full front of a galloping horse, is found in No. 165. Following this in No. 167 in the first Little Big Horn series is a drawing of a very unusual and difficult attitude, one which only an extreme realist would desire or attempt to render: a rolling wounded horse is pictured as seen from beneath. The drawing is sketchy and crude, but it exhibits a naturalism in attitude and movement which in turn bespeaks a keen observation on the part of the artist.

The most comprehensive composition in this class, as far as variety of attitudes of the human body is concerned, is found in No. 408. The subject of the drawing is the public Omaha Dance, which is still performed at Fourth of July celebrations and on other special occasions. There are profile, full-front, rear, and three-quarter-front views of the bodies of dancers. One sees in this composition, as in a few other dance portrayals in the record (see Nos. 187 and

---

[9] Roger Fry, *Vision and Design* (New York: Brentano's, 1920), p. 63.

[10] Nos. 59, 78, 228, 255, 257, 258, 264, and 365, which is a miniature drawing.

190), the stiff-backed bending of the body from the waist so common in this dance; one sees, too, the flexing of the knee and the odd, sometimes grotesque positions of arms and legs; and one who has seen the actual dance can almost feel in the drawing the effect of stiff-legged yet elastic action of the dancers. Even the sidewise turning of the head as it is seen in most of these full-front and rear-view representations is characteristic of this dance. Bad Heart Bull is drawing the thing just as he has seen it.

So far, all of my detailed discussion has concerned drawings of the nearer-view class. Several of the various attitudes, however, are to be observed among the drawings done in minute scale. These compositions possess a more "spread out" character; one is observing the action from above and at an angle, and the view is more distant. The profile is the predominating view again, but one also sees in most of these drawings a certain foreshortening effect, which is naturally an essential tendency since the angle of vision is what it is. No. 171 in the second Little Big Horn series is a fair representative of this group. Some horses are running in one direction, some in another, and others in still another; in such a situation there is bound to be fore-shortening, sometimes from one angle and sometimes from another. The pinto pony bearing Chief Crazy Horse (toward the right of the composition) is a good example of this type of execution; there is no part of the composition, however, that does not exhibit it. In No. 365 there is near the center of the drawing another, rather different example of this artistic device; the running horse is shown full front except that its head is turned toward the left.

There are also three outstandingly effective rear-view portrayals among these miniatures, portrayals which, especially in view of their minuteness, show a decided power of artistic technique. In No. 19, in the lower left corner of the composition, is a rear-view drawing of a buffalo, the head showing as it is turned slightly to the right. A similar portrayal of a horse and rider is given in No. 365 in the roundup scene; and on the same page and in No. 412 are found examples of Bad Heart Bull's unique, conventionalized representation of a cow, which is made in only four strokes but is nevertheless unmistakable. Even in these minute, distinctly stylized drawings realism is the keynote—realism coupled with keen imagination.

COSTUMES, ETC.

I shall not give time and space here to the subject of costumes, ceremonial and ritualistic articles, and weapons, for I discuss them elsewhere in connection with the manners of Dakota artistic expression.

SCALES

The scales used in the technical execution of the drawings in this record correspond so closely to the classification according to visual perspectives given in Chapter VI, Part Two, that they may be identified rather closely with the four classes named there: topographical, or beyond actual vision, with *very* minute representations of men and animals if any; minute, stylized drawings of battle and hunting scenes, containing a hundred or more figures; nearer views, containing twenty or thirty figures and giving attention to detail; and the close-up view, showing fewer figures and giving much attention to detail. I am simplifying the classification a little more, however, by making the first and second one class: miniature scale. The general scales would then be three: miniature, distant scenes; larger scale, showing nearer views; and close-up. This cannot mean, of course, that there is an absolute size or scale of drawing for each class. In the first class, for instance, the scale will range from very minute to somewhat larger miniature drawings. There are the tiny conventionalized drawings of running, ridden horses (which one does not at first suspect of being such), like those one finds in No. 61, where two large war parties are shown in action in the distance, and in No. 177[11] in the upper left corner; no one of these horses measures more than a sixteenth of an inch in length. Then there are at the other extreme the larger miniature portrayals as they are found in the second Little Big Horn series, where horses measure about an inch on the average. The range is rather wide, but the drawings all comprise a general class which is miniature. So also in the others will there be slight variations in

---

[11] This composition, which seems to be a discarded one, exhibits more variety in the absolute scale in the miniature class (scale differing to meet demands of perspective) than any other one drawing.

absolute size. Furthermore, there may be some over-lapping of the second and third classes at times, as I have suggested in my classification of the individual drawings.[12] It is only natural that in free drawing of this kind there should be slight variations of size at different times of execution and in view of different purposes, even when the type of drawing and the perspective are the same.

VARIATION OF TECHNIQUE

I have said elsewhere that the miniature drawings in all classes are panoramic in character and that they supplement the closer-view and close-up drawings which they accompany. The larger-scale drawings view the situation at comparatively close range; they show the action and the actors within the particular area chosen and give them in all the detail necessary to indicate the type of situation: kind of activity, distinguishing human physical features, costume, and paraphernalia. The miniature drawings, on the other hand, present the situation in a manner which makes its location and characterization broader in their view; they tend more to give the location and character of the whole situation, with smaller portions or episodes in the action apparent, but in very little detail and only as part of the pattern of the whole.

Take, for example, the compositions in Nos. 5, 6, and 7. All three scales may be said to be represented; 5 is miniature, 7 is closer-view, and 6 is close-up—though the only practical difference between 6 and 7 is in number of figures. No. 6 shows a Dakota man and woman on horseback followed by a horse bearing a loaded packsaddle and drawing a loaded travois. No. 7 shows another portion of the group; here there are twenty-four full-grown horses and two young colts; three of the horses bear loaded packsaddles, and two bear packsaddles and draw travois; three other horses are ridden by women, who are evidently herding both the pack animals and the others. In both drawings, Dakota riding gear and packing equipment are plainly evident. The native frame saddle, with its hooked wooden bow and similar cantle, is used by all the women.[13] The packsaddles appear to be like the riding saddle except that, of course, they do not have

stirrups; in all cases they are accompanied by orna-mented saddle blankets and are supported by decorated cruppers[14] and collars. On two of the horses (No. 7) the special ornamented blanket often used by women of the Dakota, Ute, Crow, and Sho-shoni nations[15] is easily distinguished, the beaded borders showing in front of and behind the saddle, and on all of the ridden horses the beaded and fringed saddlebag is exhibited.[16] The saddle used by the woman in No. 6 is provided, too, with both crupper and supporting collar. No detail is omitted in these drawings.

Composition No. 5, on the contrary, portrays the band moving as an organized whole. The four *waki-cunza*, or civil executives, bearing their pipe bags as symbols of their office,[17] are seen preceding[18] the group; the *akicita*, or marshals, immediately lead and flank the movement.[19] It is a general impression of a whole that is given here. Mounted horses, pack animals—some with travois, some without—and loose extra horses are indicated; and there are, besides the pipe bearers, other people on foot, but complete detail is not given. The drawing as a whole is the most highly impressionistic composition in the record. By means of varied views in varied scales, a twofold and comprehensive impression of the situation is given: in detail and as a whole.

The tendency of one scale to supplement the other or others is evident throughout the narrative, indi-cating that supplementation is the real purpose of variation in scale and in technique as technique is related to scale. As I indicated a little earlier in this discussion, the closer-view scales are the earlier ones and the miniature ones are a late development. This means that variation in technique indicates not only a difference in purpose but also a difference in the time of execution of the drawings as well.

RELATION OF CONVENTION TO SCALES

In connection with scale there comes, too, the question of conventionalization and the possible relation of one to the other. Almost immediately in the study of Bad Heart Bull's work, it becomes

---

[12] See Part Two, Chapter VI, pp. 75–77.

[13] Cf. Clark Wissler, "Riding Gear of the North Ameri-can Indians," *APAMNH*, XVII, Part I (1915), 7–14, figures 2–6.

[14] *Ibid.*, p. 17 and figure 14.

[15] *Ibid.*, figure 18.

[16] *Ibid.*, figure 19.

[17] Clark Wissler, "Societies and Ceremonial Associations in the Oglala Division of the Teton Dakota," *APAMNH*, XI, Part I (1912), 8 and footnote 1.

[18] *Ibid.*, p. 9 (top).

[19] *Ibid.*, pp. 9–10.

evident that the miniature drawings exhibit, comparatively, the greater number and the finer examples of conventionalized elements. There are bits of convention found throughout the record, however, in all the various types of drawings. It stands to reason that convention develops with a developing technique—in a sense it indicates the development and is an integral part of the finished technique—so it is only natural that as this record proceeds, conventionalizations increase in number and originality and effectiveness. This does not mean that every individual conventional element adds to the artistic effect, but that, taken as a whole, realistic conventionalization such as Bad Heart Bull's marks an artistic advance.

One convention worthy of note in Bad Heart Bull's closer-view drawings is that found in the profile portrayal of the head of the blanketed figure of a man, as it is seen particularly in the drawings relative to courting and old-time marriage scenes. In No. 112 the man and woman are under the same blanket and are seen from the back, but the man's head is turned; the hooded effect of the blanket over the man's head, a peak at the front, is the feature to which I refer. In No. 356 there are two more similar examples in the foreground; this time the couples are seen three-quarter front, but the heads are both in profile, the man's features again entirely concealed and only the hooded effect evident. In the background of this same composition the same effect is seen in miniature, both in the case of isolated single figures—lying, seated, standing, and mounted—and in the case of groups such as those to which I have referred above.

On these same pages there is evident also the Plains-wide conventionalization of the back of a woman's head: a perfectly symmetrical, horseshoe-shaped outline divided exactly in half by a perpendicular line representing the part in the hair.

In the drawings of the processionals—Nos. 124, 354, and 368, for example—one finds a conventionalization in the representation of the trotting and pacing horses. The positions of the legs of the horses are portrayed with greater or less similarity time after time; the lifted front leg is given a conventional arching, and the hind legs "move" with a certain characteristic uniformity. This does not mean that there is no variation, that a monotonously set conformation is used; there are degrees of variation that give individuality to the different drawings, but the outlines follow, more or less closely, a general

pattern. It does not mean, either, that the pattern outline or the different depictions lack realism; on the contrary, the attitudes and positions portrayed are essentially and impressively naturalistic.

Among the miniature portrayals, effective conventionalizations are numerous. Perhaps the most prominent examples are the miniature "footnotes" to which I refer in Chapter VI, Part Two.[20] Another unique example which I have mentioned elsewhere is the symbolic representation of cattle as seen from the rear (Nos. 365 and 412). The portrayal of men with rifles is noteworthy, particularly in Nos. 36 and 197; a faint impressionistic outline of head and shoulders and then a heavy straight line for the rifle barrel is all that is given, but the effect is achieved. Again, the depiction of the bonneted and mounted warrior is conventionalized; the bonnet is suggested by nothing more than a series of short, straight lines arranged side by side to represent the eagle feathers of a war-bonnet, and the leg of the warrior (usually in leggings) is the barest sort of sketched outline down the side of the horse. The horse outline in these miniature drawings is likewise a conventionalization. In fact, there are several different forms, for there are several somewhat different types of miniature portrayals. In No. 5 (to which I refer in detail elsewhere) the whole horse is suggested by a representation of only the head and shoulders and the beginning of the foreleg; a convincing effect of a row of moving horses is secured by use of this outline, the most prominent elements of which are the short, heavy, straight lines representative of the ears. In less impressionistic compositions, the horse figure is much more completely drawn. One of the characteristic conventionalizations in all these drawings, however, is omission of the lower portion of the legs of the horse; in very few instances are the hoofs drawn in. This omission may in some cases be affected to indicate concealment of the feet by dust raised in traveling (as in the travel pictures) or by grass (as in the Little Big Horn drawing No. 171); however, in many instances—and I believe that this is *often* the case—it may be prompted by no such definite intention, but may be a contingent effect of pure impressionism.

In discussing the two types of technique used in close-view drawings on insert pages, I spoke of the fact that in most cases the artist does not draw in the complete hind legs of the horses in insert series No. 2,

[20] P. 77.

and I remarked that this might have some significance in indicating the relative period of their execution. It seems to me that this technical idiosyncrasy in the drawings may point to the fact that they were done about the same time as the miniatures, either just before or just after, possibly even in the same relative period, and that its appearance in one type of drawing is due to the influence of the other type. If this is true,

and if my other conjectures are correct, my argument for considering insert series No. 2 as later than No. 1 is strengthened.

However that may be, though, the fact of varied scales of execution remains. There remains no less the fact that each scale possesses its own purpose and technique and that all together tend to a more completely comprehensive narrative.

COMPOSITION

Beyond the matter of the individual elements of the drawings and beyond the differing purposes and spirit inspiring them and dictating scale and general type of technique, there is the question of the handling of composition as such. The drawings are not mere records of history; they are as well—consciously to the recorder—expressions that demand technical balance and effectiveness of execution for their own sake; they aim not only to inform but to please by their manner of portrayal.

DECORATION

Second only to the realistic character as an outstanding feature of Bad Heart Bull's work stands the decorative quality of the individual compositions. This may be due, in part at least, to the fact that the artist is using a drawing surface of definite limits, the page of the book. But this possibility cannot be the whole explanation. Rhythm, color, spotting, and a tendency to frame the action all play a part in achieving this effect of decoration.

Rhythm. The rhythm of line and movement that most of Bad Heart Bull's portrayals of hunting, processional, and ceremonial scenes exhibit is primarily a rhythm secured by faithfulness to nature and reality, by a sympathetic interpretation of incident and activity as he has observed them, and by an appreciation of their suggestion and vitality. It is a rhythm that is aided frequently by such technical devices as color and spotting, probably used unconsciously in this case. Representative of ceremonial drawings is the depiction of the dance of victory in No. 85. The circle of the dance is given in minutest detail and according to an interesting conception of perspective. In spite of what seems at first glance to be a sort of childish crudeness in the actual drawing of outlines and details,[21] Bad Heart Bull's portrayal of

human figures shoulder to shoulder in a circular dance formation is a real accomplishment in primitive art. The circle moves. The positions of the hand drums in the hands of the braves at the right end of the line of dancers, the position of the long rear panels in the costumes farther down the line, the angles at which the scalp sticks and the lances are held, the varied angles at which the scalp locks swing, and even the slight tilt of the heads of the dancers at right and left suggest the *movement* of the dance.

Color. In the color scheme, red (favored by Indians generally) is the basic note; but relief is given by the scattered instances of purple and white and the dash of blue and yellow in the costumes, by the yellow and black of face markings, by the broken black ring suggested by the hair of the heads of the dancers, by the scattered spots of black of the scalp locks, and particularly effectively by the rhythmic appearance of black leggings or black dresses among the costumes. The feeling of balance in the composition as a whole is further increased by the unobtrusive suggestion of the tipis of the camp circle in the foreground and background and at the left side; the center of interest is framed; the incident is given location.

A portrayal of more vigorous activity is found in No. 142 in the first Little Big Horn series. The movement of the action is from right to left. The rhythms of line, mass, and motion are vigorous and effective. The page is divided, unsymmetrically in half horizontally, and the arrangement of the figures in the parallel groups suggests rhythmical thirds. Colors are varied, dark mingled with light in such a way that contrast is secured. The outstretched hind legs and doubled-up forelegs of the horses, the heavy coloring and the horizontal position of their tails, the back-tilted attitude of most of the horses' ears, the angle at which mantles and feather ornaments appear extended behind the wearers—all these details enter into the achievement of the effect of movement and vitality in

[21] A quality common to all of the closer-view drawings and to all primitive drawing of this type.

the portrayal. There is no impression of boresome symmetry in the composition, but there is a real balance.

PERSPECTIVE

In both of the drawings just cited the artist exhibits a certain definite sense of perspective, and he does it in two very different types of subject. The realistic picturing of the dance circle is a rather serious undertaking. Bad Heart Bull assumes a point of view a little above the level of the dancers and at an angle a little to the right. The fact that the scene is viewed from above is indicated by the showing of the circle as a circle, with the enclosed area visible. The fact that it is viewed from the right is shown by the difference in the attitudes of the dancers on the right and left sides of the circle; those at the right appear to lean a little to the left as one looks at the page, and the figures (all except the last two, in which a little more of the body is visible) appear to be placed almost directly behind one another; those at the left appear to lean out a little (to the left also), and much more of each figure can be seen. There are two noticeable weaknesses in Bad Heart Bull's technique, however. The first is that the striped pole, which is supposed to rise from the center of the dance circle, is placed too low on the page. It is well placed as far as right and left relationships are concerned, for it carries the correct illusion of bisecting the circle laterally when in the drawing it is actually a little more to the right; but according to the placing on the page, it would rise, not from the center of the area, but from the extreme "bottom" side. The other weakness is in the relative size of figures in the immediate foreground and those farther from the observer; instead of being somewhat smaller, the more distant figures seem to increase a little in height. The effect of the whole, however, is not seriously marred by these defects.

In the second drawing (No. 142) the effect of perspective is secured by placing the figures one behind the other, indicating close formation. Thirty-four horses are represented on this page, but in only one case does the whole figure show; in all other cases some small portion or most of the figure is concealed by another or is cut off by the edge of the page. In only four cases does the whole human figure show.

There is another compositional element in these drawings of Bad Heart Bull's that early becomes evident and demands remark. Time after time there appears a panel effect at top or bottom—or both—of the composition as a whole. This device is significant in the matter of *decoration* quite as much as in the matter of *perspective*, but I discuss it here since it belongs to both elements. I have already mentioned, in the section on decoration, Bad Heart Bull's tendency to "frame the action." The use of panels is one of his manners of "framing," of giving the action character and location. In No. 115, which is a drawing of an animal-cult ceremony, there is an example of paneling in the foreground. A row of tipis is drawn across the bottom of the page. Between the tipis can be seen the heads and shoulders of women spectators of the ceremony. Perspective as well as decoration is served—whether consciously or unconsciously—for the mere placing of the tipis and spectators tends to move the action—the ceremony—away from the observer and to suggest a certain depth in the picture. Another somewhat less effective sample of the use of this device is seen in No. 1. The four seated councilmen, flanked at right and left by the camp marshals, occupy the center of the drawing. Very simple portrayals of tipis, sketched in with pen and ink at the top, sides, and bottom of the page, represent the camp circle. The tipis in the nearest foreground, however, are the smallest of all. True perspective, as we know it, is lacking, although the artist intends to indicate by the discrepancy in proportion that the men are seated at the center of a *large* camp circle. The main purpose of the tipis, however, is to frame the action, to give it location and character. I call attention to one other example of the use of the panels, for in this composition it seems to me that both the decorative quality and perspective are especially effectively secured. In No. 356 appears one of the artist's courting scenes. Several couples occupy the foreground. In the background is a long panel in miniature, showing a portion of the camp circle and a goodly number of the inhabitants of the camp. Here in the panel also, courting is plainly going on. There is a strange air of life and reality about the portrayal. The panel is made unobtrusive by the absence of color, by the comparative faintness of its penciled outlines, and by the miniature scale in which it is drawn. Yet in spite of this unobtrusiveness, the panel figures are not vague and characterless; quite the contrary. In fact, the panel in some ways possesses more and subtler character and intriguing interest than the main part of the composition, partly because of the sense of true perspective which the three qualities named above create. The drawing is strangely realistic in effect.

Emphasis. No. 412 exhibits one of Bad Heart Bull's uniquely primitive perspective contrivances for placing emphasis. A drawing of himself, mounted, forms the center of interest in the picture. In the upper right corner of the page is a miniature representation of the government farm station. To the left of and above the central figure is the highly stylized miniature portrayal of a large herd of cattle attended by minute herders. The actual perspective is wrong; in fact, there is no actual or true perspective. But by this combination of scales and the intended suggestion of perspective, the central figure is emphasized, framed, given location.

Impressionism. Two of Bad Heart Bull's cruder examples of perspective, aided by impressionism, appear in Nos. 157 and 158 in the first Little Big Horn series. The drawings represent a part of the retreat of Reno's troops across the river. The artist's appreciation of the possibility of impressionism is evidenced by the "fading off" of men and horses in the water. Only the heads and arms, or sometimes only the heads, of the men are visible above the surface of the water. In some cases only the heads of horses can be seen; in others, hardly more than flying tail and outstretched hind legs. I have said that the drawings are crude, particularly, because of the lack of true proportion in the relative sizes of the human and horse figures and the river and because of a relative lack of balance and rhythm and realism. These are two of Bad Heart Bull's least effective compositions. But even so, the impressionism which I have just described and the effective suggestion of motion by means of the heavy spotting of outstretched horse tails and flying feather ornaments—these alone, though there were no other commendatory elements, would mark the drawings as the work of a person with some claim to artistic ability.

Groups. In all these instances, as I have tried to suggest, either directly or incidentally, the artist's manner of handling groups is one of the most significant features. Especially in the miniature compositions is Bad Heart Bull's ability to handle mass and to achieve balance and rhythm and vital movement manifested. The roundup scene in No. 365 shows this. The composition is made up of three parts: the largest herd of cattle occupies the center of the picture; a little to the right and above is a smaller herd; below and to the left is another small herd. The artist overcomes a possible lack of coherence (three absolutely separate units) by picturing a cow and calf (pursued by a cowboy) breaking away from the main herd and attempting to reach the smaller upper one, and a single animal (also pursued) breaking away from the central herd in an attempt to regain the smaller lower one. The result is a unified and coherent composition, built on a diagonal plan and well balanced.

In No. 19, the buffalo hunt shows again Bad Heart Bull's feeling for three-part balance. Whether the artist realized it or not, there is a true but unobtrusive and realistically rhythmic division of the whole into thirds: at the left the more solid and undisturbed portion of the buffalo herd, at the center the closely pursued and therefore more scattered and excited animals, and to the right the pursuing hunters. There is, of course, no break between the several sections; the three-part arrangement does not force itself upon the attention, but becomes apparent only when one studies the composition critically; the parts are organic to each other. And again Bad Heart Bull makes good use of spotting, securing a balance of tone and interest by making an individual animal, or perhaps only a tail or a head or some other portion, darker than the rest.

Enlargements. Bad Heart Bull, in his handling of various kinds of related groups, employs the enlargement to aid in making his narrative doubly clear. This trait is closely related to his tendency to use one scale or manner of technique to supplement the other, but the type of case to which I refer now is a special type with more specific purpose than was found in the discussed instances representative of the general fact. In these cases of very specific purposes, the enlargement plays a role—contrarily enough—similar to that of the miniature "footnotes" to which I have referred before: the enlargement is given in order to make clear the exact nature and perhaps the result of the encounter or other incident, whatever it may have been, or some portion of it. In No. 277, for example, there is portrayed in miniature the pursuit of three mounted Crows by a larger party of Dakotas. The story on this page is given in three separated parts: the pursuit of the three by all the Dakotas; the overtaking and killing of one of the Crows by some of the Dakotas; and the further pursuit of the other two Crows, who have swerved suddenly in their line of flight, by the rest of the

Dakotas. This is one instance, as is evident, of a sequence of drawings showing different moments in the same action, a mode of portrayal which I shall treat in greater detail later. In the present case, the prominent Crow figure is the man wearing the special wolf-head and eagle-feather bonnet. In the third part, this warrior is just being overtaken and struck by one of the Dakotas. The drawing which follows in No. 278 is an enlargement of this portion of the third part of No. 277, and connected with it is a "footnote" to leave no doubt that the bonneted warrior was killed.

Again in No. 301 a Sioux-Crow encounter is given in miniature, an encounter in which the Sioux have been surprised and overwhelmed by a war party of Crows who greatly outnumber them. The drawing in No. 302 is an enlargement of the portion showing the Dakotas as they were marooned.

Sequence of Drawings. The last instances cited are examples of a special type of sequence of drawings. They belong in that class of sequential drawings which may be called a series showing one event. The other class is a series showing different moments in the same action. These might seem to overlap at some points; but in reality they do not, for in the first I consider only portrayals which show in different manners the event or incident *at one moment.* In this class the series is comprised of portrayals in different scales in order that the nearer-view and panoramic aspects may both be secured. The last examples, those emphasizing the use of enlargement, belong in this class; so also does the travel series, which I have already described, in which the drawings in Nos. 6 and 7 give details of the move shown as a whole in No. 5. The most extensive, comprehensive example of this type of series, of course, is the double portrayal

of the Custer fight—two complete series of the same event.

In the other class, one of the longer series in closer-view scale portrays the horse-stealing expedition, Nos. 88 to 97. As I explain in Chapter VI, this series shows the whole event, step by step, from the ceremonial preparation and departure through the discovery of the enemy camp and the actual cutting of the picket ropes and leading off of the horses to the victorious return with the booty. The longest series in any scale is, of course, the first Little Big Horn series, Nos. 126 to 169. Bad Heart Bull's most effective and impressive example of this sort of treatment, however, is the second—the miniature—series of the Battle of the Little Big Horn. Nos. 171 and 172 form one composition which represents the opening of the fighting, probably the encounter between Reno's troops and the Indians; 173 pictures the situation a few moments later when the troops have been repulsed; 174 shows the growing disorder in the retreat a few minutes later still; 175 describes the time in the retreat when some of the troops and Indians have crossed the river and are flying on while others are still crossing. A definite passage of time is indicated, and the close relation between the action and that passage of time is perfectly apparent.

This series brings out particularly well a certain maplike quality which many of Bad Heart Bull's portrayals assume. The whole story is laid out before one. Comparing these compositions one by one in series to the artist's introductory topographic sketch (No. 170), one can trace without difficulty the whole line of Reno's procedure from the first meeting with the Indians to the ultimate flight to the hills. All of these sequential drawings, especially those done in small scale, markedly exhibit this cartographic trait.

PSYCHOLOGY OF THE DAKOTAS

One naturally looks to the work of such a recorder as Bad Heart Bull, dealing as he is with a life to which he is closely related, to reflect rather indirectly and subtly something of the psychological tendencies of his people. And one is not disappointed in this case. The spirit of the whole work and particularly the depiction of costume and design are closely related to tribal ideals and give evidence of the nature of those ideals. In my next chapter, "Dakotan Art and

Thought," this point will be discussed in considerable detail. It suffices here to say that costume and costume design do manifest a close relationship to the tribal ideals and philosophy of life of this people. They bespeak, through symbols of various kinds, a consciousness of determining spiritual powers and man's kinship with and dependence upon them. They bespeak, further, a conception of life as a state of activity, vigorously episodic. They are inevitably connected with war. The symbols are those which make appeal for or guarantee strength of body and spirit, or which announce the status or prowess of the wearer; they are for communication, or for protection, or for added power. In short, they are used primarily for medicine and for heraldry. And all of this means that the life of activity and danger, life with war as a constant accompaniment, was accepted by the Dakotas as the most normal sort of existence. Fighting and bloodshed were looked upon as matters of course.

Comparison with other examples of Indian art brings out more clearly than ever several points in the work of Bad Heart Bull. The three drawings of the Custer fight made by White Bird,[22] who was a Northern Cheyenne, are fairly representative of the Plains art genre to which Bad Heart Bull's work belongs. But a parallel study of these Cheyenne drawings and corresponding compositions from either of Bad Heart Bull's two series brings out some rather startling contrasts. Compare the drawing called "Custer's Fight" with the drawing in No. 146 from the first series in the Dakota account. The general spirit and basic characteristics are the same, and they indicate similar attitudes toward war and life in general; both exhibit a certain vitality and movement. But the degrees of vitality and movement, the degrees of realism, to which they attain are by no means the same. Even more evident does this difference become when one compares this same Cheyenne drawing with the corresponding one (No. 176) in the miniature Little Big Horn series, and when one compares the Cheyenne drawing called "Reno's Retreat" with a corresponding one (No. 174, for example) in this same series. I say that the difference in degree of realism obtained is more evident in these latter comparisons because the visual perspective in the second series is more like that in the Cheyenne drawings; both perspectives are inclined toward the panoramic, though the scale is very different, the Cheyenne drawings covering a much larger surface. Bad Heart Bull secures a naturalism that the other artist at no point approaches. In comparison, White Bird's horses in particular appear wooden and unlifelike; proportions and attitudes of both horses and men are unnatural, although, with the enthusiasm and abandon of a true realist, the Cheyenne artist

attempts to draw difficult and unusual positions—difficult and unusual, but quite to be expected on the battlefield. White Bird does not exhibit the impressionistic conventionalizing ability of Bad Heart Bull; he does not exhibit Bad Heart Bull's uniquely original realistic technique; and he at no time even approaches Bad Heart Bull's naturalism. In short, he did not possess an artistic genius such as the Dakota's.

The pictograph records of the older American civilizations of the Aztecs and Mayas and the inhabitants of ancient Teotihuacán show a much more highly conventionalized technique than Bad Heart Bull's—and consequently than North American Plains pictography generally—and further show a very different spirit. The codices of these older peoples exhibit intricately schematic pictographic systems. Even those records of the later people of Teotihuacán, which more nearly approach the realistic in atmosphere and purpose, bear the mark of this cultural trait. The spirit of these older records is dominantly ceremonial and ritualistic. The comparatively late Codex de San Juan Teotihuacán,[23] for example, illustrates this fact adequately. It is in records of topographic character that these older manuscripts and Bad Heart Bull's show more similarity. One may compare the "Plano de San Martín de las Pirámides," Lámina 149,[24] with the plan of Fort Robinson, No. 197. Even though this is one of Bad Heart Bull's most schematized and conventionalized portrayals, it shows much more of a tendency toward naturalism than does the Mexican drawing. In the latter, human figures, buildings, and trees are drawn in absolute profile; in Bad Heart Bull's drawing, an attempt—fairly successful—at foreshortening is plainly evident. In the Mexican drawing there is a symmetrical formalization of arrangement that the work of the Dakota does not show; Bad Heart Bull's is a freer technique. There would seem to be some slight kinship between the two, but it is the kinship of expressions of all primitive arts at certain of their stages of development. The point that stands out more impressively in these comparisons is the difference in psychological tendencies which is shadowed forth. The Mexican cultures bespeak a more strictly organized, coercive type of life and civilization; the Dakotan, a more individualistic and freer one.

In another way, Helen Tongue's copies of the

---

[22] Now in the museum of the United States Military Academy at West Point.

[23] A colored reproduction of a copy of the original is to

be found in Lámina 150, *La Población del Valle de Teotihuacán* (México, 1922), Tomo I, Volumen II.

[24] *Ibid.*

Custer's Fight

Reno's Retreat

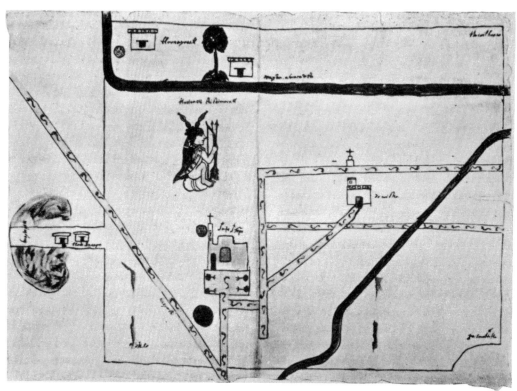

Plano de San Martín de las Pirámides

drawings of the Bushmen of South Africa[25] and Roger Fry's chapter on "The Art of the Bushman"[26] are also significant in connection with this study of the manuscript of Bad Heart Bull. Indeed, the similarity in character between some of the drawings of the Dakota artist and those of the Bushmen is striking. Like the Dakota, the Bushman drawings "represent for the most part scenes of the chase and war, dances and festivals":

> The figures are cast upon the walls of the cave in such a way as to represent, roughly, *the actual scenes.* For instance, the battle fought between two tribes over the possession of some cattle, is entirely unlike battle scenes such as we find in early Assyrian reliefs. There the battle is schematic, all the soldiers of one side are in profile to right, all the soldiers of the opposing side are in profile to left. The whole scene is perfectly clear to the intelligence, it follows the mental image of what a battle ought to be, but is entirely unlike what a battle ever is. Now, in the Bushmen drawing, there is nothing truly schematic; it is difficult to find out the soldiers of the two sides; they are all mixed up in a confused hurly-burly, some charging, others flying, and here and

there single combats going on at a distance from the main battle. But more than this, the men are in every conceivable attitude, running, standing, kneeling, crouching, or turning sharply round in the middle of flight to face the enemy once more.[27]

This might almost as well have been written of Bad Heart Bull's record. One might choose at random any one of the many battle scenes portrayed by Bad Heart Bull and find many of these Bushman traits exemplified. I have already called special attention to No. 146 and the varying attitudes of men and horses. This drawing, it is to be remembered, is taken from the first Little Big Horn series. In it, all the horses are seen in profile, most of them at a run—pursued and pursuing—one going down wounded and another bucking violently, either in pain from a wound or in fear. Two of the Indian pursuers are shown erect (or leaning a little forward in the act of firing rifles) and are pictured in profile; one is pictured in full-front view from the hips up as he has turned to kill the soldier whom he has overtaken. All of the white soldiers are seen in profile but in many

[25] Helen Tongue, *Bushman Paintings* (Oxford: Clarendon Press, 1909).

[26] Fry, *Vision and Design*, pp. 56–64.
[27] *Ibid.*, p. 58.

attitudes, some wounded or dead upon the ground, others falling forward, backward, or sidewise from their horses. Of those on the ground, several are sketched prone upon their backs, more are on their faces, one is upon hands and knees with an arrow in his back, and one is propped up in a sitting position, his arms braced behind him. This drawing is typical of practically all of Bad Heart Bull's battle scenes in the decided realism which is also so outstanding a characteristic of the Bushman portrayal. At the bottom of No. 183 there is a picture of a bit of episode which corresponds closely to the "single combats going on at a distance from the main battle" of which Fry speaks: three Indians are in hot pursuit of a single soldier who is fleeing from the battle. On the same page there are Indians in running, standing, kneeling, and crouching positions. In No. 59 there is a good example of mounted fighters (Crows) turning in mid-flight to face the enemy again. But I need not multiply cases.

Realism runs through the whole narrative like a dominant motif. Bad Heart Bull's guiding purpose is the faithful and detailed recording of the life of the Oglalas, and that demands keenness of observation and insight and a facility in transferring the actual details and effects to a drawing surface. If the result in such a case is artistic as well as scientifically and historically accurate, it is assuredly evidence of marked ability, even genius. This is what Bad Heart Bull has accomplished. Not only in his fidelity to facts but in the spirit of his art he proves himself a true realist. But even more, with this outstanding and consistent realism he couples a keen imagination. It is this which proclaims him an artist. In all probability, he did practically all of his work from memory. Most of it he assuredly did in this way. In fact, for much of it he had not even his own memory of the actual scene upon which to depend; in the drawings portraying episodes and conditions before his own time, he was utterly dependent upon the recitals of his father and uncles and others of his tribesmen and upon the constructive powers of his own imagination. And it is worthy of remark that several of his most outstanding compositions are numbered among those concerning the subjects of which he had only secondhand information. Bad Heart Bull has that striking ability of the artist to detach himself from life and incident and behold them objectively; he can see life unroll before him and can grasp at once the minute detail, the obvious or the subtle suggestion, and the artistic possibility inherent in the situation; and with it all he possesses an unusual mechanical skill and an infinite patience in execution. He is a genius among his people.

CHAPTER V

Dakotan Art and Thought

MANNERS OF SIOUX ARTISTIC EXPRESSION

WHEN I speak of Dakota *art* in this discussion, I am limiting myself to close consideration of only those expressions which may in a general way be characterized as graphic and am leaving untouched the question of drama, ritual, and song, significant though they are in the life of this people and impossible though it is absolutely to divorce any of the forms of Indian art from the other forms. Among the Dakotas, the chief manners of expression are quillwork, beadwork, featherwork, painting on skins and cloth, and, to a certain extent and in some localities, incising; one might speak, too, of the body painting of men and of horses as a certain phase of art, for it demands a real technique and bears a decided significance.

THEMES

All of these, with the possible exception of featherwork, are pictorial in character and purpose; even featherwork in reality has a symbolism which makes it closely akin to the others and consequently, in a sense, pictorial also. Among the Dakotas, as among most Plains tribes, the themes are chiefly concerned with exploit; they are closely related to the activities of war and the hunt, and it is in connection with these activities that ritualistic or ceremonial themes and symbols appear. The Dakotas were seminomadic, they were hunters and fighters; and their art tends generally toward the exaltation of the warrior and the four great virtues—bravery, generosity, fortitude, integrity—which formed the moral code of every young man who would call himself a warrior.[1] So in

the Dakotas' artistic expression the dominant motifs are those of very active life, motifs proclamatory of bravery, prowess, achievement. And when, as I have already suggested, the ceremonial or ritualistic element enters, it is almost invariably in connection with this dominating inspiration and is in a sense secondary to it, as is shown in the prayer of the Oglala Tokala Warrior Society—a prayer of invocation to *Inyan*, the spirit of bravery, generosity, and endurance:

> Help me in what I undertake.
> Be with me in my undertakings.
> Have pity on me.
> *Help me to defeat others.*[2]

USES

So the painting of buffalo or elk hide or the decoration of tipi cover and tent curtain, and frequently and in a more highly symbolized and conventionalized way quillwork and beadwork, tell the story of exploits and attainment. The robe of the Mandan chief Mah-to-toh-pa and the Crow robe described in Chapter II are examples of this Plains-wide tendency in the personal-record class. The "autobiography" made in 1873 at Grand River, Dakota Territory, by Running Antelope, a Hunkpapa Dakota chief, shows the same tendency among the Dakotas themselves.[3] Red Horse's portrayal of the Battle of the Little Big Horn, also referred to in Chapter II, is an example of the recording of incidents more general and less strictly personal in significance. The winter counts, though they serve a unique

---

[1] J. R. Walker, "The Sun Dance and Other Ceremonies of the Oglala Division of the Teton Dakota," *APAMNH*, XVI, Part 2 (1917), 62.

[2] Clark Wissler, "Societies and Ceremonial Associations in the Oglala Division of the Teton Dakota," *APAMNH*,

XI, Part 1 (1912), 20. The italics are mine.

[3] Garrick Mallery, "Picture-Writing of the American Indians," *ARBAE*, X (1888–1889), 571–575, figures 814–818 inclusive.

chronological purpose and display a unique character and technique among Dakota pictographic records, bring out no less this general tendency toward the exploit theme; they are frankly historical. I shall show in more detail a little later what must be more or less evident already—that the Bad Heart Bull manuscript is of this same nature but is more detailed and more purely illustrative in technique and impulse. There is, in all, desire to communicate.

In all cases—whether painted, embroidered, incised —the portrayal is made through the medium of images, but the motif is not in all cases *purely* communicative. In the decoration of costumes and instruments of war or ritual and of the utensils of everyday life, the expression has usually taken a more symbolic character. The beaded and quilled Dakota pipe bag described by Wissler in his paper on Indian beadwork[4] shows the fact and nature of the symbolism well, so well that I quote his explanation in full:

> The whole represents a battle scene. The white is snow. The two long green lines are to indicate the flight of arrows. The projecting lines at the end represent the wounds made by the arrows. The arrow point is represented by the triangular figures opposite the projecting lines, these being shown again as attached to the point of the arrow (*a*). The large central figure is the body of a man: the diamond-shaped portion representing the trunk, and the appendages, the head, arms, and legs. The dark blue color of the trunk-figure implies that the man is dead. The small white rectangles enclosing a red spot represent the hits or wounds that brought the man down. On the upper part of the bag the border figure (*c*) represents a victory in which the owner's horse, represented by the green diamond-shaped figure, was wounded, as shown by the red area within the horse symbol; (*b*) represents a feather, and implies that the owner of the bag was entitled to wear an eagle feather in his hair as a sign that he had killed an enemy. The figures of the pipe indicate the owner's right to carry the official peace pipe.

> The parts of this design are not new and so not original with the maker of the bag, but were selected by her to express these ideas and events, relating to the life of the man for whom she made it. Even the choice of designs was not wholly original, for it was the custom of her people to look upon certain designs as having a fixed meaning. Thus by looking at his pipe bag another Indian might read the deeds of the owner.

4 Clark Wissler, "Indian Beadwork," Guide Leaflet No. 50, American Museum of Natural History, p. 20, figure 15. The leaflet covers a series of 304 elements of bead designs, which by custom have come to have definite names and meanings; both designs and meanings are given on pp. 24–31. Although the elements are taken from Arapaho beadwork, they are, as Wissler points out, fairly representative of Plains Indian art as a whole.

Dakota Pipe Bag

Slightly different in specific purpose but similar in their main character are the medicine whistles of the Plains Indians. The Dakotas usually use them as symbols of the eagle's cry, which in turn symbolizes the thunderbird, so potent in all Indian myth and life. At stressful moments the whistle is blown to summon the thunder power to the aid of man. Bad Heart Bull has a telling picture of such an incident in No. 224.

The whistle itself is made of the wing or leg bone of the eagle and usually bears a zigzag line scratched upon it to represent lightning and therefore thunder. Wissler gives a description of an unusual Dakota specimen of this type which is now in the American Museum of Natural History:

> The whistle is from the wing bone of an eagle, and near the top is a small bag containing the medicine of the owner. The features of the yellow-winged woodpecker are attached thereto, because this bird is considered as an associate of the thunder-bird, or at least it

holds some relation to the thunder since the Dakota have observed that, when a storm is approaching, this bird gives a peculiar shrill call not unlike the sound of the whistle. . . . This they interpret as speaking to the thunder. Consequently, the features of this bird, when attached to the whistle, are supposed to put the individual also in a position to speak to the thunder. . . . Thus we have a combined charm representing the woodpecker and the eagle—two birds closely associated with the thunder.[5]

Here is a mixture of symbolism; material, form, decoration, sound all enter in. It even seems in one element, the feather, rather as if we have what might be called a reflex symbolism; the woodpecker feather is adopted because the cry of the bird resembles the sound of the whistle.

The decoration of the so-called "Ghost Shirt," worn in the ceremonies of the Ghost Dance among the Dakotas, is still another example of this tendency. The "Ghost Shirt" (or "Ghost Dress") itself was made as the result of a dream. The garment was ornamented with printed designs, chosen and arranged by the individual according to a dream or a trance vision. The design elements themselves were not new, but the arrangement was usually more or less original with the individual. And there were various elements which were repeated so frequently that they became markedly characteristic of Ghost Dance garments and other sacred objects. One of the specimens in the American Museum of Natural History amply suggests the character of these designs and their symbolism.[6] There is the crescent for the moon and hardly more than a cross for the morning star (the sun, moon, and stars always carry a peculiar potency for the Indian); there is a more or less naturalistic representation of the dragonfly, an insect which, like the eagle and the hawk, is swift in flight and difficult to hit; and there is an odd conventionalized hoofprint of a buffalo. These are only a few of the designs on the garment, but they represent the nature of the decoration. They are in reality pictographic in character.

No less do the markings of the warrior's own body make their mystic appeal to unseen powers and carry their message to those who may see them. The body painting for the Sacred Medicine Bow ceremony

serves well as an example of the form of marking. The particular emphasis in this case is upon the spiritual significance, and so does not tend especially to identify the individual as an individual. The whole body of the bow carrier was painted red, to represent the earth in a buffalo wallow, says Wissler. The face painting consisted of a black or blue band drawn in a curve from temple to temple across the bridge of the nose. This was forked at each end (i.e., on each temple), and represented lightning. A crescent was drawn upon the breast. The joints (wrist, ankle, elbow, and knee) of each dancer were ringed with blue, a mark known as the "blue stone mark" and symbolizing the wind god. Two methods of further marking arms and legs were used. In one, waved lines, forked at the end, extended downward from shoulders and thighs. The other showed but one difference: the line on one leg was straight "to signify the desire for the ability to think straight or to possess presence of mind, in contrast to the state of mind supposed to be produced by the power of the whirlwind."[7] The second form is the one which Bad Heart Bull shows very clearly in his portrayal of the ceremony.[8] Since the Medicine Bow and everything connected with it are sacred, these markings are spiritual in their primary significance; they are really prayers. But even so, in a secondary way, they are communicative not only to spirit powers but also to fellow tribesmen of the wearers and doubtless to many an Indian enemy as well.

One of the essential characteristics of the elements of decoration is evidenced by all these examples: the designs or design elements represent an active power; they are, in their inception, the intimate and personal symbol—the medicine, one may say—that can be carried with one; they are the signs of potent things and spirit powers. Sometimes only a single line is necessary, as in the case of the lightning (thunder), but a whole idea and a deep significance is expressed. And, as I have said elsewhere, they are truly *pictographic* designs. They are insignia of accomplishment, war, death, life, power; and they can and do declare to those who understand their language the status of the owner or wearer. In this way they are communicative.

---

[5] Clark Wissler, "Some Protective Designs of the Dakota," *APAMNH*, I, Part 2 (1907), 47–48, figure 22.

[6] *Ibid.*, p. 32, figure 10.

[7] *Ibid.*, pp. 51–52.

[8] Nos. 98 and 99. The latter shows the marking particularly well, for it is done in large scale.

SIGNIFICANCE

The natural question, then, is: How do the Dakotas look upon such expressions—as decoration, medicine, heraldry, or record? There can be no doubt that in most cases, other than picture writing as such, the significance is a mixed one—a mixture of all four of these impulses. In some cases, one intention will predominate; in others, another. The initial and predominant motive in the case of the pipe bag described by Wissler, I should say, is record, with heraldry and decoration secondary; of the medicine whistle, medicine, with decoration secondary; of the Ghost Shirt, medicine, with record and decoration secondary. But there can be even less doubt that almost invariably the original significance has been medicine. The ever recurring statement that an image, a form, an arrangement of images or forms, a weapon, a ceremonial object, an instrument has been made according to the dictates of a vision or a spirit voice indicates that the image, form, instrument, whatever it be, is clothed with mystery and power, that it is potency caught up in tangible form. The dictated symbol is god-given, so to speak; it is the gift to the individual from a guardian spirit, and it becomes for the individual his own personal emblem or totem. With that it takes on the character of heraldry.

As Mooney points out in a brief discussion of Indian heraldry,[9] and as I have suggested in a previous chapter, there is a definite system of military, family, and personal designation among the Plains Indians of North America. Its chief expressions are the painting and other methods of decoration of tipis, shields, and official weapons, and the body painting and other adornment of the warrior himself. The form of the designations originates in visions or dreams and is tempered by personal achievement, and both the elements and the materials of the decoration are guarded by religious taboo and by ceremony. The heraldic tipi was the property of a prominent family and passed from generation to generation by hereditary descent, each one being unique in pattern and decoration; but the shield belonged to the individual, and there might be several individuals with similar designations. The symbolism and heraldic designations of organized groups, such as the warrior societies, on the other hand, possess in some sense a somewhat wider civic significance, since they do not concern one person or one family line alone. With different heraldic expressions went specified and significant body painting and adornment, and pony painting and adornment. One could, then, be identified at a glance by a fellow tribesman or even by others.

So, as is true with all heraldry, the decoration becomes, in a certain measure, record. The tribe, clan, and personal totems tell their story, and the initiate can easily read it. Perhaps nowhere is this better shown than in the winter counts and particularly the Oglala Roster and Red Cloud Census, of which I have already spoken. But in forms of Dakota art devoted less directly and purely to pictography as such, the pipe bag to which I have referred is an excellent example. The identity, achievement, and standing of the owner are clearly indicated; and the bag is artistically decorated as well.

This leads to the last point in regard to the question of the Dakotas' feeling for the significance of their art expressions. The use of these expressions purely for *decoration* is relatively a late development. The painted, quilled, or beaded symbols and designs were always recognized as decorative, yes; but the decoration was by no means the significant element or inspiration in conception and inception of the design and its expression. The mystic symbolism and appeal, the proclamation of power and valor and achievement, the communication and record, all are more significant motives or impulses. The decorative quality in these forms of Indian expression is simply inherent in them; it is, one might say, part of the very essence of the expression. It is originally there without special intent on the part of the individual; the special conscious decorative intent comes later.

But beyond the mere image and beyond the emblematic symbol (in the above sense) is a further step, a specialization of one of these forms of imagistic portrayal or representation.

PICTURE-WRITING RECORD

The record motive carries this form of expression into pictographic portrayal of events, into historic expressions as such. This, more properly speaking, is picture writing. "In order to have true picture-writing," says Professor H. B. Alexander, "events must be given location in time and space, given location and given their character; and with this localization and characterization of events we have the

[9] James Mooney, "Heraldry," BAE Bulletin 30, Part 1, p. 544.

beginnings of history."[10] This stage of pictography presents more than image or symbol; it is illustration; it tells history in greater or less detail. "In this form it may develop and does develop into two quite different things: first, through a primary concern simply for record into a symbolic schematism which may become conventionalized into formal writing; and second, through devotion to the details of the event into the artistic picture, which becomes as much decoration as record."[11] The winter counts represent the first, among the Dakotas; the Bad Heart Bull record represents the second.

MATERIAL AND EVIDENCE IN BAD HEART BULL'S MANUSCRIPT

Picture writing is something that develops "through *devotion to the details of the event into the artistic picture*, which becomes *as much decoration as record*," Professor Alexander has said. Bad Heart Bull's story is primarily record; it is picture writing of a distinct sort. But it is record with a fullness of detail and a faithfulness to detail that carries it far beyond the schematized formalization of the ideogram; it is illustration.

Covering as it does a considerable length of time and the whole range of activities in the life of the Oglala Dakotas, it would seem probable that one would find in Bad Heart Bull's manuscript direct evidence of the tribal attitude toward the points which I have just been discussing—themes, uses, and feeling for significance of native artistic expressions.

The first outstanding fact about Bad Heart Bull's piece of work is that it is record—historical record—in character, spirit, and purpose. The artist—or historian—neglects no phase of life and begrudges no painstaking care in furnishing and portraying the details of the tribe's activity. He evidences clearly the dominant Dakota trait, the feeling for record, the historic consciousness. In this respect he shows markedly one attitude of the Dakotas for the significance of their artistic expressions. Mere reference to the table of contents of the manuscript proves this point.[12]

MEDICINE

But in that main role of record, Bad Heart Bull's narrative, as would be necessary if it is a true record, bears witness to the other aspects of Dakota art as considered by the group as a whole. Let us first consider medicine.

Organizational. The series of drawings showing the ritualistic paraphernalia of the *akicita* or warrior societies illustrates the organizational use of symbolic instruments, ceremonial objects, and other elements for medicine (see Nos. 22, 23, 25, 26, 29, and 30). No. 26 gives the regalia and lodge of the Iroka[13] (Badger) Society. At each side of the door flap of the lodge is the figure of a rampant badger, totem of the society. Like the badger, so may the warriors of the society be fierce in attack and defense. Here also the eagle-feather decorations of lances, whips, drum, and head-gear are perfectly evident: each feather is in one sense a prayer and in another the sign of a mystic rapport with the power of the thunderbird. The figure and the feathers are decorative, but that fact is secondary, is incidental. The emblem itself is an integral part of an organized ritualistic significance.

Personal. In addition to this, there is the individual, personal use of medicine, which is clearly evident in Bad Heart Bull's chronicle. I have already spoken of the fact that the shield and its adornment are the warrior's own and proclaim, to any who may see, what his personal spirit affiliations are. In No. 258 a Sioux-Crow encounter is depicted. The Sioux brave at the bottom of the page bears a shield whose character and decoration are clearly defined. A wide border portion of the upper half of the circle is colored a dark, almost purple gray, through which black zigzag lines, representing lightning, run downward. The lower portion of the shield is light yellow, probably representing early dawn. A little below the center is the bird figure in black and white, evidently a thunderbird, for from each wing downward runs a zigzag line forked at the end. Four groups of feathers —two in a group—hang pendent from the edge of the shield at equidistant intervals. On the face of the shield, placed at the lower edge of the dark section, are two rather odd symbols. They are round, button-like decorations from which hang short leather

---

[10] H. B. Alexander, "Pictorial and Pictographic Art of the Indians of North America," in *Cooke-Daniels Lectures* (Denver: Denver Art Museum, 1927), p. 22.

[11] *Ibid.*
[12] See Part Two, Chapter VI, p. 79.
[13] "Ihoka" according to Wissler's spelling.

thongs or ribbons. These may be either small cloud symbols or perhaps bags of medicine. Another shield, in No. 264, is divided exactly in half horizontally. The upper half is blue and through it black zigzag lines run downward. The lower half is yellow and is thickly sprinkled with black dots representing hailstones. In the center of the lower half a bird with outstretched wings is pictured. In No. 202 is a round shield of somewhat different character. In this case the symbolism represents achievement and unmystical experience. This shield also is divided exactly in half horizontally. The upper half is painted yellow, the lower half red. At the zenith of the circle of the shield is a set of two pendent eagle feathers, and at each side—midway between this and the horizontally bisecting diameter—are two other similar sets. At corresponding intervals on the lower half of the shield hang three groups of eagle feathers—four feathers in a group. The shield proclaims, through the red, that the bearer has been wounded by enemies in battle; through the yellow, that he has stolen horses from the enemy.

In No. 78 the insignia are worn in a little different manner. Here a mantle, falling back from the shoulders, bears the wearer's totem. A large bird with outspread wings is the central figure. Again short zigzag lines, forked at the end, extend down from the body below the wings. The ground behind and above the bird is dotted with black, while two black stars (one five-pointed and one four) occupy rather lateral positions in the hail-flecked field. Again the powers of the heavens are represented. A number of mantles of this type appear (see Nos. 142, 152, and 158, for example), always in connection with battle scenes.

The reason for the use of these designs in such relations is at least partially obvious; as the thunderbird rides the storms in safety, as the eagle, the hawk, the raven—related to the spirit bird—in the swiftness of their flight and the strength of their endurance escape the rain of hailstones and rise above the ferocity of the whirlwind, so may the bearer of their symbols go safely through battle and the various adversities of a strenuous life.

Horses. The marking of horses for medicine appears clearly and significantly also. In most cases it follows noticeably a symbolism similar to that of the shields and mantles, already described. In No. 118 the center horse bears long zigzag lines, forked at the lower end and extending down the flanks and shoulders, while shorter ones run down from the eye. The whole flank behind the one line and the shoulder and leg in front of the other line are covered with small circular markings, giving a somewhat dappled effect. These marks represent either cloud forms or hailstones; in either case, they are closely associated with thunder power. The central horse in the next drawing (No. 119) is similarly marked, and the symbolism is the same, although instead of circular marks there are small black dots. In Nos. 150 and 224 there are still other horses with like markings.

Another type of marking is found in Nos. 118, 120, 150, and 224. The outstanding symbolic element in these cases is a circular figure placed on the shoulder or flank or both. In some cases the figure is colored solidly; in others it seems to represent a hoop. In Nos. 118 and 121 the figure is colored a solid orange-yellow, while in Nos. 120, 124, 128, and 150 merely a ring is shown. In Nos. 120 and 124 the ring is purple, and in Nos. 128 and 150 it is black. The black dots, noticed in connection with the thunder symbolism before, appear in No. 120 above the hoop on the flank; in No. 124 they are below the hoops, on the legs and lower body; and in Nos. 128 and 150 they are scattered over the whole body of the horse. The circular design is connected with the medicine hoop; such designs are reputed to bear power that protects the wearer or user from all harm.[14] The fact that in most cases four of these symbols are used—one on each shoulder and one on each flank—is significant, for the number *4* is potent in the religion of all Plains Indians and in that of most others as well, especially as related to the designation of the four cardinal points—a relation which the arrangement of the symbols in these cases would seem to indicate. The horse, and consequently in large measure the rider, would thus be protected at every angle of attack.

Because it was a definitely established type of horse marking of a very significant tribal institution and includes a number of the elements noticed in the markings I have already described, I wish to mention here also the horse marking for the war-medicine ceremony of the Sacred Bow,[15] though Bad Heart Bull—oddly enough—seems not to have included a

---

[14] Wissler, "Protective Designs," pp. 40–42.

[15] See the discussion of ceremonies of war in Chapter III, p. 38.

drawing showing it. The markings of the horses were elaborate, in keeping with those of the men. In the first place, white horses were painted with red, and dark horses with white. Lightning symbols extended down the legs from withers and hips and were forked at the hoofs. A so-called "death line," also representing lightning and therefore deadly swiftness, was painted across the shoulders in front of the rider and across the hips and flanks back of the rider. Two images of birds—the red-breasted swallow—appeared inside the line in front of the rider. Two dragonfly symbols were drawn *inside* the line back of the rider. Dots or round spots, emblems of hail and storm, appeared on shoulders, hips, and flanks *outside* the "death lines." It is noticeable and significant that all symbols here are those of death-dealing agents.

In all these cases a particular phase of the Indian conception and use of medicine is suggested, a phase noted also by Wissler in one of his discussions of Dakota designs: the designs are *protective*; they are symbols of appeal to higher powers for the shielding of the wearer or user; they are not usually so much prayers for ability to overcome the enemy or other evil directly, but they are prayers for ability to elude danger, for imperviousness to bullet or arrow or magic, *in order that* the user may overcome the enemy.[16] The conquest of the foe is a secondary effect, as it were.

HERALDRY

That this medicine power and appeal is the basic element in Indian decoration of the sort just described, there can be no doubt; and Bad Heart Bull is wholly conscious of the true and original significance of such decoration. He is no less conscious, however, of the secondary and, from another point of view, no less significant heraldic meaning.

Among the most outstanding examples of heraldic designations are those of the different organizations, especially the *akicita* and other warrior societies; one can identify in every battle scene officers of various societies by headdresses, lances, or other emblems. The straight lance of the Cante Tinza, for example, is unique and easily noticed.[17] It is made with a spear at the end. Extending the length of the shaft is a strip of

red flannel, about four inches wide, which is decorated with feathers, black alternating with white at short intervals. It is a conspicuous piece of equipment, and it can be seen a number of times in the battles that are portrayed in this record. No. 250, for instance, shows one bearing a Crow to the ground. Again, at the extreme left of No. 70 one is seen. The bonnet of the Wiciska, too, is conspicuous.[18] The prominent features of this headgear are the buffalo horns. These are trimmed down for the sake of lightness and are mounted at left and right on a buckskin cap that fits the head fairly snugly. A beaded band spans the front across the forehead. Eagle down and strips of rabbit fur are bunched at the top of the crown. From the back hangs a four-inch strip of rawhide on which is mounted a length of red flannel bearing a row of eagle tail feathers. The warrior nearest the viewer at the right in No. 204 wears one; so also does the brave killing the woman in No. 252. But perhaps as conspicuous an insigne as any is the bow lance of the Tokala Society. These lances are the length of a man and are made in the form of bows but have bone points and are not flat. Ornamented deer skin covers the shaft except for the grip, which is usually wrapped otherwise. The most outstanding feature, however, is a large bunch of bird feathers hung from the tip of the bow and made more striking by an eagle feather[19] tied to a longer string[20] and so hanging even lower. In No. 165 is a portrayal of the elder Bad Heart Bull killing a Ree scout at the Battle of the Little Big Horn. It is in his capacity as a bearer of the Tokala bow lance that he is acting in this episode and in another in No. 150 (center). In the first picture the Ree is being pierced by the bow lance. Bad Heart Bull's official identification is further determined in these two pictures by the fox-skin sash and by the eagle-plume and crow-feather head decoration. Bad Heart Bull's manner of wearing the fox skin is slightly individualistic. According to some regulations,[21] the kit-fox skin was usually worn about the neck and across the shoulder of the warrior, the head in front and the tail behind (as in the case of the Indian in the upper right corner in No. 150); Bad Heart Bull wears his about the waist and hips. It is to be noticed that the fox skin is trimmed with feathers on the sides and at the head.

---

[16] Wissler, "Protective Designs," p. 53.

[17] See No. 22 and compare with Wissler, "Societies," p. 26.

[18] See No. 23 and compare with Wissler, "Societies," p. 34.

[19] Bad Heart Bull has *two*.

[20] Wissler, "Societies," p. 22.

[21] *Ibid.*, p. 16.

The other mark of identification is the head adornment which is common to all Tokala members;[22] a bunch of crow tail feathers is stuck in the hair a little toward the back of the head and at a slight lateral angle, while two eagle feathers are placed before them straight up.

The truth is that the record as a whole presents—aside from the primary historic, social, religious, ritualistic, political, and martial significance—an extensive field for study of the secondary questions of ceremonial markings and heraldic uses. The great number of scenes and episodes presented and the extreme fullness of detail furnish a wealth of evidential material on these subjects. I shall not attempt to exhaust the subject here. I wish merely to indicate the fact that Bad Heart Bull, true to Dakota feeling and tradition and practice, pictures all of these phases of life and treats them with painstaking honesty.

BAD HEART BULL'S ARTISTIC ACHIEVEMENT

In addition to the fact that Bad Heart Bull is a trustworthy student and reporter of activity and detail and is indulging in a customary Dakota method of depicting historic and other phases of the life of the tribe, one must notice that he possesses certain technical aptitudes, certain qualities of technique, that set him somewhat apart from his fellow Plains artists of similar general type.

The pictographic record of illustrative type is not peculiar to Bad Heart Bull, of course. Many pictographic robes (to some of which I have referred earlier), some tipi covers, and numerous scattered small collections or single specimens in various museums and libraries[23] belong to the same genre. The same general type of drawing is found in all of them. There are certain tendencies toward conventionalization, certain angles of vision, certain types of subject, and certain manners of treatment—attitude of mind, one might almost say—that are more or less common to all. To illustrate my meaning, take the manner of portraying the courting or old marriage custom, the man and woman under one blanket, as it is seen in Nos. 112 and 356 of Bad Heart Bull's record. This is a more or less realistic sort of depiction; yet the general shape of the outline—one head higher than the other—is a conventionalization common to Plains tribes other than the Sioux. The usual angle of vision, as is generally characteristic of primitive art, is the profile. The subjects are predominantly those of action, usually war; otherwise they are ceremonial or ritualistic in character and purpose; and they are all treated with a direct matter-of-factness that would seem to attest a decidedly commonplace attitude toward the events and suggested spirit relationships. The happenings are perfectly normal, natural activities, and the relationships are intimately real and present in the everyday life of this people. Bad Heart Bull uses the Plains type of portrayal as the basis of his depiction.

But he is advanced beyond his fellow artists in this branch of art in the degree of realism to which he attains. Even a cursory comparison of a few pages of his first series on the Battle of the Little Big Horn with those (similar in purpose and general character) of Red Horse and White Bird show this difference markedly. These two portrayals of the Custer affair are among the most highly reputed native illustrations of the battle until now known; yet they lack the definite vigor and movement that characterize Bad Heart Bull's pictures. Here is one mark of his greater genius: he is a greater realist.

But an even greater mark of genius is found in that class of drawings which I have previously designated as miniature. In these he is showing a development that is entirely his own; he is departing from the more common technique of the art genre of his civilization and is producing something quite new in character and effect. In these drawings of men, horses, and cattle, he is handling masses representing sometimes several hundred figures to the page. There are thirty-one distinct drawings of this type. In No. 5, for instance, he pictures a move by the whole band; in Nos. 18, 33, and 100, Indian battles; in Nos. 170 to 185, the whole second series of the Battle of the Little Big Horn. The effectiveness and originality of his methods of handling mass are what cause comment by artists. Here one sees particularly well that stage where picture writing develops "through devotion to the details of the event into the artistic picture, which becomes as much decoration as record."

[22] Ibid.

[23] The Ayer Indian Collection in the Newberry Library, Chicago, has a larger collection of native drawings than any other single library or museum I have seen.

The general nature of these portrayals, as I have elsewhere intimated, is panoramic. They represent the event, the movement, *as a whole*, with all the individuality of character due the whole. Even though the scale is of necessity very small, though the individual figure is very minute, the effect of individuality of the single figure is not sacrificed to the effect of the complete individual characterization of the whole—part and whole fit together to form a decided unity in variety. The vigor and movement of some of these scenes is strikingly seen in drawing No. 171 (missing), showing the Indians just as they are entering the Battle of the Little Big Horn; in the same series, it is seen again in Nos. 173 and 174, which show Reno's men in full flight at the first repulse. Bad Heart Bull has without question studied horses as they run. Even the heads of horses and Indian riders just appearing over the extreme left edge of No. 173 carry the impression of the endless numbers and sweep of attacking Dakotas as they drive back the whites. The page is full of figures; yet there is a balance and rhythm of composition that creates the effect of a truly artistic picture, a rhythm that—though balanced—possesses no burdensome symmetry.

It is in this group of drawings that one finds some of Bad Heart Bull's most striking and effective conventionalizations. Close study of the drawing of the band moving, No. 5, discloses several details that do not appear at first glance. The drawing impresses one at first as a balanced and moving composition. There is a vibrant realism about its suggestion. But notice the first row of horses and riders. A row of two short, straight lines in pairs, representing the ears of horses, is the clearest, most definite element in the depiction; a decidedly impressionistic suggestion of the head and shoulders of horses and riders, with the barest beginning of a suggestion of the foreleg of the horses, is all that is given; the bodies of men and horses are simply left out. Yet the effect is one of a row of ridden horses—*in motion*. Under close scrutiny, the whole composition shows this same sort of technique. Sometimes the portrayal is even more impressionistic than in the section I have chosen and in a few cases it is less so, but the conventionalization is seen throughout.

The same sort of thing may be seen to a degree in the Sioux-Crow fight of No. 18. In only one instance on this page is a horse drawn at all completely, in only *one* case is the animal really given legs and hoofs; and

that is the mounted galloping horse which occupies the center of the page—and incidentally is the center of the action. In the other cases, a half-dozen strokes serve to sketch in the animal; and it takes few, if any, more to place the rider upon the horse's back. But there is no doubt as to what is taking place or what tribes are involved. In No. 36 is another example of a somewhat different sort, one which is in some ways less satisfying; but it shows particularly well one detail of Bad Heart Bull's conventionalization, so I speak of it particularly. A war party is besieged on top of a butte. The numbers of the other band almost completely surround it. The whole portrayal is very impressionistic; in many cases the fighting man is represented only by faint curved lines for head and shoulders and a straight line for a gun; in numerous instances a row of short lines accompanied by light curves of the same sort represent a line of fighting men. But again, the situation is located in time and given a character. Another bit of original conventionalization of the horse is found in the roundup scene in No. 365. This is particularly unusual since it is a rear view. The figure to the left of the top bunch of cattle and the center horse and rider below the middle bunch of cattle are the best examples of this bit of portrayal. A single oddly curved line (rather horseshoe-like in outline) for the body and a heavy line for the tail are all that is needed to make a real horse. The rider, hat and all, is made with perhaps three or four lines. And the whole is entirely convincing. In this same composition, and even more in the drawing in No. 412, is Bad Heart Bull's unique, conventionalized representation of cattle as seen from the rear. The single animal is made in nearly every case with but four lines: two small curved lines for horns, a longer one for the outline of the body (and usually the beginning of the right hind leg), and a straight line for the tail. The grouping of many of these figures truly gives the effect of a herd of cattle, and, especially in No. 412, of a herd *in motion*. In all of these instances the portrayals have a certain dynamic quality; they show—impressionistic and primitive though they be—a living character and motion. In all cases the artist has given the events that "location in time and space, given [that] location and . . . character" which marks the beginning of history; and at the same time he has developed, through devotion to details, "the artistic picture, which becomes as much decoration as record."

In subtle contrast to the predominantly reverent

sense of symbolism and strongly ritualistic spirit of all Pueblo art, for instance, but in common with that of other warrior tribes of the Plains, Dakota art takes on the character of the chant of glory, bravery, triumph, or of death—the historic consciousness is shadowed forth. The shield, the garment, the paraphernalia of ceremony and of war, the buffalo robe, the tipi cover proclaim through pictures the feats and status of the owner. Action, episode, exploit are the artist's concern. So exploit is Bad Heart Bull's chief interest. The warrior rides through all the narrative. This does not mean, as I am sure is clear by now, that all sense of symbolism and mysticism so innate in Indian consciousness is lacking; it simply means that in Dakota pictorial art it is subordinated to the moving, actively dramatic sweep of episode. The brave or chief is conscious of the presence, near or far, of beings strongly akin to him in life spirit; he realizes his relationship to them and his dependence upon them. All the preparation for war, or any undertaking, through which he goes, all the instruments which he uses, the markings and adornment of his garments and of his own body and even those of his horse, in some manner are emblems of that relationship and dependence. There is a sense of the symbolic running through the whole act. But in consequence of a distinct psychological bent of mind, a dominant individualistic spirit in his philosophy of life, the Dakota feels in himself a certain power which can make *him* the significant center of the spectacle of life, in a certain sense and to a certain degree, a free agent who can move dramatically and grandly across the stage in his own right and power. So in Bad Heart Bull's narrative, *individuals* are taking part in the drama, individuals who at times can be definitely identified in the action. So, too, one feels a dynamic force and vigor that make the scenes of battle truly vivid. Even in those panoramic views done in minute conventionalized style the imagination is irresistibly caught, and one moves with the tide of events. Bad Heart Bull shows a real appreciation of mass, balance, impressionism, conventionalization, light and shade that might not be expected of a primitive artist. There is a decorative quality about some of his compositions that is unmistakable; but, taking his work as a whole, I should say that it is not *the* predominant quality. The drama, the vital movement of events is the keynote of his portrayal—life *active* is his theme. In the final analysis, he not only is writing an epic of his people; he is bodying forth their spirit, their very philosophy. He is portraying the Dakota—body, mind, and soul.

Part Two

CHAPTER VI

Introduction to the Drawings

THE Amos Bad Heart Bull record is an example of North American Indian narrative delineation, portraying in pictures the history of one period in the tribal life of the Oglala Sioux and bearing in addition numerous literal annotations, chiefly in the Oglala dialect but occasionally in English.

The manuscript (owned now by the artist's sister Dollie, Mrs. William Pretty Cloud) is an old ledger of standard type, bound in gray canvas with top, bottom, and back edged in the usual red and black imitation leather, which is gilt-trimmed. It was bought by the artist from the proprietor of a clothing store in Crawford, Nebraska, when he and his uncle, Short Bull, were located at Fort Robinson as scouts in the United States Army during the year 1890–1891.[1] The younger Indian possessed a naturally artistic tendency and a strong interest in the history of his people; so it happened that in the course of that year, aided by his uncle's interest and knowledge, he began the detailed story of the life of his band.

The ledger measures 8 by 12½ inches and has an original capacity of 300 pages of 7 by 12 dimension.[2] That capacity, however, has been considerably modified and augmented by the removal of some of the original sheets and the addition of many insert pages,

which have been carefully placed, evidently for the sake of historical sequence primarily. An exact check shows that the book contains 242 of the original ledger pages. These begin with page 61 (drawing No. 76), which, however, is out of place, the sheet being between pages 72 (No. 71) and 73 (No. 78). All are in order thereafter up to 298 (No. 411), which ends the series, except sheet 185–186 (Nos. 224 and 225), which is between 180 (No. 220) and 182 (No. 228), and 205–206, which is missing entirely. Sheets 181–182 (Nos. 229 and 228) and 237–238 are upside down, and 237 is pasted upon 239, so that the space of two pages is lost. The space available for drawings on the original ledger paper, then, is 240 pages; this means that of the 417 plates, the drawings for 177 are made on inserts.[3]

In addition to these 240 pages, there are 246 insert pages, which vary in size from one 7 by 17⅛ inches to a few 4¾ by 6, the latter bearing script only. The character and quality of the paper used for inserts also varies widely. In addition to the original ones, there are 10 other numbered ledger pages of a much cheaper paper. Pages 24 (No. 9) and 299 (No. 56) evidently come from one ledger; 101 (No. 45) and 7 (No. 316) are from a third; and 129 (No. 114) is from still a

---

[1] In No. 324 of the manuscript the artist has portrayed a mounted figure in uniform, beside which—aside from a notation in Lakota—appears the legend "Fort Robinson: Neb. U.S. Scout. 1890. Amos Eagle Lance. B. H. Bull."

[2] The paper is ruled horizontally in blue and has a triple red-blue-red ruling at the head of the page. Perpendicular rulings are all in red except a double blue ruling down the middle of the page. In addition to this marking, however, from page 201 of the original ledger paging (drawing No. 314) the page is cut horizontally a little below the middle by a blank division space an inch wide; the ruling of the upper section is finished with a double red, the lower section with a single blue, and about a quarter-inch lower a triple red-blue-red ruling.

[3] [The drawings have been renumbered consecutively. Miss Blish's numbers are listed in Appendix A. The figures given here and elsewhere regarding the number of drawings, original ledger pages, and inserts are based on Miss Blish's original pagination and numbering system (explained in Appendix A, p. 513). The discrepancy between Miss Blish's total number of drawings—417 (418, including the inside of the back cover)—and the number of drawings listed in this book—415—might be accounted for by the fact that in some instances Miss Blish may have counted as two separate drawings the halves of a two-page drawing, whereas they have been counted as a single drawing herein. See also the Note on the Editing, p. 529.—*Ed. note.*]

fourth. Besides these, there are 42 unnumbered ledger or balance-sheet pages ruled vertically in red; these are of cheap pencil paper. Another inserted series of 12 pages has evidently been removed in section from some bound ledger or journal; the pages are unnumbered, but are notched for marginal indexing; and the paper, ruled in blue horizontally only, is of very good, heavy grade. Another type of paper used for 12 of the pages was taken evidently from an old hotel ledger, for in No. 54 the printed headings of the ruled columns show plainly: "Name," "Residence," "Time," "Room," "Horses," "Remarks"; this paper is the heaviest in the book and serves very well for the artist's purpose.

In addition to ledger pages, there are several kinds of ruled paper of both good and cheap qualities. In the first place, 33 pages from an ordinary ink composition book, with rounded corners, have been used; in some cases these pages, which measure $6\frac{1}{4}$ by $7\frac{1}{4}$ inches, have been put in as single small-size pages in the ordinary position—running horizontally (Nos. 104–111, for instance). In other cases—binding staples removed—the double page has been inserted as a full-size page of the book, with rulings running vertically (No. 249, for example). A second composition-book paper, ink also but of larger size ($7\frac{1}{4}$ by 10), has been used; of this type of paper, which has a rougher finish, there are some 66 pages, used sometimes as small inserts and sometimes patched at top or bottom to make them full size (see Nos. 160 and 161). There are also in this better class of ink paper 16 pages of large-size (7 by 12) plain, blue-ruled paper, evidently sheet paper of the ordinary official size. Then there are two other cheaper pencil papers, besides a few single sheets. I find 20 pages of lined paper taken from a very cheap composition book of the same size as the first one mentioned and used in the same manner—sometimes as single pages in the ordinary position, sometimes as full-size pages (7 by 12), the double page unstapled and placed with rulings running vertically; in the case of these double pages from this book, however, very frequently the middle is reinforced by a narrow strip of paper pasted across the staple holes (see No. 246). Sixteen more pages are plain white, unruled, and measure $7\frac{1}{2}$ by 10. I am sure that I recognize in them paper which comes in large pads and which very recently was widely used in government offices and shops as scratch or note paper; I should judge, consequently, that these inserts are comparatively very recent and that the paper was secured by Bad Heart Bull from some employee at the agency or district office. The other three pages consist of one unruled, rough-finish page of pencil paper, the flyleaf of the book, and the marbled page next the inside cover—the marbled surface being covered by a white sheet pasted upon it.

In many cases, too, the original paging and the added insert paging have been changed, revisions and corrections made, by pasting other paper over whole pages or parts of pages so that all or parts of certain drawings are covered; then usually entirely new drawings or simply partial-correction drawings (as the need may be) are made upon the new paper. Of the 240 available pages of the original ledger paper, 15 are entirely covered (and in all cases one can see that there are drawings underneath), either by single sheets or by smaller patches; and in all but two of these cases new drawings have been made upon the second surface. There are comparatively few pages which do not bear at least one small patch of some shape or other, and often there are several. No. 247 is a good specimen of this patched effect: all but a small L-shaped bit, measuring around $2\frac{3}{4}$ by $1\frac{5}{8}$ by $\frac{1}{2}$ inches, of the original page is covered; there are seven patches of different sizes, shapes, and kinds of paper, some overlapping others. No. 21 bears four patches, three of which are rather large; the original drawing covered was a buffalo hunt in large scale, the large sheet covering that bears some kind of an encounter in minute scale, and this, in turn, is covered by the other three patches, which show an encounter of three Sioux and a Crow. In these cases the whole of the original page has been covered.

For the other, partial-correction sort of patching, Nos. 259 and 264 serve as fair examples. There are six small patches on No. 259, the smaller center one cut in a very odd shape in order not to cover too much of the drawing that is to be corrected. No. 264 bears four patches, the most interesting of which is the one covering a part of the yellow horse and his Sioux rider (upper left corner of the drawing); evidently the headdress was not correct, for this patch bears only the long eagle-feather warbonnet. The artist has taken occasion in a number of portrayals of later Sioux-Crow battles to make use of this patching device to change the weapons used by some of the combatants. In composition No. 228, for example, the center Sioux at the top of the page has had his lance replaced by a revolver, as one can see by holding the page to the light; and in drawing No.

274, one Sioux in the upper left corner has had his coup stick replaced by a revolver, while one of his comrades—just below—has been given an army saber instead of the bow with which he was originally striking his foe. Every kind of paper that I have catalogued as used for insert pages, besides two pages of printed blank forms pasted printed side down (Nos. 20 and 21), has been used, sometimes several kinds on one page.

As I have indicated before, all but sixty pages of the book are covered with drawings or, in some nine cases, full script notations. Incidentally, I may say that the occurrence of these blank pages, especially in those frequent instances where they are carefully *inserted* pages, taken in connection with the fact that there are a few drawings which are evidently incomplete (Nos. 177, 236, and 408, for example), would seem to indicate that the artist's plan had not been fully realized, that he had intended a number of additions in various parts of the book. All other pages of the manuscript are covered with drawings, either in color or in black and white. Some bear notations, sometimes rather full, in Oglala Dakota,[4] and a few have titles in English, especially in connection with the Custer affair (Nos. 126–185) and the later peacetime celebrations of Independence Day (Nos. 326–411). In fact, there are numerous exact dates given (twenty-nine in all) which may have been added after the record was completed, in the manner of a late editing; the earliest date given (which does not appear till No. 32) is 1856 and the latest is 1910, but there are indications that the record covers events occurring earlier and perhaps later than these dates. In all, there are 417 plates, of which 9 are script only, so that the total number of actual *drawings* is 408. Usually, one theme occupies a page; but in some cases two pages are used for a single composition, especially where the subject is more or less panoramic or topographical in character—as for instance in the case of the second Little Big Horn series.[5]

Of the entire number, 355 are in four colors or more, 32 are in three colors, 9 are in two colors, and 21 are in black and white. Brush, crayon, pen, and pencil have been used in the work,[6] varying styles and materials representing—no doubt—changing periods of workmanship. In the coloring, crayons, colored ink, indelible pencils, and perhaps in a few of the later drawings water colors have been used. Eight colors—black, red, green, brown, purple, blue, yellow, and gray[7]—are clearly distinguishable, sometimes with differences in tone, however. The first four predominate in the order in which they are named. Black appears in every drawing, for practically all outlines are in black. The source of this color is usually ink, which in most cases is put on with a pen but is sometimes applied with a brush; in some cases, however, crayon has been used. The red is often ink, sketched in with pen; otherwise it is drawn in with crayon. Crayon furnishes the blue, yellow, and green coloring entirely. Most of the brown, too, is crayon color; but in a few cases a rather heavy brown paint, perhaps a mixture of water with some dark clay or perhaps a heavy mixture of water color, has been applied with a brush.[8] The gray usually is a wash put on with a brush,[9] but sometimes is the work of a lead pencil; this color is found most noticeably in the small, stylized brush drawings, of which I shall speak more particularly later. For the last color, purple, the indelible pencil is the main source, but in a few cases crayon has been used. The black and red ink, Bad Heart Bull could easily have secured from an army or agency official or from stores at Crawford. The crayons probably came later; in fact, I am of the opinion that the crayon color in all cases, except perhaps the very latest drawings, has been added some time after the original drawings were done. Some of the brush drawings are *very* fine; in fact, many of them really demand magnification, for they have evidently been done with a single bristle or with an exceedingly fine brush. The brush drawings form one (the second in the following classification) of the four general types of drawing which are to be distinguished according to technical character.

Of the four visual perspectives employed in the

---

[4] No. 4 in the Sun Dance series, No. 53 in the Sioux-Crow wars series, and No. 112 in the courtship series, for example.

[5] See Nos. 170, 171 (missing) and 172, 173 and 174, and 198.

[6] Most of the script is done in black, but some is in red.

[7] I have been very loose in my consideration of gray in these tabulations because the gray is usually so distinctly a

mere diluting of the black that in most cases I have classed it as black, especially in the "black and white" drawings.

[8] In Nos. 6, 8, 59, 76, 84, and 96, for instance, for tails and markings of horses.

[9] In some cases this is undoubtedly a dilution of black ink, but in others it would seem to come from some other material, since it has a bluish cast.

record, the first to be considered is the topographical —i.e., beyond actual vision—with the most minute indications of men if there are any at all. Eleven of the plates are of this type. Of these, three are concerned with the Battle of the Little Big Horn;[10] three (Nos. 103, 218, and 284) are related to Crow episodes in Montana and Wyoming; one (No. 36) shows Crows besieged on top of a butte; one (No. 297) depicts a surprise attack on an Indian encampment by United States troops; another (No. 41) portrays a Dakota camp location in Montana; still another (No. 198) gives the topography of the Black Hills region in sequence following the treaty council (No. 196) concerning their disposal; and one (No. 197) shows the layout of Fort Robinson, Nebraska. One other instance, which I have not included in this count, is found as a secondary part of the picture showing the death of Crazy Horse (No. 304) included in the fourth general class; this is a drawing where the artist oddly combines in one composition two widely divergent angles of vision. All of the colors are to be found in this type of drawing, but it is quite noticeable that *many* colors are found infrequently in one drawing; in fact, nine out of the eleven drawings contain but four colors or fewer. Black predominates, of course (one in plain black and white), and in all cases ink is applied with a pen. Red is next in order, and again ink is the coloring material; it is used for crosses of location, indications of battle lines, some outlines, and —in the cases of fighting—the victims. Green is put in with crayon and marks trees and tree lines. Brown is always crayon color in this class of drawings and is used for ground, tree trunks, and—in a few cases— horses. Blue, in crayon, indicates rivers and creeks. Yellow, also in crayon, is used in the manner of high lights along the line of rivers and creeks and around the Black Hills. The gray in these drawings is usually penciled, but it is frequently also a dark wash applied with a brush, in minute figures of men and horses particularly.

The second general type I have already mentioned in passing. These are unique drawings (rather panoramic in character) of battle, hunting, and other scenes, containing a hundred or more individual figures drawn in minute scale and distinctly stylized. Thirty of the thirty-four drawings in this class have fighting as their theme: the second Little Big Horn series (twelve drawings, Nos. 171 to 182) is done in this style; eleven drawings show battles between Sioux and Crows;[11] two (Nos. 316 and 317) represent the Wounded Knee trouble of 1890; and one (No. 413) depicts the attack on the deer hunters in 1903. One early in the record (No. 5) shows a more or less panoramic view of a Sioux move. Another (No. 19) represents a buffalo hunt. And two late in the book (Nos. 360 and 365) depict roundup scenes. In all these cases the themes are those of great activity. In this class, as well as in the first, it is noticeable that highly complex color combinations are not prominent, though most of the colors are found in some places in the group. Over half the drawings have fewer than five colors; only one has seven.

Into the third class, nearer views, the greatest number of drawings fall. These present complicated battle scenes, processionals, and other scenes, drawn in detail and containing twenty or thirty figures. There are two hundred plates in this division, and they represent themes of many descriptions:[12] a council (No. 1); moves (Nos. 6, 7); dances (Nos. 10, 12, 115); camp circles and dance areas (Nos. 9, 327); hunts (Nos. 16, 17); horse-stealing expeditions (Nos. 60, 62); fighting;[13] processionals of warriors (Nos. 116, 124); and one Indian farm (No. 362) after the beginning of the new regime. This group is a colorful one; all of the eight colors, and various tones of some of them, are found in abundance. In fact, 57 per cent contain seven or eight, and none show fewer than three colors. I have already said that practically all outlines of drawings are done in black. Here I need remark further in regard to color only that, following a widely spread practice, a red splotch is used to indicate the victims of battle or violent murder.

The fourth class is made up of close-ups, drawings of few figures—men, animals, ritual objects, etc. It is sometimes rather difficult to decide which is the better class for some drawings, the third or

---

[10] No. 129 introduces the first Little Big Horn series; No. 170 is an enlargement of No. 129 and introduces the second series; No. 177 is an unfinished drawing of similar character, evidently discarded.

[11] For instance, Nos. 237, 240, 245, 277, and 301, which is semitopographical also.

[12] References in the discussion of the third and fourth classes are to a few examples from numerous possible ones, unless the text indicates otherwise.

[13] Battles and skirmishes: fifty-four showing action between Sioux and Crows (Nos. 67, 68); fifty concerning action between troops and Indians on the Little Big Horn (No. 132); and two concerning the Wounded Knee trouble.

the fourth; but I have made my choice, where the decision was at all questionable, by considering the center of interest and the emphasis in the portrayal of the theme rather than the number of figures or the outlines.[14] There are 163 plates in this group, and the range of subject matter is even greater than the third class: a council (No. 196); paraphernalia of societies and ceremonial associations (Nos. 22–31); dances and other ceremonies (Nos. 10, 13, 14); spirit or dream animals (Nos. 113, 114); costumes and furnishings (Nos. 207, 215, 312); episodes and phases of everyday life;[15] a cabin and equipment of the later period (No. 359); roundup and branding (Nos. 366, 367); fighting;[16] the death of Crazy Horse (No. 304); the artist himself or his father (Nos. 326, 332, 373, 374, 412); and so forth. Individual drawings do not partake of the complexity of action and composition that is evident in many of those of the third class. There are not so many pictures containing many colors; even so, 85 per cent show four or more colors, but only 17 drawings show seven or eight. The emphasis in these compositions is on the individual person or thing. The artist's attention and energy are concentrated on specific phases of action or aspects of persons or things; extreme accuracy of detail is his great concern.

It is in connection with this class that there occur certain unique elements which, for want of a better designation, I have termed "footnotes." These are sketches in miniature scale depicting the *result* of the action portrayed in the large compositions to which they are attached, and they are "boxed off" from the main drawing by single lines drawn with a pen. Eleven drawings bear such "footnotes."[17] In most cases, the encounters depicted are single combats between Sioux and Crows or are fights between three or four enemies. Usually the "footnote" is attached by a dotted line to the victim as he appears in the large representation of the encounter, and in all but one case it indicates the death of one of the combatants. The one exception to this general rule is No. 81; this sketch shows a Crow escaping on foot while his horse is being captured by a Sioux. In one case (No. 252), the "footnote" indicates that the woman in the episode is killed. The explanation of

No. 320 is that the murder of the four white men was the purpose and result of the visit of the four Indians to the cabin which they are just leaving. Each of the other eight instances is concerned with the death of one of the combatants in battle. In all cases, death is indicated by a red blot on or connected with the body of the victim.

This classification concerns the type of the drawings considered from the technical point of view. The book is to be divided also according to episode, so to speak. For the most part, these divisions of the record are clear-cut and follow one another in correct historical sequence. This is not, however, as is evident from the foregoing discussion, a record of historic episodes alone; in its entirety, it represents a cross section of Dakota life, the whole field of Plains Indian activity—social, political, religious, artistic, and warlike. So the contents of the manuscript fall by sequence into six main categories.

EVENTS PERHAPS EARLIER THAN 1856
Sioux Council
Moving or Traveling Series
Sun Dance Series
Warrior Societies
Buffalo Hunt Series

Of the 31 drawings shown here, 27 are in color, 4 in black and white; and of the 27, 12 have five colors besides black and gray.

This introductory section of the record, in addition to the narrative as such, builds up certain phases of the civic, social, and religious life of the Sioux as it was before the government controlled Indian affairs. There is, without any doubt, a very close relation between the five divisions under this category, not only in point of time but no less in point of general significance; these divisions are simply different steps in the organizational and administrative process.

SIOUX-CROW FIGHTS
(Earliest Dates, 1856, 1858)
By far the greatest number of drawings in the book fall into this class. All four visual perspectives are found among them, but the third class (nearer views)

---

[14] The long series of processionals connected with the Fourth of July celebrations of 1898 and 1903 (Nos. 329–354 and 376–406) might well be placed in the fourth class instead of the third.

[15] Tanning (No. 212); haying (No. 364); herding (Nos. 357, 358, 363); games (Nos. 208–209, 211, 213); courting

(Nos. 86, 87, 112); a conveyance ready for travel (No. 305).

[16] Sioux-Crow wars (Nos. 37, 50); Battle of the Little Big Horn (Nos. 179, 180); Wounded Knee (No. 321).

[17] Nos. 53 (belonging to the drawing in No. 54), 55, 79, 80, 81, 252, 254, 262, 263, 278, and 320.

predominates. Of the 151 compositions, the majority represent events following the Battle of the Little Big Horn. The drawings portray battles, skirmishes, and single combats between the Sioux and the Crows, hereditary enemies, and furnish much detail of costumes and manner of fighting. Color appears in abundance in the costumes and in decorations of horses; only 7 of the 151 drawings are done in black and white. In fact, 123 contain more than two colors, exclusive of black and gray, and 56 contain five or six. In this division, in natural connection with Sioux-Crow relations, there is included a series of drawings representing episodes in a Sioux horse-stealing expedition, episodes that portray the complete sequence of a horse-stealing expedition from the ceremonial preparation and departure (Nos. 88, 89, 90) through the preparation of camp (No. 92), the discovery of the exact location of the enemy camp and horses by the two official scouts (No. 92), and the return of the two scouts with their report (No. 94), to the actual stealing of the horses (Nos. 95, 96) and the escape with the stolen animals (No. 97).

Several notable Sioux warriors are identified in these series by the artist's notations and by personal designations in costume or other equipment.[18]

THE CUSTER AFFAIR ON THE
LITTLE BIG HORN

All four visual perspectives are represented in this group also, and colors show in abundance (82 per cent contain more than four colors). There are three series depicting the engagement: a large-scale series (a scale found in perspective classes three and four); a miniature version (noted in the second class of visual perspectives); and a series of mixed scales and perspectives. The first series consists of 46 drawings (Nos. 126–169). The second series contains 7 compositions (Nos. 170–176), 3 of which occupy two pages each. The third series contains 4 miniatures, 4 close-ups, and 1, a sort of intermediate scale, to which I shall refer below. Each of the versions has its accompany-

ing topographical drawing showing the relative positions of the Indian encampment and the troops before the battle. The third of these (No. 177) is an unfinished drawing, evidently discarded. Incongruous as it may seem, the topographical drawing (No. 170) introducing the miniature series is an enlargement of the one (No. 129) introducing the first or close-up series. Of the three series, the first two portray the part of the battle in which Reno's command was engaged; the third, a much less coherent and effective series, concerns Custer's own force. The intermediate-scale drawing (No. 183) which I have included in the series referred to above, showing the killing of Custer by Crazy Horse, is the only one of this type left open; but in several cases, if one holds the page to the light or lifts the loose edge of the paper that has been pasted over the original sheet, he can plainly see other episodes done in this intermediate scale. The artist evidently had originally intended a complete series in this scale as well as the close-up and later miniature—a series which is now replaced by the one done in miniature. This bears witness to the fact that the minute, stylized version of the battle (Nos. 170–176) is the latest one.

The episode of chief interest in the events subsequent to the Little Big Horn affair is the death of Crazy Horse (No. 304), to which I have referred elsewhere.

EARLY SOCIAL LIFE AND ITS REORGANIZATION
—TRANSITION TO AGRICULTURE AND MORE
SETTLED LIFE

This group is concerned almost entirely with the social and economic aspects of Sioux life not included in the first category. There are several scattered drawings of rituals and symbols other than those in the first Sun Dance series.[19] Some—not consecutively placed—have to do with activities of livelihood: tanning (No. 212), agriculture,[20] and stock raising;[21] numerous others represent more strictly social aspects of life;[22] and 5 describe the murder of four cow-

---

[18] Among them: Bad Heart Bull the elder, No. 238; Black Wolf, No. 35; Charging Horse, No. 294; Crazy Horse, No. 295; Iron Bull, No. 294; Little Shield, No. 294; Lone Man, Nos. 286, 296; Jack Red Cloud, Nos. 105–111; Sitting Crow, No. 286.

[19] The vigil and the skull ceremony, Nos. 188, 189; miscellaneous dances, Nos. 85, 98, 99, 186, 187, 190, 191; Omaha Dance, No. 411; spirit and dream animals, Nos. 113, 115.

[20] Cabins and farm equipment, Nos. 359, 362; haying, No. 364.

[21] Herding, Nos. 357, 358, 363; roundup, Nos. 360, 365, 367, 412; branding, No. 366; random cowboys, Nos. 368, 369.

[22] Costumes, Nos. 207, 214; games, Nos. 208, 209, 211, 213; courtship, Nos. 86, 87, 112, 210, 342, 355, 356, 361.

boys by Two Sticks and his young colleagues (Nos. 319–323). I have included here late engagements between Dakota and government military forces, since these fights are intimately concerned with the change to the new life (No. 297). This section contains relatively fewer compositions of many colors: only 26 per cent contain six or seven colors; the majority contain three or four.

THE GHOST DANCE AND THE BATTLE OF WOUNDED KNEE, 1890

The group of 6 drawings showing the Ghost Dance and the Battle of Wounded Knee is small. It includes the arrest of Sitting Bull (No. 313); a drawing of an actual dance scene (No. 314); examples of costumes, with their distinctive, symbolic decorations (No. 312); and scenes of the subsequent fighting (Nos. 316, 317). In color the series is comparatively drab.

"GREATER INDIAN SHOWS"
(July 4, 1898 and 1903)

The third and fourth visual perspectives are used here almost entirely. This long series of 72 drawings portrays one special phase of Sioux life that belongs to the newer era and still exists: the celebration of the Fourth of July. There are many pages of warriors in their colorful regalia, ready for the "warrior dancing," as Bad Heart Bull expresses it. These drawings are like representations of processionals, with men on foot or mounted following each other across the page, singly or in pairs, and moving to the right on one page, to the left on the next, etc.[23] The detail of costumes and markings on the faces of the men,[24] and in many cases markings of horses,[25] is treated painstakingly. Each series has its dance area (No. 327, 1898; No. 375, 1903) and dance ceremonies of different sorts (Nos. 328 and 338, 1898; Nos. 407, 408, 409, and 410, 1903). In addition, in the first group (1898) there is a series representing the traditional Indian custom of bestowal of gifts, a custom commonly called the "give-away."[26]

These general divisions are represented by numbers and sizes of drawings as follows:

Moves	3	(one 12 × 14; two 7 × 12)
Councils	3	(two 7 × 12; one 12 × 14)
Warrior societies	10	(mostly 7 × 12)
Sun Dance	8	(two 4⅝ × 7⅞; six 7 × 12)
Livelihood:		
Hunting		
Tanning		
Agriculture		
Stock raising	20	(mostly 7 × 12)
Social Life:		
Games		
Costumes		
Courtship		
Late encounters		
with government troops,		
etc.	73	(mostly 7 × 12)
Ghost Dance and Wounded Knee	6	(five 7 × 12; one 12 × 14)
Indian fights	151	(eight larger than 7 × 12)
Little Big Horn and sequences	62	(eight larger than 7 × 12)
"Greater Indian Shows"	72	(7 × 12)

As the initial and last dates (1856 and 1910) entered in the book show, this record covers a very active and significant period in the history of the Plains Indians. The long series of drawings depicting the constant struggles between the Sioux and Crows make up an extensive chapter, filled with detail, which throws light not only on the actual history of these fights by episode but also upon costume and manner of fighting. The wars form a background or running accompaniment to most of the action of the narrative; they interrupt at intervals all other forms of action or episode. The dramatic climax of the whole record, however, seems to be reached in the Battle of the Little Big Horn, with its several portrayals. Thence the action gradually drops to a secondary climax in the Messiah Craze and Ghost Dance religion, with its culmination on the Wounded Knee in 1890. The story ends with the setting forth of more settled and comparatively less eventful reservation life.

---

[23] For 1898, see Nos. 329–354; for 1903, Nos. 376–406.
[24] For example, Nos. 343, 404, 405, 406.

[25] For example, Nos. 326, 382, 395, 398, 402, 405, 406.
[26] See Nos. 329, 330, 331, 333, etc.

CHAPTER VII

The Drawings

An asterisk (*) at the end of a picture description indicates that a full-color reproduction of the drawing may be found in the section of color illustrations following p. 10.

No. 1

No. 1. Events Perhaps Earlier than 1856

Three notes in Lakota designating the three groups of men. Translation: 1 and 3. "Lakota marshals" (left and right). 2. "Councilmen" (center).

A close-up of a council of the head executives of the village.

The four *wakicunza*,[1] or councilmen, meet to explain the plans concerning the movements of the band and to set forth the regulations regarding the band's government. Four mounted and four unmounted head *akicita*, or marshals, wait upon the *wakicunza* to receive their directions and execute their orders; these men, the *akicita*, are in reality the principal executive officers of the camp. Each of the four

councilors has a ceremonial pipe and a beaded or porcupine-quilled pipe bag; these are symbols of his office. The pipe is used in the appeal to the Great Spirit, in the invocation to the sun, and in the general ceremonial performance of duty.

The council lodge of the *wakicunza*, larger than the rest, is shown in red in the center background, somewhat in front of that section of the tribal camp circle which is visible. Four dotted lines from the opening of the lodge to the four seated figures indicate that the *wakicunza* have proceeded directly from council in the lodge to the open center of the camp to confer with and direct the *akicita*.

[1] Cf., e.g., Clark Wissler, "Societies and Ceremonial Associations in the Oglala Division of the Teton Dakota," *APAMNH*, XI, Part 1 (1912), 7–13, and J. R. Walker, "The

Sun Dance and Other Ceremonies of the Oglala Division of the Teton Dakota," *APAMNH*, XVI, Part 2 (1917), 75–77.

Oyate Kin hekta onHan
ins Woope iciLa gapi Kin.

1   Wicaża tona WicuKRCon pi Kin
    Witu ya iyota Kapi Wicun K Canpi.

2   Oyate eKna Wica Sa eya WaRwanja
    ...pi La O Wica le pi na henca
    WaKi Cun Za pi Kta i Wan Wi Coyan Kapi
    na te Ka pi Kta natom Wica Ko gapi ____

3   Wicaża Wan ta Wi Cun Ki Ci towa Cin
    tan Kapi La O Wica le pi na he ti Kin Kakni gopi
    na he ti pi iyoKi he eyoCa ston pin na WaKi Cun Zo gun
    he na heL ti ma Sna WicunK Cun yan Kapi Kto eyopi
    an he na O Wi Co Ran gun lei O Wapi ____

No. 2

No. 2.   Events Perhaps Earlier than 1856

A note in Lakota relating to No. 1. Translation:

Rules Established by the People to Govern Them in the Past.

1. A number of intelligent men get together and plan or discuss the issue.

2. They select from among the people men of quiet and honest dispositions—four in number—and these are chosen as councilmen or leaders.

3. The tipi of a man and his wife who are very patient and freehearted is chosen and named as the council tipi, and it is decided that the councilmen or leaders will sit and plan in this tipi.

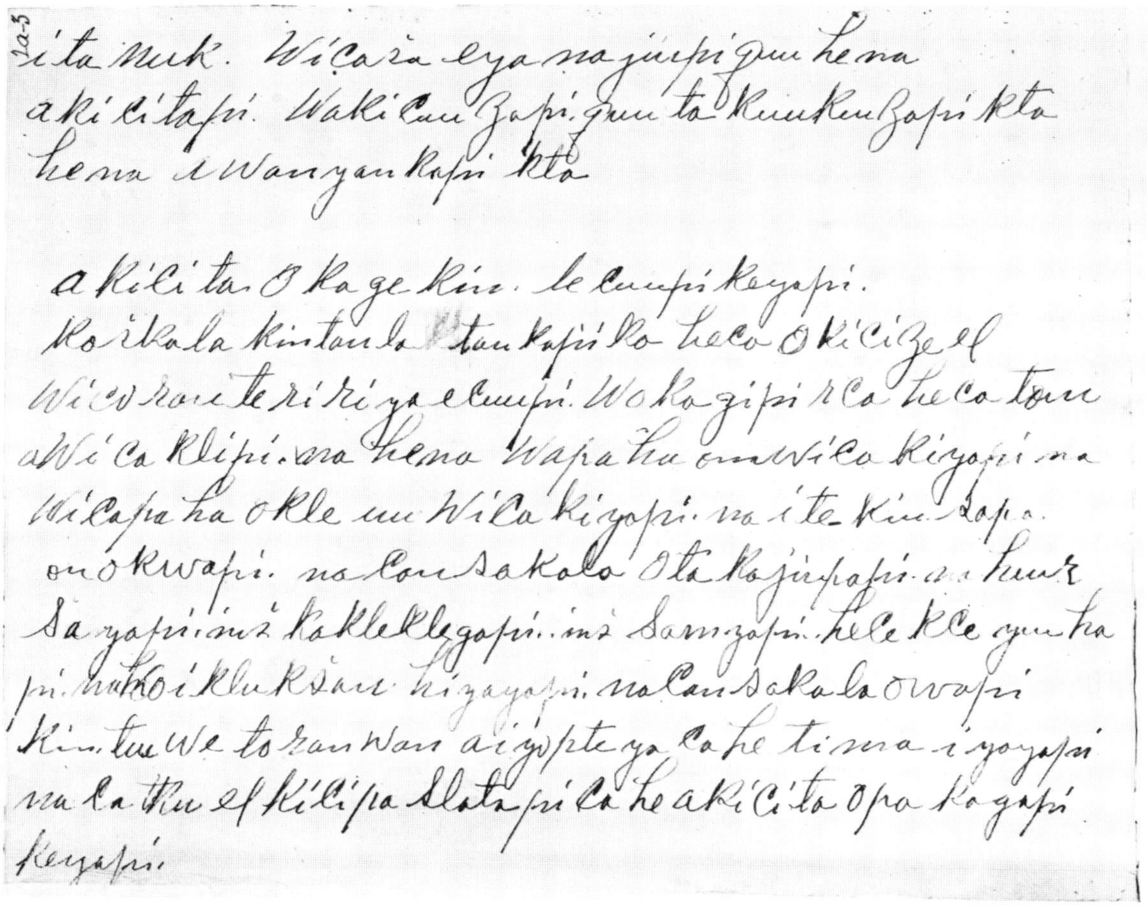

_íta muk. Wičaša eya nažiŋpi kʼuŋ hena
akičitapi. Wakičaŋzapi kʼuŋ to Kuŋkuŋzapi kta
hena i Waŋyaŋ kapi kta

akičita Okage kiŋ le čuŋpi keyapi.
Koškala kiŋtaŋla taŋkapi ko heča Okičize el
wičoraŋ teʼkiya čuŋpi. Wakagipi kta heča taŋ
awičakšipi na hena Wapaha owičakiŋyapi na
wičaša ha okle uŋ Wičakiŋyapi na ite kiŋ sapa
oŋ okwapi na Caŋsakala ota kažuŋšapi na huŋ
šayapi iŋš kakle klegapi iŋš sapŋapi kele kte kʼuŋ ka
pi hakoʼi kluk šaŋ kiyayapi na Caŋsakala owapi
kiŋ tuŋwe to žaŋ waŋ aʼiŋpte ya ča he tima iyoyapi
na ka tuŋ el Kilipa slatapi ča he akičita opa kagapi
keyapi.

No. 3

NO. 3. EVENTS PERHAPS EARLIER THAN 1856

A note in Lakota also relating to No. 1. Translation:

On each side stand two groups of men. These men are officers [similar to a constable or sergeant at arms]. They are to guard against any fights or other disturbances in camp or on the march.

The following is the manner in which these officers are chosen and installed:

Four middle-aged persons who have done great deeds in battle and who are persons to be avoided [!] are brought together, and warbonnets are placed on their heads. They are also made to wear buckskin shirts decorated with human scalps.[2] [These four must not be confused with the *wakicunza*.] Their faces are painted black. [Wissler does not mention this.] Then a great many sticks are cut to a certain length and peeled. These are colored as follows: some are painted red, some are striped black and white, others are painted black. Each design represents some deed.[3] The men are given these sticks; and, holding them, they walk in a circle around the tipi. The persons that carry sticks, designed to represent actions or deeds they have done, are permitted to enter the tipi or lodge, and the sticks are stuck in the ground in the back part of the interior of the lodge. The men are then proclaimed sergeants at arms, or constables.

[2] Wissler, "Societies," pp. 7 and 39.

[3] *Ibid.*, p. 8.

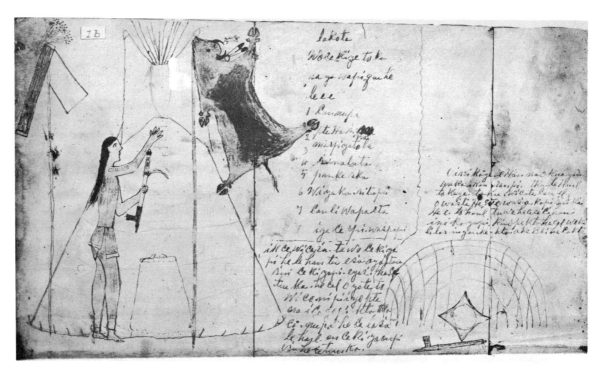

No. 4

NO. 4. EVENTS PERHAPS EARLIER THAN 1856

Three notes in Lakota. Translation:

[1] The Lakota—What They Considered a Prayer [i.e., things they considered sacred, things they used in religious ceremonies]. (1) The pipe; (2) a buffalo robe; (3) the heavens, or the firmament [literally, "blue stone" or "blue cloud stone"]; (4) a red blanket; (5) shells; (6) eagle tail feathers; (7) tobacco; (8) sacrifice [literally, "to cut off one's flesh"].

[2] The Indians of old should have kept on with their way of worship. The people might have lived and grown. At least it would have been all right to continue the use of the sacred pipe according to the original use.

[3] Used [referring to the sweat lodge] in the past for sacred ceremonies only. Now, however, used to cure any indisposition which might cause death.

In a close-up drawing, Bad Heart Bull sets forth—half diagrammatically, half realistically—some but not all of the elements used in the ceremonies of the Dakotas. At the extreme left of the drawing is the sacrifice pole, bearing at its top the "red blanket"—a strip of red flannel—and a bunch of small sticks with bits of tobacco attached. These are offerings. Next is a tipi, evidently a ceremonial lodge. Before it stands the petitioner, his body ceremonially painted. His right arm is raised in the characteristic gesture of supplication, and his left hand presents the medicine pipe to the Great Spirit. On the right upper arm appear the marks indicating incisions where he has cut out bits of flesh in sacrifice (cf. item 8 in the list above). At the right, but still before the lodge, is a red pole, from the top of which hangs a buffalo hide. This is obviously a sacred blanket: the head, horns, and hoofs are still attached; from one horn hangs a small ring bearing two eagle feathers, and from the other hangs the stuffed skin of some very small animal.

On the right side of the page, the artist gives (beneath note 3) a cross-section view of the round-topped sweat lodge, with the four-cornered altar (shown from above, however) and the pipe. Though not altogether a *sacred* thing, the sweat lodge bears a rather close relationship to the other sacred elements described here.

No. 5

NO. 5.   EVENTS PERHAPS EARLIER THAN 1856

A note in Lakota. Translation:

The Teton Lakota—The Traveling.

Whenever they are moving camp, the parties afoot go first. These are the men known as the body of councilmen, or headmen [*wakicunza*; cf. No. 1]. On each side of those that are afoot ride some on horseback. These are the Dog Soldiers, or sergeants at arms [the *akicita*;

[4] Cf., e.g., Luther Standing Bear, *My People, the Sioux* (Boston: Houghton Mifflin Co., 1928), p. 23.

cf. Nos. 1, 2, 3]; these watch over all the people. [The term "Dog Soldiers" is commonly but loosely used by Indian interpreters and early writers on the Plains Indians to refer to the *akicita*.]

Compositionally, one of Bad Heart Bull's most effective impressionistic miniatures.

The whole band is seen moving in proper organization and arrangement.[4]

No. 6

NO. 6. EVENTS PERHAPS EARLIER THAN 1856

A note in Lakota, added late probably. Translation: "Method of moving camp."

A close-up of a portion of the moving throng which is shown in No. 5. The figures are those of a man and woman, mounted, and followed by a pack animal drawing a travois. The obvious purpose of the drawing is to set forth details of costumes and trappings. The outstanding feature of the man's apparel is a kit-fox-skin cap with two eagle tail feathers attached to the crown. The skin is worn in coronet fashion, the tail hanging down behind. Without doubt this is a personal charm (*wotawe*), a symbol of a certain spiritual kinship between the man and the animal spirit. It is possible that the man was a member of the Tokala (Kit Fox) Society (cf. No. 30) and that it pleased him to effect this individual manner of wearing the fox skin. At any rate, the fox-skin cap worn in this fashion would serve to distinguish him; by it his fellow tribesmen could more or less definitely identify him in a crowd or at a distance.

This drawing presents a singularly accurate and complete portrayal of the Dakota woman's riding gear and the trappings and manner of the loading of the pack animal.[5]

The woman's saddle and the packsaddle were similar in design. The frames of both were of wood or bone, had a high-pronged pommel and cantle, and had a second prong below the pommel. Both were equipped with crupper, breast strap, and usually a single cinch (in this drawing, Bad Heart Bull shows two cinches). The woman's saddle was also frequently (as here) equipped with decorated and fringed saddlebags (*a-nuk-wo-ka-swu*). The packsaddle was loaded with painted parfleche bags and boxes, which served as trunks, suitcases, and food containers (cf. No. 212). This drawing shows, too, the old-time travois, a form of pack-carrying equipment which was used on dogs long before the coming of the horse and on horses until comparatively recent times when the government began issuing wagons to the Indians.[6] The horse travois was made of two long poles of equal length and size (often tipi poles); these were lashed together near the small end and then spread to straddle the horse, the larger ends dragging on the ground. A large, oval-shaped flat frame, crudely made of woven branches and rawhide thongs, was bound to the poles just behind the horse and held the poles firmly in place. Upon this woven frame the bulkier part of the luggage was packed. Here also the smaller children frequently rode. The Lakota name for the travois is *hupa waheyupi*—"body of, or main part of, packs"—which indicates something of its importance in the family equipment.

[5] Clark Wissler, "Riding Gear of the North American Indians," *APAMNH*, XVII, Part 1 (1915), 7–29.

[6] Cf., e.g., Clark Wissler, "North American Indians of the Plains," Handbook Series No. 1, American Museum of Natural History, pp. 30 (figure 5), 31 (figure 6).

No. 7

No. 7. Events Perhaps Earlier than 1856

A penciled title in Lakota. Translation: "The moving, according to Teton custom."

A second large-scale drawing showing another portion of the band on the march. This composition shows a group of pack horses and extra horses attended by women, mounted. The picture is true to Dakota life, for it was the women who for the most part attended to the luggage and the extra stock.

Besides the woman's saddle, the packsaddle, saddlebags, and travois, there is pictured here the typical beaded saddle blanket, shown as part of the accoutrements of two of the mounted horses.

The yellow horse (center), led by the second woman at the extreme left, is dragging a set of tipi poles.

The pinto horse at the top (left) and the buckskin horse just below wear an eagle feather apiece tied in the mane. These are luck pieces.

The two buckskin horses at the center (top) and the blue horse to the left show well the parfleche bags and cases used for clothing, ceremonial equipment, and other valuables (cf. Nos. 6 and 212). The drawing of the lower buckskin horse and his load shows more clearly than any other action picture in the record the long, cylindrical parfleche case which was used for the ceremonial eagle-feather headdress or other sacred paraphernalia.

No. 8

No. 8. Events Perhaps Earlier than 1856

A title in Lakota. Translation: "Teton Lakota Costumes of Various Types."

A drawing whose obvious purpose is simply the presentation of type costumes of different seasons.

The white, black-trimmed costumes at the extreme right and left and low foreground are winter costumes, which were made of blankets usually.

Beginning at the extreme left, I call attention to outstanding features in the outfit of each Indian pictured:

The first one carries a quiver and bow slung from the right shoulder, across the back.

The second wears a fox-skin cap decorated with eagle tail feathers (cf. No. 6) and carries a stone-headed war club; his horse wears an eagle feather in his mane.

The third wears a long head decoration of hammered silver disks strung on buckskin and hung from the scalp lock (cf. Nos. 86 and 207), and he carries a cavalry saber. His horse wears two eagle feathers tied to the forelock.

The fourth man carries a rifle in a painted and fringed rawhide case.

The fifth wears the round white hood used in winter.

The sixth (below) wears the peaked winter hood and a quiver and bow slung from the right shoulder. From the saddle horn hangs a parfleche case, fringed on one side.

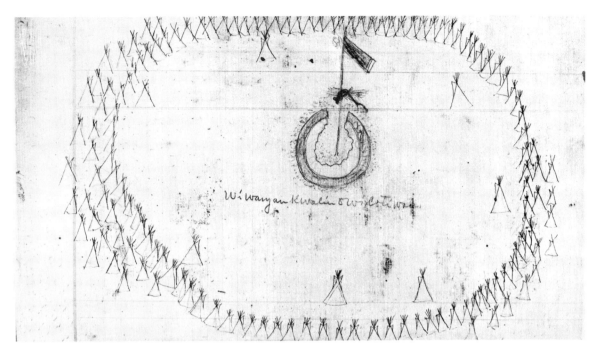

No. 9

NO. 9. EVENTS PERHAPS EARLIER THAN 1856

A note in Lakota. Translation: "The gathering, or camping, for the Sun Dance."

A diagrammatic, topographical, miniature portrayal of the Sun Dance camp and dance area.

The broken circle in green is the pine shade that surrounds the dance area proper. At the center stands the sacred pole, with the red sacrifice banner floating from the top and the sacred bundle and buffalo sacrifice placed in the crotch of the pole (see No. 12 for detail of pole and decoration).

No. 10

NO. 10.   EVENTS PERHAPS EARLIER THAN 1856

The Sun Dance

An insert bearing a panel-like portrayal of a group of women watching one of the acts of the Sun Dance ritual through the pine-bough barricade that surrounds the dance ground.

The women are seen from the rear; and several conventionalizations, common not only to Bad Heart Bull's work but to Plains art in general, are in evidence. Most prominent of these conventionaliza-tions is the back of the woman's head—a horseshoe-shaped outline filled in with black except for the light vertical line at the center, which represents the part (Plains Indian women generally wear their hair parted in the middle, from forehead to neck, and hung in two tight braids over the shoulders). Aside from the head, however, there is a type form used to represent the body outline also.★

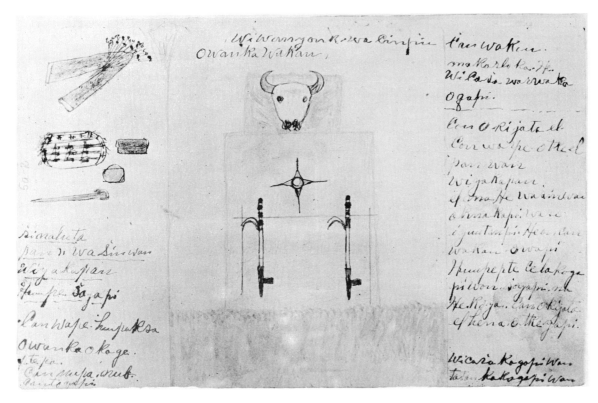

No. 11

The Sun Dance

Several brief notes in Lakota. Translation:

[Center] The sacred ground of the Sun Dance [i.e., the altar].

[Right] [1] The hole for the sacred pole is dug by a man of good habits.

[2] In the forks of the tree is placed a large pouch with a smaller pouch inside it containing the pemmican. Another pouch contains red paint. It is used to paint the sacred pole.

[3] A short picket pin painted red is also included and hung with the other things in the fork of the pole.

[4] An image of a man. An image of a buffalo.

[Left] [1] Red flannel.

[2] Pemmican pouch.

[3] Moccasin painted red.

[4] Branch of a tree with leaves.

[5] The prepared ground.

[6] Skull of a buffalo.

[7] Two pipes.

[8] Pole or stick painted blue.

A rather diagrammatic drawing of the "sacred ground," or altar, and a few sacred objects (left) which go into the Sun Dance bundle. The script simply enumerates these various elements and a few others.

Beginning at the top (left), there is first of all the red flannel banner which was invariably used as an offering in the Sun Dance ceremonies and was frequently found in others. To it are attached small offerings of tobacco tied to twigs.

Below the banner are several of the objects that were placed in the sacred bundle, which was hung in the crotch of the sacred pole.

The altar[7] holds the center of interest here. At the head is a buffalo skull (with a blue mark on the forehead) resting on a bed of sage and sweet grass and facing east. In front of this is a rectangular section of "mellowed earth" (i.e., ground cleared of grass, stones, etc., and worked till it was fairly pulverized). In it is the cross of the four quarters. The cross was drawn ceremonially by the priest and consisted simply of two intersecting trenches about sixteen inches in length, into which offerings of tobacco and kinnikinnick (used for smoking by the Indians) were dropped. Near the edge of this space a light frame ("stick painted blue"; see above) was placed, against which the two sacred pipes leaned, stems up, their bowls resting on buffalo chips. And in front of this another bed of sagebrush was spread.

[7] See Frances Densmore, "Teton Sioux Music," BAE Bulletin 61, p. 122; Alice C. Fletcher, "A Study of Omaha Indian Music," *Papers of the Peabody Museum of American Archaeology and Ethnology*, I, 5 (June 1893), 54 (or 284), reproduced by J. O. Dorsey in "A Study of Siouan Cults," *ARBAE*, XI (1889–1890), 451, figure 189, in connection with "Bushotter on the Sun Dance"; and Walker, "Sun Dance," pp. 69–70.

No. 12

NO. 12. EVENTS PERHAPS EARLIER THAN 1856

The Sun Dance

A note in Lakota. Translation: "At the beginning of the dance, they hold offerings. Sticks decorated at one end with porcupine quills are worn in the hair. Eagle-bone whistles, with plumes fastened at the end, are blown throughout the dance."

This is the dance to which a very brief note scribbled on the otherwise blank page opposite No. 12 refers: "The welcome dance," or "good dance," i.e., the opening ceremony of the Sun Dance.

The dancers are naked from the waist up except for the so-called "otterskin cape"[8] (see dancers at right end). The only other article of apparel worn by these dancers (not mentioned in the note) is the buffalo armlet, seen on the upraised arm.[9]

The colored streamers in front of the dancers are the individual sacrifice banners attached to saplings stuck into the ground. Leaves are still attached to the tops of these.

Rising from the midst of the dancers is the sacred pole of the Sun Dance. The red banner at the top, the red coloring of the pole, and the bundle and buffalo head at the crotch of the pole are all plainly visible.

Throughout this ceremony the performers gazed steadily at the sun and blew upon their eagle-bone whistles.

The movement of the dance is described by one observer as "a slow but steady rising on the ball of the foot and dropping back on the heels, which was the only movement of the 'dance' proper."[10] This was continued, the dancers sounding their whistles each time the drum was struck and gazing at the sun, until one of the performers fainted.[11]

[8] Walker, "Sun Dance," p. 112.

[9] *Ibid.*

[10] Edgar Beecher Bronson, *Cowboy Life on the Western Plains: The Reminiscences of a Rancher* (New York: Grosset and Dunlap, 1910), p. 240.

[11] Standing Bear, *My People*, p. 120.

No. 13

NO. 13. EVENTS PERHAPS EARLIER THAN 1856

The Sun Dance

Three notes in Lakota. Translation:

[1] Buffalo-skull carrier dancing [upper left].

[2] The singers for the Sun Dance use a tom-tom beater made from a piece of tanned hide tied to a stick with hair [lower left].

[3] Tied to stakes on one night of the dance [right].

A drawing showing the drummers (or singers) and the first two forms of the Sun Gaze Dance (the torture ceremonies).

The artist might very well have called attention to the peculiar drum as well as to the special drumstick. For the Sun Dance, the drummers sat around a buffalo hide which was stretched taut upon the ground and staked. Upon this dried skin they beat with their long sticks.

The dancer at the left is performing the first form of the Sun Gaze Dance. The flesh of his shoulders has been pierced and wooden skewers have been inserted, to which thongs bearing buffalo skulls have been tied in such a way that they hang halfway down the body. Leaning upon a forked staff and blowing his whistle,

the performer danced until the flesh was torn loose and the skulls fell.

The second dancer is performing the second form,[12] which is a little more severe. Some say that this was not necessarily a part of the Sun Dance ritual but that it was traditionally performed at that season. In this form, the devotee danced midway between four posts set in a small square. Each post was forked at the top. At the crotch was the offering—banners of red and, in this case, other colors, bits of tobacco arranged in the usual way, and bunches of sage. From each crotch, too, hung a leather thong which was fastened to skewers run through the flesh of the shoulders (as in the first form) and the chest. In such position this man also danced until the motion freed him of his bonds.

In these forms as well as the others, a long leather skirt, painted red, was worn; the upper part of the body was left naked; the hair was decorated with small painted or otherwise decorated wooden pins at the crown of the head; and an eagle-bone whistle was held in the mouth and blown continually.

[12] Walker, "Sun Dance," pp. 61–62.

No. 14

NO. 14.   EVENTS PERHAPS EARLIER THAN 1856

The Sun Dance

A note in Lakota. Translation: "Piercing the chest."

The third form of the Sun Gaze Dance.

This is the most commonly known form, the one which is popularly looked upon as the Sun Dance proper. Of the more widely used forms, it was most dramatic in quality, for several people, sometimes quite a numerous body, performed it simultaneously around the sacred pole itself. As is apparent from the drawing, the costuming and equipment correspond closely to those already discussed.

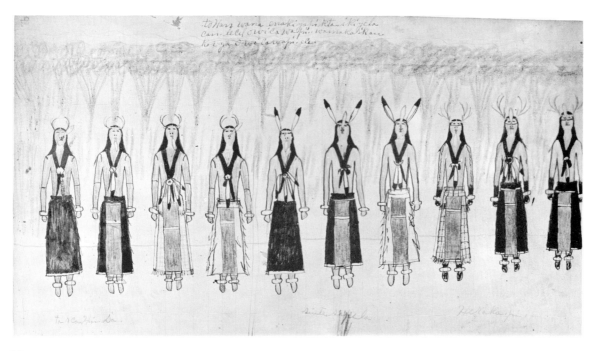

No. 15

NO. 15. EVENTS PERHAPS EARLIER THAN 1856

The Sun Dance

A note in Lakota. Translation: "When they are about through, they are decorated to represent some kind of animal."

The last ceremony of the Sun Dance ritual.

After the participants in the Sun Dance had endured the extreme torture and been ceremonially cleansed and purified, they arrayed themselves to represent various kinds of animals and so performed the last dance. In this case, the four dancers at the left represent the red deer (*tarca hin sa*); the next three, the black-tailed deer (*sinte sapela*); and the last three, the elk (*heraka*). The headgear and the body painting indicate the animal represented. The variations in the skirts and in the tie ornaments are simply matters of individual taste, or of accomplishment in the case of the latter.

A representation of the pine-bough sunshade is visible in the background.

No. 16

No. 16. Events Perhaps Earlier than 1856

Notes in Lakota. Translation: 1. "Taking the hide off." 2. "The whole hind quarters. From shoulder forward. Middle."

A close-up showing the butchering of buffalo.

Four men are preparing to butcher two buffalo. The apparel of the men would indicate that the season is winter. The buffalo at the right is a splendid illustration of Frances Densmore's explanation of how an animal was butchered when the hide was desired *whole* for use in making a lodge:

> If the hide were to be used for a tent it was removed whole instead of being cut along the back. In this process the animal was turned on its back, the head being turned to the left so it came under the shoulder and the horns stuck in the ground so that the head formed a brace.[13]

The Indians named each part and each muscle of their food animals (therefore the terms in the second note above). In butchering, they began at the back and took out each part, removing it from the bones, first along one side and then along the other.

The practice referred to in this bit of interesting information seems to correspond in a certain measure to the practice of counting coup: in the old days, though he did not kill the buffalo in a hunt, the man who first tied a knot in the tail of the animal was entitled to a certain definitely prescribed and generous portion of the meat.

[13] Densmore, "Teton Sioux Music," pp. 443–444.

No. 17

NO. 17. EVENTS PERHAPS EARLIER THAN 1856

A note in Lakota. Translation: "To come home with meat."

The sequel to the episode of which No. 16 is a part.

Four pack horses with packsaddles are carrying home the spoils of the chase. The "green" hide (hair side down) is hung across the saddle and the meat is piled upon it and fastened in place.[14] Two of the hunters follow the pack horses, seated upon two other new hides which have been thrown double across the saddle blankets.

[14] Standing Bear, *My People*, p. 55; see also Densmore, "Teton Sioux Music," p. 444.

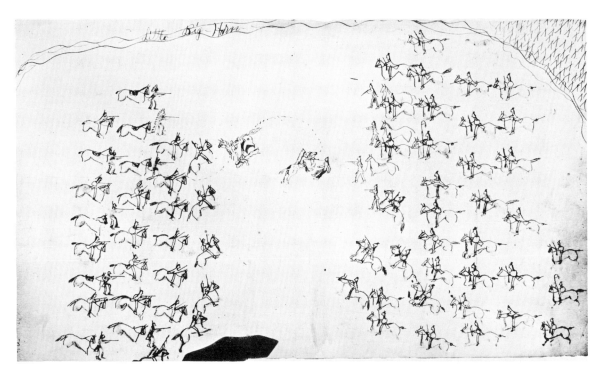

No. 18

No. 18. Events Perhaps Earlier than 1856

A miniature portrayal (in black and white) of an encounter between the Dakotas and the Crows.

The center of interest in this drawing is the single combat fought between the lines of the opposing forces, a characteristic type of fighting among these Indians. The bonneted Sioux warrior has gone out on horseback from the force at the left to meet and count coup upon the dismounted Crow (right center). He charges and counts coup upon him very close to the Crow line, then circles back toward his comrades (the dotted line shows the path of his dash back to his own people). A second Crow, however, fires at him just as he is striking the dismounted Crow. The

Crow's aim is good evidently, for the Dakota falls from his horse as he reaches his own line.

The counting of coup, that is, the striking of an enemy with one's weapon, was a very important point in Indian warfare. More honor attached to counting coup upon an enemy than to killing one. Especially great was the honor if this were done to a live enemy; consequently, warriors not infrequently risked their lives, with apparent foolhardiness and often with fatal results, as in the case pictured here, in an attempt to touch the living enemy (cf. also Nos. 54 and 55).

No. 19

No. 19. Events Perhaps Earlier than 1856

A note in Lakota. Translation: "To chase the buffalo."

A miniature portrayal of an attack upon a herd of buffalo.

At the extreme right are the extra riding horses and pack animals, probably kept by older men[15]

while the hunters, on their best horses, run the buffalo.

I have spoken in Part One, Chapter IV, of the three-part rhythm of this composition and of the movement from right to left, with its gathering momentum.

[15] Cf. Standing Bear, *My People*, p. 62.

No. 20

No. 20. Events Perhaps Earlier than 1856

A note in Lakota. Translation: "This is a hill. It is called 'They-Flee-Around-It.' The Crows were chased around it and some were killed. A person who wore four horns was killed."

A miniature, impressionistic drawing of the attack upon a Crow camp by a party of Hunkpapa Dakotas. Red figures here and there indicate the Crows killed. A creek flowing past this butte was for a long time known as "The Creek Where They Cleaned Up the Village." It runs between Tongue River and the Big Powder, emptying into Tongue River near the mouth.

At one time, before He Dog's day (He Dog is about ninety-five years old at the time of this note—1929), a Crow village was attacked and captured by the Sioux. The Crows fled around the butte in an attempt to escape, but some were killed and many were taken captive.

No. 21

The Lakota note on No. 20 concludes with the sentence: "A person with four horns was killed."

This drawing is a close-up of the killing of that man. His headdress shows the "four horns."

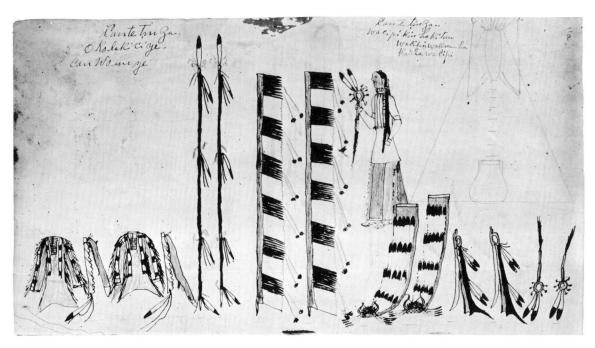

No. 22

NO. 22. EVENTS PERHAPS EARLIER THAN 1856

Cante Tinza Society[16]

Two brief notes in Lakota. Translation:

[1] Symbols of office of the Braves, or Brave Heart Society [left].
[2] In the Brave Heart Society dances, the members are all dressed in full regalia and all rattle the *wakmuha* [medicine rattle] as they dance [right].

The paraphernalia from left to right consist of:

(1) Two fringed shirts. These were worn by the leaders. Wissler does not mention the shirts in his discussion of Oglala societies. Such differences, however, can usually be accounted for by the fact that the various bands were likely to differ somewhat in the matter of paraphernalia.

(2) Two whips. These "have broad, flat handles with saw-like edges, lashes of rawhide, and guards of otter skin. Their owners wear two eagle feathers at the back of the head."[17] The shirts, whips, and two eagle feathers were all symbols of the same office. At one time He Dog held this office in the society and so wore and carried these badges of office.

(3) Four lances. He Dog and Short Bull say that in their band (Amos's was the same band, of course) there were six lances—the four straight ones shown

by Amos in the drawing and a pair of crooked ones which Wissler mentions also. Of the straight lances, however, Wissler describes only the second type given in this manuscript, lances made "with a spear on the end and a piece of red flannel about four inches wide the full length of the spear with a row of black feathers alternating with a row of white at short distances."[18]

(4) Two feathered headdresses. These were made with a tight cap of buckskin as the base. A buffalo horn, split to make it light, was fastened to each side. The front was decorated with a bit of beadwork. The tail of the bonnet was made of a long strip of red flannel about six or eight inches wide, to which rows of eagle feathers were fastened horizontally.

(5) Two swords with black otter-skin guards. Wissler does not mention these.

(6) Medicine rattles. The rattles, made in the shape of a ring,[19] were carried by all members of the society.

The figure of the man represents the costume worn by the members in peacetime dances and shows the manner in which the rattle was held and shaken.

---

[16] Cf., particularly, Wissler, "Societies," pp. 25–31, 67, 68 (figure 3c); see also Densmore, "Teton Sioux Music," pp. 320–325.
[17] Wissler, "Societies," p. 26.

[18] *Ibid.*
[19] For a slight variant, see Densmore, "Teton Sioux Music," Plate 45 (Standing Rock Sioux).

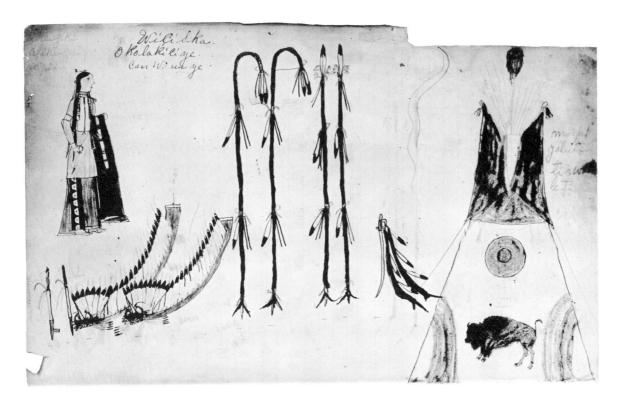

No. 23

NO. 23. EVENTS PERHAPS EARLIER THAN 1856

Wiciska Society[20]

Notes in Lakota. Translation:

[1] This is the style of the costume worn when they dance [left].

[2] The symbols of office of the Wiciska Society [center].

[3] This shows the style of Red Cloud's tipi [right].

The left portion of the page is given over to a close-up of paraphernalia of the Wiciska Society, or "society of those–who–carry–something–white" ("something white" refers to the feathered bonnets).

Paraphernalia of officers from left to right:

(1) Two pipes.

(2) Two warbonnets. The cap is made much like that of the Cante Tinza (No. 22); but as the drawing plainly shows, the feathers of the tail are arranged differently.

(3) Four lances: two crooked ones wrapped with fur and decorated with eagle feathers[21] and two straight ones similar to two of those pictured for Cante Tinza. The latter do not correspond in manner of wrapping to Wissler's description, however.[22]

(4) A sword with a double black otter-skin guard. Short Bull says that there were two swords. The two swords make the correct number of officers (i.e., ten).

Wissler does not mention swords for this society. He does, however, speak of two whips, which Bad Heart Bull does not show and which He Dog and Short Bull do not mention.

The figure of the man shows the peacetime dance costume.

The right portion of the page bears a drawing of the lodge of old Chief Red Cloud (*Marpiya Luta*).[23] The rainbow, at each side of the lodge cover, was Red Cloud's personal emblem. The red disk represents the sun, and the encircling yellow ring, its halo. The black at the top of the tipi represents the heavens at night. The dark color at the bottom (it looks black or brown but should be green) represents the earth. The buffalo is obvious (the yellow on the hump indicates old hair not yet shed: the hump sheds last). In his lodge decoration, Red Cloud thus appealed to the Great Spirit through several of the mightiest spirit powers.

[20] Wissler, "Societies," pp. 34–36, 67, 68 (figure 3a).

[21] *Ibid.*, p. 67.

[22] *Ibid.*, p. 35.

[23] See James H. Cook, *Fifty Years on the Old Frontier* (New Haven: Yale University Press, 1923), p. 216, for a drawing of Red Cloud's lodge made by his son in 1909.

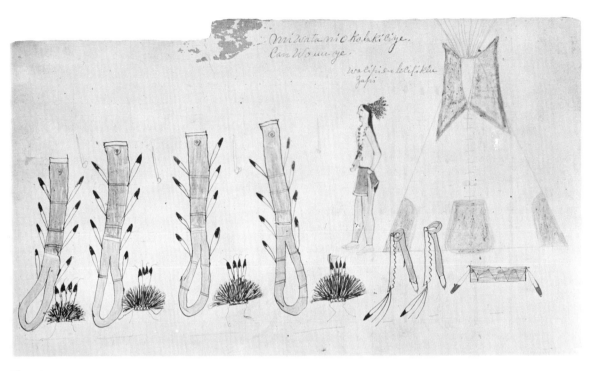

No. 24

No. 24. Events Perhaps Earlier than 1856

Miwatani Society[24]

Notes in Lakota. Translation: 1. "Symbols of office of the Miwatani Society" (left). 2. "This is the way they dress when at a dance" (right).

From left to right the paraphernalia consist of:

(1) Four feathered headdresses (Wissler mentions but two)[25] and four stake sashes (four small stakes have been penciled in near the end of each sash). The wearers of the headdresses were very important and their position was most precarious, for, in the front of battle, they were obligated to stake themselves down (with the stake pin run through the small hole in the end of the sash; see drawing) and so remain unless a fellow member could fight back the enemy sufficiently to pull up the stake and so release his comrade. The Miwatani are generally conceded to be the first to institute this no-flight regulation (see also Cante Tinza, No. 22, and Kangi Yuha, No. 29).

The headdress is made of crow feathers centered with eagle feathers.

(2) Two whips similar to those of the Cante Tinza.

(3) A drum.

According to He Dog and Short Bull, there were two other officers whose paraphernalia are not shown here. The symbols of office were two rattles made of antelope dewclaws. A wooden frame about sixteen inches long, made in the general shape of a long-handled gourd, was first decorated with beadwork and porcupine quillwork, and then the head was thickly hung with the dewclaws.

With these two officers, there were nine in all in the society.

Again the figure of the man shows the peacetime dance costume. A bunch of spotted-owl feathers is worn in the hair.

A feature of the dance peculiar to this society was the regulation that no one of the members could be seated after the drumming and singing stopped until he had been touched by the whip bearer, nor could he resume his dancing when the music started again until he had been touched by that officer.

There was also a special feature in the initiation of the sash bearers. At the time of their taking the oath of office, they were painted entirely red. Then they

[24] Wissler, "Societies," pp. 41–48, 69 (figure 5), 71–74 (tale of origin); see also Densmore, "Teton Sioux Music," pp. 326–329.

[25] Wissler, "Societies," p. 42.

stood in a row and buffalo grease was rubbed in the palm of the right hand of each one. Immediately the "servant" of the society placed a live coal in the palm of the right hand of each. Then each walked to the consecrated ground at the back-center of the lodge and slowly placed the coal upon that sacred space.

He Dog and Short Bull can give no explanation of the red and green decoration of the society lodge (right) other than that it was given in a vision. They know little about the organization and its symbolism, for it was one of the oldest societies and they were comparatively late (He Dog is about ninety-five years old—in 1929); but they were familiar with the dress and paraphernalia.

The name of the society is foreign in origin and has—so it seems—no translation in Dakota; it is a Mandan word used by the Dakotas to designate that tribe. Some other tribes show evidences of a similar organization or of the borrowing of parts of such an organization. The Omaha tribe in particular has a society known by a slight variant of the same name (*Ma-wa-da-ni*), a society which possesses a dance called the "Mandan dance."[26] Quite plainly, there is a very real relationship between the two; for, as J. O. Dorsey points out, the Omahas borrowed this society from the Poncas, who in turn had taken it from the Dakotas.[27] Alice C. Fletcher seems to indicate that, in part at least, the Omahas may have borrowed the institution directly from the Sioux when she says, "The Omahas took from the Sioux the *Ma-wa-da-ni* songs."[28] Her explanation of the purpose of the initial banding of the group, in her tale of origin, is an interesting comment on the general precepts of the Omaha society and reflects well the general character of the Dakota:

> The men . . . banded themselves together in order better to serve their people, to present to the young men of the tribe an example of generosity in time of peace and of steadfast valour on the field of battle.[29]

[26] J. O. Dorsey, "Omaha Sociology," *ARBAE*, III (1881–1882), 354.

[27] *Ibid.*

[28] Fletcher, "Omaha Indian Music," p. 9 (or 239).

[29] Alice C. Fletcher, *Indian Story and Song* (Boston: Small, Maynard and Co., 1900), pp. 39–44.

No. 25

Sotka Yuha Society[30]

Notes in Lakota. Translation: 1. "Symbols of office of the Sotka Yuha Society" (center). 2. "The costume worn in the dance" (right).

As Wissler points out, it is difficult to secure a good translation for the name of this society:

> It is said to imply a smooth, unadorned stick; hence, they that have empty lances, referring to the custom of investing certain members with plain lances to which they may tie feathers if coups are counted.[31]

The paraphernalia shown, from left to right, consist of:

(1) Two pipes.

(2) Six lances—two crooked and four straight. The crooked pair are fur-wrapped and closely resemble those of the Wiciska (No. 23). The third pair resemble the straight fur-wrapped lances shown for the Cante Tinza (No. 22) and Wiciska. The second pair seem to resemble the pair of straight lances described by

Wissler for the Wiciska,[32] except that instead of being wrapped with "a strip of red flannel [and] a strip of blue flannel . . . so that the blue and red showed in succession," these have black and red showing in succession. Blue and black are frequently used interchangeably, however.

(3) Two fringed buckskin shirts.

(4) Two whips similar to those described earlier. He Dog points out that the shirts and whips belonged to the same officer.

(5) A sword with a double black otter-skin guard.

(6) A drum.

The figure of the man represents the peacetime dance costume. A noticeable part of this equipment is the long scalp-lock decoration trimmed with silver disks (cf. Nos. 86 and 210; the Lakota form of the name for this ornament is *pe-co-kan-iyu-kmu-pi*).

This is said to be a very old society, coming between the Miwatani (No. 24) and Cante Tinza in age.

[30] Wissler, "Societies," pp. 33–34.
[31] *Ibid.*, p. 33.

[32] *Ibid.*, p. 35.

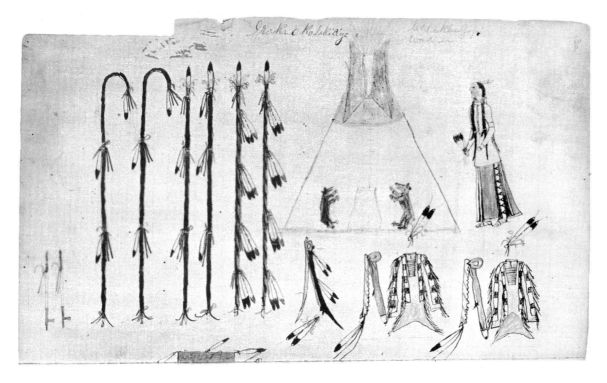

No. 26

No. 26. Events Perhaps Earlier than 1856

Iroka Society[33]

Notes in Lakota. Translation: 1. "Symbols of office of the Iroka Society" (left). 2. "The dance costume of the society" (right).

Paraphernalia of the Iroka, or Badger, Society consist of:

(1) Two pipes.

(2) Six lances—two crooked, two straight and fur-wrapped, two straight with black and red alternating as in the Sotka Yuha drawing (No. 25). Wissler lists "4 lances, two crooked" and then adds "2 lances, buckskin wrapped," which must be the red and black ones.

(3) One drum.

(4) One sword with black otter-skin guard.

(5) Two fringed buckskin shirts.

(6) Two whips. Evidently, again the shirt wearers and whip bearers are the same men.

(7) Two head decorations of two eagle tail feathers each. These also belong to the whip bearers.

The society lodge bears a rampant badger at each side of the door flap. This is the society's totem.

The man shows the peacetime dance costume.

[33] Wissler, "Societies," pp. 13, 31–32, 67; see also Densmore, "Teton Sioux Music," pp. 327–328.

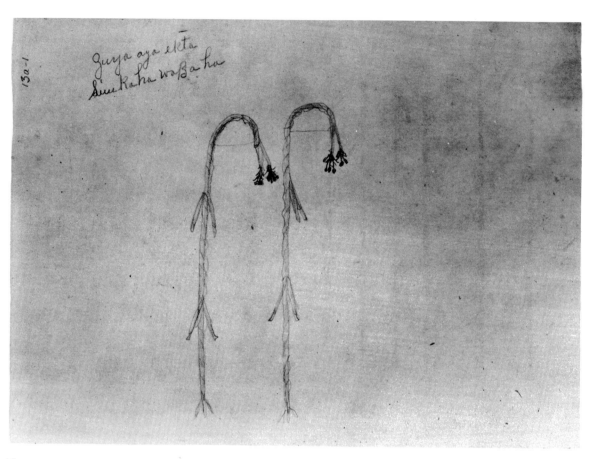

No. 27

No. 27.   Events Perhaps Earlier than 1856

Iroka Society

A note in Lakota. Translation: "When going to war, they carry wolf-skin banners."

A penciled sketch of two crooked lances.

He Dog and Short Bull explain that these lances were carried on horseback by men especially deputized as lance bearers in cases of emergency (hard battles) when more officers were needed. The lances had to be made in great haste and from green wood. They were wrapped with wolf skin and were bound with cord, for since the timber was green, the crook would not stay in place unless it was tied.

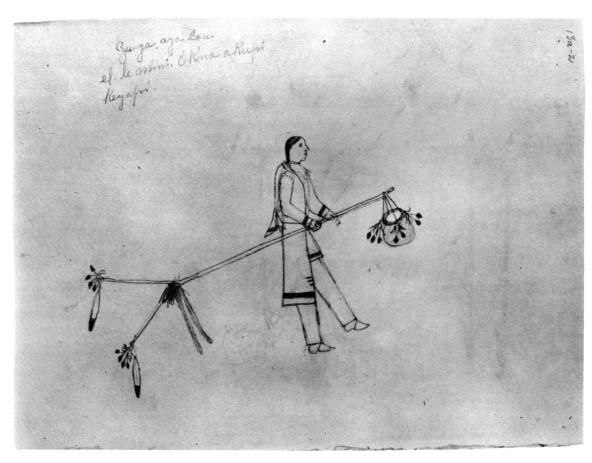

No. 28

NO. 28. EVENTS PERHAPS EARLIER THAN 1856

Iroka Society

A note in Lakota. Translation: "When going to war, this is the water bag that is used to carry water."

A penciled sketch of the "waterboy"[34] of the group.

A boy was made the water carrier of the organization. In order to test his courage and to develop it, when the group was out on the warpath, this boy was often sent, after dark, over rather dangerous paths, to get water for the older men.

[34] Wissler, "Societies," p. 60 (figure 2).

His water bag, shown in the drawing, was of a special type. The sack itself was called a "heart bag" and was made from the sac-covering of the buffalo heart. Tied in four places, with feathers at the places where the cords were tied, it was hung from the large end of a stick about five feet long, which had a short forking at the opposite end. Decorations of feathers and other small objects were suspended from the ends of and at the two branches of the fork and from the fork itself.

No. 29

No. 29.   Events Perhaps Earlier than 1856

Kangi Yuha Society[35]

Notes in Lakota. Translation: 1. "Symbols of office of the Kangi Yuha Society." 2. "The dance costume of the society."

Paraphernalia of the Kangi Yuha, or Crow Owners, Society:

(1) Two pipes.

(2) Two short lances (see text accompanying No. 30, last paragraph).

(3) Two crow–skin or crow–feather lances (straight). These form the especially distinguishing feature of the Kangi Yuha paraphernalia. A spearhead was bound to one end of each lance. The shafts were ceremonially painted (one blue, one red), and then both were wrapped with otter skin. An eagle feather and a few owl feathers adorned the upper end of the shaft, tied a little below the top. Finally the lances'

real mark of distinction was affixed: the stuffed skin of a crow,[36] the feathers still intact, was bound to each pole just above the spearhead.

A no–flight regulation went with these lances (cf. Nos. 22 and 24); the bearers staked themselves down before the enemy. He Dog and Crazy Horse had been given the crow-feather lances just before the severe battle "When They Drove Them into Camp" (see Nos. 219–284), so their trial came with promptness and with fury!

(4) Two official rattles. These were large and globular, and each bore the image of a human face (cf., especially, the Tokala rattle, No. 30).

(5) Two bows, and two arrows with blunt tips.

(6) Two feather bustles (cf. No. 31). (These Wissler does not mention.)

---

[35] Wissler, "Societies," pp. 13, 23–25, 67, 68 (figure 3b), 69 (figure 14). See also Densmore, "Teton Sioux Music," pp. 318–320, 384, 394, Plates 40, 44; Alice C. Fletcher and Francis LaFlesche, "The Omaha Tribe," *ARBAE*, XXVII (1905–1906), 441–442, Plate 55; Robert H. Lowie, "Dance Associations of the Eastern Dakota," *APAMNH*, XI, Part 2 (1913), 109, 199, 309; and Clark Wissler, "Societies and

Dance Associations of the Blackfoot Indians," *APAMNH*, XI, Part 4 (1913), 392.

[36] Wissler describes the lance with only the neck and head of the crow ("Societies," p. 24). But He Dog's people (as Bad Heart Bull shows in the drawing), in common with others, used the whole bird.

The man figure represents the peacetime dance regalia.

The lodge shows a crow, the totem of the organization, on the door flap.

Wissler points out that no large drum was owned by the society but that small hand drums were borrowed on ceremonial occasions. Bad Heart Bull would seem to bear out this finding, for he pictures no drum as part of the paraphernalia. And He Dog and Short Bull mention none.

The feather bustles were worn by two officers who were called "servants" but who seem to have been very important functionaries, for they directed the singing and gave the signals for the dancing at the ceremonies; and they were also responsible for securing food for the whole group. In connection with these duties, they carried, respectively, the rattle and the bows and blunt-tipped arrows (*miyostake*). When the band was moving, these two men shot their blunt arrows at parfleche food cases which they knew were well filled, thus obligating the owners to the donation of a pot or two of choice dried buffalo meat for the society at its next dance and feast; or they hit, upon the thigh, certain men, thus obligating them to the gift of choice food—dog flesh or special cuts of jerked buffalo meat; or, again, they chose and hit a particular dog, whose master was thus obligated to have the dog killed and cooked for the society's feast. These same officers, too, at the time of a society dance, kept the members in proper activity by shooting any who lagged or showed a tendency to stop in the performance of the dance.

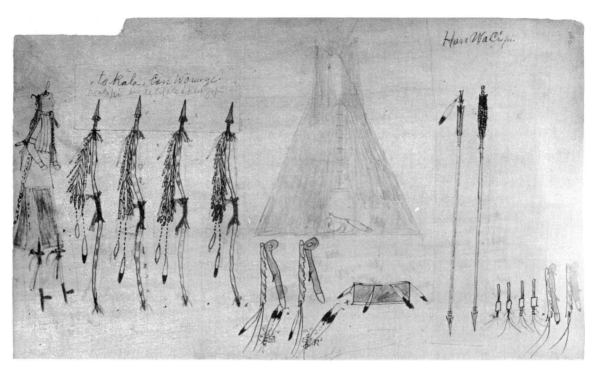

No. 30

NO. 30.   EVENTS PERHAPS EARLIER THAN 1856

Tokala Society[37]

Notes in Lakota. Translation: 1. "Symbols of office of the Tokala Society" (left). 2. "Dance costume of the society" (left). 3. "The dance of the night" (right).

Paraphernalia of the Tokala, or Kit Fox, Society, as shown from left to right, consist of:

(1) Two pipes.

(2) Four lances. The lances are the distinguishing feature of this organization. Unlike the lances of any of the other societies, these were made in the form of bows which strongly resembled the Sacred Bow of the tribe (cf. Nos. 98 and 99) but were unstrung. The shaft was trimmed with beadwork and the grip wrapped with colored sinew. At one end was a large spearhead. From this same end, bound to the shaft a few inches below the spear point, hung a long banner made of feathers ingeniously attached to a strip of rawhide, from the tip of which dangled two eagle

tail feathers. Short Bull was at one time invested with the Tokala bow lance, a signal honor and at the same time a precarious position, for the Tokala bow carriers were men who had proved themselves among the bravest and who were expected to take their places unflinchingly in the front of battle. The artist's father was also a Tokala lance carrier, as is shown by the drawing which portrays him striking a Ree scout with the bow lance in the Battle of the Little Big Horn (No. 165).

(3) Two whips similar to those of other societies.

(4) Two eagle-feather headdresses consisting of two eagle feathers each, which are worn by the whip bearers.

(5) One drum.

The man shows the peacetime dance costume. The long scalp-lock decoration, bearing silver disks, is again a prominent feature (cf. Sotka Yuha, No. 25).

The word *hanwacipi*, meaning "dance of the

---

[37] Wissler, "Societies," pp. 14–23, 67, 70 (figure 6), 71–74. See also Densmore, "Teton Sioux Music," pp. 316–317, 365, 414–415; George A. Dorsey, "The Cheyenne. I. Ceremonial Organization," Field Columbian Museum Publication 99, *Anthropological Series*, IX, 1 (March 1905), 15 ff.; Fletcher and LaFlesche, "The Omaha Tribe," p.

486; Lowie, "Dance Associations," p. 195; Robert H. Lowie, "Societies of the Crow, Hidatsa, and Mandan Indians," *APAMNH*, XI, Part 3 (1913), 155, 253, 296; and James Mooney, "The Cheyenne Indians," *Memoirs of the American Anthropological Association*, I, 6, 412.

night" or "night dance," indicates a change of mind on the part of the artist. Evidently he had intended to make a drawing showing the "night dance," which was common to many of the Plains tribes and was nothing more than a social dance, chiefly for the sake of the young people. There is no drawing whatever, though, concerning this subject.

He Dog says that according to his experience in watching the Tokala dances, the medicine-rattle carrier[38] had an unusually large black rattle. (Amos fails to picture the rattle in this case.) The head of it, which was made of rawhide, had been shaped, while it was still wet, into the form of a man's face and head. The carrier was painted entirely black and danced by himself, seemingly more vigorously than the others. He was commonly spoken of as the "black man." The rest of the dancers arranged themselves according to him. His position formed a very small segment of a circle. A little space was left at both his right and his left, and then the circle was continued and almost completed by two large, balanced segments made up of dancers in close formation. Directly opposite the "black man" was a

[38] I have found no mention of this figure in published material on the Tokala.

[39] Wissler does not mention the whips, but my inform-

break in the ring—a very small open space corresponding to his position. Quite obviously, according to this, the official Tokala dance was a circular one.

The Tokala, it seems, was the most prominent and one of the oldest of the warrior societies among the Oglalas. Traditionally, the members of the group were noted for their watchfulness over the band in times of peace as in times of war, for their dauntlessness in the face of danger, and for a constant readiness to meet any exigency, all of which is reflected in their song:

> I am the kit fox,
> I live in uncertainty.

The two spears, four rattles, and two whips[39] shown at the right in this drawing do not belong there but should be shown in the preceding drawing; they represent part of the paraphernalia of the Kangi Yuha. These drawings of the spears show the two so-called short lances of the society. One was made of ash and was painted blue and black; the other was cherry and was painted red. The four rattles are similar to the two shown in No. 29, but are smaller. The two whips are like those of the other societies.

ants say that there were two officers whose emblems of office were both the shirt and the whip (see text accompanying No. 29).

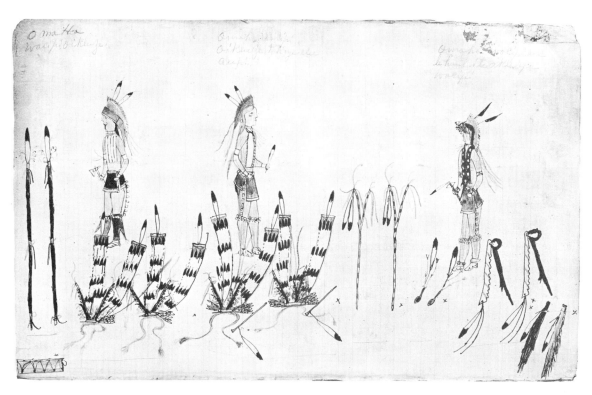

No. 31

Omaha Society[40]

Three notes in Lakota above the three figures of men. Translation:

[1] The customary way of dressing for the Omaha Dance.

[2] The original customary way of dressing for the Omaha Dance.

[3] Now their faces are covered when they are dancing the Omaha.

The paraphernalia as shown by Bad Heart Bull consist of:

(1) Two short lances wrapped with otter skin—similar to the short lances of the Kangi Yuha but lacking the crow skin.

(2) One drum.

(3) Four feather bustles (cf. Kangi Yuha, No. 29). These are technically referred to as "the crow" by Alice C. Fletcher and Francis LaFlesche, who give the history of their significance.[41]

(4) Two whistles (below second two bustles).

(5) Two ornamented forked spears.

(6) Two rattles (different from any so far shown).

(7) Two whips.

(8) Two horse tails decorated with an eagle feather apiece. Only men who had had their horses shot down under them had the right to carry these.

The Omaha Society is clearly an importation, probably from the Pawnees through the Omahas.

Among the Oglalas it was originally distinctively a warrior society quite similar in general outline to the others described. A remnant of it still exists in the popular and now social dance called, from the society name, the Omaha Dance. The most significant part of the original dance ceremony was the more or less ritualistic Grass Dance (see No. 408).[42]

As a significant incidental phase, a healing ceremony developed in the Omaha Society, in which the Grass Dance played a significant part. In fact, this healing ceremony came to be considered one of the most important social elements of the organization and was looked upon as one of the chief methods of securing supernatural aid for bringing about the recovery of someone who was ill.

[40] Wissler, "Societies," pp. 48–52. See also Densmore, "Teton Sioux Music," pp. 468–477; H. M. Chittenden and A. T. Richardson, eds., *The Life, Letters, and Travels of Father Pierre Jean DeSmet, S.J., 1801–1873* (4 vols.; New York: Francis P. Harper, 1905), III, 1059–1060; J. O. Dorsey, "Siouan Cults," p. 463; Fletcher and LaFlesche,

"The Omaha Tribe," p. 459; Lowie, "Dance Associations," p. 130; and Wissler, "Societies and Dance Associations," pp. 451–456.

[41] Fletcher and LaFlesche, "The Omaha Tribe," pp. 441–442 and Plate 55.

[42] Cf. No. 408 and Wissler, "Societies," pp. 50–51.

No. 32

No. 32.   Sioux-Crow Fights. Earliest Dates, 1856, 1858

Three short notes in Lakota. Translation:

[1] There were Oglalas and some Miniconjous.

[2] They took a stand under a projecting rock along the cliff.

[3] In 1857 at Captive Butte, the Sioux killed ten Crows. The only damage the Crows did was to wound a horse.

The butte, known to the Dakotas as Captive Hill (*Wayakapaha*), is located northwest of Ghost Butte (cf. No. 198) near Spearfish, South Dakota, at the head of Moreau River (Owl Creek). The Sioux ran the Crows into a cave here and killed ten.

The date given is 1856. The seeming discrepancy between this date and the reference in note 3 can be explained by the fact that a year in the winter counts represents parts of two of our calendar years; thus the year would be 1856–1857.

Bad Heart Bull's conventional portrayal of the butte is plainly shown here. The Crows are seen on top, while the Sioux surround the hill and scramble up the sides.

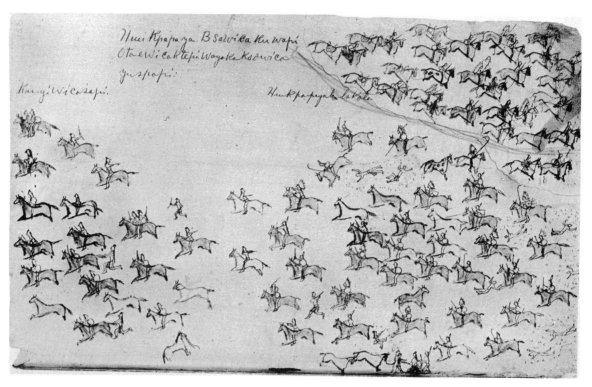

No. 33

No. 33. Sioux-Crow Fights. Earliest Dates, 1856, 1858

A note in Lakota. Translation: "The Hunkpapas were chased and many were killed and many were taken prisoners."

A miniature of the latter part of a fight in which a band of Hunkpapas attacked a party of Crows.

The Dakotas were repulsed and lost quite a number killed and captured. They were chased back so fast, in fact, that they did not dare return to their "moccasin carriers" (women and baggage carriers), who had been left far behind when they attacked, but had to take another route. During the struggle, another group of Sioux appeared and the Crows were in turn driven back. It is this latter part of the struggle that is pictured here. The upper right corner shows that portion of the Dakota party which is leading back several captive Crow women (the figures in yellow) and a number of captured pack horses. The many hoofprints around each of the fallen figures (lower right) indicate that the fight was a fierce one and that several warriors have counted coup upon each victim. In the immediate foreground (right), two Dakotas are scalping a Crow.

No date is given, but according to He Dog and Short Bull, this skirmish took place before the killing of Yellow Robe (see No. 35), i.e., before the year 1858.

No. 34

NO. 34.   SIOUX-CROW FIGHTS. EARLIEST DATES, 1856, 1858

A miniature showing another bit of the fight portrayed in No. 33.

It was at this time [sic] that Yellow Robe (*Tasi Nagi*) was separated from the rest of the Crows and was killed (cf. No. 35).

No. 35

NO. 35.   SIOUX-CROW FIGHTS. EARLIEST DATES, 1856, 1858

A note in Lakota. Translation: "Yellow Robe and his son were killed."

A close-up of the killing of Yellow Robe by the Hunkpapa Black Wolf (*Sunkmanitu Sapa*).

Yellow Robe and his son, a mere boy, were both killed when they and their fellow tribesmen invaded the Dakota camp.

The date given is 1858. The Short Man winter count gives "1858. The killing of His Yellow Blanket," which confirms the date, for "His Yellow Blanket" is but a variant of "Yellow Robe."

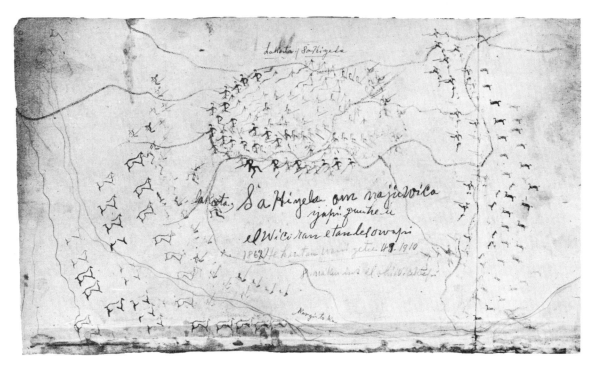

No. 36

NO. 36.   SIOUX-CROW FIGHTS. EARLIEST DATES, 1856, 1858

A note in Lakota. Translation: "This is when the Sioux and Cheyennes were attacked."

A highly impressionistic miniature showing a concerted attack on a party which has been driven to a butte.

Below the Big Horn River where it empties into the Missouri, a war party of Crows caught a small band of Sioux and Cheyennes under a bank (wall of a butte). They fought for some time, but finally the Sioux and Cheyennes maneuvered so that the Crows were put to flight. One half-breed Dakota-Cheyenne was the only person lost on the one side, but the Crows lost over ten.

The event is dated 1862.

No. 37

NO. 37.   SIOUX-CROW FIGHTS. EARLIEST DATES, 1856, 1858

Notes in Lakota give the names of Dakotas counting coup on the Crow warrior. Translation: 1. "High Hollow Horn," and the nickname "Old Spider" (left). 2. "Iron Hawk," and the nickname "Contradicter," or "One Who Mixes Things Up" (middle). 3. "Young Man Afraid of His Horses" (right).

High Hollow Horn (*Herlogeca Wankatuya*; see No. 196 for nickname, *Iktomila*), a half-brother of Red Cloud, has caught the Crow's horse; Iron Hawk (*Cetan Maza*; see No. 326 for nickname, *Wayajuju*) is counting coup on the Crow, with a saber; and Young Man Afraid of His Horses (*Tasimke Kaki Papi Ici Nupa*) is riding up to count coup next.

The fight is the same as the one shown in No. 36.

No. 38

NO. 38.   SIOUX-CROW FIGHTS. EARLIEST DATES, 1856, 1858

A note in Lakota. Translation: "Young Man Afraid of His Horses takes the bow from another Crow in the same fight. It was said that the Crow had stolen the Sacred Bow" (see Nos. 98 and 99 for the Sacred Bow).

No. 39

No. 39.   SIOUX-CROW FIGHTS. EARLIEST DATES, 1856, 1858

A note in Lakota. Translation: "Young Man Afraid of His Horses took the gun away from another Crow [in the same fight] and killed him in midstream."

The two are shown in close-up view in midstream. He Dog and Short Bull say that there is a mistake here, that it was a Cheyenne, not Afraid of His Horses, who killed this Crow.

No. 40

NO. 40.   SIOUX-CROW FIGHTS. EARLIEST DATES, 1856, 1858

No record for this number—evidently the same as
No. 39.

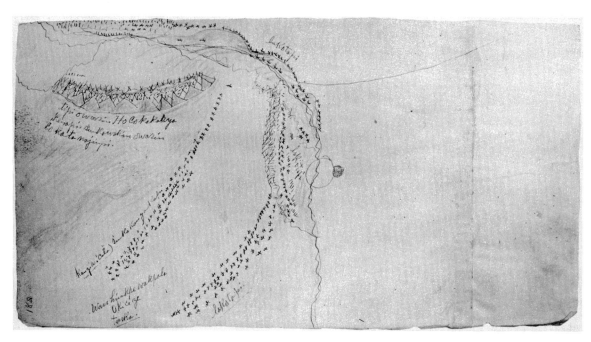

No. 41

NO. 41. SIOUX-CROW FIGHTS. EARLIEST DATES, 1856, 1858

First Arrow Creek Fight

Brief notes in Lakota. Translation:

[1] All tipis were erected in a circle with all horses in the center [upper left].

[2] Crow Indians riding horseback [center left].

[3] Arrow Creek fight—a big battle [lower left].

[4] Lakota [repeated several times from top around right to bottom, to indicate that all these besiegers are Lakota people].

A very small topographic miniature introducing the first or Upper Arrow Creek fight (Nos. 41 to 48; see also No. 218). The episode is also sometimes designated as "Defending the Tent" (*Tiyonajin Wicayapi*) because—as note 1 indicates—the Crows set up their lodges as a barricade and thus defended their camp. The lodges, in a circle, are seen upper left; below and to the right are some of the Crows out in battle line to meet the Sioux ("riding horseback," as note 2 has it). The Dakotas are strung out from lower right all along the creek suggested at the right.

The Sioux force was made up of Oglalas, their allies the Cheyennes, and a few Miniconjous—chiefly Oglalas.

The two forces charged back and forth: the Sioux tried to storm the barricade and unseat the Crows but were unsuccessful; the Crows tried to drive the Sioux back across the river but were not sufficiently strong to carry the point. Finally the Dakotas had to give up and withdraw after a loss of five Oglalas and five Cheyennes.

No. 42

No. 42. Sioux-Crow Fights. Earliest Dates, 1856, 1858

First Arrow Creek Fight

A note in Lakota. Translation: "In Montana. The time the Crows made a barricade with their tents. This Crow was killed first. These are Cheyennes. This was in 1863. Oglalas, Miniconjous, and Cheyennes were together."

A close-up of three Cheyenne warriors pursuing a single Crow. The foremost Cheyenne (seen in the act of counting coup upon the unfortunate Crow) is High Back Bone (*Canku Wankatuya*); the second is Poor Elk (*Heraka Tama Heca*); and the third, Swinging Lame, or Limping (*Kapemini Huste*).

The stuffed bird (a blue hawk) worn by High Back Bone is his personal charm (*wotawe*).

The three names here given are the same as those of three prominent Dakota warriors who are mentioned elsewhere in this record, but these are Cheyenne allies.

No. 43

No. 43. SIOUX-CROW FIGHTS. EARLIEST DATES, 1856, 1858

First Arrow Creek Fight
A note in Lakota. Translation: "A Cheyenne. Brave Wolf is brought in pierced with arrows."

Another close-up, showing the Crows in pursuit.

Brave Wolf (*Sunkmanitu Ohitika*), a Cheyenne warrior who was with the Dakotas, charged into the ranks of the Crows, circled, and rode out again, followed by a hundred Crows. This was one of those reckless feats of so-called courage so dear to the hearts of the Plains fighters. Escape would have been a miracle. As the note indicates and the drawing shows, he was pierced by numerous arrows (*okagaga aupi*, "shot full of arrows"). He fell in midstream on his dash back toward his own lines. His comrades rushed to his rescue, but he was dead.

No. 44

NO. 44.   SIOUX-CROW FIGHTS. EARLIEST DATES, 1856, 1858

First Arrow Creek Fight

A close-up showing Brave Wolf charging the Crows.

This drawing should precede No. 43. Brave Wolf is seen lower right, riding toward the Crows. He Dog says he saw him thus and then saw him come back covered with Crow arrows.

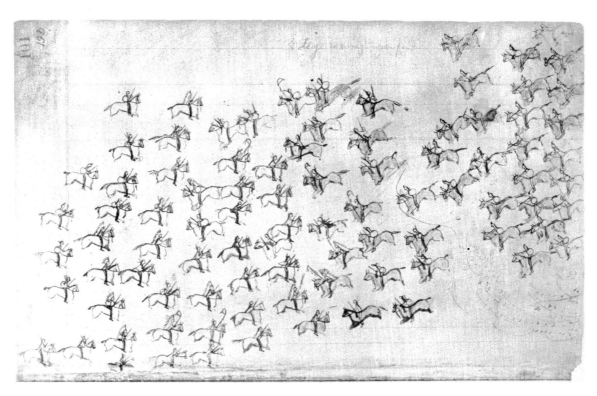

No. 45

NO. 45. SIOUX-CROW FIGHTS. EARLIEST DATES, 1856, 1858

First Arrow Creek Fight

A note in Lakota. Translation: "Attacked them right at their lodges."

A miniature showing the Dakotas and Crows op-posed, the Crows turning back the foremost Sioux.

This is the moment when the Dakotas have driven the Crows to their very doors, only to be stopped (cf. No. 41).

No. 46

NO. 46.   SIOUX-CROW FIGHTS. EARLIEST DATES, 1856, 1858

First Arrow Creek Fight
  Another portion of the fight shown in miniature;
again one of the charges in which the Sioux have the
advantage.

No. 47

NO. 47.   SIOUX-CROW FIGHTS. EARLIEST DATES, 1856, 1858

First Arrow Creek Fight

A note in Lakota. Translation: "This relates to when they [the Crows] were attacked in their lodges. Young Man Afraid of His Horses killed, at the camp, one who had his face painted black. His horse was wounded."

A close-up of Afraid of His Horses counting coup upon a Crow.

It happened that a few days before the Arrow Creek fight, a party of Crows had successfully attacked a party of Cheyennes and Arapahos. The

black paint on the face of the Crow here pictured was a sign of victory (quite generally practiced among Plains tribes). This warrior was one of the members of the previous war party and had done much killing. During this later fight, however, he was killed in one of the charges on the Crow camp. It is generally agreed that Afraid of His Horses was the man who killed him, because the Dakota's horse, with two bullet wounds in the breast (see drawing), was found lying dead beside the body of the Crow.

No. 48

NO. 48.   SIOUX–CROW FIGHTS. EARLIEST DATES, 1856, 1858

First Arrow Creek Fight

A note in Lakota. Translation: "He Dog killed a Crow with spotted hair."

Another close-up of a single exploit in the battle.

The expression "spotted hair" refers to the special hair decoration of porcupine quillwork or beadwork so often found among the Crows.

Although the drawing does not indicate it, He Dog says that this Crow was unusually richly arrayed. From the Crow's horse he secured a silver-mounted bit, and from the man himself a good warbonnet, a shield with eagle feathers, a sword (slightly bent!)—very likely the one with which he is counting coup upon him—and other less important bits of accoutrements.

No. 49

NO. 49. SIOUX-CROW FIGHTS. EARLIEST DATES, 1856, 1858

Notes in Lakota. Translation:

[1] Montana. They killed four Crows. They shot the horse of one. This was done by a Sioux. This was the one that charged and fell down. He almost stabbed one to death.

[2] 1864. Oglalas and Miniconjous.

[3] High Back Bone. Buffalo Head. One who was stabbed. Buffalo Walks in Sight.

A large-scale drawing showing an engagement in which a party of Dakotas overpower and kill four Crows.

High Back Bone (*Canku Wankatuya*), the mounted warrior who occupies the center of the drawing, killed one (for another characteristic costume worn by High Back Bone, see No. 42). Buffalo Walks in Sight (*Tatanka Tan Inyan Mani*) killed the second; he is seen striking him with a sword (right). This Crow had already stabbed a Dakota severely, cutting him from shoulder to hip (note the scarred figure at the right, labeled *le capapapi*, which means "this one was stabbed"). He Dog and Short Bull are of the opinion that it was Shawnee Horse (*Sawala Tasunke*) who killed this Crow, thus saving the life of the stabbed man; but the drawing indicates that Buffalo Walks in Sight was the man. Shawnee Horse is first named in the next drawing.

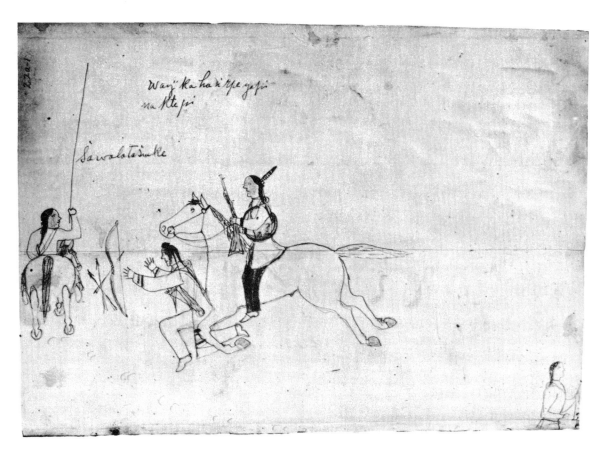

No. 50

NO. 50.   SIOUX-CROW FIGHTS. EARLIEST DATES, 1856, 1858

Two notes in Lakota. Translation: "Shawnee Horse. The captive was disrobed and killed."

A close-up of another exploit in the same fight.

Shawnee Horse ran down a Crow who was about to kill a Dakota. He is shown in the very act of running over the Crow.

No. 51

NO. 51.   SIOUX-CROW FIGHTS. EARLIEST DATES, 1856, 1858

Notes in Lakota. Translation: 1. "Four Crows were killed. No Dakotas lost their lives." 2. "He Dog of the Big Road band." 3. "This one also was captured."

Another close-up of the killing of a Crow.

This would seem to indicate that five Crows were killed. The note on No. 49 and the one on this drawing, however, state that there were four. The explanation without doubt is that He Dog (not the uncle of Bad Heart Bull, it is to be noticed; the latter had a band of his own) also counted coup upon one of the Crows.

No. 52

NO. 52.   SIOUX-CROW FIGHTS. EARLIEST DATES, 1856, 1858

A miniature of the complete engagement of the preceding drawings.

The first note on No. 51 belongs with this drawing also; it is half on one page, half on the other.

The four Crow figures (much elongated) can be seen stretched out between the two divisions of the Dakota party.

No. 53

No. 53.   Sioux-Crow Fights. Earliest Dates, 1856, 1858

A note in Lakota. Translation:

The intention in surrounding the three Crow Indians was to kill them, but only two were killed. One had a short carbine with which he shot and killed a chief by the name of White Tail Feathers [a Miniconjou]; he then made his escape [see No. 56]. At the present the names of those that were killed are to be seen written where they are lying. 1868.

The note introduces another fight series (Nos. 53 to 56).

At the right is a close-up of the Miniconjou warrior Buffalo Man (*Tatanka Wicasa*), who carries the official lance of the Sotka Yuha Society (cf. No. 25).

At the upper left is a "footnote" that really belongs to the following drawing (No. 54), to which it is connected by a red line.

No. 54

NO. 54. SIOUX-CROW FIGHTS. EARLIEST DATES, 1856, 1858

A note in Lakota. Translation: "Buffalo Man (nickname, Plume on Head) killed a Crow by stabbing him."

A close-up showing the Dakota stabbing the Crow. The "footnote" (in the upper left corner of No. 53) indicates that the Crow was killed and stripped.

No. 55

NO. 55.   SIOUX-CROW FIGHTS. EARLIEST DATES, 1856, 1858

Two short notes in Lakota. Translation: 1. "Was killed without doing any damage" (left). 2. "Three in company killed" (right).

A close-up of the killing of one of the three Crows.

The first note indicates that this Crow was put out of the way before he could do any damage to the Sioux.

The second note is not particularly significant to this drawing but is a general remark regarding the whole encounter: three people were killed in the skirmish—two Crows and a Dakota chief (see Bad Heart Bull's notes for Nos. 53 and 56).

No. 56

NO. 56. SIOUX-CROW FIGHTS. EARLIEST DATES, 1856, 1858

Two notes in Lakota. Translation: 1. "This one escaped and disappeared from sight" (left). 2. "White Tail Feathers" (center).

A close-up of the killing of the Miniconjou chief White Tail Feathers (*Situpi Ska*) by the Crow who afterward escaped.

According to He Dog and Short Bull, White Tail Feathers could easily have killed the Crow, but he wished to show his great bravery by counting coup upon him with the coup stick while he was yet alive.

He misjudged the time, the distance, and the Crow, however; the result was fatal. The Crow then escaped to the timber (timber is suggested in the usual way, by the thickly grouped ink marks in the upper left corner; the path of the escaping Crow is indicated by inked dashes).

A series of conventionalized hoofprints mark the path of White Tail Feathers in his circling of the Crow.

No. 57

NO. 57. SIOUX-CROW FIGHTS. EARLIEST DATES, 1856, 1858

Notes in Lakota. Translation:

[1] A war party killed two women. They probably were Crow women. One had a child.

[2] The warrior wearing the warbonnet is Charging Eagle.

[3] The other's name is White Calf.

[4] These two men were not related at the time, but later Charging Eagle married White Calf's sister.

[5] Oglala and Miniconjou.

A close-up of the two Sioux pursuing the women on horseback and striking them with Tokala bow lances.

The child is in a cradle hung from the saddle horn of the woman at the right.

It is said that there was a white man with these women, who was killed also, but the drawing does not show him. It is possible that he was married to one of the women. All of them were killed, however, even the baby.

The Crows were much incensed by the affair and ran the Sioux into the mountains as a result.

Charging Eagle (*Wanbli Watakpe*), the Miniconjou, is riding a pinto horse which was noted far and wide for its beauty, speed, and endurance. Short Bull remarks that this picture does not do it justice, that it was evenly marked in black and white and was an exceptionally good horse.

No. 58

NO. 58.   SIOUX-CROW FIGHTS. EARLIEST DATES, 1856, 1858

A large-scale drawing showing a battle in which the Dakotas are in hot pursuit of the Crows.

There is no note to identify the action. He Dog and Short Bull think that this and the next two drawings, which form a series, probably belong to the portrayal of the "Battle of the Big Dust," which follows (Nos. 61 to 78). I am inclined toward this conclusion also, for the general technique is much the same.

No. 59

No. 59.   Sioux-Crow Fights. Earliest Dates, 1856, 1858

A continuation of No. 58.

No. 60

NO. 60.   SIOUX-CROW FIGHTS. EARLIEST DATES, 1856, 1858

A large-scale drawing of two Dakotas driving off stolen horses.

This drawing would seem, without doubt, to belong to the following episode, though it is out of order (cf., especially, No. 62).

No. 61

NO. 61.   SIOUX-CROW FIGHTS. EARLIEST DATES, 1856, 1858

The Battle of the Big Dust
A note in Lakota. Translation:

Oglalas, Miniconjous, Sans Arcs, and Brulés on the warpath discovered a lone Crow herder with a large herd of horses. Red Shirt took after him and killed him; then he found that he was only a boy. The Sioux started to run off the horses. The Crows received news of what had happened and came in force to meet the Sioux. The Sioux lost twenty men, among them several chiefs—two shot from their horses.

A combination of extremely conventionalized miniature and close-up. Red Shirt (*Okle Luta*) killing the boy herder in the foreground; Crow camp and Sioux and Crow battle lines in background.

So many horses were being run off and so many men were taking part in the vigorous running fight that the dust rose in clouds "almost like smoke from a prairie fire"; consequently, it is frequently designated as the "Battle of the Big Dust."

The Miniconjous and Sans Arcs had combined against the Crows in this undertaking. Purely by accident, four Oglalas took part in the fight, having happened along, en route home from another horse-stealing expedition, just in time to join the party. The four Oglalas were Only Man (*Isnala Wica*), a brother of He Dog, Short Bull, and the elder Bad Heart Bull; High Hollow Horn (*Herlogeca Wankatuya*; see No. 37); Red Shirt (*Okle Luta*); and Crazy Horse (*Tasunke Witko*), not the famous leader but another man of the same name, a brother of Little Wound.

The translation of the note gives the main points of the encounter. That the battle was long and furious is evidenced by the following drawings, in which Bad Heart Bull presents details of the fighting.

The engagement took place in Montana where the Assiniboin Reservation now is, running from the upper Missouri River down to Dry Creek. Both He Dog and Left Heron agree that this fight took place before either Arrow Creek fight (consequently, it is somewhat out of chronological order). Left Heron places it definitely as sixty-eight years ago, i.e., 1861.

No. 62

NO. 62. SIOUX-CROW FIGHTS. EARLIEST DATES, 1856, 1858

The Battle of the Big Dust

A large-scale drawing showing three Dakotas driving off Crow horses, and an impressionistic miniature (upper right) showing a portion of the Crow camp.

No. 63

No. 63.   Sioux-Crow Fights. Earliest Dates, 1856, 1858

The Battle of the Big Dust
  Large-scale drawing of fighting.

No. 64

NO. 64. SIOUX-CROW FIGHTS. EARLIEST DATES, 1856, 1858

The Battle of the Big Dust

A close-up showing an exploit of Buffalo Walks in Sight (*Tatanka Tan Inyan Mani*); he is counting first coup on a Crow. Brave Bear (*Mato Ohitika*), designated here by his nickname, Sells His Gun (*Hunte Lo Wiyapeya*; see also No. 80), runs up from behind the first Dakota to count second coup with the bow lance of the Tokala.

No. 65

NO. 65.   SIOUX-CROW FIGHTS. EARLIEST DATES, 1856, 1858

The Battle of the Big Dust
   A close-up of two retreating Dakotas.

In the lower left corner is seen the Miwatani head-dress and "stake robe" (*wicicaske*; cf. No. 24).[43]

[43] Wissler, "Societies," pp. 41–46.

No. 66

NO. 66.   SIOUX-CROW FIGHTS. EARLIEST DATES, 1856, 1858

The Battle of the Big Dust

A large-scale drawing showing Dakotas fleeing from Crows.

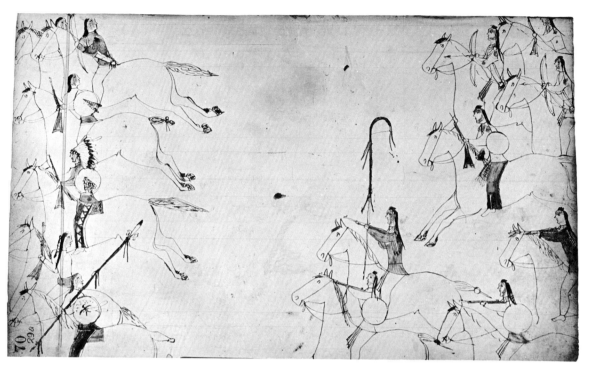

No. 67

No. 67.   SIOUX-CROW FIGHTS. EARLIEST DATES, 1856, 1858

The Battle of the Big Dust
  Dakotas still in retreat.

No. 68

NO. 68. SIOUX-CROW FIGHTS. EARLIEST DATES, 1856, 1858

The Battle of the Big Dust

A large-scale drawing intended to show that there was much running fighting—some in the valleys and some on the ridges. The separation of valleys and ridges is indicated by wavy division lines across the page. The lower portions of men and horses at the top of the page are not visible, a fact which indicates that high ground intervenes between the figures in the foreground and those in the background.

At the top (center) a Sioux is being scalped by Crows.

No. 69

No. 69.   Sioux-Crow Fights. Earliest Dates, 1856, 1858

The Battle of the Big Dust
   Another large-scale drawing showing the scattered fighting on both sides of the ridges (cf. No. 68).

Two Crows are preparing to scalp a Dakota (top right).

No. 70

NO. 70.   SIOUX-CROW FIGHTS. EARLIEST DATES, 1856, 1858

The Battle of the Big Dust
  Dakotas fleeing from Crows.

Here and throughout this series the face painting of the Crow warriors is plainly evident. The face is circled with red paint.

No. 71

NO. 71.   SIOUX-CROW FIGHTS. EARLIEST DATES, 1856, 1858

The Battle of the Big Dust
   The Dakotas seem to be holding the Crows for a
moment.

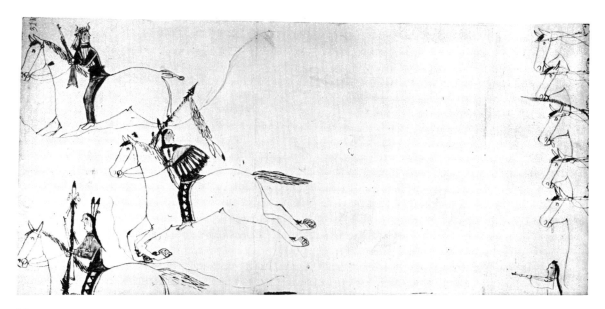

No. 72

NO. 72.   SIOUX-CROW FIGHTS. EARLIEST DATES, 1856, 1858

The Battle of the Big Dust
   Dakotas fleeing.

No. 73

NO. 73.   SIOUX-CROW FIGHTS. EARLIEST DATES, 1856, 1858

The Battle of the Big Dust

No. 74

NO. 74.   SIOUX-CROW FIGHTS. EARLIEST DATES, 1856, 1858

The Battle of the Big Dust

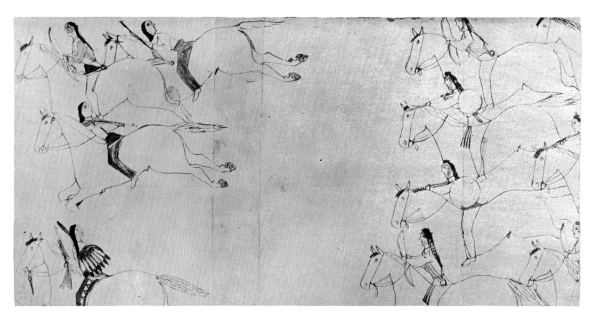

No. 75

NO. 75.   SIOUX-CROW FIGHTS. EARLIEST DATES, 1856, 1858

The Battle of the Big Dust

No. 76

NO. 76. SIOUX-CROW FIGHTS. EARLIEST DATES, 1856, 1858

The Battle of the Big Dust

A note in Lakota. Translation: "No particular happening shown."

Shows manner of fighting.

Drawing of Crow at upper right indicates the way in which the quiver was carried in battle.

No. 77

NO. 77.   SIOUX-CROW FIGHTS. EARLIEST DATES, 1856, 1858

The Battle of the Big Dust
  [The description for No. 78 erroneously was also

used for No. 77 in Miss Blish's manuscript.—*ed. note*]

No. 78

NO. 78.   SIOUX-CROW FIGHTS. EARLIEST DATES, 1856, 1858

The Battle of the Big Dust
    The eagle-feather head decoration and the fringed shirt of the Chiefs Society (lower left).[44]

Mantle bearing individual designation (upper left).

[44] Wissler, "Societies," p. 39.

No. 79

No. 79. Sioux-Crow Fights. Earliest Dates, 1856, 1858

A note in Lakota. Translation: "The deeds of Fool Heart, son of Lame Deer. He killed a horse thief near Powder River."

Miniconjous discovered a Crow stealing a horse. Fool (Crazy) Heart (*Cante Witko*) struck him first; Ghost Heart (*Cante Wanagi*) struck him second.

The "footnote" (lower left) is connected with the sketchy portrayal of the tipis of the Dakota camp and shows the dead or dying Crow horse thief lying prone upon his face while two Miniconjous take final shots at him.

The Lame Deer mentioned here is the prominent Miniconjou chief who headed the band of "hostile" Sioux that longest resisted General Nelson A. Miles in the campaign of 1877, in which Miles attempted to persuade or force all the still-roaming warrior Indians of the Northern Plains to surrender to government officials and take up reservation life (see No. 305 for an episode in this campaign).

The skirmish resulting in the death of Lame Deer—and, according to my Dakota informants, of this same son, Fool Heart—occurred "ten years after the killing of the Crow horse stealer." (This statement, of course, gives some idea of the time of the latter event, since we know that Miles's campaign was carried on in 1877.)

The story of the incident as I receive it from He Dog and Short Bull differs in certain details from Miles's own story of it[45] but agrees in several essential points. They agree that the time was the spring (May) "following Custer's death"; that the Sioux village was surprised by the troops; that Lame Deer fired at Miles but missed him and killed a soldier just behind the General; and that Lame Deer was killed. Miles describes what appeared to be an auspicious opening to the meeting. The troops made their surprise appearance with no show of belligerence, he says; and, at his command, the Indian scouts with him called out to the Dakotas that the troops were friendly and that no shot would be fired if no resistance were offered. Miles immediately rode up to Lame Deer and extended his hand. The Indian responded by giving his. But at that moment an ill-advised white scout behind Miles covered the Indian leader with his gun. Suspecting treachery, Lame Deer jerked away his hand and fired at Miles. The result was tragedy, of course.

Miles gives the number of Indians killed as fourteen and mentions no casualties among the troopers except the orderly who received the bullet from Lame Deer's gun at the first shot.

He Dog and Short Bull do not describe the amicable beginning of the scene. Neither do they mention any casualties among the Dakotas other than Lame Deer and the son, Fool Heart. They do report, however, that each of these two killed a trooper.

In spite of what appear to be slight discrepancies in detail, both accounts suggest a certain definite importance—and a certain element of tragedy—attaching to the event.

45 Nelson A. Miles, *Serving the Republic* (New York: Harper and Bros., 1911), pp. 160–163.

No. 80

No. 80.   Sioux-Crow Fights. Earliest Dates, 1856, 1858

A note in Lakota on bottom half of drawing. Translation: "One of two Crows who had entered the camp to steal Sioux horses was killed. The first person to strike him was Charging Eagle. Sells His Gun struck him second, on foot. 1857. Miniconjous."

Scattered notes in Lakota on top half of drawing.

Translation: 1. "Charging Eagle counted coup first." 2. "Killed a horse thief." 3. "At a place this side of the Little Powder River." 4. "One hiding" (extreme left).

Five Dakotas attack a Crow. Charging Eagle (*Wanbli Watakpe*) is counting coup upon him.

Sells His Gun (*Hunte Lo Wiyapeya*), whose proper name is Brave Bear (*Mato Ohitika*; see No. 64), is shown (lower right) approaching the Crow on foot to count coup second.

Roan Bear (*Mato Hinrata*), whose name is given in abbreviated form in the drawing (behind the Crow), is the mounted warrior (lower left) who counted

coup third. This man was an Oglala; the rest were Miniconjous.

At the extreme top (left) is seen a miniature mounted warrior making his escape ("the one hiding who escaped with his life," according to the note). This is the other of the two Crow horse thieves (see Bad Heart Bull's note on bottom half of drawing).

According to He Dog and Short Bull, this occurred about the time that Yellow Robe was killed, i.e., 1858 (cf. No. 35). The date here given is 1857. Obviously the drawing is out of chronological order.

No. 81

No. 81. Sioux-Crow Fights. Earliest Dates, 1856, 1858

Notes in Lakota. Translation: 1. "One Bear, an Oglala." 2. "The forks of the Missouri rivers. 1862."

One Bear (*Mato Wanjila*), an Oglala, met a Crow at the forks of the Missouri rivers and gave chase. Bad Heart Bull's "footnote" (lower left) indicates that One Bear did not kill the Crow but that he

captured the latter's horse and allowed the warrior to escape. Short Bull says, however, that the Crow was killed.

Short Bull and He Dog say further that One Bear is given special attention here because in this one year he killed a Shoshoni, a Ute, and a Crow.

No. 82

NO. 82. SIOUX-CROW FIGHTS. EARLIEST DATES, 1856, 1858

A note in Lakota. Translation: "Coming back with stolen horses."

A large-scale drawing showing the return of the Dakotas from a horse-stealing expedition.

The fact that there has been fighting is evidenced by the scalps hanging from the scalp sticks.

According to Short Bull, this expedition took place in about 1878.

No. 83

No. 83.   Sioux-Crow Fights. Earliest Dates, 1856, 1858

Large-scale drawing of the beginning of the triumphant entrance into the village on the return from the horse-stealing expedition (cf. No. 82).

Scalp locks are in evidence again.

He Dog and Short Bull believe the leading warrior to be Brave Wolf (*Sunkmanitu Ohitika*, literally "Brave Dog-of-the-Wilderness"), for this is his headdress. The last warrior, in fox-skin cap and purple tunic, they think is Little Bird (*Zintkala Cigala*), for he dressed in this fashion.

No. 84

No. 84. Sioux-Crow Fights. Earliest Dates, 1856, 1858

A note in Lakota. Translation: "It is generally the custom on the return from a successful war expedition for the returning warriors to charge at a run around the camp, firing guns as they go."

No. 83 continued.

A large-scale drawing showing a part of the charge, in the foreground. In the background, in semi-miniature, a portion of the camp circle, with women watching the charge.

It was the custom for the members of a returning war party to stop at some distance from the camp and garb themselves in battle array, and then to circle the camp at a run, shouting, firing guns, and displaying their trophies of war, to the admiration of those at home, especially the women.

According to Short Bull, the leading warrior in this portrayal is Bad Heart Bull the elder; his fox-skin charm (*wotawe*), falling from his left shoulder, is particularly noticeable here.

The last warrior in the line is Short Bull himself. On this particular expedition he captured a pinto horse, which he is riding, and secured a scalp with very long hair.

The second man in the line is Black Deer (*Tarca Sapa*). A flute, a personal charm (*wotawe*), hangs at his left side. The striking thing about it is that a bunch of feathers—arranged somewhat as for the banner on the Tokala bow lance—is suspended from the flute. This was at first intended for a banner on a lance, but since he had no wood for the lance, Black Deer tied the feathers to his flute. He, too, is riding an enemy horse.★

No. 85

No. 85. Early Social Life and Its Reorganization

A note in Lakota. Literal translation: "Kills and comes back. This is the way the Tetons dance for it."

This is a large-scale drawing of the Oglala version of the famous, Plains-wide Victory, or Scalp, Dance.[46] The interchangeableness of these two names and the literal translation of the Oglala name for the dance—"kills and comes back"—leave no doubt at all as to what constituted victory for the Indian.

The portrayal here follows the preceding charge in natural sequence.

A scalp, a hand, and a foot of enemies hang from the dance pole; the men (drummers) are grouped together in the circle (right); and many women—some bearing scalp sticks—take part in the dance.[47] The women are relatives of warriors lost in battle. A brief general discussion of the ceremony is to be found in Chapter III, p. 38; a technical discussion of Bad Heart Bull's composition is in Chapter IV, p. 52.*

[46] See, for example, Frances Densmore, "Chippewa Music. II," BAE Bulletin 53, p. 118, and "Teton Sioux Music," pp. 361–363; J. O. Dorsey, "Siouan Cults," p. 526; A. B. Skinner, "War Customs of the Menomini Indians," *Am. Anthrop.*, XIII (NS), 2 (1911), 309–310; Standing Bear, *My People*, p. 57; and Wissler, "Societies," pp. 27, 44, 80.

[47] Miss Densmore, J. O. Dorsey, and Skinner give considerable detail regarding the ceremonial preparation of the scalp.

No. 86

No. 86. Early Social Life and Its Reorganization

A note in Lakota. Translation: "How courting was done long ago."

A close-up showing three young men paying court to a Dakota girl in front of the family lodge.

As Richard I. Dodge puts it:

> It not infrequently happens that two or more lovers are paying their addresses to the same girl at the same time ... each possibly in plain view of the others, but each presumed by the fiction of the custom to be entirely concealed from all the world. The girl appears. A rush is made. A lover seizes her.[48]

[48] Richard I. Dodge, *Our Wild Indians* (Hartford: A. D. Worthington and Co., 1882), p. 196.

[49] Cf., e.g., Clark Wissler, "The Whirlwind and the Elk

If she does not accept the advances of the first, the next takes his turn, etc. Usually, as the drawing shows, several await their turns.

The rich attire of the young men shows that they possess some means. The hair ornament of the second one is a prominent detail in the sketch. This is an antelope-horn decoration called *wopeknaka*, and is a love charm (see also Nos. 8 and 207). The fork-horned animals are closely associated with love among the Dakotas.[49] Consequently, elk, deer, and antelope love charms are by no means uncommon.

in the Mythology of the Dakota," *Journal of American Folk-Lore*, XVIII, 71 (October–December 1905), 261–268.

No. 87

No. 87. Early Social Life and Its Reorganization

A note in Lakota. Translation: "Customs of the past."

Another large-scale drawing of a courting scene. Again several young men are waiting their turns. The outstanding and seeming incongruous item here is the umbrella.

The mounted hide thrown over the back of the first horse is a mountain-lion skin. These were much used in the early days but were rare at the time of this record.

No. 88

No. 88.   Sioux-Crow Fights. Earliest Dates, 1856, 1858

Two notes in Lakota. Translation: 1. "When on scouting trips, it is customary to go on foot. Women also go along." 2. "The one that carries the pipe is the leader."

The medicine pipe was always carried and used ceremonially on these expeditions. Here the leader presents it to the Great Spirit as the party sets forth.

The wolf- or coyote-skin headgear was a characteristic part of the paraphernalia of many scouts. It served to conceal the scout, especially when he was peering over the top of a ridge to see if enemies were in sight. The Plains Indians considered wolves and coyotes quite in the manner of friendly spirits.

Nos. 88 to 97 are a series depicting those activities which have to be governed by the *blota hunka*,[50] or leader, of a horse-stealing expedition.

[50] See Wissler's discussion (he uses the spelling *blotaunka*) in "Societies," pp. 54–61.

No. 89

NO. 89. SIOUX-CROW FIGHTS. EARLIEST DATES, 1856, 1858

Notes in Lakota. Translation:

[1] The place where the war party is resting [upper right].
    [2] Butchering the buffalo [left].
    [3] Cooking with paunch or tripe [right].
    [4] Heating the rocks [center right].
    [5] The cooked meat [lower right].

Scouting parties could not be burdened with kettles and other cooking utensils; consequently a special technique was developed for cooking on these expeditions. Frank Grouard gives a graphic and accurate description that serves well to accompany Bad Heart Bull's illustration of the way in which the problem was solved.

> After making a big fire with the buffalo chips, the Indians put rocks in the fire. Next they took the paunch out of a buffalo, and, after emptying it of its contents, turned it inside out and filled it about two-thirds full of water—it must have held fifteen or twenty gallons. Then they took four bows, stuck them in the ground and fastened them together at the top, and suspended the paunch . . . between the bows. As the stones were heated they were put into the water-filled paunch, and the same result was obtained as if the water had been placed in a tea-kettle . . . on top of a stove or over the fire. The stones were constantly changed. . . . The meat was put into the boiling water and cooked.[51]

A faint irregular border of green and brown in the background marks the line of a creek. Immediately in front of that, in miniature to indicate perspective, can be seen a group of temporary shelters of a sort erected on such occasions (cf. No. 92).

The foreground shows, in large scale, the operations in quartering and cooking the buffalo in order that the war party may be fed.

The notes explain quite effectively the various elements in the drawing. I shall need to call attention to but one or two details. The drawing shows that on occasion the paunch was hung from sticks other than bows (cf. Grouard). Beside the pile of rocks (right center) can be seen the forked sticks which were used for lifting the hot stones. After the meat was cooked, the pieces were dipped out and laid on branches and leaves near the fire (lower right).

[51] Joe DeBarthe, *Life and Adventures of Frank Grouard* (St. Louis: Combe Printing Co., 1894), p. 170.

No. 90

No. 90. Sioux-Crow Fights. Earliest Dates, 1856, 1858

A note in Lakota. Translation: "How a war party goes on foot."

A large-scale drawing very much resembling No. 88.

Miss Densmore explains thus the white blanket and hoodlike headdress that appear as common articles of apparel in both of these portrayals:

> When warriors were acting as scouts or wished for any reason to be unobserved [cf. horse-stealing episodes, Nos. 95 and 96], each wore a white cloth arranged like a blanket and frequently having eagle feathers fastened at the shoulders. Sometimes a separate cloth covered the head [sometimes in the form of a peaked hood, as Bad Heart Bull shows]. . . .
>
> If an open fight was expected the warriors put on their gayest regalia.[52]

[52] Densmore, "Teton Sioux Music," p. 350, Plates 51 and 59.

No. 91

No. 91.   Sioux-Crow Fights. Earliest Dates, 1856, 1858

A large-scale drawing showing one of the scouts
shooting an antelope.

No. 92

NO. 92. SIOUX-CROW FIGHTS. EARLIEST DATES, 1856, 1858

A note in Lakota. Translation: "A place where a war party is resting."

The temporary grass shelter (*pejin wakeya*; cf. No. 89) is plainly seen in the foreground. Long ago, warriors, when camping on scouting trips, made huts out of brush and bark covered with long grass. Sometimes these shelters were constructed so that a bank served as one wall.

Coyote and fox skins hang from the shoulders of the two scouts of the expedition (see scouts peering over hilltop with telescopes, right). As I have intimated elsewhere (see No. 88), these were often used for purposes of disguise. Skins were most valuable parts of warriors' equipment; they were used for masquerading purposes and for bed and covering.

No. 93

NO. 93. SIOUX-CROW FIGHTS. EARLIEST DATES, 1856, 1858

A note in Lakota. Translation: "A war party on horseback."

A large-scale drawing breaking into the strict sequence of the scouting series. The artist shows a mounted war party, that is, a war party proper, not a preliminary scouting party.

As the drawing indicates, in a mounted war party, the warrior leads his best horse, keeping him in reserve till a time of emergency.

No. 94

NO. 94.   SIOUX-CROW FIGHTS. EARLIEST DATES, 1856, 1858

Notes in Lakota. Translation: 1. "Scouts returning with news." 2. "Buffalo chips."

The leader, with the pipe, and the other members of the party are waiting in a group for the two returning scouts and the ceremonial giving of news. In the lower left corner is an odd, rather diagrammatic sketch indicating what has taken place preceding this meeting. There is a rounded object around which, leading from right to left, are footprints. The small rounded figure represents a particular hill in the vicinity (here the naïve disregard for perspective, for the sake of suggesting several steps in an episode, is evident). Around this hill the two scouts have made their way on their scouting trip.

Now they are returning to report their findings. Before reaching the group, they give the call of the coyote to announce their return (cf. Young Iron's return, Nos. 301 and 302). The drawing shows in the foreground, before the leader, a small pile of buffalo chips (*pte cekin heca*). The scouts approach and, without a word, kick or bow to the chips to show that they have performed their duties faithfully and will report truthfully. Then the pipe ceremony follows, in which the scouts smoke the pipe in silence in further guarantee of their truthfulness, before the actual recital of news.

The two scouts can be identified by their costumes as the head scouts of the preceding pages.

No. 95

NO. 95.   SIOUX-CROW FIGHTS. EARLIEST DATES, 1856, 1858

A large-scale drawing of the result of the scouting activities of the preceding pages.

The Dakotas are stealing horses at the very lodges of the enemy.

No. 96

NO. 96.   SIOUX-CROW FIGHTS. EARLIEST DATES, 1856, 1858

A note in Lakota. Translation: "Stealing at night."

Further portrayal of the actual stealing of the horses.

There is no doubt of the risks that are run on such expeditions as this. The scouts of the scouting party just described are leading in the work; they approach the enemy camp near enough to cut the tethers of the horses that have been tied to the tent-pins of the lodges themselves.

No. 97

NO. 97.   SIOUX-CROW FIGHTS. EARLIEST DATES, 1856, 1858

The Dakotas driving off the stolen horses. The
expedition has been a success.

No. 98

No. 98.   Early Social Life and Its Reorganization

A note in Lakota. Translation: "The Sacred Bow racing."

A miniature, diagrammatic drawing showing the performance—the "racing"—of the Sacred Bow ceremony.[53]

Stakes indicating the four cardinal points are set up at the inner edge of the camp circle; these represent enemies. The sacred lodge and the sweat lodge are placed at the center of the camp circle.

The Sacred Bow is looked upon with a decided awe, even a reverent fear. The bow itself and the ceremony are really strong medicine, charms for the accomplishment of important ends—usually in war.

There were among the Oglalas four such bows and four hangers which were used to support them when they were not in use. The bows were entrusted only to certain carefully chosen men, and numerous strict rules governed the bestowal and the entertainment of such an honor. The assignment of hangers was second only to the giving of the bows in solemn considera-

tion. The eight men (bow and hanger bearers) held office as long as possible. The duration of the term was usually not long, however, for the demands made upon the holders of the offices were so heavy that men could not long endure them; but the posts were vacated only by death or resignation. Quite in keeping with the fact that the organization was a military one, and that war medicine was its chief concern, was the stipulation that each officer must (1) lead in battle, (2) show great bravery, and (3) strike at least one or two enemies with the bow or hanger (this last was an especially serious undertaking, since in order to approach closely enough to touch an enemy with such an instrument—which, incidentally, was *not* a weapon—one opened himself to the possibility, almost the certainty, of being struck or shot himself). The life, needless to say, was a most strenuous one; and after proving himself unquestionably, the officer sometimes returned the bow—or hanger—to the shaman at the head of the organization, in symbol of his resignation. It was at such a time that the ceremony

[53] Clark Wissler, "Some Protective Designs of the Dakota," *APAMNH*, I, Part 2 (1907), pp. 50–52. For most of the data here, I am referring to unpublished notes of my

own, made on the Pine Ridge Reservation during the summers of 1928 and 1929.

usually was performed—as a combined resignation and initiation (for the newly appointed officer) ritual.

The race was run also, however, when new members who were not officers were received; in such cases it was for these new members especially a pledge of faith and fidelity. At the same time, however, it might be the fulfillment of a vow to a spirit power for the recovery of someone who was ill, or a prayer for power to fulfill vows, or a prayer for protection in time of great danger or power and protection in some great undertaking. This last is the chief purpose of the ceremony. For instance, the performance portrayed by Bad Heart Bull occurred shortly after the battle "When They [the Crows] Drove Them into Camp" (see Nos. 219–284). As part of the preparation for an expedition of revenge, the Dakotas danced the Sacred Bow.

Wissler gives a brief summary of some of the main features of the bow and the ornamentation and symbolism in the paraphernalia of the officers of the organization,[54] so I shall limit myself here, for the most part, to a sketching of the *form* of the *public ceremony*. After the usual rites of purification at the hands of the shaman (in the sweat lodge and sacred tipi), the runners of the race left the sacred lodge, ran to the west, struck and circled the post, ran back and circled the lodge, then ran to the north, struck and circled the post, returned to the center, and so on, till all four quarters had received homage. Then, as the last step, at the end of the race, the dancers

[54] Wissler, "Protective Designs."

entered the sanctified sweat lodge, where they received a final purification.

The ceremony was really more or less an endurance test for the performers, for the camp circle was large (sometimes a mile or more in circumference) and the performance was in truth a race. There was no regulation concerning the maintenance of a regular order in which the performers must run after the start, and one might pass others; the first man in won the race.

He Dog points out that the outstanding forces invoked symbolically in this rite were all death-dealing agents: the lightning, the wind, the hail, the snake, the bear; they show no mercy, and all of them are powers from the above except the last two. He also points out the importance of the swift-winged creatures of the air, as does Wissler; their use was in reality a prayer that the warrior might, like them, be swift in flight and hard to hit.

As is usually the case in the founding of ceremonies and organizations and various other sacred practices, this institution of the Sacred Bow came into existence as the result of a dream, in this case the dream of a powerful Dakota shaman, Black Road.

Probably, however, the original Sacred Bow organization was founded among the Southern Cheyennes as part of their Arrow Prophet tradition; thence it spread to a few Dakota bands which were in friendly contact with the Cheyennes. These Dakota organizations, however, possessed their own distinctive characters, for the new organizations were always tempered by the dream of the founding shaman and by traditions of the individual tribes.

itaži̇pa wakan yu Hakii yankapi

No. 99

No. 99.   Early Social Life and Its Reorganization

A note in Lakota. Translation: "The Sacred Bow racing."

Close-up of the opening of the Sacred Bow ceremony.

The four bow carriers, the four hanger carriers, and two extra men (probably the official club bearers of whom He Dog tells me but whom Wissler does not mention), who are to perform the ceremony, are shown in the opening rite. Just emerged from the sacred lodge, they stand facing the west, the right hand raised in appeal to the Great Spirit. Then they will start on their race toward the west.

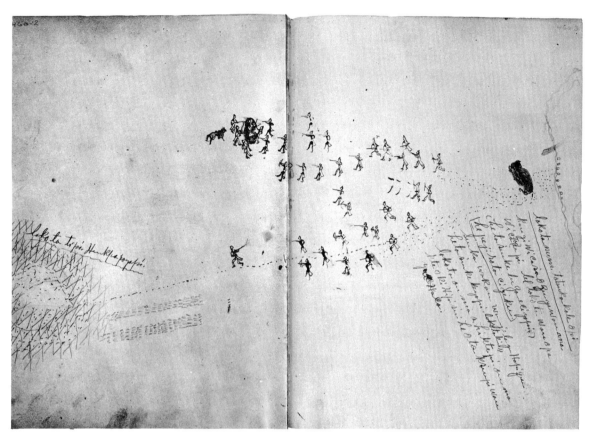

No. 100

No. 100. Sioux-Crow Fights. Earliest Dates, 1856, 1858

A note in Lakota. Translation:

Two Sioux killed this buffalo and were dressing it when they were surrounded by the Crows. A Sioux by the name of Fast Horse was with the Crows; he was a brother of Sage. The Crows had only one horse, and it is claimed that this horse belonged to Fast Horse. The Crows killed one of the Sioux, but the other got away because he had a good gun.

A two-page miniature of an attack upon two Dakotas by a war party of Crows.

The Sioux camp is seen in the lower left corner. At the extreme right the Crows are appearing over the brow of a hill. The center of interest is the two Dakotas and the dead buffalo.

Two Hunkpapa (Standing Rock) Sioux have killed a buffalo. While they are preparing to butcher it, a large party of Crows discover them and attack. One Dakota is killed, but the other, who has a very good repeating rifle, escapes to the home camp with news of what has happened.

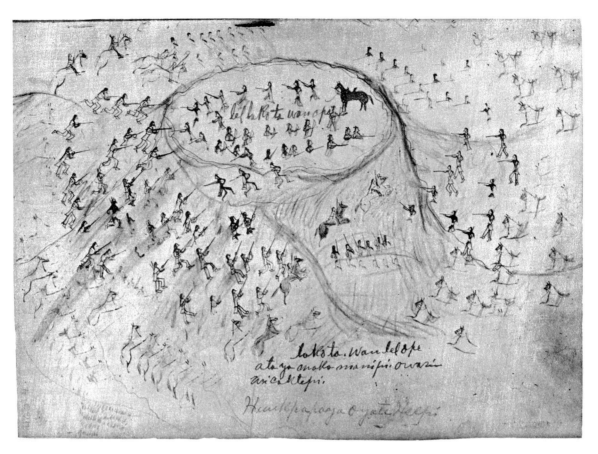

No. 101

No. 101. Sioux-Crow Fights. Earliest Dates, 1856, 1858

Notes in Lakota. Translation: 1. "A Sioux belonged in their party." 2. "They were all afoot [i.e., the Crows] and the whole party were killed."

A miniature sequel to No. 100.

The fight is the result of the previous attack by the Crows. The escaped Dakota returned to camp and reported what had happened. The thirty Crows and Fast Horse, an allied Dakota, had by that time left the scene of battle. The Sioux followed them all that night and the next day and night and finally, the next morning, chased them to the top of a butte (known as Sheep Mountain) at the mouth of Tongue River. There they besieged the Crows and finally killed them all, as well as Fast Horse and his horse.

According to Short Bull, this fight took place sixty-two years ago (1867), the year that Amos was born [sic].

No. 102

NO. 102. SIOUX-CROW FIGHTS. EARLIEST DATES, 1856, 1858

A note in Lakota. Translation: "Fast Horse and his horse."

A close-up of No. 101, inserted especially to show Fast Horse (*Tasunke Luza*), the traitorous Sioux, and his horse.

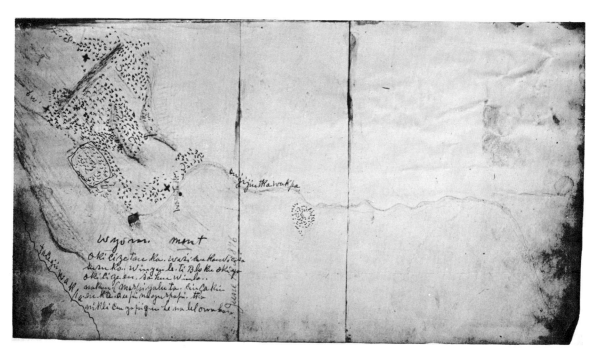

No. 103

No. 103. Early Social Life and Its Reorganization

The Battle of the Rosebud
   Notes in Lakota. Translation:

   [1] Rosebud Creek.
   [2] Tongue River.
   [3] Along the Rosebud and Tongue Rivers a fierce battle was raging between the white men and Shoshonis on one side and the Sioux and Cheyennes on the other. This Cheyenne woman helped her brother through the battle. Also about the same time, Red Cloud's son had coup counted upon him and was dragged from his horse but escaped with his life. These are pictured on this page. [And then somewhat parenthetically:] It was Crow Indians that treated Jack Red Cloud so.

A very small-scale miniature, in topographical, diagrammatic style, showing Crook's famous fight on the Rosebud, June 17, 1876.[55]

According to this version, the Sioux and Cheyennes were surprised by the troops and their Crow and Shoshoni scouts.

It is said that in this fight a Cheyenne girl entered the strife to help her brother. Her courage aroused the admiration of all who saw her. It is thought that the red crosses in this sketch mark the places where the girl performed particularly bravely.

[55] For an account of the battle from the Indian point of view, see George Bird Grinnell's *The Fighting Cheyennes* (New York: Charles Scribner's Sons, 1915), pp. 324–331. In tone and emphasis, this account is a fit companion for Bad Heart Bull's pictured version of the fight. For a general discussion, see John G. Bourke, *On the Border with Crook* (New York: Charles Scribner's Sons, 1892), pp. 311–318; Patrick E. Byrne, *Soldiers of the Plains* (New York: Minton, Balch and Co., 1926), pp. 52–57; and DeBarthe, *Frank Grouard*, pp. 233–242.

No. 104

No. 104. Early Social Life and Its Reorganization

The Battle of the Rosebud

A close-up showing the Cheyenne girl and her brother.

This fight is quite commonly known among the Dakotas as the "Fight Where the Cheyenne Girl Showed Great Courage."[56]

The two outstanding features of the battle, from the Indian point of view, are the Cheyenne girl's courage and the capture and escape of Jack Red Cloud (see Nos. 105 to 111).

[56] For another example of a girl's entering the fight, see Rain-in-the-Face's description in *The Teepee Book* (Sheridan, Wyo.: Mills Co., 1926), Official Publication, Fiftieth Anniversary, Custer Battle, National Custer Memorial Association, a souvenir booklet reprinted from *The Teepee Book*, II, 6 (June 1916), published by Herbert Coffeen of Sheridan, Wyoming.

No. 105

No. 105. Early Social Life and Its Reorganization

The Battle of the Rosebud
  A note in Lakota. Translation:

   This shows a fight that took place on the headwaters of Rosebud Creek in Montana against the Crows and Shoshonis. The enemies struck the son of Red Cloud, took his gun away from him, even pulled him from his horse. But he finally escaped.

Jack Red Cloud, son of the famous chief of the Oglalas, meeting a Crow scout in the Battle of the Rosebud.

No. 106

NO. 106. EARLY SOCIAL LIFE AND ITS REORGANIZATION

The Battle of the Rosebud
   The name Jack Red Cloud in English.
   A close-up of Jack retreating from the scouts.

No. 107

No. 107.   EARLY SOCIAL LIFE AND ITS REORGANIZATION

The Battle of the Rosebud
  The name Jack Red Cloud in English.
  A close-up of Jack being overtaken by a Crow.

No. 108

NO. 108. EARLY SOCIAL LIFE AND ITS REORGANIZATION

The Battle of the Rosebud

A note in Lakota. Translation: "Buffalo Hard to Hit."

The name Jack Red Cloud in English.

A close-up of Jack and the Crow, Buffalo Hard to Hit, fighting each other with their quirts in a running fight.

No. 109

NO. 109. EARLY SOCIAL LIFE AND ITS REORGANIZATION

The Battle of the Rosebud
Notes similar to those of No. 108.

A close-up of Jack being disarmed and dragged
from his horse by the same Crow and another.

No. 110

NO. 110.   EARLY SOCIAL LIFE AND ITS REORGANIZATION

The Battle of the Rosebud
   Notes the same as in Nos. 108 and 109.

A close-up of Jack's miraculous escape from the Crow scout.

No. 111

No. 111.   Early Social Life and Its Reorganization

The Battle of the Rosebud
   A note in Lakota. Translation: "Seven days after Jack's escape, Custer made his fatal charge."

The name Jack Red Cloud in English.
   A close-up of Jack riding back to his own people after his escape.

No. 112

NO. 112.   THE BATTLE OF THE LITTLE BIG HORN

Two notes in Lakota. Translation:

[1] A controversy arose among the Sioux. Some insisted that Custer charged on them the morning after the second night of their encampment on the Little Big Horn; others maintained that he came the first morning. *Milala* [Knife], whose correct name is King of the White Buffaloes [*Pte San Yatapi*], claims and proves that it was the morning after the second night, for on the first night he courted his wife and on the second she consented and eloped with him. He was not in the fight [left].

[2] This shows *Milala* eloping with his bride toward Fort Laramie. Next morning they could hear the roar of battle north of them [right].

A symbolic but at the same time realistic close-up. The left half shows *Milala* courting his wife; the right half shows them eloping the next night.

No. 113

No. 113. Early Social Life and Its Reorganization

A close-up, symbolic drawing of the "dream elk," or "spirit elk."

This is a bit from one of the visions that inaugurate a cultic performance.[57]

[57] Cf., e.g., Densmore, "Teton Sioux Music," pp. 172–198, and Wissler, "Protective Designs," pp. 43, 48–52, "Societies," pp. 81–99, and "Whirlwind and Elk," pp. 257–268.

No. 114

NO. 114. EARLY SOCIAL LIFE AND ITS REORGANIZATION

Another close-up of the "dream elk," or "spirit elk," associated with No. 113.

In the drawings of all three of these "spirit animals," the odd symbolic mark on the side of the body is plainly evident. Wissler says of this symbolic element:

> Another idea seems to be connected with the conception of the medicine-hoop, and that is the appearance of certain mythical animals with openings through their bodies where their hearts should be. The conception seems to be, that an animal without a heart is immortal and supernatural: at least this is the way the mythical elk was described.[58]

The elk was closely associated with the Indian idea of love and sexual passion (cf. No. 191). Supernatural power lay behind manifestations of sex desire; consequently, numerous mythical creatures were thought to control such power, and of these, the bull elk was the most important. The spider was another of these creatures of influence, one possessing special power over women because of its cunning.[59] Both elements in these "spirit" drawings by Bad Heart Bull are thus explained.

[58] Wissler, "Protective Designs," p. 43.

[59] Wissler, "Whirlwind and Elk," pp. 261–262.

No. 115

No. 115. Early Social Life and Its Reorganization

A medium-scale drawing of the performance of the cultic ceremony of the elk dreamers (for other portrayals of cultic animal-dreamer ceremonies, see Nos. 186, 187, 190, and 191).[60]

Such performances are given in response to someone's dream or vision in which he is told to test his medicine and the guardianship of the particular animal seen in vision.

He Dog says that before the fight on the Rosebud (see Nos. 103 to 111), some of the Dakotas performed a ceremony, which he saw, imitating the black-tailed deer, long-tailed deer, elk, and bear (the various animal dreamers usually combined in one celebration). This drawing is evidently the representation of a part of that ceremony (that of the black-tailed deer).

The time set apart for such a performance was known as a "Medicine Day."

The two female figures represent the "holy women," creatures who are characteristically a part of this sort of ceremony and who, incidentally, are regarded with a certain superstitious fear by the

[60] For animal-dreamer cults, see, for example, Wissler, "Societies," pp. 81–99.

people because of magic powers which they are supposed to possess. They carry the sacred medicine pipes in the ceremony, thus making an offering to the Great Spirit.

The erect, robed male figure (upper right) is the medicine man, the priest of the ceremony.

The squatting figure (lower left) is the "magic shooter," another medicine man, who tests the medicine power of the dancers. They attempt to dodge whatever he shoots at them, but if their medicine is strong, no injury will result even though they are hit. The "magic shooter" is really the evil-spirit element in the performance, and he is often put to flight by the onslaughts of dancers whose faith in their medicine or whose animosity adds strength to their courage and power.

These three dancers are all imitators of the black-tailed deer. The blue and black coloring indicates this conclusively. The headgear, the eagle feather in the right hand, and the hoop in the left hand are all characteristic of all the deer cults. The slight variations in the headgear and hoops of the individuals is a matter of personal dreams and tastes. The black figure (left) carries a small hoop and wears another larger one upon his head. The small circle at the center of this head hoop and those in the hand hoops of the other two dancers contain small mirrors. The mirrors, so it is said, possess the power to detect and track ill-feeling, so they are of great value, especially in such cases as this where the evil spirit is present to harass one and test his strength and power. At any rate, the mirror and the hoop have become closely associated as powerful medicine among the Dakotas.[61] The hoop (*cankle skan*) is the embodiment of the circle, which is the emblem of the fork-horned animals and is always prominent in their ceremonies.

Upon the hoop was placed the so-called "ammunition" of the dreamer (dancer), that is, the emblem of that with which he combated evil powers; this "ammunition" came in such forms as bear claws, eagle claws, grasshoppers, deer hoofs, and so forth—parts of animals or insects whose protective powers are especially potent for the particular individual.

The circle is again clearly seen in this drawing, painted on the body of the dancer at the extreme right.[62] It is doubtless painted upon the bodies of the other two dancers but is not here visible. In elk and deer imitations the circle must be worn "to make things complete," says He Dog, unable to explain further. A dancer could be hit on this spot by any kind of weapon or missile, and—if his medicine were really potent—he would not be killed. The name of this circle is *onte*, which means "causes death" (i.e., *to the one who tries to hit it*).

The small, leafy branches stuck into the ground bear offerings to the Great Spirit in the form of the purple or red banners which hang from them.

Relatively few people, says He Dog significantly, see visions which require the public ceremony and the subsequent practice of medicine.

[61] Wissler, "Protective Designs," pp. 40–43.

[62] *Ibid.*, p. 41.

No. 116

No. 116. Early Social Life and Its Reorganization

A note in Lakota. Translation: "A charge around camp before departure for battle."

Nos. 116 to 125 form a series of close-up drawings depicting the typical charge that took place before a large party went out on the warpath.

The formation and equipment in the charge are exactly as for entry into battle. After departure from camp, when the men are out of sight of the village, they halt and remove their finery and put it away in rawhide cases for safekeeping. Just before battle, they again halt and array themselves in their gayest and most complete regalia. This latter operation requires considerable time because of the numerous regulations and taboos regarding the equipment of society officers.

The stream indicated in the drawing is the Greasy Grass (*Peji Sla Wakpa*), i.e., the Little Big Horn. This might possibly indicate that the charge was somehow related to the Custer affair. He Dog and Short Bull, however, think that the young artist was simply portraying a typical charge, not a particular one. Whatever his intention, he shows in great detail the manner of behavior and of costume and adornment. Lances of various societies are evident, types of headdress, scalp decorations on bridles, painting of men and horses, shields, and so forth appear in the various drawings.

No. 117

NO. 117.   EARLY SOCIAL LIFE AND ITS REORGANIZATION

The charge around camp before departure for war.

The leading rider on the left wears the headdress and the feather bustle of the Omaha Warrior Society (cf. No. 31);[63] the second rider on the right carries the bow lance of the Tokala (cf. No. 30);[64] the third rider on the right, the straight lance of the Kangi Yuha (cf. No. 29).[65]

[63] Wissler, "Societies," pp. 49–52.
[64] *Ibid.*, pp. 14–23.

[65] *Ibid.*, pp. 23–25.

No. 118

No. 118. Early Social Life and Its Reorganization

Charge around camp before departure for war.

The hoofprints on the flank of the first horse on the right indicate that the warrior has brought in that many captured enemy horses. The two center riders belong to a group made up of men who, through a vision, have received their powers from the sky gods, the storm gods. All the markings of face and body and of the body of the horse represent storm forces; even the decoration in the men's hair and the forelocks and tails of the horses is a small leguminous plant which is closely associated with the thunder power. The peculiar arrangement of the hair is supposed to represent the manner in which the light-ning arranges the hair when it strikes a person. Instead of appareling themselves in rich garments, as is quite characteristic of Dakota warriors generally, the braves of this cultic group go into battle almost naked, wearing only moccasins and breechcloth; for the rest, the painting of the body is their only covering. The spots painted upon the neck, shoulders, and flanks of the horses represent hail. The forked-lightning symbol down the shoulders and flanks of the horses is obvious. This symbol appears, too, on the faces of the men. The spots on the faces and chests of the men represent rain or hail (cf., e.g., Nos. 121, 122, etc.).

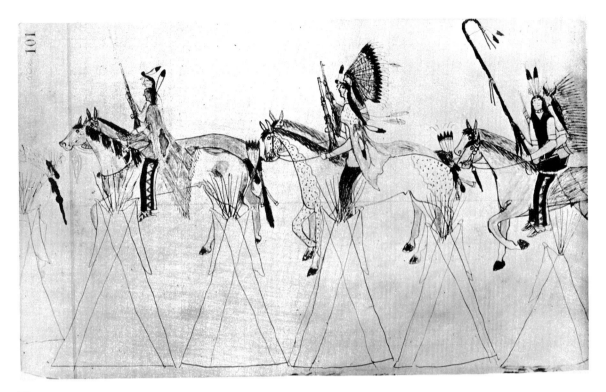

No. 119

NO. 119. EARLY SOCIAL LIFE AND ITS REORGANIZATION

Charge around camp before departure for war.

No. 120

NO. 120. EARLY SOCIAL LIFE AND ITS REORGANIZATION

Charge around camp before departure for war.
The first horse (right) bears the mark of the Sacred
Hoop upon shoulder and flank (cf. No. 115).

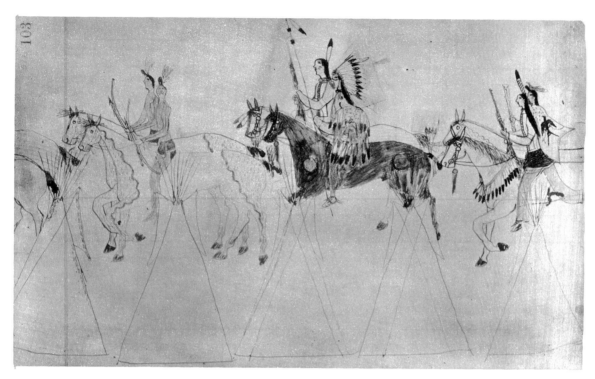

No. 121

No. 121. Early Social Life and Its Reorganization

Charge around camp before departure for war.
Parallel lines on the flanks of horses indicate the
number of enemies killed by the rider.

No. 122

No. 122. Early Social Life and Its Reorganization

Charge around camp before departure for war.

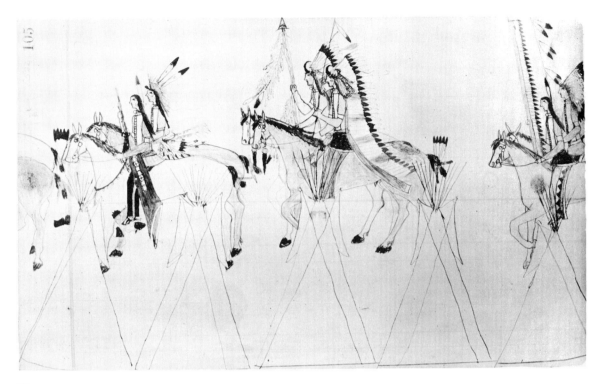

No. 123

NO. 123.   EARLY SOCIAL LIFE AND ITS REORGANIZATION

Charge around camp before departure for war.

No. 124

NO. 124. EARLY SOCIAL LIFE AND ITS REORGANIZATION

Charge around camp before departure for war.

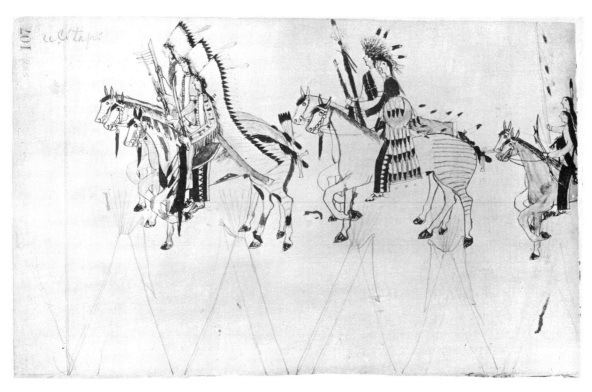

No. 125

No. 125. EARLY SOCIAL LIFE AND ITS REORGANIZATION

A note in Lakota. Translation: "Charge around camp."

The rider at the right in the second rank wears the owl-feather headdress of the Miwatani Warrior Society (cf. No. 24).[66]

[66] Wissler, "Societies," pp. 41–48.

This completes the charge series.

According to He Dog and Short Bull, these charges before battle were led by four men who had led in battle, and they were concluded by a rear guard of four equally brave men. This distribution was intended to show that brave men lead in battle and that brave men guard the rear.

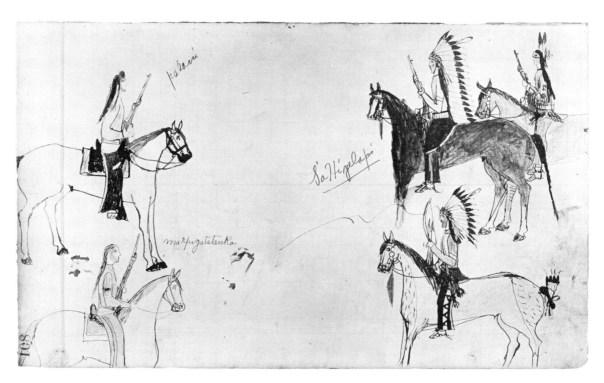

No. 126

No. 126.   The Battle of the Little Big Horn

Lakota words. Translation: 1. "Ree." 2. "Buffalo Cloud." 3. "Cheyennes."

A close-up of rather symbolic nature, apparently representing the various tribes of Indians, other than the Dakotas, that opposed each other in the Custer fight.

At the upper left is a Crow scout, distinguishable by the Crow hair arrangement. The word *Palani*, meaning "Ree," which appears beside this figure should accompany the lower figure (left). This Indian was a Ree, also a scout, whose name, as another note shows, was Buffalo Cloud (*Marpiya Tatanka*). The three warriors opposite them are Cheyennes. These latter, of course, were allied with the Dakotas.

The Ree scout, Buffalo Cloud, according to He Dog, took part in the Reno fight and retreat. He probably was especially noticed in the fighting and is given special attention here because he spoke Dakota.

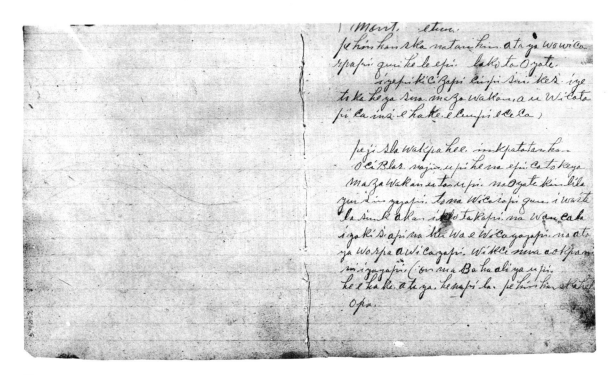

No. 127

NO. 127. THE BATTLE OF THE LITTLE BIG HORN

Notes in Lakota introductory to the drawings which portray the battle. Translation:

[1] In Montana. When Long Hair [i.e., Custer] came charging on us, all of his men were killed. This is they [referring to ensuing drawings]. The Indian nation did not wish to fight; it is always they [the whites] that start shooting first and the Indian who starts last.

[2] Along this [stream, outlined in pencil] is the head of the Greasy Grass. They came in this fashion [see No. 128], all abreast. This is they who started shooting first and surprised the Indian tribes. All those who pretended to be men got their horses and got ready and met them with a shout and charged. The battle followed. In the first battle [Reno's first charge] perhaps ten got away. In another battle [the fight with Custer's command] all of those who came along the ridge were killed. Long Hair was with them.

No. 128

No. 128. The Battle of the Little Big Horn

A note in Lakota. Translation: "Long Hair came with a challenge."

The opposing forces drawn up as facing. The names of General Custer, Crazy Horse, and Sitting Bull are written in, in English.

The drawing is, of course, not literal, but symbolic, designed as a pictorial title to indicate the principals in the action.

Many reports of the battle say that Sitting Bull was not in the actual fighting but that he was out in the hills "making medicine."[67] This seems reasonable, since he was not primarily a fighting man but a medicine man and an agitator. However, He Dog insists that Bad Heart Bull's record is correct in showing Sitting Bull as in the battle; he says that the Hunkpapa leader did take part and that he himself saw him during the fighting. Red Cloud, according to He Dog, was the only prominent chief who was not engaged.

According to numerous reports,[68] the troops on their way to the fatal encounter discovered a Sun Dance field which had been but recently used. Sitting Bull was the notable devotee in this performance of the ritual, says He Dog, and it was in connection with this dance that he received the vision which caused him to prophesy the coming of the forces of General Custer and their defeat by the Indians. Certainly Custer's approach and the attack were not a surprise, in spite of the implications of the introductory note, No. 127.★

[67] See, for example, "Lost and Won," by Colonel Charles Francis Bates, reprinted from the *New York Times* of June 20, 1926, in a pamphlet of reprints entitled *Fifty Years After the Little Big Horn Battle*, prepared for the anniversary of 1926 by the National Custer Memorial Association.

[68] See, for example, Edward S. Godfrey, "Custer's Last Battle," *Century Magazine*, XLIII, 3 (January 1892), 358–384.

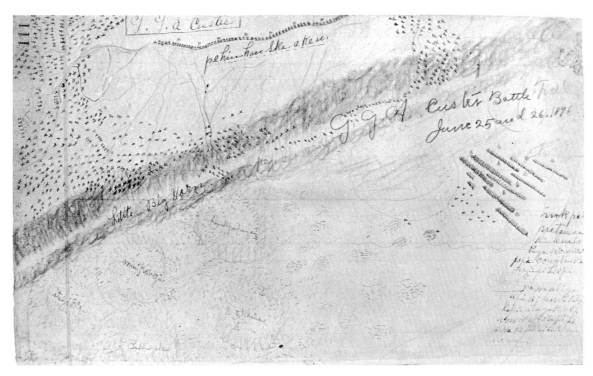

No. 129

No. 129. The Battle of the Little Big Horn

Notes in Lakota at the right margin:

[1] The ones [Indians] who were shot off their horses in the charge upstream were Big Design and Large Wound with Guts.

[2] They [the white soldiers] were surrounded on a hill and all of them were killed. [This was Custer's command, of course.]

[And at the top center:]

[3] Again comes Long Hair.

A topographical and quite conventionalized and schematic sketch showing the river, the position of the Indian camps, Reno's first charge, Custer's approach along the ridge (upper center), and the last, entrenched position of Reno's troops from which they were rescued by Terry's column (upper right).

Five camp circles plainly visible near bank of stream (lower left): the *Itazibco*, or Sans Arc Dakotas; the *Minikowoju*, or Miniconjou Dakotas; the *Hunkpapaya*, or Hunkpapa Dakotas; the *Sahiyela*, or Cheyennes; and the *Oklala*, or Oglala Dakotas.

At right center, red-inked and penciled marks in rows form a conventionalized portrayal of Reno's troop, with colors flying, marching to the attack of one end of the village.

Upper center, a conventionalized representation shows Custer's column advancing along the top of the ridge above the river, in plain view of the Indians.

The odd, massed crosses scattered from the upper left down and along the river are highly conventionalized mounted Indian warriors. It is to be noticed that they greatly outnumber and almost surround Custer's command.★

[215]

No. 130

NO. 130. THE BATTLE OF THE LITTLE BIG HORN

A note in Lakota designating individual figures. Translation: "One of the leaders."

A drawing showing Crazy Horse and Sitting Bull (cf. footnote 67, page 214) mounted before their warriors.

Mounted horsemen frame the composition on three sides: right, left, and bottom. The immediate foreground bears the portrayal of a row of mounted horsemen seen from the rear—one of Bad Heart Bull's panel effects.★

No. 131

No. 131.   The Battle of the Little Big Horn

A Lakota note relating to ranks of mounted cavalrymen followed by two Sioux. Translation:

These are the ones from up the river [Reno's command]. This is the way the Indians met them [the word used implies that the soldiers were shot from their horses].

The three who met them first were Kicking Bear [*Mato Wanartaka*], Hard to Hit [*Oosicela*], and Bad Heart Bull [*Tatanka Cante Sica*].

Kicking Bear was a member of Big Road's band, the *Oyurpe*, and is the same man who was prominent in the fighting in the Bad Lands at the time of the Ghost Dance trouble of 1890 (cf. No. 315).★

No. 132

No. 132. The Battle of the Little Big Horn

A two-page sequel to No. 131 in subject and technique. The only notations are the names of the three Dakota heroes at the right, the first two given in English, the third in Oglala: Bad Heart Bull, Kicking Bear, and *Oosicela* (see No. 131).

The note on the preceding drawing rightfully should accompany this larger drawing, for this composition shows the three Indians actually turning the troops back; the ranks are broken, and the soldiers are retreating at a gallop, many of them firing into the air.

No. 133

NO. 133.   THE BATTLE OF THE LITTLE BIG HORN

This drawing and Nos. 134, 135, and 136 constitute a sequence, homogeneous in character and technique, which continues the two compositions immediately preceding.

This group belongs to the artistically inferior group of drawings which, in my discussion of Bad Heart Bull as an artist, I have called insert series No. 2

(see Chapter IV, pp. 45–46).

From No. 133 to No. 169, Reno's retreat is being portrayed in its various stages, the confusion and utter demoralization becoming more and more evident. I shall not discuss every page in detail but shall confine myself to those drawings which bring out particularly interesting or significant points.

No. 134

No. 134.   THE BATTLE OF THE LITTLE BIG HORN

The retreat of Reno's command.

No. 135

No. 135.   THE BATTLE OF THE LITTLE BIG HORN

The retreat of Reno's command.

No. 136

No. 136.   THE BATTLE OF THE LITTLE BIG HORN

The retreat of Reno's command.

No. 137

No. 137.   The Battle of the Little Big Horn

The first of four drawings of insert series No. 1 (see Chapter IV, pp. 45–47, and cf. No. 133).

The colors in these compositions are less vivid than in most of the large-scale drawings, and the outlines are somewhat heavier in general.*

No. 138

NO. 138. THE BATTLE OF THE LITTLE BIG HORN

A note in English: "Custer Battle Field. June 25 and 26, 1876."

The leading Indian horse, with the rider wearing the red mantle, and the unmounted cavalry horse (upper right) are evidently late additions to the page, for they belong to insert series No. 2 instead of to the one in which they are found (see No. 133).

No. 139

NO. 139.   THE BATTLE OF THE LITTLE BIG HORN

A warrior in the eagle headdress and the fringed shirt of a shirt wearer of the Ska Yuha Society (lower right); appropriately, too, he rides a white horse, characteristic of the Ska Yuha members, or White Horse Owners.[69]

On this page also there have been inserted (left) several horse heads of the type found in insert series No. 2.

[69] Cf., e.g., Wissler, "Societies," p. 41 (see also pp. 38–41).

No. 140

No. 140. The Battle of the Little Big Horn

The retreat of Reno's command.★

No. 141

NO. 141.   THE BATTLE OF THE LITTLE BIG HORN

The retreat of Reno's command.

No. 142

NO. 142.   THE BATTLE OF THE LITTLE BIG HORN

The retreat of Reno's command.

No. 143

No. 143. The Battle of the Little Big Horn

The retreat of Reno's command.★

No. 144

No. 144.   THE BATTLE OF THE LITTLE BIG HORN

The retreat of Reno's command.*

No. 145

NO. 145.   THE BATTLE OF THE LITTLE BIG HORN

The retreat of Reno's command.*

No. 146

NO. 146.   THE BATTLE OF THE LITTLE BIG HORN

A note in English reads: "Custer Battle Field. June 25 and 26, 1876."

Below this is a mounted warrior marked "Crazy Horse" (cf. drawings of Crazy Horse, Nos. 128, 130, 171, and 183).

Again, several horse heads have been inserted at the left.*

No. 147

NO. 147.   THE BATTLE OF THE LITTLE BIG HORN

A note in English reads: "Custer Battle Field. June 25 and 26, 1876."

A warrior (upper left) counting coup on a soldier with his bow.

Numerous inserted horse heads (left).★

No. 148

No. 148. The Battle of the Little Big Horn

A trooper is being dragged from his horse by a Dakota on a green horse (extreme right).

James Wilber, a survivor of the Custer fight, says, in speaking of the Reno retreat: "It was a wild rush for the river with Indians on all sides, yelling like devils, shooting into our ranks, and even trying to drag men from their horses."[70]★

[70] Colonel Henry Hall, "Reminiscences," in *The Teepee Book* (Sheridan, Wyo.: Mills Co., 1926), Official Publication, Fiftieth Anniversary, Custer Battle, National Custer Memorial Association, a souvenir booklet reprinted from *The Teepee Book*, II, 6 (June 1916), published by Herbert Coffeen of Sheridan, Wyoming.

No. 149

NO. 149.   THE BATTLE OF THE LITTLE BIG HORN

The retreat of Reno's command.★

No. 150

No. 150. The Battle of the Little Big Horn

Two manners of wearing the fox-skin charm (*wotawe*).

The first warrior (upper right corner) wears his hung from his neck down his back.

The second warrior (top center) wears his around the waist, head and tail meeting in the back. This, very likely, is Bad Heart Bull the elder, for quite characteristically he wore his fox skin (the Tokala emblem) in this fashion (see also Nos. 132 and 165).

No. 151

No. 151.   The Battle of the Little Big Horn

The retreat of Reno's command.*

No. 152

No. 152. The Battle of the Little Big Horn

The retreat of Reno's command.

No. 153

NO. 153. THE BATTLE OF THE LITTLE BIG HORN

The retreat of Reno's command.

No. 154

NO. 154.   THE BATTLE OF THE LITTLE BIG HORN

The retreat of Reno's command.

No. 155

NO. 155. THE BATTLE OF THE LITTLE BIG HORN

The retreat of Reno's command.

No. 156

NO. 156. THE BATTLE OF THE LITTLE BIG HORN

The retreat of Reno's command.

No. 157

NO. 157. THE BATTLE OF THE LITTLE BIG HORN

The troopers being driven across the river.

The effectiveness of this composition is seriously minimized by the artist's insertion of many of the large, clumsy horse heads of the type of insert series No. 2. They appear noticeably all along the left portion of the river, as though the animals were just emerging from the water. The result is an effect of technical confusion (cf. my discussion in Chapter IV, pp. 46–47).

No. 158

NO. 158.   THE BATTLE OF THE LITTLE BIG HORN

A companion piece to the preceding: troopers being driven across the river.

The composition is essentially like No. 157. At the upper left, particularly, a mass of ungainly horse heads has been inserted. Confusion is the outstanding note.★

No. 159

NO. 159.   THE BATTLE OF THE LITTLE BIG HORN

A sketchy drawing showing numerous half-stripped dead soldiers lying about the field.

No. 160

No. 160. The Battle of the Little Big Horn

Notes in Lakota. Translation:

[1] Running Eagle shot him [from the rear] [lower left].

[2] Young Skunk killed him [meaning that Young Skunk, the warrior in the fringed mantle, first struck the enemy's body, thus counting coup upon him] [upper center].

[3] Runs Fearless [the warrior on the black horse] struck second [lower right].

Center left, a Ree scout (*Palani heca*).

Upper left, an unhorsed Cheyenne warrior (*Sahiyela*). The hoofprints of his horse lead past the fallen Ree and to the left. Probably the Ree shot the Cheyenne as he dashed past trying to count coup upon him.

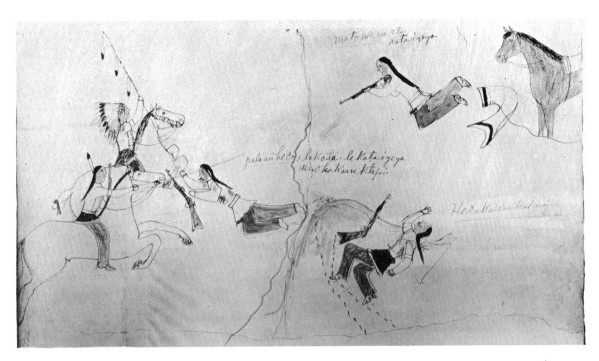

No. 161

No. 161. The Battle of the Little Big Horn

Notes in Lakota. Translation: 1. "This is a Ree Indian who shot a Sioux and then was killed or struck afterward" (center; cf. No. 160). 2. "Elk Stands Above" (right).

The irregular brown lines and the knoll-like formation at the center of the drawing would seem to indicate that this episode took place in the rough ridge country back from the river.

The center, fallen figure is the Ree scout. Four Dakotas have surrounded and attacked him. He has succeeded in killing one, whose name is Elk Stands Above, but the others kill him. The red dotted lines leading up the hill mark the paths of the two Indians who have been killed.

No. 162

No. 162.   THE BATTLE OF THE LITTLE BIG HORN

The retreat of Reno's command.★

No. 163

No. 163. The Battle of the Little Big Horn

A penciled note in Lakota. Translation: "A Ree."
The portrayal of a mounted Ree scout beset by a party of Dakotas and Cheyennes (above).

Four Dakotas leading back captured cavalry horses (below).

No. 164

NO. 164.   THE BATTLE OF THE LITTLE BIG HORN

Two of Reno's most belated troopers being overtaken by Dakota warriors.

The bird head decoration is a stuffed dark hawk. This, like the fox skin, was worn as a personal charm (*wotawe*). It was the characteristic head adornment of the Oglala warrior Soldier Hawk (*Cetan Akicita*). Such articles of adornment, since they were individualistic in character and appearance, played no small part in deciding questions of identification during fights or on other occasions.

No. 165

NO. 165. THE BATTLE OF THE LITTLE BIG HORN

Notes in Lakota. Translation: 1. "Bad Heart Bull, killing" (left). 2. "Ree" (i.e., Arikara). Bad Heart Bull the elder is counting coup upon one of the Ree scouts and killing him.

Here again Bad Heart Bull's personal charm, the fox skin, can be seen worn in his characteristic and peculiar manner.

No. 166

No. 166.   THE BATTLE OF THE LITTLE BIG HORN

Warriors leading back captured cavalry horses.★

No. 167

No. 167.   THE BATTLE OF THE LITTLE BIG HORN

A portion of the field (Reno's fight) covered with
dead troopers and wounded troopers and horses.

No. 168

NO. 168.   THE BATTLE OF THE LITTLE BIG HORN

A portion of the field after Reno's retreat. Bodies
of troopers are strewn about the ground. Warriors
are capturing and leading away horses of the troopers.

No. 169

NO. 169.   THE BATTLE OF THE LITTLE BIG HORN

A portion of the field after Reno's retreat. The
half-stripped bodies of troopers lie about the ground.
Warriors are leading away captured cavalry horses.

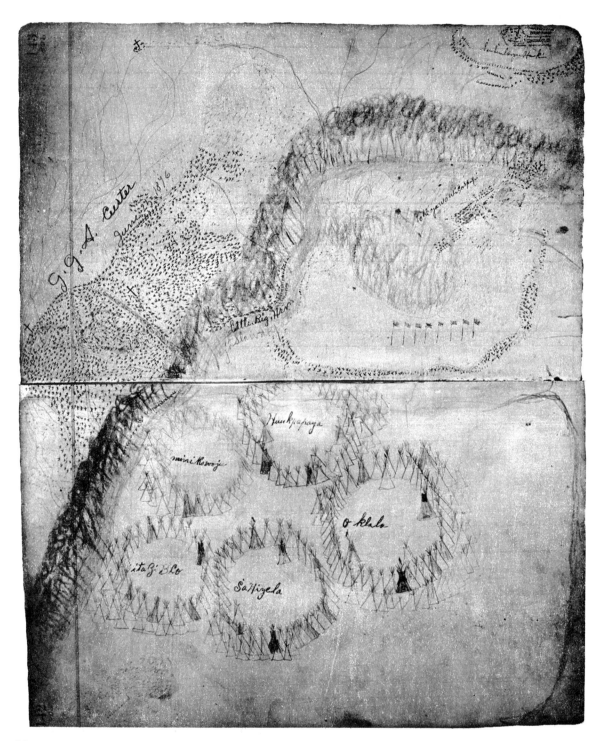

No. 170

No. 170.   THE BATTLE OF THE LITTLE BIG HORN

A second topographical portrayal of the Little Big Horn battleground, introducing the second Custer series. This is practically a replica of the first (No. 129) but is drawn in a somewhat larger scale, shows one or two additional details, and bears one or two more notes in Lakota.

Translation of note at right: "The first ones killed," or, literally, "The first ones shot off their horses."

The literal expression indicates the conclusive way in which the Indians overpowered the whites. This note accompanies the series of ranked dots in red which mark the path of Reno's approach and retreat.

Translation of inscription in upper right corner: "The ones who have the mules," i.e., the pack train.

A group of very small, clustered red and black marks represents the barricaded remnant of Reno's troops and the pack train in the besieged position from which Terry's command later rescued them. The circle of small black crosses surrounding them represents the line of mounted attacking warriors.

The red crosses lower on the page and at the left concern the scene of the fight of Custer's own command. They without doubt mark spots where the fighting was particularly heavy or where some of the most prominent men fell. The lone cross at the top of the page probably marks the place where the last white man alive (according to Dakota tradition) killed himself (see Nos. 184 and 185).

No. 171.   The Battle of the Little Big Horn

Dramatic portrayal of the gathering of the Indian fighters for the charge against Reno. Before the curved line of battle, Sitting Bull (left) and Crazy Horse (right) face their warriors with right arms upraised in appeal or admonition, while other leading fighters dash back and forth inspiring the warriors to action.

A heavy blue line in crayon along the left side of the page marks the river.

At least a hundred miniature horses and riders appear in this composition. Most of the figures are outlined with indelible pencil, so that a dull purple is the prevailing color tone of the drawing. A number of the figures before the battle line are sketched in black ink, however. All of the coloring, aside from the purple of the indelible pencil, is done with crayons.

[Drawing No. 171 is missing from Miss Blish's manuscript and from all other known collections of reproductions of Amos Bad Heart Bull's drawings.— *ed. note*]

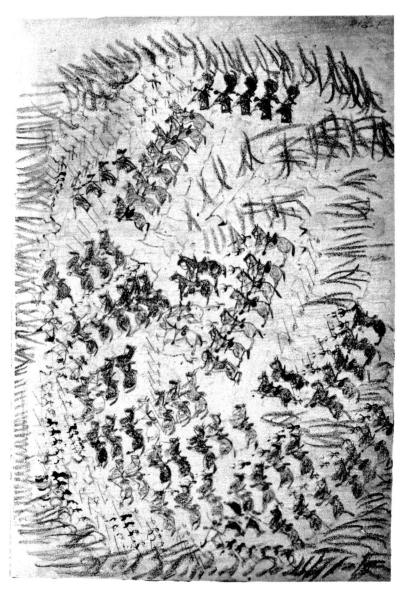

No. 172

No. 172.   THE BATTLE OF THE LITTLE BIG HORN

Reno's force dismounted and fighting from cover
of timber after the first volley has been answered.

No. 173

No. 173. The Battle of the Little Big Horn

The next moment in the Reno episode.

Hard pressed by the onsweeping Dakotas, the troopers desert the cover of the wood and, on horseback and on foot, run for the protection of the rough country across and back from the river, while the Indians follow close at their heels.

No. 174

No. 174. The Battle of the Little Big Horn

The retreat has become a mad rout. Many of the cavalry horses are now riderless, and the Indians are thoroughly mixed with the fleeing troopers as they approach the river.

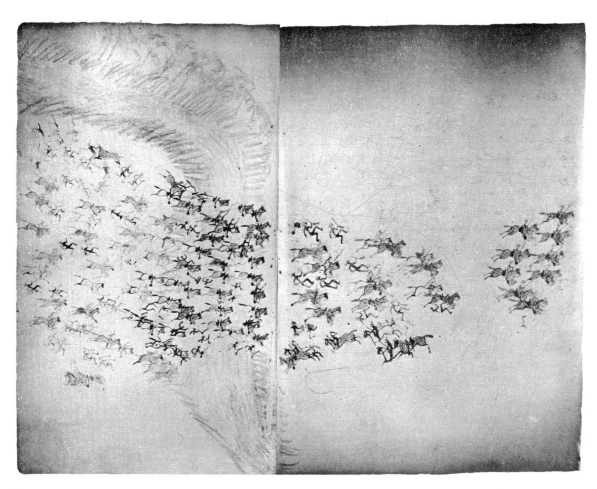

No. 175

NO. 175.   THE BATTLE OF THE LITTLE BIG HORN

A two-page composition telling the story of the last stages of the retreat. The soldiers are being driven across the river. Many an Indian can be seen riding back, leading a captured cavalry mount or attempting to capture one of the riderless horses. Dead soldiers lie strewn about; other troopers struggle in the water. Only nine soldiers, still mounted, escape to the ridges beyond the river.

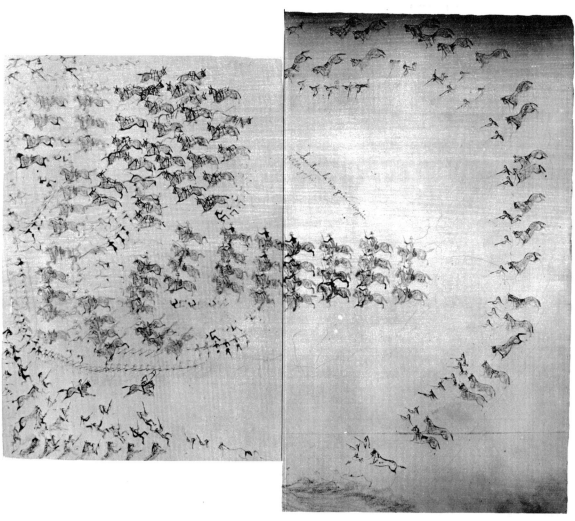

No. 176

No. 176. The Battle of the Little Big Horn

Another two-page composition portrays Reno's last part in the fight—the barricaded defense of the remaining troops and the pack train on a high ridge back from the river. Here the hard-pressed force, composed of the remnants of Reno's command and the members of Benteen's, held out against the gradually weakening onslaughts of the Indians until the approach of Terry's column caused the besiegers to withdraw.

The single Lakota note means: "Attacking the pack train." The mules are easily distinguished from the horses in this drawing.

One Dakota explains the Indians' prompt withdrawal at the approach of Terry's command thus:

In that fight, where the Indians tried to clean up the pack train, as they tell about it themselves they could have got all the ammunition and might have cleaned up on the whole army, but they saw infantry and they don't seem to like them—they bury themselves in the ground like badgers and it's too slow fighting.[71]

The circle of the Indians, the position from which most of them are firing (as implied by the impressionistic sketches), the positions of the individual horses in relation to their owners, and the wavy lines marking the outline of the soldiers' stronghold indicate that the Indians are attacking a position entrenched on the top of a hill. Most of the Indians are crouching or lying flat and firing over the edge of rising ground.

[71] John Colhoff, letter of April 7, 1929.

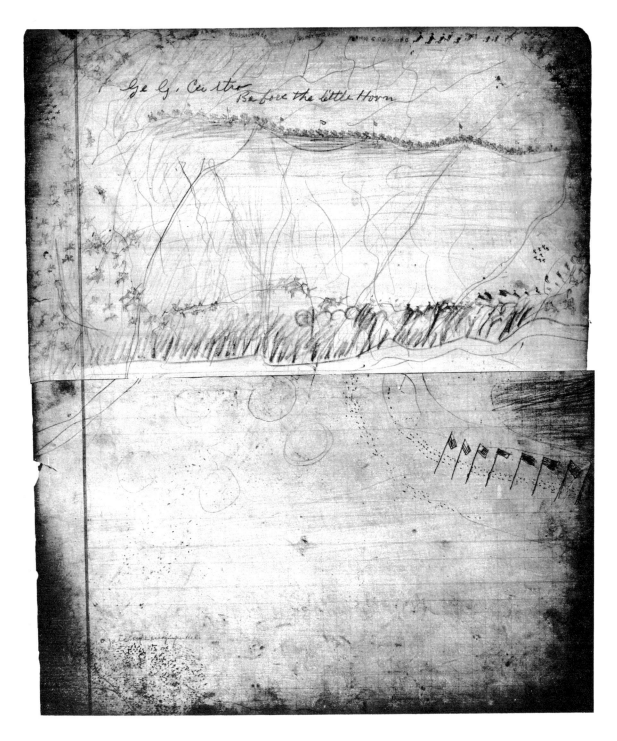

No. 177

No. 177.   The Battle of the Little Big Horn

An unfinished pencil sketch, evidently discarded, corresponding slightly to the preceding topographical drawings of the battlefield (Nos. 129 and 170). This one, however, indicates a position farther down the river and centers around the approach of Custer's command and the position which it later assumed.

Custer's column is shown moving along the top of a high ridge in plain view of the Indians, who are shown on all the surrounding ridges.

In the lower left corner are numerous dots and small marks with an inscription which means: "People making ready to flee." This refers to the Indians (mostly women, of course), who, at the first attack, began to prepare for flight.

The sketch is a very rough one, done for the most part in pencil in mixed miniature scales and with mixed perspectives. The artist probably was not satisfied with it, for it has been scratched over with long pencil marks, and, as I said before, is not finished.

The fact is that this third short Custer series can in no way compare with the others in effectiveness. It would appear that the artist was not particularly interested in portraying the annihilation of Custer's command, for that is the subject of this brief and rather heterogeneous series.

No. 178

No. 178. The Battle of the Little Big Horn

A miniature drawing showing Custer's men on foot, fighting against overwhelming numbers of mounted Indians. Dead soldiers are scattered over the field. Most of those who are still living are firing from a kneeling position.

The scale in this drawing is the same as that used in the second series, but the composition is far less effective, although it does create the impression of great confusion and desperation.

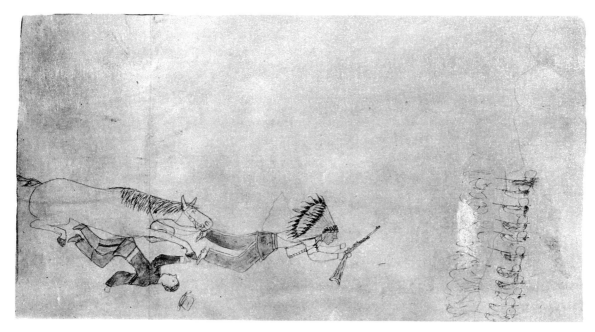

No. 179

No. 179. THE BATTLE OF THE LITTLE BIG HORN

A large-scale drawing showing a bonneted Sioux crawling away from a fallen trooper and toward another group of soldiers. Only the heads and arms and rifles of the latter show.

No. 180

NO. 180.   THE BATTLE OF THE LITTLE BIG HORN

A drawing similar in scale and general character to the preceding one, showing one of two retreating troopers shooting a pursuing Indian from his horse. A third soldier lies dead behind the horse.

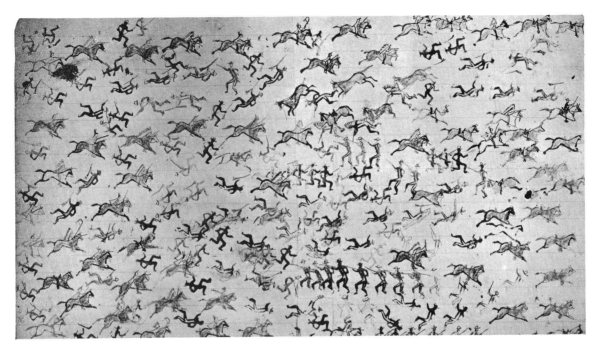

No. 181

NO. 181.   THE BATTLE OF THE LITTLE BIG HORN

Miniature drawing similar in character and technique to No. 178.

No. 182

No. 182. The Battle of the Little Big Horn

Portrayal of one of the last moments in the Custer fight.

This is the last miniature of the series. In character and technique it is one with that immediately preceding and with No. 178.★

No. 183

No. 183. The Battle of the Little Big Horn

Intermediate-scale drawing of the last moment in the Custer fight, showing the killing of General Custer by Crazy Horse (center) and the momentary escape of the one trooper (lower right).

The only inscriptions here are two in English: 1. "Last of General Custer." 2. "Ge. G. Custer. June 26, 1876."

This is the only "uncovered" drawing in this

intermediate scale (see Chapter VI, p. 78). Contrary to most of the drawings in the record, this one has been made on the vertical plane of the page; thus the composition is a vertical panel instead of a horizontal one.

From a purely technical point of view, even though there were no other reason, this is an interesting composition. In the first place, it vividly suggests the confusion that must have reigned at that moment. The movement of the whole scene is but accentuated by the suggested quietness or arrested motion of the fallen figures. It is rich in its variety of postures and angles of vision and in the phases of fighting portrayed (see Chapter IV, pp. 48 and 59).

No. 184

NO. 184.   THE BATTLE OF THE LITTLE BIG HORN

Two-page drawing showing the next moment after that of 183, the moment when the last man in Custer's command took his own life. It is tradition among the Dakotas that this man could have saved himself but that, maddened by what had taken place and not realizing his opportunity, or being unwilling to take it, he raised his gun and fired a shot through his temple.

No. 185

NO. 185.   THE BATTLE OF THE LITTLE BIG HORN

The sequel to No. 184. The Indians have come up to the fallen body. One has captured the horse and is holding the reins, while a second takes the soldier's coat and a third sits and shoots arrows into the lifeless body. It is to be noticed that the soldier was not scalped. This restraint is due to the fact that the Indians had such a supersitition with regard to suicides that they considered the body untouchable.

The Lakota note indicates that this was the end of Custer's command. It reads further: "The long guns taken away from them were counted, and it is said they numbered more than seven hundred." This would have to mean guns taken in both the Custer and the Reno encounters.

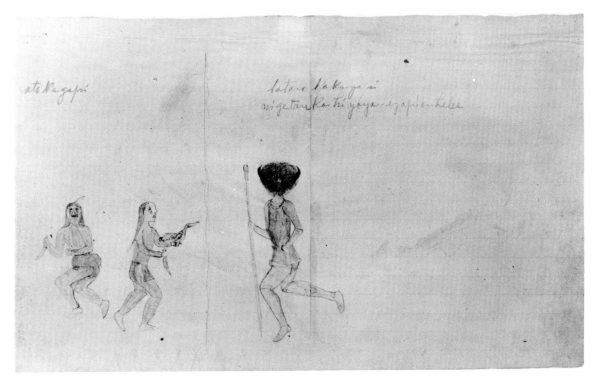

No. 186

No. 186. Early Social Life and Its Reorganization

Cultic performance of animal dreamers (cf. No. 115). The two figures at the left are bear dreamers; the one on the right is a buffalo dreamer. One bear dreamer carries a bird in his hand. This emblem was of the duck family, known as *huntka* by the Indians. The bird was skinned, then ground up, bones and all, with a special medicine, and then eaten by the dreamer. The stuffed skin was thereafter carried in the public ceremony as a medicine charm.

The performance here portrayed, as the note indicates, is that of *Nige Tanka* (Big Belly Buffalo), whose nickname was *Nuni* (Lost). It was given in the country above the Black Hills, on a creek that is still known as Big Belly Creek.

No. 187

No. 187. Early Social Life and Its Reorganization

A deer dreamers' ceremony (cf. No. 115). The long-tailed deer, black-tailed deer, and elk dreamers are shown here. The long-tailed deer dancers are painted red, the black-tailed deer dancers blue and black, and the elk dancers yellow.

The two deer species show marked similarities. The elks show a few features differing from the former; for example, the elks carry large, plain hoops, unadorned by visible medicine or the spider-web lacing seen in the smaller hoops of the deer dancers. Instead of the feathers borne in the right hand, the elk dreamers carry long canes with green leaves at the top.

The medicine man is again seen, at the right (top); at the lower right is the "medicine shooter."

No. 188

NO. 188. EARLY SOCIAL LIFE AND ITS REORGANIZATION

Hanble ceyapi, the vigil, or retreat, a common and significant rite among the Dakotas and, in one form or another, among most North American Indians.

This is one of the extreme forms of sacrifice among the Dakotas. It is a personal and individual sacrifice made for the sake of some great need, frequently in fulfillment of a promise made to the Great Spirit for the recovery of a stricken relative, frequently also simply for the securing of the great vision which will give the individual his personal medicine and make known to him the nature or identity of his mystical guardian. In any case a vision is sought, a mystical experience is desired, and the rite is performed in strictest reverence and most sincere devotion; the seeker stands before his god and the spirits of the world in humble supplication.

The devotee is prepared, physically, mentally, and spiritually, by solemn rites at the hands of a shaman; then he proceeds, barefooted and alone, to the top of some high and lonely hill, where he holds his fast until the vision comes.[72]

Bad Heart Bull shows here the seeker in his ceremonial buffalo robe, on top of a high hill, presenting the sacred pipe in supplication to the Great Spirit. The colored streamers around him are sacrifice banners.

He Dog points out that some people receive nothing from this experience but that some receive much.

[72] See Frances Densmore's description in "Teton Sioux Music," pp. 274–275.

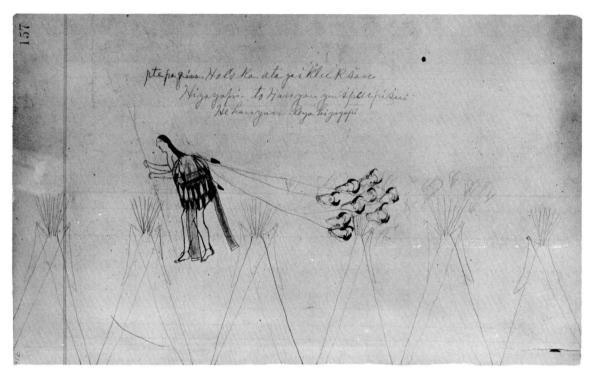

No. 189

No. 189. Early Social Life and Its Reorganization

The rite of propitiation of the buffalo gods.

A man, nude except for the breechcloth and breechpanels, is shown dragging a cluster of buffalo skulls. His only paraphernalia are a long staff and a highly decorated shield.

A note in Lakota reads: "The one that carries the buffalo skulls by thongs slipped through the pierced flesh of the back goes around the center of the entire camp."

This is a rite performed in fulfillment of a promise to the buffalo spirit when help in stealing horses was sought. Consequently, it does not strike the high note felt in the preceding rite.

The devotee usually came from the wilderness, from a medicine lodge in the hills where a shaman had attended to his initial purification and preparation. The man was painted entirely white. Usually, four or five buffalo skulls were used, but Bad Heart Bull shows more.

This skull-dragging ceremony reminds one of the torture of the first form of the Sun Gaze Dance (see No. 13). There is this technical difference, however: in the former, the skulls drag upon the ground; in the latter, the thongs are short, the skulls do not touch the ground, and the weight is borne entirely by the pierced flesh.

No. 190

No. 190. Early Social Life and Its Reorganization

Lakota notes. Translation:

[1] Making [or imitating] buffalo.
[2] What is called "making wounded."
[3] Making [or imitating] "strange dogs" [i.e., coyotes] or wolves.
[4] This is the place where the buffalo was "killed."

A dream-cult ceremony featuring the buffalo dreamer. This is the buffalo-dreamer dance, which was performed correctly according to He Dog (see also Nos. 115, 187, and, especially, 186). In this particular performance, coyotes ("strange dogs") and wolves and *heyoka* dancers also take part, but merely as secondary actors in the episode; the buffalo is the center of attention and significance.

Wissler's description of the buffalo-cult performance gives briefly the main points. Bad Heart Bull's drawing illustrates the description well:

> There was a group of men and occasionally a few women, known as the buffalo dreamers. When they had their dance, a shaman would appear in the head and skin of a buffalo. As he ran about the camp a nude young man stalked him, while the cult followed singing. At the proper time the hunter discharged an arrow deeply into a spot marked on the buffalo hide [see Bad Heart Bull's drawing]. The shaman would then stagger, vomit blood and spit up an arrow point. The wolf cult would then pursue him [this is the stage of the ceremony portrayed in this drawing]. Later, another shaman would use medicine (*pejuta*), pull the arrow out and at once the wound was healed.[73]

The association of the wolf or coyote dreamers and the *heyoka* is explained to a degree by Wissler's explanation that when those who dream of the wolf are to give a dance and feast, "a herald shouts out the invitation around the camp; he also *notifies the heyoka* to get ready as 'soon there will be a wolf coming over the hill.' "[74]

The wolf dreamers "have wolf skins over their backs and on their arms and legs. On the head they wear a rawhide mask with holes for the eyes and one for the mouth through which the whistle is sounded. Symbols of the owner's dream may be painted on the mask. The legs and arms are painted red, the bodies white. Some carry an imitation snake from which

[73] Wissler, "Societies," p. 91.

[74] *Ibid.*, p. 90.

they shoot *wakan* influence."[75] Some also carry the pipe.

The outstanding feature of the costume of these dreamers is the rawhide mask, which bears a rather striking resemblance to some of the masks of the Indians of the Southwest.

The *heyoka* dreamers are the clowns of the cultic organizations. The main fact regarding their actions is that they are consistently anti-natural. Those people are *heyoka* who have dreamed of *heyoka*, "clown beings," and must immediately after such a dream go through a public performance lest they be killed by lightning. According to some informants, they bear some relation to the weather; and on special days of feasts and ceremonies, if the skies begin to look threatening, the *heyoka* are called out to perform and propitiate the sky spirits.[76]

Bad Heart Bull is portraying the correct buffalo-dreamer performance given on the South Platte in the spring of "The-year-they-got-burned-out-in-the-fall," when He Dog was a mere boy. All the other dancers are shown engaged in harassing and attacking the buffalo. In this the "hunter" (i.e., the "magic shooter," who was testing the power of the buffalo's medicine) used arrows and then finally a gun. The "hunter" is shown in the lower right corner of the drawing, and the two arrows which he has shot can be seen sticking in the buffalo hide. The buffalo, however, did not stop until he had completed the circle of the camp again. Then he lay down near the medicine tipi. Meanwhile, the "hunter" had concealed himself in the brush near the animal; and as the buffalo lay still, he fired a bullet at him. With a roar the buffalo leaped to his feet and ran into the medicine lodge. The shaman there immediately began to work with him, and finally the buffalo dreamer coughed up the bullet. So the dreamer's faith was vindicated, for the great *buffalo power* is resistance to bullets and other such evils.

Guns were not usually used in these ceremonies, however. Quite evidently this was an unusual performance, and the recital of the tale, one that was frequently given.

Relative to the snake and the pipe borne by wolves in this drawing, He Dog says that Old Blunt Horn (*Hewotaka*) and Swift Bird (*Zintka Oranco*) were wolves on this occasion. One carried a snake, the other a red pipe. These two men were noted for stealing horses from the enemy. The snake, as frequently occurs in such cases, represents a rope, which in turn symbolizes proficiency in horse stealing. In this case the pipe has the same significance. So personal prowess is indicated.

[75] *Ibid.*
[76] See, for example, *ibid.*, pp. 82–85; Lowie, "Dance Associations," pp. 113–117; and J. O. Dorsey, "Siouan Cults," pp. 468–471.

No. 191

No. 191. Early Social Life and Its Reorganization

A single note in Lakota. Translation: "Indian love flute."

The central figure in the drawing is that of a man; he is robed in a decorated buffalo skin, his face is painted yellow with two red diagonal stripes on the cheek, he wears an eagle feather in his hair, and he plays a flute. This figure is framed by a circle, the right half of whose circumference is red, the left, yellow. The wavy blue line reaching from the oddly represented *sound*, issuing from the flute, to the yellow ring of the circle indicates that this man's music possessed spiritual powers not usually found in flute music. Behind the figure, just outside the circle, are eight women's heads; in front, outside the circle, are more.

The explanation given is this: In the old days each man followed some special interest, usually war and the chase, of course. This man, however, followed the *elk activity* (see text accompanying No. 115), that is, his greatest interest was playing with the affections of women.

He was a player of the flute, the instrument of love,

[77] Wissler, "Whirlwind and Elk," pp. 261–268.

and elk medicine[77] had made the call of his flute irresistible to women throughout the whole circle of his world (therefore the circle about him). The eight heads outside the circle and behind him are like notches on a gun butt: they represent eight women who have already fallen victim to his charms. The heads before him represent victims yet to come.

According to Dakota tradition, hundreds of years ago a man (not a Sioux and not a Cheyenne) appeared in the land of the Dakotas, bringing the magic love flute. It is the belief of He Dog and Short Bull that this is the being represented in young Bad Heart Bull's drawing.

The red of the enclosing circle, they say, shows that this being was Indian, though no one knows to what tribe he belonged.

The significance of the yellow of the circle is not known.

This being used, as part of his equipment, split deer-hoof rattles on his ankles. Here He Dog adds this whimsical bit from his own experience: When they were camped on Cheyenne River, they used to hear a sound like that of deer hoofs rattling, and they thought it was this old being walking.

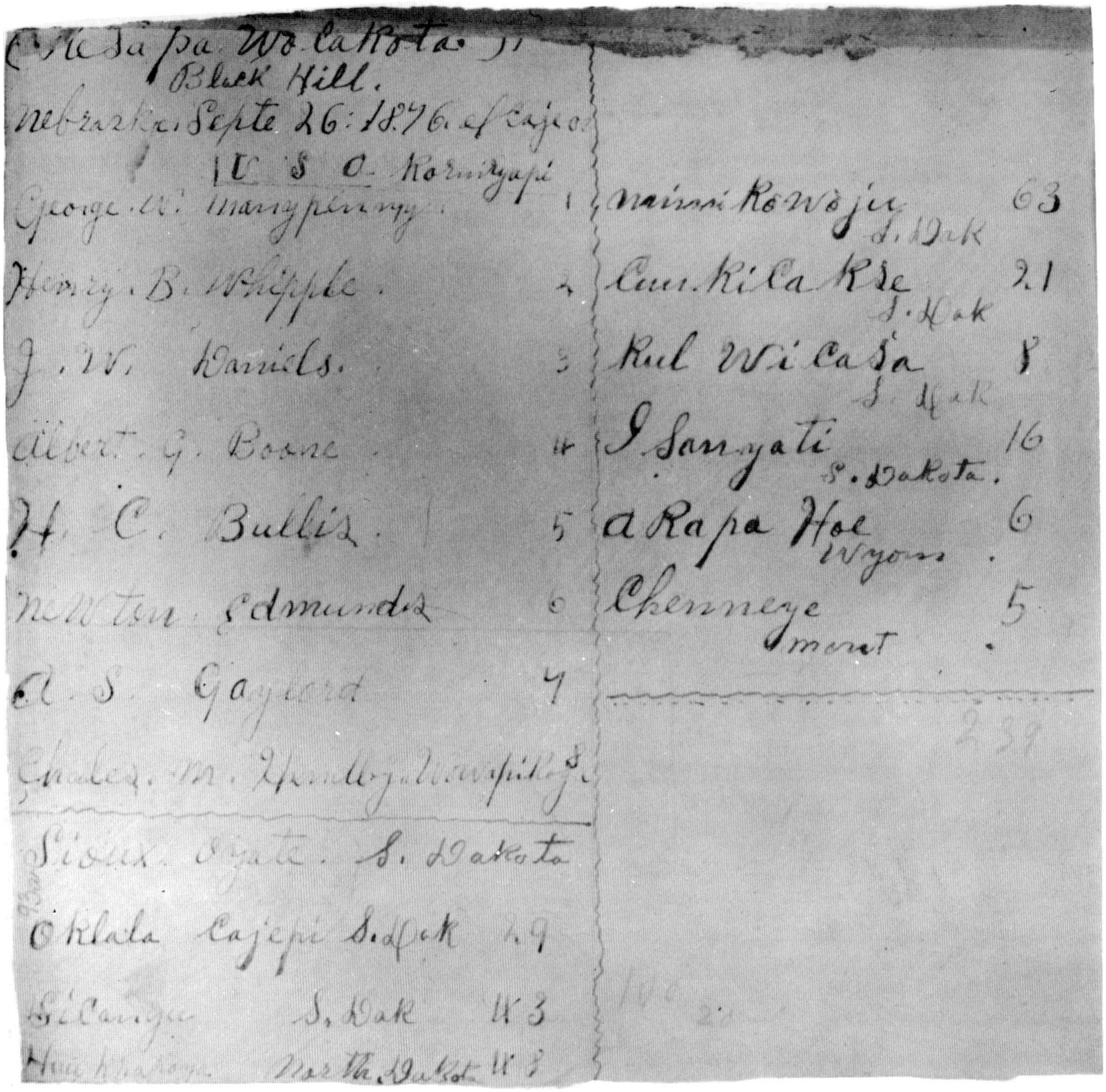

No. 192

No. 192. Early Social Life and Its Reorganization

A note in Lakota. Translation:

Black Hills Peace Talk.
September 26, 1876.
George W. Manypenny   1
Henry B. Whipple   2
J. W. Daniels   3
Albert G. Boone   4
H. C. Bullis [misspelling of "Bulis"]   5
Newton Edmunds   6
A. S. Gaylord   7
Charles M. Hendley   8
. . . .
Sioux Nation, South Dakota

Oglala names, South Dakota   29
Rosebud names, South Dakota   43
Standing Rock names, North Dakota   48
Miniconjou names, South Dakota   63
Crow Creek names, South Dakota   21
Brulé names, South Dakota   8
Santee names, South Dakota   16
Arapaho names, Wyoming   6
Cheyenne names, Montana   5

No drawing—merely the foregoing lists.

Nos. 192 to 197, inclusive, form a series concerning the conference of 1876 which had to do with the ceding of the Black Hills (*Re Sapa*) to the United States government.

According to the report of the act of ratification in Chapter 72 of *Acts of the Forty-fourth Congress— Second Session, 1877*,[78] the agreement was "dated and signed at Spotted Tail Agency, Nebraska, September 23, 1876."[79] Bad Heart Bull gives the date as three days later, but the discrepancy is insignificant. The names of the commissioners and tribes concerned agree. All the tribes named, however, did not meet at Spotted Tail. The commissioners met the Crow Creek, Standing Rock, Brulé, and Santee delegations at their own agencies.

[78] Charles J. Kappler, comp. and ed., *Indian Affairs, Laws and Treaties* (2 vols.; Washington: Government Printing Office, 1904), I, 168–172.

[79] *Ibid.*, p. 171.

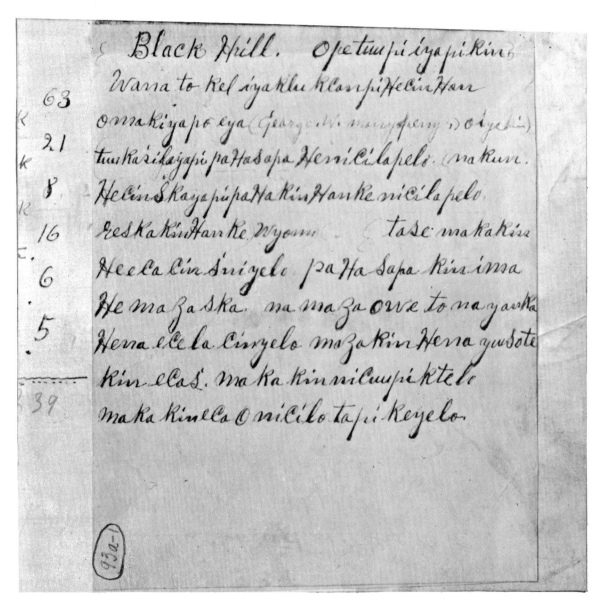

No. 193

No. 193. Early Social Life and Its Reorganization

A note only, in Lakota. Translation:

The Talk on Purchasing the Black Hills.
George W. Manypenny said: "Now, I want to know what you have decided to do. The Great Father has asked you for the Black Hills, also part of the Big Horn Mountains, also part of the White Mountains of Wyoming. He doesn't want the soil, but the gold and other metals that may be in the Black Hills are what he wants. After he has mined all the mineral from them, he will give you back the soil. He only wants to lease the land, or soil. This is what he says."

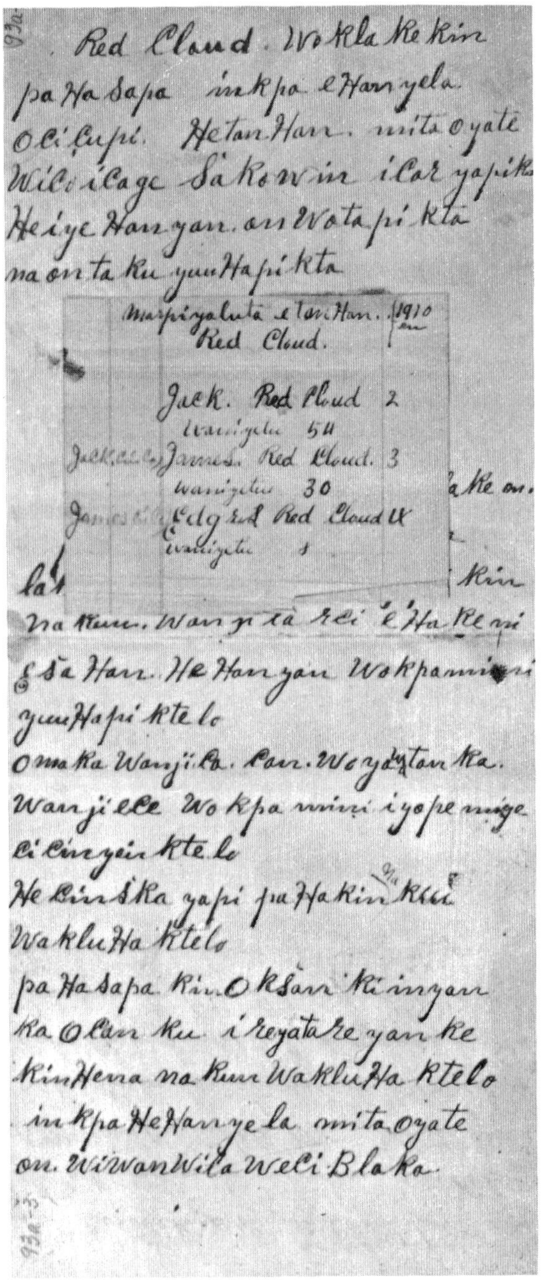

No. 194

NO. 194. EARLY SOCIAL LIFE AND ITS REORGANIZATION

Notes in Lakota. Translation:

[1] The speech of Red Cloud [chief of the Oglalas]: "I will lease you only the surface of the Black Hills. Seven generations of my people shall eat and have something from this lease."

[2] Direct male line of descent of Red Cloud, in 1910:

Red Cloud	
Jack [his son]	54 years
James [Jack's son]	30 years
Edgar [James's son]	8 years

[3] The speech of Spotted Tail [chief of the Rosebud Dakotas]: "From the Black Hills, so long as the Indians may exist, even though it be only one that is

living, so long shall they be entitled to a distribution of necessities. Every year you shall expend for my benefit at least $1,000,000 for necessities.

"I also want to reserve part of the Big Horn Mountains.

"I also reserve the foothills around the Black Hills.

"I am speaking for my people in this leasing of the hilltops or surface of the hills only."

The meaning of Red Cloud's statement seems to be that he was willing to lease for seven generations, during which time the members of the tribe were to be fed and clothed by the government.

As Spotted Tail indicated literally, the mining equipment was not to come farther down than the "Race Track" (*Ki Inyanka Ocanku*; cf. No. 198), the Dakota designation of the foothills immediately circling the Black Hills.

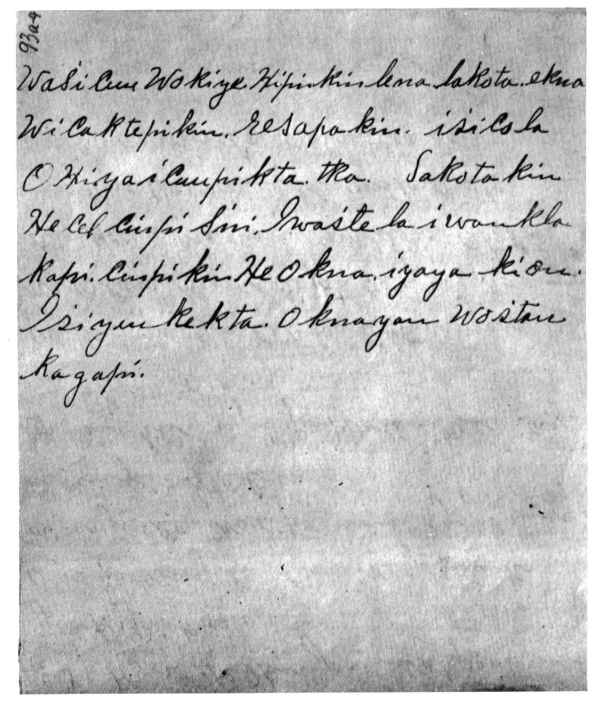

No. 195

No. 195. Early Social Life and Its Reorganization

A note in Lakota giving another bit of a speech by Spotted Tail. Translation: "If the United States had tried to take the Black Hills by force, they would have lost. But as it is, by using peaceful methods, they secure them, and the Indians are able to get some return also."

No. 196

No. 196. EARLY SOCIAL LIFE AND ITS REORGANIZATION

A Lakota heading and the names of four sergeants at arms stationed about the room at the Black Hills conference.

[1] The Black Hills Peace Talk. Red Cloud and Spotted Tail are in the center.

[2] Spider, [i.e., High Hollow Horn (*Herlogeca Wankatuya*; cf. No. 37) (upper left)].

[3] Can't Walk [a nickname for American Horse (lower left)].

[4] Young Man Afraid of His Horses [upper right].

[5] Keeps the Sword [more familiarly known as Sword (lower right)].

A close-up showing the white commissioners and the Indian leaders sitting in council.

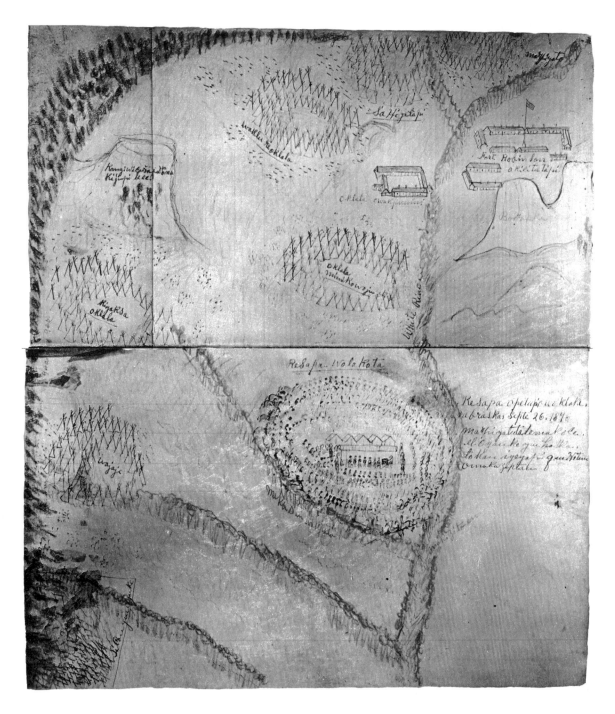

No. 197

No. 197. Early Social Life and Its Reorganization

Notes in Lakota. Translation:

[1] September 26, 1876. Red Cloud talking about the buying of the Black Hills. Red Cloud had chosen this place for his reservation, but he was taken away

from there five years afterward.
[2] Black Hills Peace Talk.

A somewhat topographical, diagrammatic sketch

showing the setting of the Black Hills conference of 1876.

The center of interest is the circular group (center) designated "Black Hills Peace Talk." This council is sketched in highly impressionistic style, and is placed at the fork of two streams: (right) *Maki Zita En*, "On Smoking Earth," i.e., White River (cf. No. 198); (left) *Maka San Wakpapa*, "White Earth Stream," i.e., White Clay Creek. (Two creeks by this name empty into White River. This is not the one referred to in No. 321.)

The several camp circles range from above Fort Robinson proper (upper right) along the foot of the ridge (shown upper left and left) to a point somewhat below the conference ground and somewhat at the left. There are seven camps in all. At the upper extreme right appears the camp of *Marpiyato*, "The Blue Clouds," i.e., the Arapahos;[80] next is *Sahiyelapi*, "Red Teeth People," i.e., the Cheyennes; close by is *Waklu Re Oklala*, the "Hang Around" or "Loafer" band of the Oglalas (Red Cloud's band [sic]); at a greater distance and directly below is *Oklala Miniko-*

woju, a combined group of Oglalas and Miniconjous; directly west from this is the camp of *Kiyaksa Oklala*, the Kiyuksa or "Cut" band of the Oglalas; below this is *Wajaje*, another Oglala group of that name; and below this appears *Sicangu Oyanke*, the place where the Brulés, or "Burned Thighs," were camped on Beaver Creek.

The buildings of the fort appear at the upper right immediately below the Arapaho encampment. The group is labeled *akicita tipi*, "soldier lodges."

Directly to the left of the fort buildings is another group, labeled *Oklala owakpamini*, "the place of distribution of Oglala annuities," i.e., the government Indian agency.

Immediately below the fort itself is the representation of a butte, which is designated as *Baha Ska*, White Butte. It is noticeable that the artist shows this point white, whereas all the other portions of the diagrammatic portrayal are shaded.

Opposite *Baha Ska*, to the left, is another butte, flat-topped, marked *Kangi wicasa paha ona kijupi le ee*, which, translated, is "the refuge butte of the Crows." Both of these buttes are well-known landmarks in this section of the country. Crow Butte is especially prominent, both in appearance and in fame.

[80] Hugh Lenox Scott, "Early History and Names of the Arapaho," *Am. Anthrop.*, IX (NS), 3 (1907), 557.

No. 198

No. 198. Early Social Life and Its Reorganization

A double-page, typically imaginative, topographical representation of the Black Hills region.

The yellow band is the traditional "Race Track" (*Ki Inyanka Ocanku*), which circles the Black Hills (cf. No. 194).

According to this sketch, the south branch of the Cheyenne River skirts the lower extent of the Black Hills, small tributaries feeding into it from the Hills, but the upper branch flows through the northern region of the range, running past *Mato Tipi Paha*,

Bear Lodge Butte, familiarly known to the whites as Devils Tower. Just outside the Black Hills proper, at the extreme north in this drawing, is *Baha Zizipela*, Slim Buttes, and almost directly opposite, to the east —as Bad Heart Bull shows it—is *Makiyan Paha*, Thunder Butte. Within the circle of the Hills, at their northernmost reach, is *Baha Sapa*, Black Mountain or Black Butte, fittingly colored in this picture. South and somewhat east of this is *Mato Tipi Paha*, Bear Lodge Butte. The drawing of this butte indicates the towering cylindrical column of the strange formation and bears near the base the sketchy outline of a bear's head. Directly below this is *Re Sla*, Bare Mountain ("Old Baldy" on most maps), portrayed as a barren, rounded hill. Due west of Bare Mountain is *Hinyankaga Paha*,[81] Ghost Butte, pictured as an odd, horned head. Straight east of Ghost Butte and Bare Butte but just outside the circle of the Hills is *Mato Baha*, Bear Butte, represented here as a bear's head.

South of Bare Mountain, far to the south on one of the branches of the lower Cheyenne River, is a rectangular designation; this is *Mini Kata*, Hot Springs, the place of the bubbling up of numerous natural hot springs, where the town of Hot Springs, South Dakota, now stands. Southeast of this point, a square opening into the circle of the Hills' circumference is shown. This is *Pte Tali Yapa*, Buffalo Gap, the opening into the Hills.[82]

At the right, just outside the circle of the "Race Track," is a small circle marked "Rapid City" and *Miniluzahan*, which means "fast water." The complete Lakota name for Rapid City is *Miniluzahan Otunwahe*; Bad Heart Bull simply uses an abbreviated form.

South of the Black Hills and a little to the west, along a southern tributary to the Lower Cheyenne, appears the designation *Wapaha Kagapi*. Translated, this is "Making the Warbonnets." This is the place where, it is said, the warbonnets for the various warrior societies were originally made. The stream is now known as Hat Creek, perhaps a prosaic interpretation of the warbonnet association.

Somewhat south and east of this creek, Bad Heart Bull represents a long, elliptical formation labeled *Winurcala Wanti*, "The Place Where the Old Woman Lives." There is a vague bit of legend about an old woman, frequently seen in these parts in the distant past, who invariably disappeared completely— seemingly into this hill—when pursued by wandering bands of Indians. Finally it was concluded that she was a ghost; as a result, the place was shunned.

To the right of these latter two landmarks appears *Maka Izita*, White River, literally "Smoking Earth River" (cf. No. 197). (The correct spelling is *Maka Izita*; the spelling in No. 197 is an abbreviated form.) In the old days, it is said, smoke used to rise from various places all over the country which this stream drained; consequently it was called "Smoking Earth River."

Ghost Hill (or Butte) calls for some explanation, especially its peculiar portrayal here. The story is that it was near this butte that the Indians (Cheyennes, probably, for it is said that they named it) first sighted a particular buffalo bull. Again and again they saw him, but they could never catch him; he always disappeared into this particular butte, it seemed. Consequently they thought he must be a ghost or spirit animal, so they named the place Ghost Butte. This explains Bad Heart Bull's graphic depiction; he is representing a *spirit buffalo*.

Needless to say, this representation of the Black Hills and the various geographic points is not accurate; the relative positions are not true. The discrepancies are not serious, however, when one considers the diagrammatic purpose of the portrayal. The outstanding inaccuracy here is the location of Bear Lodge Butte (Devils Tower), which, in reality, is not in the Black Hills but rises abruptly from a level plain across the state boundary line in Wyoming.

[81] John Colhoff spells this *Hinhan Kaga Paha*.

[82] Standing Bear, *My People*, p. 17.

No. 199

No. 199. EARLY SOCIAL LIFE AND ITS REORGANIZATION

The first of another series (Nos. 199 to 205, inclusive) portraying the *uci tapi*, or "charge around camp," which precedes the departure for war (see also Nos. 116 to 125).

This is probably the charge that preceded the battle known as "When They Drove Them Back to Camp." The long portrayal of this battle follows, after an interruption, in Nos. 219 to 284.

It should be remembered that in these charges before battle, the warriors appear in all their battle regalia. It must be remembered further that usually the Indian warrior wished to die as richly dressed as possible. It is to be expected, then, that these portrayals of charges will disclose a rich assortment of splendid costuming and paraphernalia. They are given here chiefly for this reason. It will be to some of the details of this equipment that I shall refer, for the most part, in my notes on the series.

The clubbed tails of the horses and the face markings of the warriors are the prominent features in the first drawing.

Noticeable, too, however, is the black otter-skin, feather-bedecked charm worn from the left shoulder of the young warrior in the foreground (left). The relatively small size of this brave and the fact that he carries no insigne of office and no noticeable marks of achievement would seem to indicate that he is a mere boy, going out, perhaps, on his first war expedition.

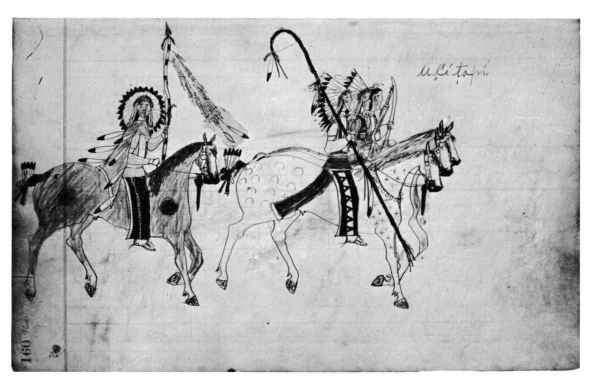

No. 200

No. 200. Early Social Life and Its Reorganization

The leading warrior in the immediate foreground carries the ceremonial crooked lance of the Iroka Society (No. 26). It appears, too, that he is wearing the bone-tube breastpiece often worn by members of the society.[83]

The following brave carries the bow lance of the Tokala (No. 30).[84] Another prominent feature of this Dakota's apparel is the feathered red mantle worn from the shoulders. This is an especially interesting figure from the point of view of technique because it gives the fairly rare full-front view of the head.

[83] Wissler, "Societies," p. 32.

[84] *Ibid.*, pp. 14–23.

No. 201

No. 201. Early Social Life and Its Reorganization

Tanned-hide quiver worn across left thigh of leading rider.

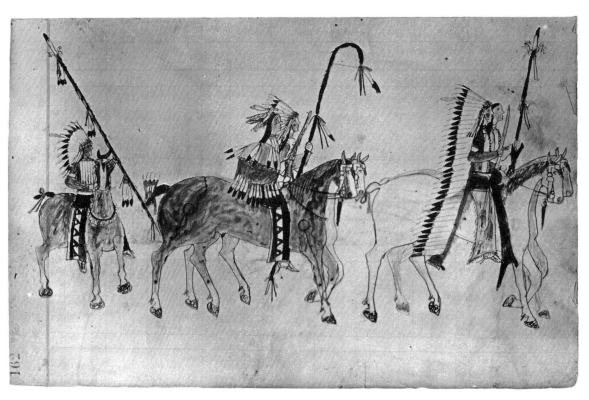

No. 202

No. 202. Early Social Life and Its Reorganization

Lances of two different societies appear in this one group. The leader in the background carries the straight, short lance of the Kangi Yuha Society (No. 29); the crow skin is plainly visible below the bearer's hand.[85] The warrior immediately behind him carries the crooked lance of the Iroka (Nos. 26 and 200).[86] The last man bears the straight, striped lance of the same society. Both of these Iroka warriors and the one shown in No. 200 wear two short, parallel black marks on the cheek.

Prominent are the stuffed blue-hawk head decoration and the large, heavily feathered shield of the middle warrior.

The interesting feature technically is the fore-shortened, three-quarter-front view of the last horse.★

[85] Wissler, "Societies," pp. 23–24.

[86] *Ibid.*, p. 32.

No. 203

NO. 203. EARLY SOCIAL LIFE AND ITS REORGANIZATION

The foremost rider wears a black otter-skin cap (*ptan ha wapastan*) decorated with eagle tail feathers.

The next warrior has, thrown across his horse's neck, a black otter-skin charm (*wotawe*).

To the right of the latter rides the bearer of a lance which resembles but is not identical with the lance of the Cante Tinza shown by Bad Heart Bull in No. 22. It is, however, like Thunder Bear's drawing of the Cante Tinza lance accompanying Wissler's article.[87]

The last rider, in the background, wears the brown-hawk head charm (*wotawe*).

[87] Wissler, "Societies," p. 68 (figure 3c).

No. 204

NO. 204. EARLY SOCIAL LIFE AND ITS REORGANIZATION

The first warrior, beside the Tokala bow-lance bearer, wears the official headgear of the Wiciska Society (No. 23).[88]

[88] Wissler, "Societies," pp. 34–36.

The detail that first catches the eye is the large shield, with its red "skirt."

Noticeable, too, for the sake of technique, are the two running horses seen full front at the left.★

No. 205

NO. 205.   EARLY SOCIAL LIFE AND ITS REORGANIZATION

The foremost of the second pair of riders wears the
headdress and feathered bustle and carries the straight,
short lance of the Omaha Society (see No. 31).[89]

[89] Wissler, "Societies," pp. 48–52.

No. 206

No. 206. Early Social Life and Its Reorganization

The first of a series of eight drawings portraying Oglala Dakota games.

The first game: *itaipa ape*, i.e., "striking the bow."

As the drawing indicates and as He Dog and Short Bull and Standing Bear[90] agree, the players are divided into two groups.

A bow is hung by one end from a pole that has been propped at an angle from the ground. At a distance of some eight or ten feet has been placed a brush pile, into which a single arrow has been thrown for a target. Each player in turn, the two sides alternating, stands beside the bow and throws one of his arrows at the taut bowstring so that it will be shot into the brush pile. The way in which the shot arrow falls in relation to the target arrow determines the count, various shots tallying differently. At the bottom of the page, Bad Heart Bull has made a diagram to show the relative value of the shots. The unnumbered arrow (red in the original drawing) is the target. The others are numbered according to the way in which they tally. Shot No. 1 is like a "grand sweep," for it takes everything; one No. 1 shot wins the game.

Like all Indian contests, this is a betting game. Both individual and group bets may be laid before the play starts.

On the same page (upper right), a small sketch has been made of two little girls "playing house," as white children might express it. Each has a small, loaded travois which she is pulling.

[90] Cf., e.g., Standing Bear, *My People*, pp. 38–39.

No. 207

No. 207. Early Social Life and Its Reorganization

A Lakota inscription. Translation: "Customary kinds of wearing apparel."

Besides wearing apparel, however, the artist gives detail regarding the arrangement of some of the furnishings of the tipi.

The young men ranged in a row exhibit typical costumes, especially costumes suitable for courting, for at that time a young man dons his choicest peacetime finery. The second and fourth robes show the beaded-belt effect often found on the finest robes of young men. The third one is quilted with porcupine quillwork. Such a blanket would be especially valuable. On the second man is visible a bit of the deerhorn love charm and the silver hair ornament which I have described before (Nos. 8 and 86). The fourth figure gives the complete view of such a decoration, however. The deer or antelope horn forms the top and is fastened to the scalp lock. The circular parts of the piece are silver disks, usually slightly convex.

The first youth wears fringed buckskin leggings; all the others, flannel, decorated in one way or another.

In the background is a section of a lodge interior. The typical Plains Indian bed is clearly pictured. The foundation of it consists of two odd pieces of furniture called *can-kazuntapi*, "wood strung together side by side." These *can-kazuntapi* are made of small, straight branches stripped of their bark and strung on cords of rawhide, the lengths of wood shorter at the top and gradually increasing in length toward the bottom, so that the outline of the whole is that of a triangle, slightly truncated. The rawhide cord is arranged at the top in such a way that there is a loop by which the *can-kazuntapi* are hung from forked single posts or from tripods, so that the wide halves lie flat on the ground, meeting each other to form the bed proper, while the upper halves slope abruptly to form the head and foot of the bed. The *can-kazuntapi* are usually painted in stripes and consequently are decorative (the drawing shows them striped red and white). Over this foundation, blankets and buffalo robes are laid; and, from head and foot, robes are draped to make a soft, comfortable resting place. As is quite apparent from Bad Heart Bull's portrayal, special equipment and wearing apparel are hung from the head- and foot-posts. At the left can be distinguished leggings, a dark belted blanket, a pair of moccasins, a rifle, and a quiver; at the right, a feather ornament (perhaps a warbonnet only partly visible, perhaps an eagle-feather handpiece), a white bone-tube breastpiece, a revolver and cartridge belt, and an otter-skin charm (*wotawe*).

Behind the bed, and between it and the curved tipi wall, is a curtain, decorated with porcupine quill-work, which runs the length of the bed.[91] The tassels of quillwork and perhaps beads, at the top, and the colored rows running lengthwise are the decorations on this curtain.

Immediately behind the bed and in front of the curtain are the parfleche cases and boxes, which correspond in purpose and use to our suitcases, bureau drawers, cupboards, etc. The larger rawhide cases (*wakpan*), which are placed at the bottom of the pile, contain the family's winter store of dried meat and sometimes dried vegetables. A somewhat cruder bag of the same general type (*wizipan*) is used for any kind of food, usually food for immediate consumption. All of these are decorated with geometric painted designs. (Women did this kind of painting. Men painted the war articles.) On top of these food cases are seen the smaller, more highly decorated bags (most commonly called *pan-kinpi* but known also as *pan ipatapi*). These are finer pieces made of tanned skins and beaded or quilted with porcupine quill-work.[92] They are used as receptacles for valuable clothing and possessions. Frequently, smaller boxes or cases of varying shapes are also found which contain such things as women's tools, porcupine quills, paints, etc.[93] The warbonnet was kept in a special tubular case; it was not placed, however, with the usual pile of cases but was hung from one of the bedposts.

The figure at the extreme right is simply the representation of another bed, seen from the end.

[91] Standing Bear, *My People*, p. 14.
[92] Cf., e.g., Wissler, "North American Indians," p. 64 (figure 23).
[93] Cf., e.g., *ibid.*, p. 63 (figures 21, 22).

No. 208

No. 208. Early Social Life and Its Reorganization

Lower Half of Drawing

Second game: *ba inyankapi,* i.e., "to make it run," "to push it," in this case the hoop.

Two men play this game. The equipment consists of a large wooden hoop (*cankleska*) and a pair of double throwing sticks or wands (*cansakala*). The hoop is about twenty-four inches in diameter and is made of a single rounded branch of ash, about an inch in thickness, which has been bent into a circle and the two ends ingeniously fitted and bound. Four marks upon it divide it into quadrants. Each mark has a distinct name: the joint in the hoop is called *can-hute,* "end of timber"; opposite that is *okajayi,* a mark like an X; at the left of *can-hute* (if this is at the top) is *wagapi,* "many marks"; and opposite that, *sap-yapi,* "black mark." *Okajayi* is a cross cut into the outer surface of the hoop; *wagapi,* a series of short, parallel straight lines drawn crosswise on a short space on the outside of the hoop; and *sap-yapi,* a short space on the outside of the hoop cut down slightly to a flattened surface and painted black. These various marks are most significant in making scores.

The throwing sticks are really four in number, but are used in pairs. The two sticks of each pair are fastened together at the middle by a narrow rawhide thong, so that there is a length of about five inches of rawhide between the two sticks. About halfway between the middle binding thong and the ends, each stick is wrapped with rawhide for a space of about six inches. Near the middle of each stick, also, is fastened a small banner of flannel about an inch wide and five or six inches long, red for one pair, blue for the other. Before the game starts, each player decides which mark on the hoop is to be his high mark and what the rank of the others will be, and together they decide upon the count of each.

Both men play at once; the umpire throws the hoop. (According to some methods, sometimes, probably in less important matches, they play by turns.) The players run after it, each attempting to make his throw first. The object of the throw is to trip the hoop in such a way that it will fall upon the throwing stick so that some of the markers are covered by the bound portion of the sticks, the flannel banner, or the joining thong. If the bare wood of the stick touches the marker, it does not count.

The game was a very popular one with the Dakotas and with some other tribes.[94] In fact, whole bands sometimes visited each other in order to engage in such a contest; on such occasions excitement and wagers ran high.

Walker points out the probable ceremonial origin of the game; evidently, he says, the hoop was the Sacred Hoop of the Sioux and is significantly related to the ancient ceremony relating to the securing of buffalo.

Upper Half of Drawing

Third game: *okle cekutepi*, "game of coat shooting."

A supplementary note in Lakota. Translation: "Shooting their best."

This second notation helps to bear out the fact that this is a game for developing and exhibiting skill rather than a game played for points.

Several men or boys might join in this sport. The equipment consisted of the "coat" (*okle*), the bow (*itazipe*), and arrows (*wanhinkpe*). *Okle* is a symbolic name used to designate the target arrow. This usually is painted black or wrapped with a black strip of buckskin and bears a small tag which represents the "coat." It is shot high into the air so that it falls at a distance of about fifty or seventy-five yards. Then the players shoot at it. The exact and original significance of the term "coat" in this game does not seem to be clear.

Wissler makes reference to this game in his discussion of the Oglala societies: "Then some [of the men who made up a society closely related to the Braves] played the game of shooting-coat and were named accordingly."[95]

[94] Stewart Culin, "Games of the North American Indians," *ARBAE*, XXIV (1902–1903), 503–504, 508–509, and 514 and figures 664–666, 673, 674, and 679; Standing Bear, *My People*, pp. 42–43; J. R. Walker, "Sioux Games. I," *Journal of American Folk-Lore*, XVIII, 61 (1905), 278–283.

[95] Wissler, "Societies," p. 28.

No. 209

No. 209. Early Social Life and Its Reorganization

Lower Half of Drawing

Fourth game: *tahunka cankleska unpi*, "playing buckskin-hoop game."

The equipment for play consists of short lances, forked at the end, and several small hoops, varying in size and webbed with buckskin thongs. There may be any number of hoops, provided there are at least four. Two parallel lines are drawn about fifty feet long and about fifty feet apart. The players choose sides (a great number may take part) and decide upon the number of innings.

Briefly, the game is this: The players take their positions outside the parallel lines. According to one method of play, one hoop at a time is thrown (by a player), the sides alternating in putting a hoop into play. The hoop must be thrown so that it crosses both parallel lines, either rolling on the ground or passing through the air. Then those toward whom it is thrown try to spear it. If the hoop is speared through the "heart" (that is, the center, larger hole in the buckskin web) while it is in the air, the count is five;

through some other hole while in the air, two; through the "heart" while rolling on the ground, three; through some other hole while rolling on the ground, one. According to the other method, all the hoops are thrown at once; the opponents keep the speared hoops and return those not speared, to be thrown again. When all the hoops have been speared by one side, that side chases its opponents, throwing the hoops at them. The game ends when one of these hoops is speared in the air by one of the pursued players.

Speaking of the boys' game by the same name, J. O. Dorsey says that when the hoop is rolled back into play after being returned to the owners, the players raise the shout: "Ho! there a buffalo is returning to you!" And he adds that Bushotter says this is an obsolescent game.[96]

It is said that the game is of Cheyenne origin. It is a matter of fact that the Cheyennes use a hair ornament representing the hoop[97] as a reward of victory in the game.

[96] J. O. Dorsey, "Games of Teton Dakota Children," *Am. Anthrop.*, IV, 4 (1891), 334.

[97] Culin, "Games," p. 505, figure 564.

Upper Half of Drawing

Fifth game: *raka umpi,* "the playing of the elk game."

The implements necessary for playing the game are a peculiarly constructed stick and a small ring wrapped with rawhide. The stick is between thirty-five and forty inches in length. A curved piece of sapling is bound to the end, the points curved toward the handle of the stick, and lashed into position. Two short bars of wood are fastened to the stick at intervals, and immediately below each is another short sapling, curved toward the handle in the same manner as the one at the top. The curved sapling at the end of the stick and the shaft of the stick to a point just below the last crosspieces and the handle are painted; and a small flag, corresponding in color to the crosspieces and the point, is fastened to the

[98] *Ibid.,* pp. 504–505.

curved piece at the end of the stick. The flags, of course, represent the colors of the two sides playing. In Bad Heart Bull's drawing, one stick bears a red flag, the other a blue one.

The stick is held just above the first crosspiece and below the curved strip at the end (see the drawing).

The ring is tossed into the air. The object of the game is then to spear the hoop with the stick. If the ring is caught on the point, it counts ten; if on the nearest spur, five; and on any other, one. The number of points making a game is previously decided upon by the players.[98]

Just as the Cheyennes used a miniature gaming-wheel hair ornament as a prize in the preceding game, so the Dakotas used the same sort of ornament as a prize in this game.[99]

In origin, this game is related to the elk ceremony.

[99] *Ibid.*

No. 210

No. 210. Early Social Life and Its Reorganization

A note in Lakota. Translation: "Courting customs according to the Tetons."

The only new article of apparel in this courting scene (cf. Nos. 86, 87, and 207) is the hood. The wearing of the hoods would indicate that this scene took place in the winter season.

No. 211

No. 211. Early Social Life and Its Reorganization

Sixth game: *huta nacute* (Bad Heart Bull spells it *hunta*), "feathered bone glider."[100]

A note in Lakota. Translation: "*Hunta nacute* is made out of a buffalo rib and two sticks, with feathers attached, wedged into the inside of the bone. The side that slides it farthest wins."

The costumes, especially the hoods and the footgear, of the players here shown indicate that the game was played in the winter.

The player shown at the right in this picture is throwing one of his darts into the air to see whether or not it is properly balanced. If the feathers are properly adjusted, the dart will come down straight, bone point down.

Walker briefly summarized the Oglala game thus:

Any number may play. Each player may have from two to four winged bones, but each player should have the same number. A mark is made from which the bones are thrown so that they may strike or slide on the ice or snow. The players throw alternately until all the bones are thrown. When all the bones are thrown the player whose bone lies farthest from the mark wins the game.[101]

In Bad Heart Bull's drawing, the individual markings of the feathers of the different players' darts are quite plainly visible.

[100] Culin, "Games," pp. 415–419, figures 537, 541, 542; J. O. Dorsey, "Games of Teton Dakota Children," p. 343; Standing Bear, *My People*, pp. 30–31 and drawing opposite

p. 30; J. R. Walker, "Sioux Games. II," *Journal of American Folk-Lore*, XIX, 75 (1906), 31.

[101] Walker, "Sioux Games. II," p. 31.

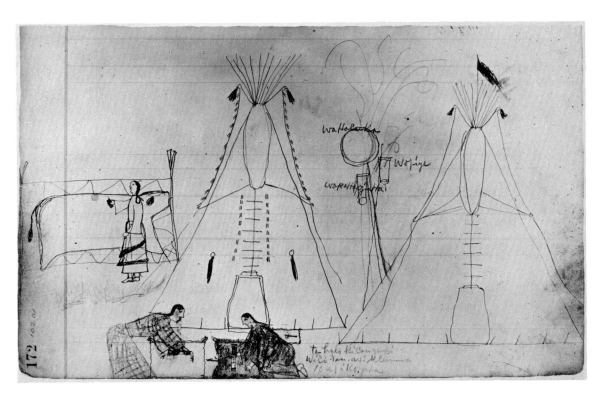

No. 212

No. 212. Early Social Life and Its Reorganization

Tanning done by women.[102]

A brief note in Lakota. Translation: "Handling the raw hides. There are ten doings [operations] connected with this."

The two women in the foreground are shown fleshing and cleaning small hides that have been stretched and pinned to the ground. The woman at the left and in the background is working a buffalo or cow hide that has been hung from a temporary frame.

The ten operations to which Bad Heart Bull refers in his note include the butchering of the animal as well as the tanning proper. In order, these operations are: (1) *wapatapi*, taking the hide off; (2) *wajujupi*, butchering and separating the parts of the animal; (3) *wakablopi*, jerking the meat; (4) *tahalo okatanpi*, stretching the hide over the ground with pins; (5) *parpapi*, fleshing (woman at right in the drawing); (6) *waha ktapi*, cleaning still more, i.e., removing hair,

etc. (woman at left in foreground); (7) *iyutunpi* or *yurunpi*, "working against it," i.e., pulling the skin back and forth across a cord or timber; (8) *kpanyanpi*, putting the white mixture on the hide to make it pliable; (9) *taha zujapi*, "making it yellow," i.e., the tanning proper; and (10) *hanpsicu*, the finished products for tents, moccasins, cases, etc.[103]

Standing Bear's description helps to make the processes clearer. I quote him in full:

> As soon as the hides were brought in, the women spread them on the ground and pegged them out while they were yet fresh, with the flesh side up. Three or four women would then commence to remove all superfluous bits of meat from the hide. In this work they used a piece of flint or a sharp stone before steel and iron came into use among them. These "fleshers" were shaped like a crowbar with teeth in the end. The handle was covered with buckskin, with a buckskin string attached to tie up around the wrist, which

---

[102] Cf., e.g., Dodge, *Our Wild Indians*; Walter McClintock, *Old Indian Trails* (New York and Boston: Houghton Mifflin Co., 1923); Maximilian, Prince of Wied, *Travels in the Interior of North America*, Vols. XXII–XXIV in R. G. Thwaites, ed., *Early Western Travels*, 1748–1846 (Cleveland:

A. H. Clark Co., 1906); Wissler, "North American Indians," pp. 56–66 (figures 18–22); and Standing Bear, *My People*, p. 19.

[103] John Colhoff.

helped to hold the instrument [cf. woman at right, No. 212].

After all the meat was removed from the skin, and it had dried out, it was turned over with the hair on top. Then, with a tool made of elk-horn, they scraped off all the hair. This instrument, clasped in both hands, was used by the women, who worked it toward them. They were very expert in this work [cf. woman at left in foreground, No. 212].

When the hair had all been scraped off, it showed a layer of skin which was dark. This was also removed, showing another layer of white. This the women took off carefully in little flakes, and it was used in making a fine soup. The brains and liver of the buffalo were cooked together, after which this mixture was rubbed all over the skin. It was then folded into a square bundle for four or five days. Several of these bundles of skins would be piled on top of each other.

A frame was now built on which to stretch the skin after it was opened. This frame was made of round poles tied together at the four corners with rawhide thongs. When the skin was opened, it was damp. It was fastened to the frame with rawhide rope run through the peg-holes around the edge of the hide [cf. figure at extreme left, No. 212]. The mixture of brain and liver was now all scraped off, and the skin washed with water until perfectly clean. The women then went all over the skin with a sandstone, which made the hide very soft.

A braided sinew was then tied to a naturally bent tree, and the other end fastened to a stake driven in the ground. This made the sinew taut, like a bowstring. The skin was then taken off the frame and pulled back and forth on this sinew, by the women, until it was very soft. The effect of this was to produce a beautiful white tan.[104]

To the right of the center of the page, between the two lodges, Bad Heart Bull shows three labeled objects. These are three of the things made from rawhide: *waha canka*, a shield; *wopiye*, a bag; and *wapha ojuha*, a warbonnet case.

[104] Standing Bear, *My People*, pp. 19–20.

No. 213

No. 213. Early Social Life and Its Reorganization

Seventh game: *pte heste umpi*, i.e., "using, or playing with, buffalo horn tips."[105]

An additional note in Lakota. Translation: "Many pieces of wearing apparel were lost in this game."

The instruments for playing are throwing arrows which are considerably shorter than the throwing sticks (cf. *baslohanpi*, No. 217) but which, like them, are tipped with buffalo horn, as the first note indicates. Any number of boys may play the game, and the players may use any number of arrows, provided each player has the same number of arrows. To the unpointed end of the arrow several feathers are bound with sinew. These serve as ornaments and as aids to balance adjustment. Louis L. Meeker points out that these arrows were thrown underhand. And Luther

Standing Bear emphasizes the fact that care must be exercised in making the sticks straight so that the direction of their flight might be nicely controlled, for "they were much heavier than the 'hu-ta-na-cu-te' [cf. No. 211], and if they hit you they might kill."

As the costumes in Bad Heart Bull's drawing indicate, the game is a winter one. It was played either on ice or snow, the purpose being to make the arrows glide as far as possible. The players throw alternately. The one who has thrown farthest is the victor and wins all the other arrows.

The second note merely shows conclusively that this, like the rest, is a betting game and that articles of apparel formed a common medium of exchange.

[105] Cf., e.g., Culin, "Games," p. 416; J. O. Dorsey, "Games of Teton Dakota Children," p. 338; Louis L. Meeker, "Ogalala Games," *Bulletin of the Free Museum of*

Science and Art, III (1901), 33, 35; Standing Bear, *My People*, pp. 31–32; and Walker, "Sioux Games. II," p. 32.

No. 214

NO. 214. EARLY SOCIAL LIFE AND ITS REORGANIZATION

Women's costumes.

Five women are shown, two from the rear, three from the front. The first wears a dress made of a heavy wool material, a sort of flannel commonly used by the Dakotas for dresses, leggings, and sometimes blankets. The belt, with its long tail, is made of leather trimmed with silver disks, much like those, already described, found on the long hair ornament worn by men (cf. Nos. 8, 86, and 207). The second woman has a blanket decorated with porcupine quillwork. The third is wrapped in a Navaho blanket.

The fourth wears a cloth dress similar to that worn by the first. This one, however, is decorated at the top with elk teeth, a not unusual but rich manner of trimming in the old days. This woman wears also a belt similar to that of the first woman. The new feature in this figure is the wrapped braid. The fifth woman wears a fringed buckskin dress trimmed with beadwork at the top. She, too, wears the characteristic women's belt, but hers is of a somewhat different type, one without any silver ornaments.

No. 215

NO. 215. EARLY SOCIAL LIFE AND ITS REORGANIZATION

Eighth game: *inyan kawacipi*, "making rock dance," or *can kawacipi*, "making wood dance."

The necessary equipment for each player is a top and a whip with a deer-skin lash. As the names given show, the tops are sometimes made of stone and sometimes of wood. The stone top is an older type. It was usually made of red pipestone and was decorated by incising. The wooden top of the Oglalas was very frequently made of cedar "because many people like the loud buzzing sound that it makes when it spins."[106] Frequently, however, it was made of ash because the weight of ash makes it possible for the top to "kick" others out of the square in a "kicking" match.[107]

This game, as the costumes of the boys show, was a winter game and was usually played on the ice. A square of about five feet was marked (in one way or another) on the ice, one side being left open. The tops were lined up outside the open end of the square and were all started spinning at once.

According to Meeker's description,[108] the players raced to see who could first whip his top into the square through the open end. The boy who invaded the square held it against the others as long as he kept his top spinning within the boundaries of the square. Whenever the top stopped spinning or spun out of the square, the other boys attempted to whip theirs in.

Neither Meeker nor any other of the writers listed in my bibliography,[109] however, mentions the "kicking" match referred to in my first paragraph; but John Colhoff says that this was the sort of play most common in his experience with the game. The three sides of the square were made by laying down lengths of small timber heavy enough so that the spinning tops could not move them. A semicircular entrance mark was then drawn before the open side of the square. Three round marks were made in a row near the side of the square opposite the entrance. These were usually slightly dished so that a top could get into them and continue to spin or could be pushed

[106] John Colhoff, letter of March 2, 1929.
[107] *Ibid.*
[108] Meeker, "Ogalala Games."
[109] Culin, "Games," pp. 745-747, figures 994-1000;

J. O. Dorsey, "Games of Teton Dakota Children," p. 33; Meeker, "Ogalala Games"; Standing Bear, *My People*, p. 32; Walker, "Sioux Games. II," pp. 33-34.

out by another top. Once driven into the enclosure, the tops were not whipped again. The top which stopped spinning on one of the markers last won the game.

Walker describes a form of the game very much like this. The only difference was that there were no markers. The top that was lying nearest the side opposite the entrance when all the tops were "dead" won the game.[110]

This last version seems most nearly to correspond to the drawing, for Bad Heart Bull shows no round markers in his square; there is, however, a line running parallel to the side of the square where the round markers would be.

[110] Walker, "Sioux Games. II," p. 34.

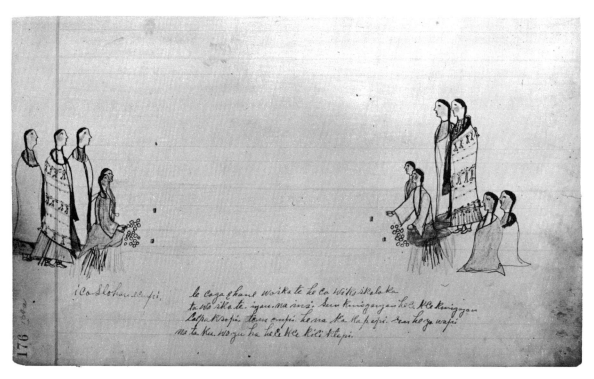

No. 216

No. 216. Early Social Life and Its Reorganization

Ninth game: *ica slohan ecunpi*, i.e., "a game of bowls or marbles."

An additional note in Lakota. Translation:

> During the winter, when the ice is good, this game is played. It is a young women's game. Round stones or something similar are used to roll at the targets. Some sticks are made for counting. Many articles are bet in this game.

This is a little like the game of tenpins, but was played on the ice by opposing teams of two and two, three and three, four and four, etc. The targets were small blocks of wood called *on-pa-pi*, "movable targets." These were about 1½ by 2½ inches in measurement and were painted red and black—in slightly varying fashions. Rounded stones were used for rollers. The women seated themselves on brush seats (see the drawing) on the ice about twenty or thirty feet apart. Each player had her target set a short distance in front of her on the ice. One at a time the stones were rolled. The first player rolled; if she hit the opposite marker, her opponent threw over her first bet, which happened very frequently to be a string of beads. If this bet happened to hit the first player's target, the bet was not yet forfeited but must be returned to the owner. The first player again rolled, and if she again struck the target, the bet was hers. So the game proceeded.

Walker and Standing Bear agree with this description by He Dog and Short Bull, though Walker adds a few minor points in regard to technical rules and Standing Bear mentions a very slight change from the others in the matter of turn of play.[111]

[111] Walker, "Sioux Games. II," p. 29, and Standing Bear, *My People*, p. 33.

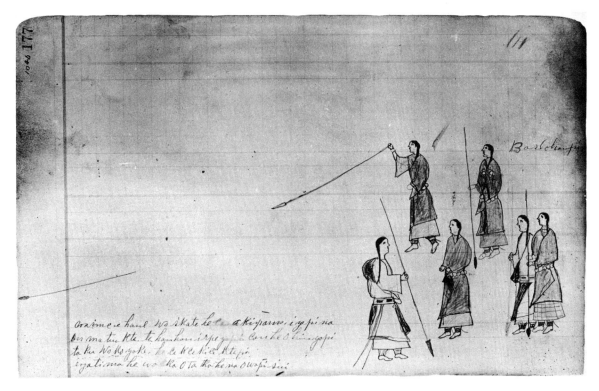

No. 217

No. 217. Early Social Life and Its Reorganization

Tenth game: *baslohanpi*, i.e., "to make it slide (or crawl)," as, for instance, creeping up on an enemy. An additional note in Lakota. Translation:

When there is plenty of snow, this game is played most. They take sides, and whichever side slides the farthest wins. Many useful articles are bet on this game. Although there are indoor games, this one is preferred above all.

The game pictured by Bad Heart Bull is the women's *baslohanpi* game. It was sometimes played by both boys and girls, however, and there was as well a boys' or men's game of the same name which differed but slightly.[112] The game is sometimes designated by the expression "horned-javelin game," for the playing instrument is a long stick—usually willow—tipped with horn. The game, it seems, was played sometimes in the fall, sometimes in the winter, and sometimes in the spring, when the willows were green and easily peeled.

The sticks (javelins) were held by one end and thrown, in the girls' or women's game, from the shoulder (the boys and men frequently shot their sticks from across some rest, such as the hand, arm, foot, a stump, etc.).

Meeker points out that in the girls' game the sticks were thrown high in the air,[113] but He Dog and Short Bull (and Bad Heart Bull's drawing) indicate that the javelin was thrown in such manner that it glided along the ground—or ice or snow, as the case might be. He Dog and Short Bull, in describing the game as played by both boys and girls, say that on a straightaway, boys were better than girls because of their greater strength, but that on a crooked trail, girls were better because the boys' sticks, thrown too hard, frequently jumped the track.

These old men point out further that there were individual bets but a collective score in this game.

112 Cf., e.g., Standing Bear, *My People*, pp. 40–41, and Walker, "Sioux Games. II," p. 31.

113 Meeker, "Ogalala Games," p. 36.

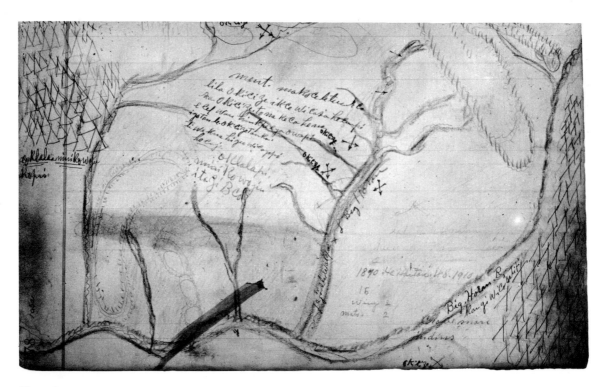

No. 218

NO. 218. SIOUX-CROW FIGHTS. EARLIEST DATES, 1856, 1858

A note in Lakota. Translation:

Montana. In this country great battles were fought by the Indians. Wherever a great battle was fought, you will note the arrows.

The name of this battle is "When They Retreated into Camp."

The last sentence in this note seems somewhat ambiguous, for among the arrow-marked locations of battles fought, this fight is not listed. However, the entry is explained by the fact that the pages immediately following this (Nos. 219 to 284) depict this famous battle. Evidently the fight "When They Retreated into Camp" is the one most prominently in the mind of the artist at the time of his preparation of the page, however, for the date noted at the lower right is the correct date (1870), the place ("along the Little Big Horn") is right, and the camps of the enemy people are shown clearly in the upper left and the lower right corners (Dakotas and Crows, respectively).

The main object of the artist in making such a sketch, however, is the representation of the great hunting ground and battleground of the Dakotas, a section of the country which witnessed many of their fights with other Indians and much of their final stand against the whites. The sketch is a purely topographical one except for the representations of the camps, to which I have already referred. Beginning in the upper right corner and running down through

the foreground of the sketch is the Big Horn River. Above that extend the four prominent tributaries, in order from left to right: the Powder, Tongue, Rosebud, and Little Big Horn (Greasy Grass) rivers; the last is the only one named by Bad Heart Bull, however.

The large potato-shaped and bristled mass at the upper right represents the Big Horn Mountains and is fairly accurately placed. Similar masses at the lower left must be the Rosebud Mountains, in which case they are much too far north (too low in this sketch).

In his attempt to make the map compact, Bad Heart Bull has had to sacrifice somewhat in accuracy and clearness. The river running up and down at the extreme left of the page is the Powder River, according to He Dog and Short Bull (and corresponds in general trend and comparative length to official cartographic representations of it). This river does not, however, empty into the Big Horn, but into the Yellowstone, into which, at a more western point, the Big Horn itself empties. I believe, especially since he has placed the name "Big Horn R." so far to the right, that the artist intended the left-to-right stream here to represent the Yellowstone part way across the page to a point where the Big Horn branches off (somewhere to the left of the mouth of the *Little* Big Horn) but that he failed to continue the Yellowstone, since he had no more use for it at this time.

No. 219

No. 219. Sioux-Crow Fights. Earliest Dates, 1856, 1858

Brief note in Lakota. Translation: "Running off with the Crow horses."

Four Dakota warriors, variously garbed, are driving off a bunch of horses. This marks the beginning of the long series of drawings (Nos. 219 to 284) depicting the battle familiarly known as "When They Retreated into Camp," "When They Chased Them Back to Camp," or "When They Drove Them Back to Their Lodges."

The engagement was precipitated when the Crows discovered the Dakotas driving off the stolen horses. Immediately, of course, the Crows gave chase. The Dakotas promptly scattered on both sides of the ridges, and a long running fight followed. The succeeding pages show the scattered fighting and bring out specifically individual episodes and personal exploits. Many pages will not need particular comment, since frequently page follows page only to suggest the precipitancy of the action and the general character of the running fight.

No. 220

No. 220. SIOUX-CROW FIGHTS. EARLIEST DATES, 1856, 1858

Sioux fleeing from the Crows.

No. 221

NO. 221. SIOUX-CROW FIGHTS. EARLIEST DATES, 1856, 1858

Insert page showing the Dakotas still in flight.

Again Bad Heart Bull naïvely indicates the fighting *on both sides* of the ridges by letting wavy lines represent the tops of the ridges. Only the heads of men and horses are visible above the topmost ridge; the legs of the horses are not visible behind the second ridge. Thus he suggests perspective.

No. 222

NO. 222.   SIOUX-CROW FIGHTS. EARLIEST DATES, 1856, 1858

Sioux shield, upper left. The waved lines covering
the upper half represent lightning and rain; the
thunder beings are symbolized.

No. 223

NO. 223.   SIOUX-CROW FIGHTS. EARLIEST DATES, 1856, 1858

Another insert.

Double mount, lower left. Roan Eagle (*Wanbli Hinrata*), an Oglala, is rescuing a Miniconjou relative by the name of Bald Eagle (*Anukasan*) whose horse has given out.

The following warrior, who is acting as rear guard, is the elder Bad Heart Bull.

No. 224

NO. 224. SIOUX-CROW FIGHTS. EARLIEST DATES, 1856, 1858

Sioux still fleeing from Crows.

The warrior in the immediate foreground, lower left, has in his mouth an eagle-bone whistle, with which, in his extremity, he is appealing to the swift-winged beings of the air to protect him.[114]

[114] Cf., e.g., Wissler, "Protective Designs," p. 47.

The warrior just above him evidently depends strongly upon the thunder beings, for he wears the forked-lightning symbol upon his face and has painted his horse with a similar symbol, as well as with the hailstone marks of the storm forces.

No. 225

NO. 225.   SIOUX-CROW FIGHTS. EARLIEST DATES, 1856, 1858

Moccasin Top (*Hanpi Ska*), above, and Spotted Deer (*Heraka Kle Ska*) defy the enemy; they alone turn back to face the Crows in the thick of the fight.

Moccasin Top carries the straight, feathered lance of the Cante Tinza Society.[115]

[115] Cf. No. 22 and Wissler, "Societies," pp. 25–31, 67, and 68 (figure 3c).

No. 226

NO. 226.   SIOUX-CROW FIGHTS. EARLIEST DATES, 1856, 1858

Brief note in Lakota. Translation: "This relates to
'When They Ran Them into Camp.'"
The Crows still have the advantage.

No. 227

NO. 227. SIOUX-CROW FIGHTS. EARLIEST DATES, 1856, 1858

A note in Lakota. Translation: "While chasing, this person was shot off his horse."

The Dakotas have at last made a stand against the Crows, and the foremost Crow is seen falling from his horse. There is some dispute as to whether the elder Bad Heart Bull or Ghost Bear shot this Crow; the bird head charm was worn by both. If this is Bad Heart Bull, he has left off his fox skin on this occasion.

No. 228

No. 228. Sioux-Crow Fights. Earliest Dates, 1856, 1858

At one point in this running battle, the Crows are really being halted. Though some of the Sioux are still in flight, some have stopped and are effectively turning back the enemy. At the upper right a Crow in full retreat is seen from the rear. For the rest, at this particular point, only the heels and tails of the horses are visible at the edge of the page.

Though Wissler states that the members of the Chiefs Society did not go out on war parties,[116] He Dog insists that the warrior in the lower right corner of this drawing is an officer in the Chiefs Society, as is evidenced by the fringed blue shirt and the eagle-feather head ornament, and he identifies him as Brave Heart (*Cante Okitika*), who was noted for taking the front.

Other society affiliations are plainly indicated on this page. To Brave Heart's left is a Tokala bow lance. At the top of the page and a little to the left is a Miwatani sash wearer; he wears also the headdress of

owl feathers peculiar to his office.[117] The feathered, panel-like piece of equipment floating out behind him is the so-called sash. A large loop at one end slipped over the head, and the sash then hung down across the body from the left shoulder to the right side below the arm. By this sash, the wearer staked himself down before the enemy. He could not be released from this precarious position until he had counted coup upon an enemy or until a fellow tribesman could fight back the enemy sufficiently to pull up the stake and free his comrade.

At the extreme left (above), is a bonnet wearer of the Cante Tinza (Braves) Society. The buffalo horns at each side of the headpiece, and the long feathered tail, are the characteristic features of this headdress.[118] These officers also staked themselves down before the enemy.[119] On this occasion, they seem not to be living up to their obligations.

[116] Wissler, "Societies," p. 41.
[117] *Ibid.*, pp. 41–48.

[118] *Ibid.*, pp. 25–26.
[119] *Ibid.*

No. 229

NO. 229. SIOUX-CROW FIGHTS. EARLIEST DATES, 1856, 1858

At some points in this scattered fighting the Crows still have the advantage. A warrior wearing a special bear warbonnet leads the attacking Crows. This man appears again in Nos. 277 and 278.

No. 230

NO. 230.   SIOUX-CROW FIGHTS. EARLIEST DATES, 1856, 1858

Sioux in flight.

Lower left, a Kangi Yuha short-lance bearer. The crow skin is visible just above the point of the lance.[120]

[120] Cf., e.g., No. 29 and Wissler, "Societies," p. 24.

No. 231

NO. 231. SIOUX-CROW FIGHTS. EARLIEST DATES, 1856, 1858

A note in Lakota. Translation: "Two Sioux were killed."

The man with the bow and arrows is Dog Chief (*Sunka Yatapi*).

The other one is Cottonwood Tree (*Wagalan*).

No. 232

No. 232. Sioux–Crow Fights. Earliest Dates, 1856, 1858

Two very brief notes in Lakota. Translation:

[1] They say he shot him through the ear [i.e., the upper Crow].

[2] Stuck an arrow in his skin [i.e., an arrow was shot from a bow and struck so that it stuck up in the flesh. This arrow is to be seen in the right leg of the lower warrior].

Dog Chief (*Sunka Yatapi*) is the Sioux who has thus wounded the Crows. Evidently he succeeded in doing this much before he himself was killed (cf. No. 231).

No. 233

No. 233. SIOUX-CROW FIGHTS. EARLIEST DATES, 1856, 1858

The Dakotas are still in flight.
Typical Crow costumes are plainly evident.

No. 234

NO. 234.   SIOUX-CROW FIGHTS. EARLIEST DATES, 1856, 1858

The Sioux have been driven across the river.

No. 235

NO. 235.   SIOUX-CROW FIGHTS. EARLIEST DATES, 1856, 1858

A brief note in Lakota. Translation: "The one who killed the mule, they say, was wounded again."

Who this person is, is not clear.

The drawing shows two pack mules (probably trophies of the Custer fight [sic]) drinking at the river. The foremost Crow warrior is striking one of them. On the opposite side of the river, the Dakotas have turned back to face the enemy. Evidently the leading Crow is the one who killed the mule. The headmost Dakota is firing at him.

No. 236

No. 236. Sioux-Crow Fights. Earliest Dates, 1856, 1858

A note in Lakota. Translation: "This is the man who killed the mule. They are taking him away."

Two Crow warriors, one on each side of him, are helping a third from the field. It is necessary for them to hold him on his horse. This is an example of the way in which the Plains Indians rescued their wounded and killed on the field of battle.

No. 237

NO. 237. SIOUX–CROW FIGHTS. EARLIEST DATES, 1856, 1858

A miniature, panoramic presentation of the moment when the Dakotas have crossed the river (cf. No. 235) and a few halt to try to stop the Crows.

No. 238

NO. 238.   SIOUX-CROW FIGHTS. EARLIEST DATES, 1856, 1858

A note in Lakota. Translation: "This is Muskrat. When they killed him, they didn't come any farther."

A close-up view of the scene of No. 237.

Bad Heart Bull the elder, mounted, and Muskrat (*Sinkpe*), creeping toward the enemy, are meeting the Crows alone.

Muskrat (*Sinkpela* is the full spelling) was the last man killed by the Crows before they were forced to retreat.

No. 239

NO. 239.   SIOUX-CROW FIGHTS. EARLIEST DATES, 1856, 1858

Bad Heart Bull and Thunder Tail (*Wakinyan
Situpi*) charge into the Crows as the tide of battle
turns.

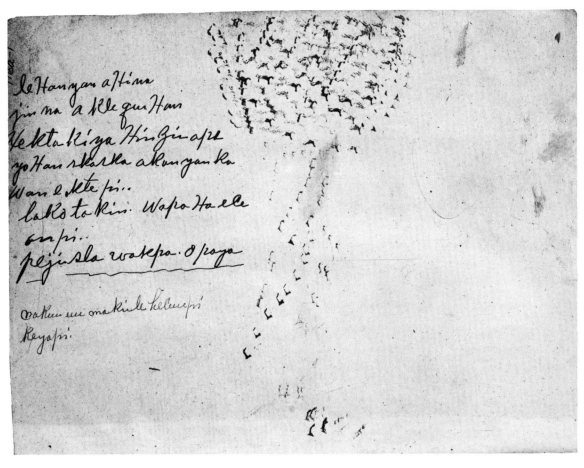

No. 240

No. 240.   Sioux-Crow Fights.   Earliest Dates, 1856, 1858

Insert page bearing a note in Lakota. Translation:

They [the Dakotas] made a stand thus far. Then they started back. One [Crow] riding a buckskin horse with a white mane was killed [cf. Nos. 242 and 243]. The Sioux all wore warbonnets [the following close-ups, Nos. 242, 243, and 244, show this]. This was along the Little Big Horn.

This is a very small-scale, highly impressionistic portrayal of the turning point in the battle. The statement that "the Sioux all wore warbonnets" refers to the second party of Sioux warriors, who returned to camp just in time to save their people from utter defeat.

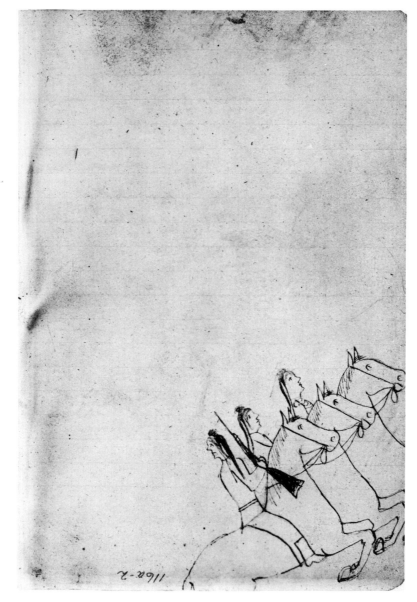

No. 241

No. 241.   SIOUX-CROW FIGHTS. EARLIEST DATES, 1856, 1858

Three mounted Crows making their escape.

No. 242

No. 242. Sioux-Crow Fights. Earliest Dates, 1856, 1858

A note in Lakota. Translation: "This is Charging Eagle. He should have been the one to first strike the Crow. He was accused of missing him."

Portrayal of a Dakota warrior on horseback about to strike a dismounted Crow with the Tokala bow lance. This Crow is the one who tried to escape on his "buckskin horse with a white mane" (see No. 240). Some Dakotas insisted that Charging Eagle (*Wanbli Watakpe*) did not strike the Crow and consequently was not entitled to coup credit. But Short Bull says that he saw the lance banner touch the Crow. The buckskin pony is seen in the lower left corner.

No. 243

No. 243. Sioux-Crow Fights. Earliest Dates, 1856, 1858

A sequel to No. 242. A note in Lakota. Translation: "They were made to retreat to their lodges. He was killed at the rear."

This time it is the Crows who are retreating to their lodges; the tide of battle has changed, and this Crow is one of the men who were covering the retreat. Charging Eagle is riding away on his pinto war horse. He has killed and scalped the Crow.

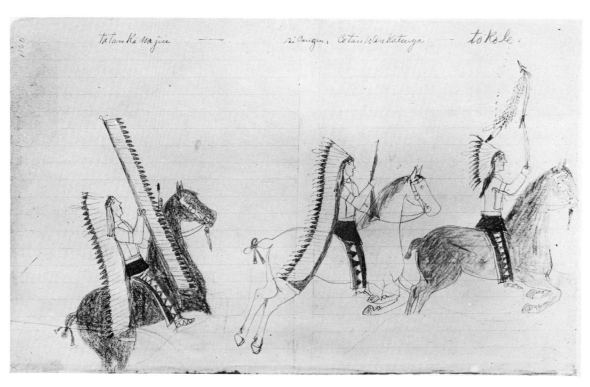

No. 244

No. 244. Sioux-Crow Fights. Earliest Dates, 1856, 1858

Three of the prominent Dakota warriors; left to right: Standing Buffalo (*Tatanka Najin*), a Miniconjou; High Hawk (*Cetan Wan*) or Yellow Thigh (*Sicanzin*), a Rosebud; and Hunts Enemy (*Tokole*), a Sans Arc. Later the Miniconjou and the Sans Arc were killed. They came in mortally wounded and were later buried on a high cedar butte.

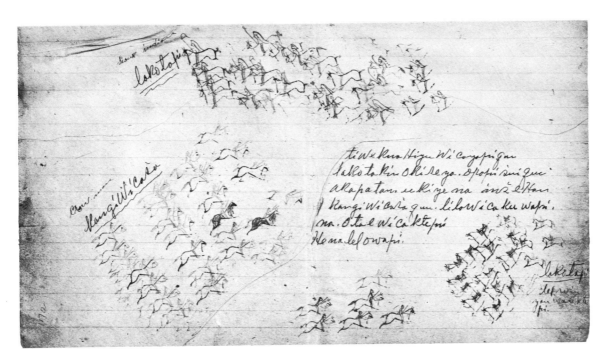

No. 245

No. 245. Sioux-Crow Fights. Earliest Dates, 1856, 1858

Another impressionistic miniature of the change in the fortunes of the two forces.

Two notes in Lakota. Translation:

[1] When they were forced to retreat to their lodges, half of the Sioux were not present; but shortly after this they returned and in turn made it miserable for the Crows and killed a lot of them.

[2] Here a woman was killed [lower right].

As is evident from what has preceded, this drawing is somewhat out of natural order. The party of Crow warriors (lower left and foreground) are riding toward the Dakota camp (Sioux pack horses are seen lower right). Then the second Sioux war party is seen appearing over the ridge (top).

No. 246

No. 246. Sioux-Crow Fights. Earliest Dates, 1856, 1858

First of a series of large-scale drawings showing the retreat of the Crows.

The center Sioux warrior, wearing a short red mantle and an odd cap to match, is High Back Bone (*Canku Wankatuya*), whose name is sometimes mis-translated "Big Breast" (see also Nos. 254 and 279). He was later killed by the Shoshonis.

No. 247

NO. 247.   SIOUX-CROW FIGHTS. EARLIEST DATES, 1856, 1858

Crow flight continued.
Variety of costumes, but no identifiable warriors.

No. 248

NO. 248.   SIOUX-CROW FIGHTS. EARLIEST DATES, 1856, 1858

Crow retreat becoming a mad rout.
  Peculiar Crow head decoration, lower right corner.
Porcupine-quill ornaments are woven into the hair.

No. 249

NO. 249.   SIOUX-CROW FIGHTS. EARLIEST DATES, 1856, 1858

The Crow flight continued.
Bad Heart Bull shows a row of five horses, bearing

Crow riders, seen at full gallop from the rear.
Composition and perspective are not good.

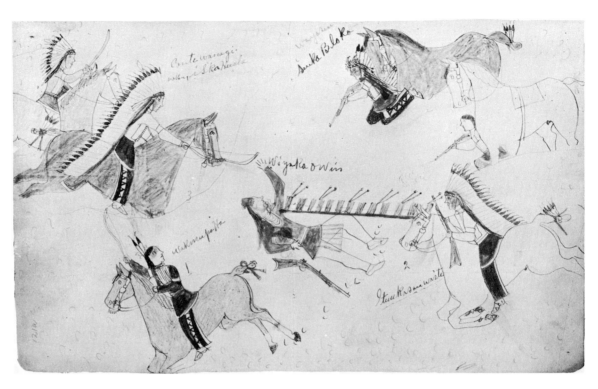

No. 250

NO. 250.   SIOUX-CROW FIGHTS. EARLIEST DATES, 1856, 1858

Several Dakota warriors counting coup upon an enemy whom they have unhorsed and surrounded.

Beginning at the upper left and reading down and around, they are: Ghost Heart (*Cante Wanagi*); Feather Ear Ring (*Wiyaka Owin*); Pumpkin Hill (*Wakmu Paha*); Good Weasel (*Itunkasan Waste*);

Charging Bear (*Mato Watakpe*), familiarly known as Little Big Man but not named in the manuscript; and He Dog (*Sunka Bloka*). Good Weasel is striking the Crow with the feathered lance of the Cante Tinza. He Dog wears a horned and feathered headdress and, from his left shoulder, a fox skin.

No. 251

NO. 251.   SIOUX-CROW FIGHTS. EARLIEST DATES, 1856, 1858

Crows still in flight. Their horses are becoming exhausted.

The odd portrayal at the bottom of the page is a conventional representation of unhorsed Crows seeking refuge in the timber. The same sort of portrayal appears many times in the following pages; usually the trees are shown in green, but here black ink is used.

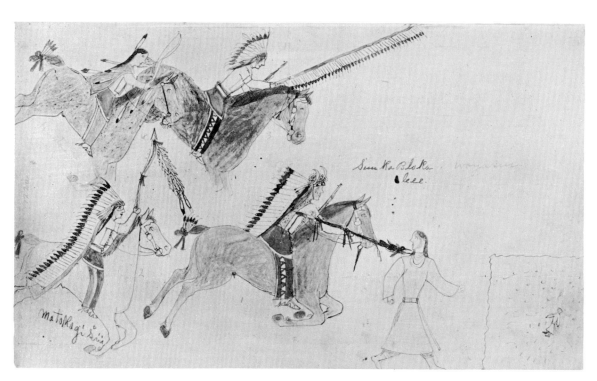

No. 252

NO. 252. SIOUX-CROW FIGHTS. EARLIEST DATES, 1856, 1858

The killing of a Crow woman (see Lakota note 2 of No. 245).

He Dog (*Sunka Bloka*) is striking the woman. (After his name the word *wayasin* is written in pencil. The word means "judge" and is here intended to further identify He Dog, who was later, for years, a judge in the Indian court at Pine Ridge.) He says that he was so enraged at finding his fellow tribesmen so beset by the Crows that he did a thing he had never done before and never did again—he killed a woman. (The "footnote" shows that she was killed.) The instrument with which he is striking the woman is the crow lance of the Kangi Yuha Society, of which he had just been made the bearer. Chief Crazy Horse was the other carrier of the crow lance at the time.

Fearless Bear (*Mato Kagi Sni*) (lower left) counted coup on her second with the Tokala bow lance.

No. 253

NO. 253. SIOUX-CROW FIGHTS. EARLIEST DATES, 1856, 1858

Crow flight continued.

No. 254

No. 254. Sioux-Crow Fights. Earliest Dates, 1856, 1858

High Back Bone (*Canku Wankatuya*) counting coup upon a Crow (cf. Nos. 246 and 279). Three other Dakotas approach to strike the enemy also. The "footnote" (right) shows the dead, stripped body of the Crow.

No. 255

NO. 255.   SIOUX-CROW FIGHTS. EARLIEST DATES, 1856, 1858

Crows still in flight. One (upper right) stops and turns to fire into the pursuing Sioux.

A great variety of costumes and weapons is shown. Bad Heart Bull portrays the horses in at least three distinct positions: one Dakota horse (upper left) has been brought to an abrupt halt in order that the rider may meet the fire of one of the Crows; the horse to its right is caught in a rearing, foreshortened position; and most of the rest are seen at full gallop.

No. 256

NO. 256. SIOUX-CROW FIGHTS. EARLIEST DATES, 1856, 1858

Next to the rear view of the Crow warrior (left), to which I have referred before, the outstanding feature of this composition is the variety of positions of the horses and men.

No. 257

NO. 257.   SIOUX-CROW FIGHTS. EARLIEST DATES, 1856, 1858

Crow retreat continued.
Three-quarter foreshortened rear, full-profile, and
full-front views of horses.

No. 258

NO. 258.   SIOUX-CROW FIGHTS. EARLIEST DATES, 1856, 1858

Crows causing a momentary halt of a group of
Sioux.

No. 259

No. 259. Sioux-Crow Fights. Earliest Dates, 1856, 1858

The Dakotas again assume the offensive.

A Dakota warrior counts coup upon and kills an unhorsed Crow. The name of the Sioux, as here given, is *Huca Se Slasla*, sometimes translated "Rattling Leggings" but more literally "Skin Garters with the Hair Worn Off."[121] This is the

[121] John Colhoff.

Dakota's nickname, however. The proper name is Afraid of Thunder (*Wakiyan Kakipapi*).

Another dismounted Crow is running for the shelter of the timber.

A noticeable feature of this page is the number (five) of patches used in making corrections or additions in the drawing.

No. 260

No. 260.   Sioux-Crow Fights. Earliest Dates, 1856, 1858

Sioux still attacking.

The center of interest here is the Miwatani sash and bonnet wearer (cf. No. 24).[122]

[122] Cf. also, e.g., Wissler, "Societies," pp. 41–48, 69 (figure 5), and 71–74.

No. 261

NO. 261.   SIOUX-CROW FIGHTS. EARLIEST DATES, 1856, 1858

Sioux firing at the Crows, from both sides of the
ridge.

Little regard for perspective is evident.

No. 262

NO. 262.   SIOUX-CROW FIGHTS. EARLIEST DATES, 1856, 1858

The exploit of Sun Eagle Feather (*Wiwanblupi*).

Another case of the reckless bravado common to Plains warriors. Sun Eagle Feather (wearing a fawn-skin charm) had already counted coup on the Crow. To further show his great bravery, however, he wished to do it again. He circled the Crow (see hoofprints) and killed him, but in so doing he was so badly wounded by the Crow that a few moments later he fell from his horse (see miniature figure, upper center).

Perspective in this instance is suggested by the diminutive size of the fallen figure of the Dakota.

The "footnote" indicates the Crow's end.

No. 263

No. 263. Sioux-Crow Fights. Earliest Dates, 1856, 1858

The exploit of Iron Magpie (*Onkcekira Maza*). This warrior (who, like Sun Eagle Feather, wears a fawn-skin charm) also counts first coup on a Crow, but he himself is not hurt.

No. 264

No 264. Sioux-Crow Fights. Earliest Dates, 1856, 1858

The Crow retreat continued.

By means of a long, narrow patch, Bad Heart Bull has given the Sioux warrior (upper left) a full-length eagle-feather warbonnet in the place of headgear of a less pretentious kind.

No. 265

NO. 265.   SIOUX-CROW FIGHTS. EARLIEST DATES, 1856, 1858

Crows in riotous retreat.

Confusion is the chief effect in this drawing. A number of Crows (unhorsed) are seeking shelter in a thicket (center). Several others (lower left), bent low over the necks of their horses, are making a hard run to escape the pursuers. In the center foreground, two Crows are attempting to escape on one horse.

This page shows a number of the late type of horse heads, and even whole horses, of which I have spoken elsewhere.

No. 266

No. 266.   Sioux-Crow Fights. Earliest Dates, 1856, 1858

The Crows still in flight.

The center of interest is the horse with the double mount and the unhorsed warrior who attempts to aid in his escape by grasping the tail of the already overloaded animal.

This is another drawing from the second insert series, which lacks the vigor and general effectiveness of the other series.

No. 267

NO. 267. SIOUX-CROW FIGHTS. EARLIEST DATES, 1856, 1858

Crow flight continued.
Drawing from second insert series.

No. 268

NO. 268.   SIOUX-CROW FIGHTS. EARLIEST DATES, 1856, 1858

Crow flight continued.

No. 269

No. 269.   Sioux-Crow Fights. Earliest Dates, 1856, 1858

Crow flight continued.
A much patched page bearing a drawing from the
second insert series.

No. 270

NO. 270.   SIOUX-CROW FIGHTS. EARLIEST DATES, 1856, 1858

The Crow flight continued.

Runs Fearless (*Kagi Sni Inyanka*; see also Nos. 277, 278, and 287 to 293) is counting coup upon an un-horsed Crow. Other Crows have sought refuge in clumps of timber (foreground and extreme left).

No. 271

NO. 271. SIOUX-CROW FIGHTS. EARLIEST DATES, 1856, 1858

Crows still beset by Dakotas.

An unidentified Sioux warrior counts coup upon a Crow boy, while three other Sioux ride up to count the second, third, and fourth coups. Lest the observer should not realize from the size of the unfortunate Crow that he is a mere boy, the artist has labeled the figure "Boy."

Two other Crows, hiding among trees, are seen at the left.

No. 272

NO. 272.   SIOUX-CROW FIGHTS. EARLIEST DATES, 1856, 1858

The Crows still in hurried flight.

No. 273

NO. 273.   SIOUX–CROW FIGHTS. EARLIEST DATES, 1856, 1858

The flight continued.

No. 274

NO. 274. SIOUX-CROW FIGHTS. EARLIEST DATES, 1856, 1858

Crows still retreating.

A very brief note in Lakota attached to central horseman. Translation: "This is his battle," meaning that *he* was the hero of the episode. Probably High Back Bone (see also Nos. 246, 254, and 279) is meant, for he was the hero of such a momentary episode as this.

There is more action, more suggestion of dynamic motion in this composition than in the two preceding. This one belongs to the series on original ledger pages, the others to the second insert type of drawing. The right end of this composition, however, has been added later on a large patch and the technique is that of the later insert series.

No. 275

NO. 275. SIOUX-CROW FIGHTS. EARLIEST DATES, 1856, 1858

Crows in flight, seeking protection of timber, and fighting on foot.

Struck by an arrow which has been shot by a Crow in hiding, a Sioux horse stops suddenly, almost throwing the rider (lower left). To the right, a Dakota warrior counts coup on a dismounted Crow.

No. 276

NO. 276.   SIOUX-CROW FIGHTS. EARLIEST DATES, 1856, 1858

Three Dakotas kill and count coup upon a lone
Crow (see part 2 of No. 277).

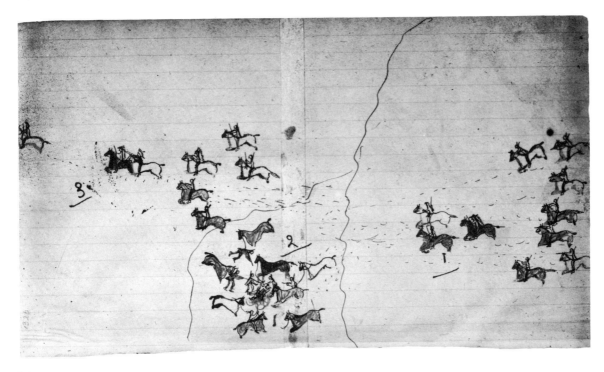

No. 277

No. 277. Sioux-Crow Fights. Earliest Dates, 1856, 1858

A single-page composition showing three moments in the pursuit of three Crows (see also Nos. 276 and 278).

In his peculiar miniature style, Bad Heart Bull portrays the three parts of this episode, separating the parts by wavy lines.

A party of seven Dakotas pursue three Crows, the most prominent of whom is the warrior with the bear warbonnet, referred to in No. 229 (see part 1, extreme right). The Crow on the dark horse finally breaks off to the left and is overtaken by several of the Sioux, who kill and scalp him (see part 2, center, and compare the close-up No. 276). Bear Warbonnet (so called by the Dakotas because of his distinctive headgear) and the third Crow continue to their right, followed by the rest of the Sioux. The third part of the drawing shows the foremost Dakota warrior overtaking and counting coup upon Bear Warbonnet before killing him, while the third Crow makes his escape (see Chapter IV, pp. 54–55).

No. 278

NO. 278. SIOUX-CROW FIGHTS. EARLIEST DATES, 1856, 1858

Killing of Bear Warbonnet. A close-up of part 3 of the preceding miniature.

Runs Fearless (cf. Nos. 270, 277, and 287–293), justifying his name, has outstripped his fellow tribes- men and is the first to count coup upon the Crow; he strikes him with his bow. The "footnote" indicates the fate of the Crow.

No. 279

NO. 279.   SIOUX-CROW FIGHTS. EARLIEST DATES, 1856, 1858

General flight of the Crows continued. High Back Bone (*Canku Wankatuya*) is again distinguishable by his red mantle and cap (cf. Nos. 246 and 254).

No. 280

General flight of the Crows continued.

No. 281

NO. 281.   SIOUX-CROW FIGHTS. EARLIEST DATES, 1856, 1858

Episode in flight of Crows.

A Crow has been overtaken and dragged from his horse and is being stripped and scalped. This shows very well the Dakota manner of scalping.

The Dakota at lower left has captured the Crow's horse.

No. 282

No. 282. Sioux-Crow Fights. Earliest Dates, 1856, 1858

Episode in Crow rout.

Fifteen mounted Dakota warriors circle a lone Crow at a run while a sixteenth counts coup upon him with a lance and another rides in from his rear to strike him with a bow.

Rear, full-front, profile, and somewhat foreshortened views are all seen in this drawing. It is effective in composition, atmosphere, and the suggestion of action.

No. 283

NO. 283.   SIOUX-CROW FIGHTS. EARLIEST DATES, 1856, 1858

One of the last moments in the retreat of the Crows.

They have been driven back practically to their camp, and the Sioux are becoming less ardent in their pursuit. In fact, one Dakota (upper right) is riding toward the rear, leading a captured horse. Many of the Crows are afoot.

The general effect of the composition has been ruined by the insertion, in the left half, of numerous horse heads of the style of the second insert series.

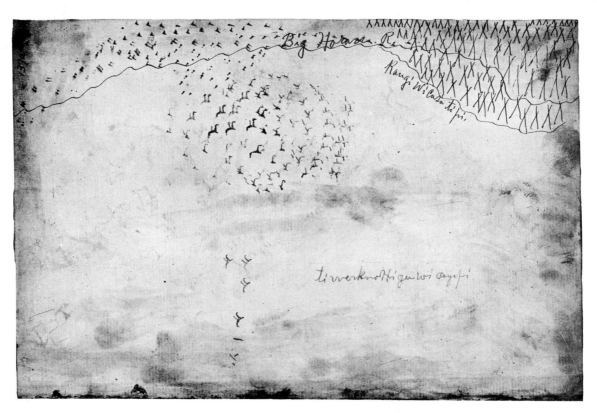

No. 284

No. 284. Sioux-Crow Fights. Earliest Dates, 1856, 1858

Two notes in Lakota. Translation: 1. "They ran them [the Crows] into the village" (lower right). 2. "Lodges of the Crows" (upper right).

A very small impressionistic miniature summarizing the result of the battle; the last of the series.

The Big Horn River is indicated. Beyond it is the Crow village. Below, the Crows are retreating toward the lodges.

No. 285

No. 285. Sioux-Crow Fights. Earliest Dates, 1856, 1858

The killing of a Crow by three Dakotas, one of whom is counting coup with a bow.

The latter's name appears above him in Lakota. In translation it means "Buttock on Both Ends," and more properly should be spelled *Anuk Onze*. This, however, is a nickname borrowed from a famous warrior relative. The proper name of the Dakota here pictured is Fire Thunder (*Wakiyan Peta*). The exact event represented here is not clear. This warrior, however, gained considerable honor at one time by counting first coup on two Crows in one year. The feat was considered such a striking one that one of the Oglala calendar years is known as "Anuk Onze killed two Crows."[123]

[123] Short Man winter count, 1872.

No. 286

No. 286. Sioux-Crow Fights. Earliest Dates, 1856, 1858

Two unmounted Dakotas wearing eagle-feather warbonnets occupy the center of the drawing. At the left are two mounted warriors designated in English as Sitting Crow (*Kangi Iyatake*) and Lone Man (*Išna Wica*), and at the right is another whose name is not given. The unmounted warrior to the left is labeled in Lakota: "It never was known where he was killed."

A penciled note on the otherwise blank page preceding reads thus: "Sitting Crow, Only Man, No Tears, and a Lower Brulé. These warriors were killed by the Crows in a fight."

Since the notes on No. 286 give the names of the two warriors at the left as Sitting Crow and Lone Man, these are evidently the men referred to in the note from the preceding page. The time of the killing of these men was "when Runs Fearless killed the four Crows." This would place the drawing as but slightly out of order, since the battle in which Runs Fearless distinguished himself, the second Arrow Creek fight, immediately follows (Nos. 287 to 296).

The fifth warrior remains unidentified.

No. 287

No. 287. Sioux-Crow Fights. Earliest Dates, 1856, 1858

A note in Lakota. Translation: "Costume worn by Runs Fearless [*Kagi Sni Inyanka*] when they were being killed off."

A mounted warrior is pictured. His garb is the same as that worn on all other occasions when he is shown (cf. Nos. 270, 277, 278, 289 and 290–293): leggings of a heavy flannel-like material much used by the Indians for leggings and blankets, beaded the length of the legging at the outer side; a bright yellow shirt; a bone-tube breastplate; and an eagle-feather war-bonnet. His horse is a dark buckskin with black mane and tail—the tail decorated with three eagle feathers.

This introduces the second Arrow Creek fight, which occurred, according to Left Heron and Short Bull, in the year 1872—in July or August because, as Short Bull has it, "chokecherries were ripening."

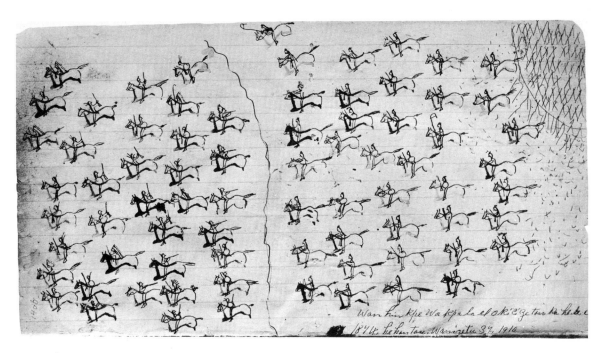

No. 288

NO. 288.   SIOUX-CROW FIGHTS. EARLIEST DATES, 1856, 1858

Second Arrow Creek Fight

A note in Lakota. Translation: "This relates to the big fight at Arrow Creek."

The artist has dated this 1874; but, as I have already pointed out, the two old men place it two years earlier.

In a miniature-scale impressionistic drawing in black and white, Bad Heart Bull shows a large war party of Crows driving a similar body of Dakotas before them. The Crow camp is represented at the upper right behind the Crow force.

No. 289

No. 289. Sioux-Crow Fights. Earliest Dates, 1856, 1858

Second Arrow Creek Fight

A note in Lakota. Translation:

> He [Runs Fearless] turned and made a charge at them, but his horse was shot down. This happened at the Arrow Creek fight. It may be that they shot each other's horses. It was reported that he was attacked and was struck three times but that each time he shot one [Crow].

Another notation lists the Oglala, Miniconjou, and Sans Arc Dakotas as participants in this engagement.

Bad Heart Bull portrays again in miniature one of those uniquely Plains Indian single-combat episodes between the lines of opposing forces. As the preceding drawing shows, the Dakotas are in full retreat before the Crows. Then, after crossing the creek (marked by the penned lines to indicate light timber along the banks), several turn and make a stand to support the singlehanded charge of Runs Fearless. The pictorial effect is rather cinematic in spirit and quality, several moments in the action being represented in the one composition. As the note shows, four Crows in rapid succession attack the lone Dakota. The hoofprints show the path taken by each combatant. Runs Fearless can be identified by his yellow shirt and brown horse.

The Dakota charged the Crows. One rides out to meet him, and both men are unhorsed (see encounter, extreme right, Runs Fearless beside his horse shooting at a fleeing Crow). A second Crow dashes out and charges the dismounted Runs Fearless. He counts coup upon the Dakota but is shot and later falls from his horse (see the figure marked *1*, lying prone, top of page). Before this Crow has fairly been dispatched, another (marked *2*, just below *1*) strikes the hard-pressed Runs Fearless, but he also is shot. Finally a fourth Crow on a red horse (marked *3*) overtakes the Dakota when he is halfway back to his own line; he succeeds in counting coup upon him, but he, too, is shot, and Runs Fearless succeeds in reaching his own party. He has vanquished four enemy warriors.

The mounted Dakota warrior covering Runs Fearless' retreat is Sitting Hawk (*Ceta Iytaka*). Iron Thunder (*Marpiya Maza*), lower left, attempted to ride to Runs Fearless' rescue, but his horse was shot down and he was forced to retreat.

The numbers mark the Crows killed by Runs Fearless. The first Crow to attack, who was unhorsed at the same time as the Dakota, did not strike Runs Fearless, it is to be noticed, and was not himself shot.

No. 290

NO. 290. SIOUX-CROW FIGHTS. EARLIEST DATES, 1856, 1858

Second Arrow Creek Fight

A close-up of the first encounter—the unhorsing of both Runs Fearless and the Crow.

A crude attempt at perspective for the purpose of giving prominence to the main actors is seen in the row of miniature Sioux horsemen at the left.

No. 291

NO. 291. SIOUX-CROW FIGHTS. EARLIEST DATES, 1856, 1858

Second Arrow Creek Fight

Close-up of Runs Fearless' second encounter (see No. 289).

Perspective similar to that on the preceding page is seen here in the representation of a row of Crows at the right.

No. 292

NO. 292. SIOUX-CROW FIGHTS. EARLIEST DATES, 1856, 1858

Second Arrow Creek Fight
Close-up of Runs Fearless and his second victim.

No. 293

NO. 293. SIOUX-CROW FIGHTS. EARLIEST DATES, 1856, 1858

Second Arrow Creek Fight
Close-up of the shooting of the third Crow.

No. 294

NO. 294. SIOUX-CROW FIGHTS. EARLIEST DATES, 1856, 1858

Second Arrow Creek Fight

Episode in the more general fighting that followed.

A close-up of five Dakota warriors rushing up to count coup on a fallen Crow (only the first four in any encounter can be tallied, however, so Bad Heart Bull numbers the fortunate warriors).

He Dog disagrees with the artist's indication (by number) of the order in which these braves struck the Crow (a point which is very important in Indian calculations concerning bravery and prowess). The older man's opinion should be more reliable than the other's. Bad Heart Bull may simply have made an error in entering the names and information given

him by his uncles, for he received much of his material from them; or perhaps there is a difference of opinion among various informants. Bad Heart Bull's enumeration can be seen in his drawing. I give He Dog's also: (1) Chasing Horse, i.e., Hunting Horse or Hunts Horses (*Iwakuwa*), extreme left; (2) Iron Bull, which should be translated "Iron Buffalo" (*Tatanka Maza*), right, riding the black horse shown full front; (3) Little Shield (*Wahacanka Cigala*), a brother of He Dog's, who wears a red mantle and carries the Tokala bow lance; and (4) Turtle Ribs (*Keya Tucuha*).

No. 295

NO. 295.   SIOUX-CROW FIGHTS. EARLIEST DATES, 1856, 1858

Second Arrow Creek Fight
   A close-up of Crazy Horse (*Tasunke Witko*) leaving
his wounded horse.

No. 296

NO. 296. SIOUX-CROW FIGHTS. EARLIEST DATES, 1856, 1858

Second Arrow Creek Fight

Another coup-counting incident.

The fallen Crow has been shot in the back with arrows. Dakotas surround him. Lone Man (*Isna Wica*) is counting coup upon him with a bow.

The topmost Sioux (right) is Iron Magpie (*Onkce-kira Maza*). Below him is Old Eagle Warbonnet (*Ruyowapostan*). At the left (above) is Weasel Bear (*Itunkasan Mato*), whose nickname, given here, is About the Waist (*Wite Hepi*). Below him, leading the Crow's horse, is Red Crane or Heron (*Pehan Luta*),

known also by the nickname Wish Sunshine (*Maste Ko*).

Lone Man (or Only Man, as the name is sometimes translated), referred to here by an identifying nickname—Crawler (*Slohan*)—as well as his proper name, is a nephew of He Dog, the elder Bad Heart Bull, Little Shield, Short Bull, and Lone Man, and was named for his famous uncle of the same name.

He Dog remarks, in connection with the episode here pictured, that after Lone Man had struck the Crow he scalped him and took his two six-shooters, but that Red Crane got the horse.

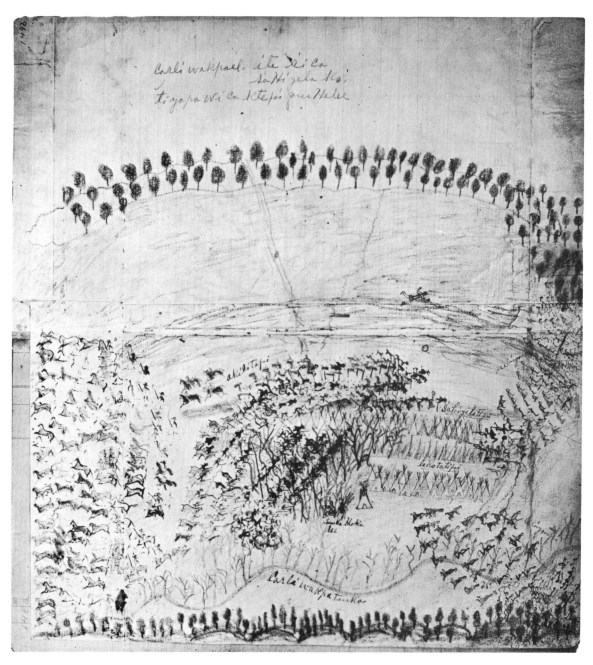

No. 297

No. 297. Early Social Life and Its Reorganization

A note in Lakota at the top of the page. Translation: "This relates to the massacre of the two [?] Cheyennes on Powder River."

A two-page portrayal in miniature, panoramic style showing an attack on an Indian village.

The stream in the foreground is Big Powder River (*Carli Wakpa Tanka*). The drawing indicates hilly

ridges covered with evergreens (evidently evergreens, since they are green while the trees along the creek are bare) at both sides of the camp (top and bottom of page), hemming it in. Representations of leafless trees follow the line of the river and form a wood in the center of the drawing.

Toward the right of the center is a group of tipis

marked "Lakota tipi," i.e., Dakota lodges. Above them is another group marked "Sahiyela tipi," i.e., Cheyenne lodges.

In the lower right of the drawing many women (*Winyanpi*, i.e., "These are women") are fleeing. Above is another group similarly marked, whose retreat is being covered by a few men with rifles.

A little to the right of the center of the drawing a crouching figure is shown shooting from behind a tree. This is He Dog (*Sunka Bloka le e*), who seems to have been the hero in this affair.

Mounted men can be seen making their way into the wood and surrounding it on two sides. The Lakota word *akicitapi* (upper center) indicates that these are soldiers. Bad Heart Bull's usual conventional portrayal of the troopers' hats confirms the labeling. Other soldiers can be seen driving off a large herd of horses (left).

A prone figure of an Indian man is visible at the upper right, quite removed from the center of the confusion.

Near the lower end of the wood is a group of fallen troopers, evidently dead, for they are surrounded by red coloring.

This portrayal represents the surprise attack of Crook's troops against the Dakota-Cheyenne camp early on the morning of March 17, 1876.[124] Authorities agree that the results, as far as the troops were concerned, indicated gross misunderstanding or mismanagement on the part of the leader. Instead of securing the food, blankets, and other useful goods with which the camp was supplied, he had the whole village burned. The soldiers succeeded in driving off a very large herd of Indian ponies, but these were recovered, for the most part, a few days later.

According to He Dog's story, he was one of the comparatively few warriors left in camp when the attack came; most of the fighting men had gone north on a war expedition. The charge of the troops was sudden and unexpected. The village had been left thus relatively unmanned because the Indians felt unwarrantedly secure. The position of the camp was difficult of approach and entrance, since it was hidden in a gorgelike spot almost wholly surrounded by steep cliffs and rough ridges. Scouts had reported the

presence of troops in the vicinity; but, feeling that the location was well-nigh impregnable, the Sioux and Cheyenne inhabitants had paid little attention to these reports. Then on this day, early in the morning, came the surprise attack. He Dog chose a position rather well protected by trees from which to meet the charge and, if possible, hold back the troopers while his wife and the other women made their escape. He had as weapons two rifles, a six-shooter, and a bow and quiver of arrows. From his hidden position he succeeded in stopping the soldiers sufficiently to allow for the escape of the others. Fortune was with him, as he himself points out, for the nature of the country made it very difficult for the troopers to approach the camp; they could enter, he says, only by a very narrow pass. The pictured group of dead soldiers already referred to probably represents He Dog's victims.

After driving the Indians from the village, the soldiers drove off, in the opposite direction, all of the large herd of Indian horses.

"One sleep" later, the other Sioux warriors returned. Immediately they set out on the trail of the troops and in a short time recovered over three hundred of the horses (cf. Grouard).[125]

The Indian casualties, as He Dog gives them, were one old Cheyenne woman shot while in her tipi, one boy—probably Sioux—out looking for horses (perhaps the one referred to by Byrne),[126] and one Cheyenne man shot from a great distance through the abdomen (probably the prone figure in the drawing, upper right). The episode is consequently sometimes referred to as "The massacre of the two Cheyennes on Powder River."

The composition itself gives evidence of a decided sense of balance and an effective use of spotting. The tense action is concentrated in the skirmish at the center. But this is flanked and framed by the directly opposed movements of the horse herd and soldiers at the left and the fleeing women at the right, while bounds are set at top and bottom by the conventionalized pine-crowned cliffs and ridges. In technique, the drawing is highly impressionistic, a fact which seems to intensify rather than to lessen a certain decidedly dynamic quality.

---

[124] Cf., e.g., Byrne, *Soldiers of the Plains*, pp. 35–52; DeBarthe, *Frank Grouard*, pp. 182–198; etc.

[125] DeBarthe, *Frank Grouard*.
[126] Byrne, *Soldiers of the Plains*.

No. 298

NO. 298. SIOUX-CROW FIGHTS. EARLIEST DATES, 1856, 1858

Brief notes in Lakota. Translation: 1. "This is Bear Louse [*Mato Ta Heya*] killing a Crow." 2. "In Montana. 1874." 3. "Charging Eagle [*Wanbli Watakpe*]."

The center of interest is a group of three Dakotas killing a Crow. Bear Louse is counting coup upon the fallen enemy. Charging Eagle is riding in on horseback to count second coup.

Off in the distance to the left (distance suggested by the use of impressionistic miniature), two women on horseback, one on foot, and an unmounted Crow man who is covering the retreat are making a hurried escape with several pack horses.

The incident has not been completely identified.

No. 299

No. 299. Sioux-Crow Fights. Earliest Dates, 1856, 1858

Two notes in Lakota. Translation:

[1] This is Crow Head [*Kangi Pa*] killing a horse stealer. His son-in-law counted coup. His name is written here [see figure labeled *Mato Wanagi*, i.e., Ghost Bear]. 1875.

[2] It was said that they were stealing horses, so they were immediately killed.

The fact that the Sioux were Oglalas is indicated by the penciled word *Oklalapi* at the bottom of the page.

A party of Crow warriors made a horse-stealing raid on the Sioux camp at night but were driven back. In the fierce fight, however, the excited Crows left their horses, for they had dismounted in order to enter the camp quietly on foot. After the Crow flight, Running Eagle (*Wanbli Inyanke*) and Short Bull (*Tatanka Ptecela*) were sent out to bring the Crow horses into camp.

In this drawing, which represents an incident that followed the raid, one of the Crows, with his horse, has ventured from the protection of the lodges barricaded with brush (miniature, lower left). He is being attacked and killed. Crow Head strikes first (left); Ghost Bear, second (right); while two more Dakotas (immediate foreground) are rushing up to count the third and fourth coups.

Technically, the horse is disappointing. It is stiff and lifeless and is placed with no regard for perspective or naturalness.

An interesting example of conventional technique in the drawing, however, is the row of large-size footprints (moccasin prints) leading from the miniature lodge to the place where the Crow is killed.

No. 300

No. 300. Sioux-Crow Fights. Earliest Dates, 1856, 1858

Notes in Lakota. Translation: 1. "These are the horses belonging to the Crow war party." 2. "Run-ning Eagle and Short Bull. Oglalas."

Related to the episode in No. 299.

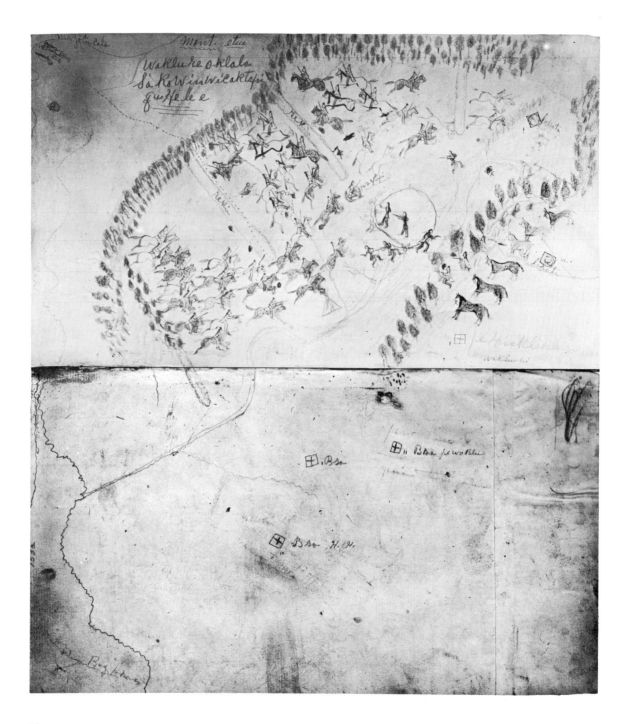

No. 301

NO. 301.   SIOUX-CROW FIGHTS. EARLIEST DATES, 1856, 1858

A note in Lakota. Translation: "In Montana. This refers to the time when seven Loafer Indians of the Oglala tribe were killed."

A miniature of combined topographical and realistic character, with mixed perspectives.

Graphically and rather diagrammatically, Bad Heart Bull presents a serious and tragic engagement between the Crows and a small party of Oglalas of the so-called Loafer band.[127]

[127] Cf. Short Man winter count, 1875.

I give the story of the episode according to Short Bull, who was the first to hear it. The prologue to the incident here portrayed is this: A few days before, a Crow party had come to a Dakota camp, bent on stealing horses; the Sioux had surprised them, however, and had killed one of their number; the rest had fled back to the main encampment of Crows (of the existence of which the Dakotas knew nothing), leaving their horses, baggage, etc., in the temporary camp from which they had sallied on this expedition; a small party of Dakotas under the leadership of Young (or Little) Iron (*Maza Cincala*) had planned a trip before the Crow episode; after the Crows had departed, this party set forth according to previous plans; they were watched and followed, however, by a large party of the Crows, who were fired with a desire to avenge the death of their comrade.

In Nos. 301 and 302, Bad Heart Bull gives the sequel, which Short Bull explains thus:

He (Short Bull) was out near the village looking for his horses when he saw Young Iron, wrapped in his blanket (for it was winter) and carrying his gun (cf. No. 302), come afoot over the top of a hill. Surprised, he called to him to come over and have a smoke (the proper friendly greeting and preface to any serious talk). After the ceremony of a few minutes' exchanging of the pipe, Young Iron said that he thought his comrades—there had been seven in the party besides the leader—had all been killed.

They had been encamped in a horseshoe-shaped bend in the mountains. Young Iron himself had gone out in the morning to scout and had watched all day from a high point on one arm of the horseshoe, but he saw no enemies and heard no disturbing sounds. After dark, he made his way back toward the camp. As he drew near, he gave the customary wolf-howl signal of approach. There was no response, a fact which seemed most strange to him, so he crept cautiously forward. By feeling, he discovered that the ground was covered with horse-hoof tracks. Then, he said, he discovered lying on the ground at one side an arm in the sleeve of a coat that had been worn by one of his men. (This was never found by others investigating the spot afterward, but the body of the Sioux who wore the coat was found *whole*. Young Iron, in the dark and in his excitement, evidently made a mistake.) The young leader did not wait to investigate further but fled, for it was evident that a terrible battle had been fought.

The first day, he stopped and hid on Rosebud Creek, the second, on Tongue River, for he traveled only at night. Each time a voice woke him, saying, "Ready. It is time for us to start." But when he awoke, he found no one; the ghosts of his comrades were following him. So, finally, he had reached his own people again.

There was something strange about the whole affair; and, Short Bull says, many people doubted Young Iron and thought he had deserted his men, for it is not usual for a leader to return when all his party has been slain. But there was no way of proving anything. Short Bull and He Dog, however, are very charitable in their feeling toward Young Iron.

In the drawing, the Big Horn River runs up and down. To the right of the river and following its general line is pictured a ridge covered with evergreens, which curves to the right at the top of the page. Farther to the right and running more or less parallel for a distance is another ridge covered with evergreens; this curves to the left, toward the other ridge at the top of the page, both ridges meeting in a high hill. Extending to the right of the first ridge and perpendicular to it are three odd formations marked *rekin*, a word which means "mountains" or "hills"; these are lesser dividing ridges breaking up the basin of the horseshoe formed by the main tree-covered ridges. This is the horseshoe to which Young Iron refers as the place where they were encamped.

The tipi in the sketch (center) is the lodge in which the Oglalas were camped. It was here that the seven were surprised. Marks to indicate footprints lead from it, off at an angle to the right in the direction in which the Dakotas fled. As the drawing shows, the party of Crows was overwhelming in numbers. These men swooped into the horseshoe from its open end and down upon the Dakotas.

Near the bend in the horseshoe, on higher ground, were a spring and a willow thicket (suggested by a bristle of pencil marks perpendicular to the bare mountain, upper right). If the Sioux could have reached this point, their tribesmen think, they probably could have defended themselves. Perhaps they tried to do this, for most of them started out in this general direction, and one almost reached the place (see the red square marked *Lakota*, upper right). The Dakotas were all very young, they were without doubt utterly surprised by the attack, and, lacking their leader, they probably lost their heads; or, judging from the numbers of attacking Crows, perhaps they could not have done better had they been seasoned veterans. They fought so well at first that the Crows were forced to withdraw from their first attack (notice the confusion of the Crows between the smaller ridges directly opposite the fighting Dakotas), and part of the number formed a barricade on somewhat higher ground which overlooked all the Sioux (see dismounted Crows on ridge, right).

There is no doubt that the young Dakotas fought well; signs on the field and the bits of testimony secured later from the Crows bear witness to the fact.

The red circle (center) indicates a cut bank, probably in an old stream bed, beneath which some of the Sioux tried to protect themselves; five of them are plainly visible in its vicinity. The two red squares marked *Lakota* (extreme right and upper right) mark the places where two of the Dakotas were killed— one probably the man shown running toward the willow thicket and the other the Dakota seen, to the right of the cut bank, facing the barricaded Crows. Four Dakotas fell beneath the cut bank (hence the red). One was separated far to the left and can be seen, in a crouching position, firing from a thicket between two of the *rekin*.

The red dots and crosses mark places where Crows are supposed to have been killed. Just opposite the cut bank at the left in a red semicircle is a crouching Crow marked *warpapi*; the word means "shot from his horse." It was thought that he fell from his horse, killed by a Dakota bullet, but the body was not found, a fact which is not strange if one considers the way in which the Plains Indians made every attempt to remove the bodies of their comrades from the battlefield, even under fire.

The note at center right simply gives the nickname and description of the Crow whose death called forth this act of vengeance. He is designated as "The one with the striped hair" (i.e., whose hair was decorated with beadwork or quillwork). The nickname Bead Work (*Wakśunpi*) is given also. His real name, however, was Charging Crow (*Kangi Watakpe*).

The Crows insist that they lost no men in this encounter with the seven Oglalas. They do not like to talk about the event, however, for it reflects no glory on them, since they found that the Oglalas were all very young and were without their leader. Whether any Crows were killed or not, the profusion of bloodstains in the snow gave ample proof that the young Sioux did much damage.

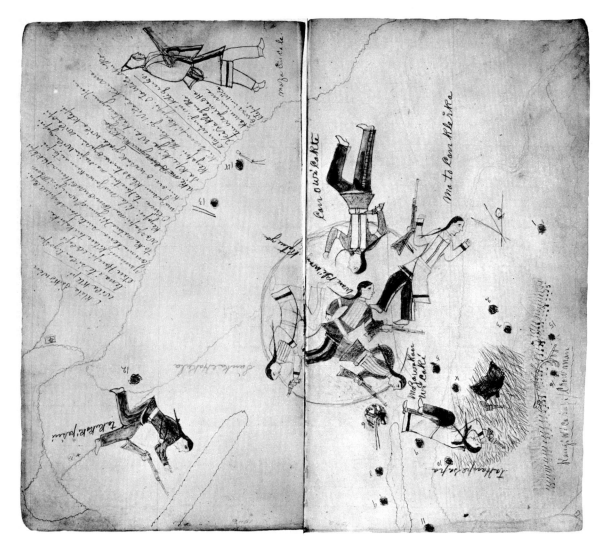

No. 302

NO. 302.   SIOUX-CROW FIGHTS.   EARLIEST DATES, 1856, 1858

A two-page close-up of the struggle of the Loafer Oglalas (No. 301).

In order to view this drawing from the same angle as that found in No. 301, Bad Heart Bull's ledger book must be turned upside down. Then the barricaded Crows, shown in an odd, highly conventionalized miniature and marked *Kangi wica sapi Crow man*, will appear at the right, as shown here.

To the extreme left is Not Afraid of the Enemy (*Toka Kapi Pesni*). To the right, near the barricade, is Black Moccasin (*Tahanpe Sapa*); perhaps, with a crude twist of perspective, Bad Heart Bull intended this to be the man who was killed near the willow thicket. The rest, under the cut bank, are labeled:

Maza Wakan Wicaki (Takes the Gun Away, i.e., from the enemy), *Mato Cankleśka* (Bear Hoop), *Canowica Kte* (Kills in Timber), *Wanbli Wankatinya* (High Eagle), and *Sunka Chakela* (Last Dog). *Maza Cincala* (Young Iron) is seen departing, with his gun beneath his arm.

The impressionistic depiction of the barricade is worthy of notice. A whole row of Crow warriors fighting with rifles is indicated by vague suggestions of ovals for heads and straight lines for rifles. The curved, branchlike object running through this line is an example of a common way, according to Short Bull, of indicating a pine log used as a barricade.

As in the preceding composition, the red spots

[399]

indicate places where Crows were killed or wounded.

The number *6*, near the cut bank, marks a place where the snow showed marks of a hard struggle and of blood. Two ramrods were found here (see two straight lines). The Sioux did not use these, so a Crow must have left them.

The number *13* shows more ramrods.

The number *14* shows a Crow quirt, left behind.

Just above the head of Bear Hoop (*Mato Cank-leśka*), the artist indicates a water bag still hanging from its tripod. The water bag and tripod were found so after the fight—another sign that the attack was a complete surprise.

NO. 303.   SIOUX-CROW FIGHTS.   EARLIEST DATES, 1850, 1858

A note in Lakota. Translation: "This is the striped-haired Crow that Beadwork shot and then counted coup on first. The Crow, in defending himself, shot two. One was Iron Crow."

A small war party of Dakotas gave chase to two Crows. One Crow stopped to fight, but the other fled, leaving his partner alone (see hoofprints and miniature horse and rider, left). Though beset by several Sioux, the Crow defended himself well. Iron Crow (*Kangi Maza*), who was nearest to the Crow, sustained a serious gunshot wound in the shoulder. Finds Horses (*Sunkiyeya*), a Rosebud Dakota, received a shot in the jaw and died about a month later. Beadwork (*Wakśunpi*), a Miniconjou, however, put an end to the affair by creeping up on a rise of ground (depicted in semiminiature) and shooting the Crow

in the back. He also counted coup on him first.

This is one of the very few times in the record where we see men using a gunrest while firing.

Those here shown are among Bad Heart Bull's best portrayals of galloping horses as seen from the rear.

The Crow in this drawing is a compelling figure. True to Crow tradition, he is colorful. He wears dark leggings, the typical square patches or inserts at the bottom of which are bright red. The characteristic apron panel is striped black and white. His long blanket coat is a vivid green with black stripes at the bottom and at sleeve cuffs. The long hair is ornamented with beadwork and quillwork. And the artist has managed to give the figure a suggestion of the debonair and of appealing vitality.

This event occurred in the fall of 1876.

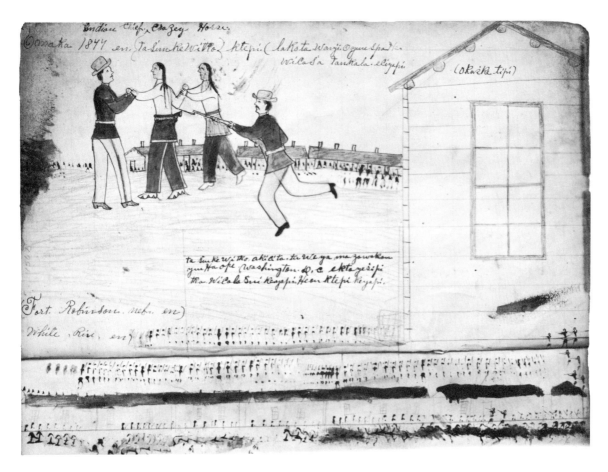

No. 304

No. 304. Early Social Life and Its Reorganization

Brief notes in Lakota. Translation:

[1] In the season of 1877 Crazy Horse was killed. A Lakota seized him. His name was Little Big Man [cf. No. 250].

[2] The soldiers and scouts used guns on him. They asked him to go to Washington, but he refused. For this he was killed.

[3] Guardhouse.

[Notes in English:]

[1] Indian Chief Crazy Horse.

[2] Fort Robinson, Nebr. White River.

The four central figures—Crazy Horse, one Indian guard, and two soldiers—and the guardhouse (right) are given in close-up scale. All of the rest, both the background and the foreground, is given in very highly impressionistic miniature.

Within the walls of the fort, rows of soldiers are lined up. Outside the walls (immediate foreground) there are many horses and numerous human figures;

these are probably Indians. The effect here is one of confusion and excitement.

The drawing shows Crazy Horse in front of the guardhouse, held firmly on one side by a soldier and on the other by an Indian scout, while another soldier runs at the captive from behind with fixed bayonet. The suggestion of cold-blooded murder seen here reflects the attitude which must have been held by some of the Indians.

The story of two Indians of good repute who were on duty at the time do not confirm the implications of this drawing, however. I give here the story of the Oglala scout Plenty Wolves, familiarly known and referred to in reports as Yankton Charley. His story is corroborated in every detail by that of Yellow Horse (*Taśunke Hinzi*), an Eastern Dakota son-in-law of Red Cloud. The two reports were secured independently (by John Colhoff).

Crazy Horse had been arrested and was brought in to the fort. There he was asked to go to Washington to talk over the situation of his people and himself with a view to settlement of difficulties. He refused and reached for the revolver in his holster. Fortunately, Plenty Wolves had just removed the weapon. Crazy Horse did manage, however, to get his knife before the guards could seize his arms. Little Big Man (*Wicasa Tankala*),[128] the Indian scout on his right, realized the futility of the chief's opposition and appealed to him, calling him "nephew" (a truly *appealing* manner of speech of the Dakotas), to take the whole matter calmly. But the captive would not listen.

[128] His proper name is Charging Bear (*Mato Watakpe*).
[129] See, for example, DeBarthe, *Frank Grouard*, and E. A.

Knife drawn, Crazy Horse struggled with the two guards. The soldier placed on guard behind him, with drawn bayonet, backed away to avoid touching the Indian with his bayonet. He moved back so far that, without his realizing it, the butt of his rifle almost touched the wall. A sudden, violent struggle on the part of the captive chief threw him heavily against the bayonet. Of course, the result was fatal; the blade was run through his body.

This is simply one more version of the story of the death of the great war chief; varied versions are by no means lacking.[129]★

Brininstool, ed., "Chief Crazy Horse, His Career and Death," *Nebraska History*, XII, 1 (January–March 1929).

No. 305

No. 305. Early Social Life and Its Reorganization

Two notes in Lakota. Translation:

[1] This refers to Brave Wolf when they retreated toward the east. While they were out killing game, a charge was made. These two were killed.
[2] An Oglala of the Bad Face band [i.e., He Dog's band]. A Hunkpapa woman.

A close-up portraying a woman leading away a horse with a travois (to the right), and a warrior, mounted on a brown horse, charging, with raised rifle, in the opposite direction.

The incident is a part of the Little Creek (*Wakpa Cigala*) fight, near the Canadian border, in the vicinity of Poplar, Montana, during General Miles's campaign of 1877, when he was attempting to round

up the "hostiles." The troops, with whom were Crow, Cheyenne, and a few Dakota scouts, came upon a band of Hunkpapas and Oglalas who were out hunting. A fight was immediately precipitated, and the troops were finally driven back.[130]

In the fight, however, Brave Wolf (*Sunkmanitu Ohitika*), an Oglala of the Bad Face (known also as the Sore Back [*sic*]) band, courageously but vainly met the attack of Crow and Cheyenne scouts in an attempt to save the life of a Hunkpapa woman. Both he and the woman were killed. But his act is commemorated here and in the tribal calendar.

[130] This event in Miles's campaign, of course, would have preceded the death of Lame Deer (cf. No. 79).

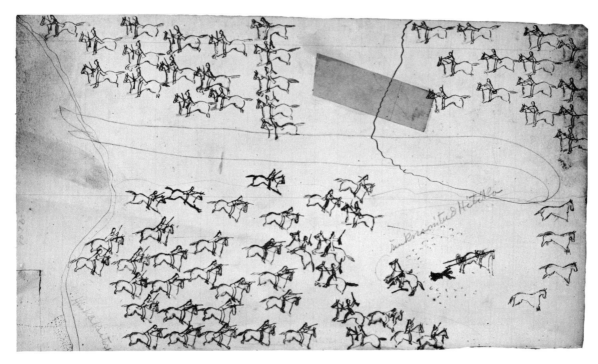

No. 306

No. 306. Early Social Life and Its Reorganization

Two brief notes in Lakota. Translation: 1. "Brave Wolf, the hero" (right). 2. "Bay, bald face" (left).

This second note must refer to the horse of Brave Wolf, for the close-up (No. 305) shows his horse to be a bay with a white face.

The drawing is a miniature in black and white showing the panoramic view of the episode of which Brave Wolf's feat was a part and of which No. 305 is a close-up. The Indian scouts seem divided into two groups (upper and lower); the larger party (foreground) is the one which Brave Wolf meets single-handed. The drawing represents the moment at which the Dakota falls from his horse; the woman lies dead beside her travois. The Dakotas (upper right) have forced the upper group of scouts to retreat, and the leaders of the second (lower) group are already turning back.

No. 307

No. 307. Early Social Life and Its Reorganization

A note in Lakota, below. Translation: "This refers to the lone Crow Indian who was chased and killed by Hard to Hit."

And above, the single Lakota word *Sahiyela*, i.e., "Cheyenne."

The occurrence is another single event following the Brave Wolf episode, but belonging also to the Little Creek fight.

This is a miniature panoramic portrayal of the same character as No. 306. The effect is rather double-barreled, however. The Dakotas have given chase to two scouts. At the lower right is Hard to Hit (*Oosicela*, as Bad Heart Bull has it) killing a Crow scout who has been overtaken and surrounded. Above is a Cheyenne scout by the name of White Weasel (*Itunkasan Ska*) being driven into the creek by another part of the Dakota group. The Cheyenne's horse mired in the heavy mud of the creek and the scout was killed.

No. 308

No. 308.   Early Social Life and Its Reorganization

Two notes in Lakota. Translation: "This is where a Cheyenne was chased and caused to bog down in mud."

And below the Cheyenne, a penciled notation which is translated thus: "The brother-in-law of Little Creek."

A close-up of the upper part of No. 307 (see also No. 309). Three Dakotas are shown in hot pursuit of a Cheyenne scout on a bay horse. The Cheyenne is the brother-in-law of Little Creek (*Wakpa Cigala*).

No. 309

No. 309. EARLY SOCIAL LIFE AND ITS REORGANIZATION

Notes in Lakota summarizing the action of the preceding pages. Translation:

[1] Where Brave Wolf was killed. There a Cheyenne was killed also.

[2] This relates to where a Crow Indian was killed. It also relates to where Hard to Hit struck him and was shot.

[3] This relates to where a Cheyenne was chased and ran into a soft place where his horse bogged down. He was killed.

[4] Grinder [*Wokpan*] was allowed to have the honor of striking him.

The drawing is a close-up sequel to No. 308 and the upper portion of No. 307. The horse is shown mired in the mud up to the body. The Cheyenne has dismounted and is attempting to make his way through the mud on foot, while several Dakotas fire at him from the bank of the creek. As the last note indicates, Grinder was the first to count coup upon him.

Bad Heart Bull suggests the churned aspect of the mud, where horse and man struggle in it, by dark pencil shading around the two figures.

No. 310

NO. 310. EARLY SOCIAL LIFE AND ITS REORGANIZATION

Another exploit of Hard to Hit, the Oglala   No. 309).

(*Oosicela, Oklala*; cf. No. 307 and Lakota note 2 of   A close-up of the shooting of Hard to Hit.

The drawing is a very uncompact two-page composition. The reason for the lack of aesthetic unity and balance is a practical one: expression is being sacrificed to idea. Space had to be allowed to make possible the indication of the charge of Hard to Hit, a charge whose course is indicated by the hoofprints to the right. Evidently, both Hard to Hit and the warrior (upper left) charged side by side up to a certain point; then the one warrior swerved off to the left (see one line of hoofprints). Hard to Hit meanwhile charged the Crow, missed him, and circled back (see hoof-

prints to right). The Crow was more accurate in his aim, however, and before the Dakota could get his gun into action after turning back, the Crow had shot him. The other Dakotas rescued their comrade, but he died the next day. Holy Cloud (*Marpiya Wakan*), a Yankton Dakota, killed the Crow.

The hoofprints serve as the main elements of unity in the composition, bringing into relationship as they do the Sioux (upper and lower left) and the center of interest, i.e., Hard to Hit and the Crow.

No. 311

NO. 311. EARLY SOCIAL LIFE AND ITS REORGANIZATION

A note in Lakota. Translation:

This relates to the killing of Spotted Tail. It is said that he sold some land and received and used the proceeds himself. This was the charge against him. On the other hand, it was reported that he was charged with having taken someone's wife from him and having refused to give her up. He was killed for one of these reasons. He had three wives.

A close-up portrayal, on an extra-size page (lengthened by pasting an addition to one end of the page), of Crow Dog (*Kangi Sunka*) shooting his fellow tribesman and chief, Spotted Tail (*Sinte Kleska*).

At the left is a team of horses hitched to a wagon from which the box has been removed. Beside the team stands Crow Dog firing at Spotted Tail with a rifle. Witnesses in plenty are pictured in the foreground, and two others appear running toward the scene of action (upper right).

The drawing of Spotted Tail, on hands and knees,

a revolver in one hand, would seem to suggest that the chief was approaching stealthily and with questionable intentions.

The note suggests that the reason for Crow Dog's action was a desire to avenge a personal wrong as well as wrongs committed against his people. Dr. Charles A. Eastman, the well-known educated Dakota, explains it as the result of "a solemn commission received from his people. . . . Crow Dog was under a vow to slay the chief, in case he ever betrayed or disgraced the name of the Brulé Sioux. There is no doubt that he had committed crimes both public and private, having been guilty of misuse of office as well as of gross offenses against morality; therefore his death was not a matter of personal vengeance but of just retribution."[131] Whether or not there was a greater element of personal animosity than Eastman indicates, this is true: Crow Dog was tried for murder, condemned to be executed, retried, and acquitted.[132]

[131] Charles A. Eastman, *The Soul of the Indian* (New York and Boston: Houghton Mifflin Co., 1911), pp. 111–112.

[132] *Ibid.*, pp. 112–113.

No. 312

NO. 312.   THE GHOST DANCE AND THE BATTLE OF WOUNDED KNEE

A note in Lakota. Translation:

Our Father saw the common people mourning the world over. For this reason he took pity on them. He was among the people long ago and said that the people should gather together. He presented himself in person and taught them a dance and told them what costume to wear. And he told them to live peaceably. But the Indians went too far and a great many died, so he did not wait for them. They have now forgotten it.

Drawings of three typical Ghost Dance costumes.

[133] Cf., e.g., Wissler, "Protective Designs," pp. 35–38.
[134] See James Mooney, "The Ghost Dance Religion and

Among others, now familiar in this record, there appear noticeably the four-pointed star, the moon, the butterfly (see mantle, left), and the dragonfly. The Ghost Shirts (middle and right figures) exhibit the characteristic V yoke.[133]

The tragedy of the Ghost Dance would naturally be felt keenly among the Oglalas and mention of it would belong to a complete record of the tribe, for it was on their reservation that the fighting and deaths incident to the religion occurred.[134]

the Sioux Outbreak of 1890," *ARBAE*, XIV (1892–1893), Part 2, 653–1111.

No. 313

NO. 313. THE GHOST DANCE AND THE BATTLE OF WOUNDED KNEE

Lakota notes. Translation: 1. "Crow Foot was killed in his sleep" (upper left). 2. "In the season of 1890. Sitting Bull was killed at his home."

At the top of the page appears the title in English: "Sitting Bull." At the bottom is the English notation "Standing Rock, North Dak.," followed by the Dakota *en*, meaning "at" or "in."

Bad Heart Bull describes the arrest and death of

Sitting Bull and of his son, who is still in bed, at the hands of the Indian police.[135]

At the top of the page he has painted a cross section of the roof of a log cabin to show that this is an interior scene.

Again Bad Heart Bull's naïve attempt at suggesting perspective is seen in the diminutive bed (left).

[135] Cf., e.g., James McLaughlin, *My Friend the Indian* (New York and Boston: Houghton Mifflin Co., 1910), pp. 218–221, and Mooney, "Ghost Dance Religion," pp. 867–879.

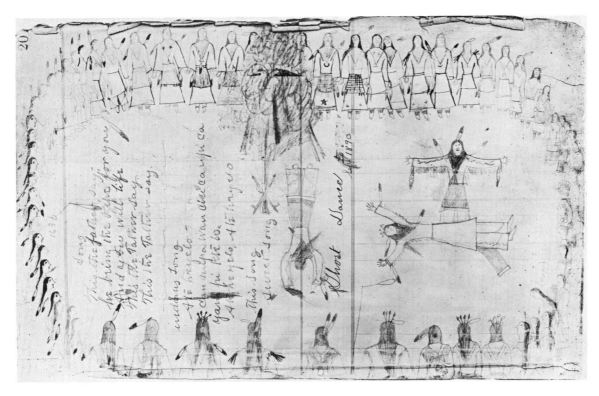

No. 314

No. 314. The Ghost Dance and the Battle of Wounded Knee

A graphic representation of the dance circle at an actual performance of the ceremony of the Ghost Dance.

Words of the Ghost Dance song,[136] in both Lakota and English:

> *Ate heyelo*
> *Can nupa wan cicica upi ca*
> *Yani pi kte wa*
> *Ate heyelo, ate heyelo.*
>
> This the Father say,—
> He bring the pipe for you
> And you will live.
> This the Father say,
> This the Father say.

The page is framed by the circle of dancers, men and women. In the center is the sacred tree, bearing sacrifice banners. Two sacred pipes are crossed at its foot. Near the tree lies a man in a trance. A little farther to the right lies another. Behind him is a third. One cannot be sure whether this last man is also supposed to be lying in a trance or whether he is haranguing the other dancers. Probably he is in a trance.

Inscription in English: "Ghost Dance. Sep. 1890."

Distorted perspective is evident, figures in the parts of the circle at left and right being much smaller than those in the background.

[136] Cf. the Ghost Dance song of Short Bull in Natalie Curtis Burlin, ed., *The Indians' Book* (New York and London: Harper and Bros., 1923), p. 47.

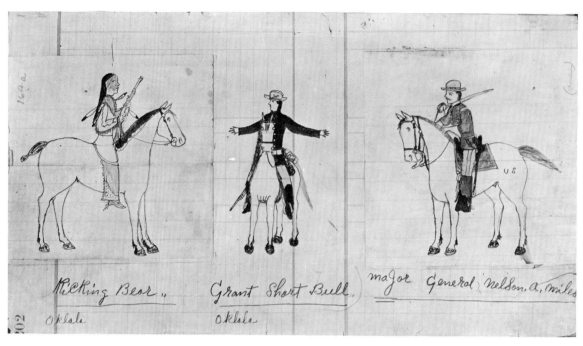

No. 315

No. 315. THE GHOST DANCE AND THE BATTLE OF WOUNDED KNEE

A close-up, rather symbolic drawing of the representative of the United States government, General Nelson A. Miles (right); Kicking Bear (*Mato Wanartaka*), the Oglala representative of the Indians; and Grant Short Bull, Oglala scout.

The figure of Grant Short Bull (my informant, whose name should be translated "Short Buffalo"), an arm outstretched toward each of the two representatives of the opposing forces, might be said to represent the spirit of conciliation. Short Bull carried dispatches between the two leaders.

Kicking Bear wears a Ghost Dance costume.★

No. 316

NO. 316. THE GHOST DANCE AND THE BATTLE OF WOUNDED KNEE

Notes in Lakota. Translation: 1. "This refers to the killing of Big Foot." 2. "This was worse than the Custer battle. They even killed a great many children."

An impressionistic miniature portrayal of the attempted disarming of Big Foot's followers at Wounded Knee Creek.

The drawing shows a circular group of Indians at the center (some standing, some squatting and smoking pipes), surrounded by a ring of infantrymen with raised rifles, who in turn are surrounded by mounted cavalrymen with raised rifles. It represents approximately the moment just before the hotheaded young Dakota gave the signal that precipitated the terrible slaughter.[137]

The impressionistic horses in this composition are noticeably effective. The human figures are inclined to be rather wooden.

[137] See, for example, Mooney, "Ghost Dance Religion," and DeBarthe, *Frank Grouard*, pp. 396–475.

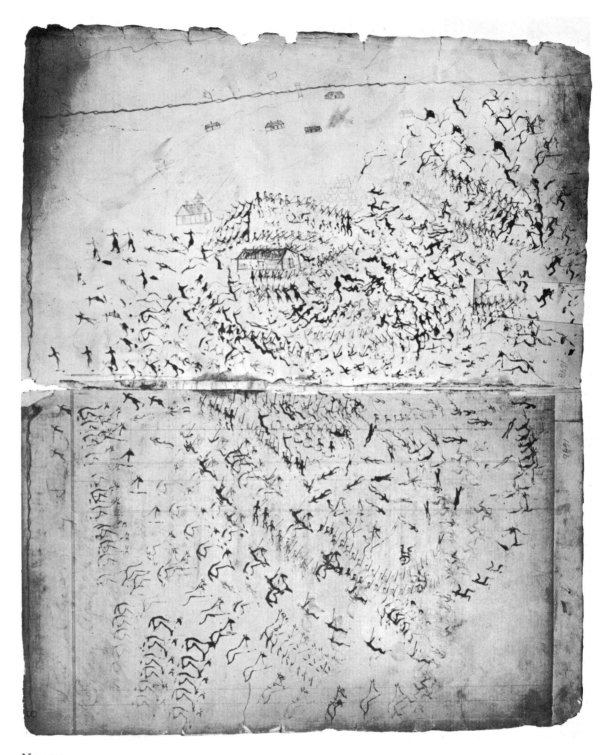

No. 317

No. 317. THE GHOST DANCE AND THE BATTLE OF WOUNDED KNEE

A two-page, highly impressionistic miniature of the fight which followed the event of No. 316.

The artist suggests the utter confusion of the occasion; but as an artistic composition, the drawing is relatively ineffective.

No. 318

NO. 318. EARLY SOCIAL LIFE AND ITS REORGANIZATION

A note in Lakota. Translation: "The Horse Dance."

A two-page, large-scale drawing of the Horse Dance of the members of the horse cult.

At the center is the ceremonial lodge. Before it stand the four official drummers; these are the musicians of the ceremony. The small hand drum, as the drawing shows, is the type used in this dance.

Contrary to the practice in other dream-animal dances (cf. Nos. 115, 186, 187, 190, and 191), there is no "medicine shooter" in the Horse Dance. Only seven of the eight appointed riders are represented in the drawing, probably because of lack of space; there should be two horses and riders for each color—

black, white, red, and gray. The feather decorations at the top of the masks represent ears. The lightning and thunder decorations of both men and horses point to the fact that thunder, as well as the horse, is a significant element in this cult.[138]

[138] Cf., e.g., Wissler, "Societies," pp. 95–98.

No. 319

No. 319. Early Social Life and Its Reorganization

A close-up drawing of the interior of a room in which a wood range is more or less surrounded by the sprawled bodies of four dead young men.

The first one (upper right) stretched out on the floor, is marked *Koska tokan tanhi*, i.e., "a visiting young man"; the second (right), also on the floor, is

labeled *Hokśila*, "a boy"; the third, evidently prone on a bed, *Koska*, "young man"; and the fourth (left), sprawled across a bed, *Wohela*, "the cook."

The explanation of this event is given in the note to No. 320.

No. 320

No. 320. Early Social Life and Its Reorganization

Note in Lakota. Translation: "These are the cowboys that Two Sticks killed. This is the way they were lying dead."

Penciled notation at top of page: "Feb. 2, 1893."

A close-up.

A log cabin and two green haystacks are shown, situated in a horseshoe bend of White River. In the distance, across the river, are *Baha Canweknayanka* (Hill-in-the-Timber) and a smaller butte. In the center of the composition appear four young Indians, armed and walking single file away from the cabin. At the left of the drawing is a miniature copy of drawing No. 319; this represents the interior of the cabin which the Indians are leaving.

The two sons of Two Sticks (*Can Numyuha*), an old Miniconjou chief, and two companions have murdered four cowboys.

The cabin is located in the district to which the artist belonged, not many miles from his own home. As it happened, Bad Heart Bull was the one who discovered the bodies of the murdered men, and he immediately reported to the government officials.

The four young Indians fled southwest on White River and then south on White Clay Creek. It was on White Clay, at a point some twelve or fifteen miles north of the agency, that the Indian police finally met the fugitives. A battle took place, for, of course, the murderers resisted arrest. One of Two Sticks' sons (young Two Sticks) was killed while giving battle, singlehanded, to the police. His companion, Has the White-Faced Horse (*Sunkpaska Yuha*), sustained a broken leg, shattered by a bullet, while attempting to go to young Two Sticks' rescue. The other two young Indians fled. They were joined by the old chief, Two Sticks, himself; he had met the young men on White Clay after the beginning of their flight.

The old man was later arrested, tried at Deadwood, South Dakota, and hanged in 1894. The three young men were freed because they were all very young and because it was shown that old Two Sticks was the instigator of the crime. Lingering rancor resulting from the Wounded Knee tragedy of 1890 was the reason for his desire for murder, it seems.

No. 321

No. 321. Early Social Life and Its Reorganization

A brief note in Lakota. Translation: "The killing of young Two Sticks."

A two-page close-up of the short fight between the Indian police and the fugitive murderers on White Clay Creek (see the text accompanying No. 320). young Two Sticks is charging the police. His companion, Has the White-Faced Horse (designated by the abbreviated form of his Lakota name), who wears a buffalo headdress, is attempting to rush to his assistance. *Sintepi* ("mere striplings") and Chief Two Sticks (*Can Numyuha*) are trying to escape down the creek (left).

The sketchy lines at the left represent brush and timber upon which the fugitives were depending for concealment and protection.

The wagon shown beside the lodges is one of Bad Heart Bull's most grotesque misrepresentations of perspective. It is supposed to be a full-size lumber wagon. In relation to the size of the men and the lodges, however, it would seem to be a toy.

No. 322

No. 322. Early Social Life and Its Reorganization

A second close-up showing the killing of young Two Sticks. This shows him at the moment that he is hit and drops his gun. Presumably it was The Big-Bellied Sorrel (*Hinsa Nige Tanka*), familiarly known as Joe Bush, whose bullet struck him first, for this is the only name given (in pencil, right).

Judging from the great activity of the policemen (upper right), I am of the opinion that they must be attempting to intercept and arrest the fleeing criminals while the rest attend to young Two Sticks.

It is to be noticed that the young Miniconjou wears a Ghost Dance costume.

No. 323

No. 323.   Early Social Life and Its Reorganization

The most confused, heterogeneous page in the record.

A Lakota note heads the page. Translation: "The killing of Two Sticks."

This is followed by the date: "Feb. 2, 1893."

There seem to be parts of several compositions here. In the lower left is a miniature portrayal of the scene in No. 321. Above this, on a large patch which partly covers the top of the miniature, is a larger-scale drawing of six armed and mounted Indians (scouts, presumably) in three-and-three formation. At the right of this, in slightly smaller scale, is the band of

Indian police, looking somewhat disheveled (one has his head bandaged). Below them in larger scale are Amos Bad Heart Bull and a companion, both mounted. All the parts, however, have some connection with the Two Sticks affair.

Perhaps the artist intended this to be a rough and sketchy summary. Evidently in the beginning, however, he intended to make it a miniature of the killing of Two Sticks and the pursuit of the rest, for several patches have been placed on the page, some of them covering part of the miniature (lower left).

No. 324

NO. 324. EARLY SOCIAL LIFE AND ITS REORGANIZATION

A note in English: "Fort Robinson: Neb. U.S. Scout. 1890. Amos Eagle Lance. B. H. Bull."

A note in Lakota. Translation: "Pine Ridge, S.D. The time of the trouble or battle [i.e., the Wounded Knee fight]. Amos B. H. Bull. Belonging to the Indian scouts, Fort Robinson, Neb. The drawing of the way the Sioux [scouts] dressed."

A close-up, equestrian drawing of the artist as a scout.

No. 325

No. 325.   EARLY SOCIAL LIFE AND ITS REORGANIZATION

An isolated, close-up drawing bearing no relation
to any other composition, apparently. It appears to
represent a horse race.

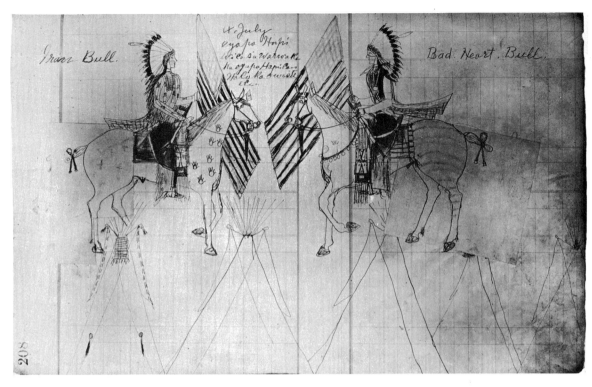

No. 326

No. 326. "Greater Indian Shows," July 4, 1898 and 1903

A list of names in Lakota. Translation:

Wrecker [*Wayajuju*, a nickname for Iron Hawk, see the next name and also drawing No. 37].
Iron Hawk [*Cetan Maza*].
Bad Horse [*Tasunke Sica*, a nickname].
High White Man [*Wasicu Wankatuya*].
American Bear [*Wasicu Mato*, which should be literally translated "White Man Bear"].

A close-up drawing introducing a series (Nos. 326 to 354, inclusive) depicting the celebration of the Fourth of July, 1898, by the Oglala band, the *Ite Sica*

(Bad Faces) or *Canka huran* (Sore Backs) [*sic*]. These celebrations belong distinctly to the postwar period in Dakota life.

This page bears the likenesses of the two "chiefs" of the occasion, Iron Bull (*Tatanka Maza*) and Bad Heart Bull (*Tatanka Cante Sica*), the artist's father, mounted and bedecked with their complete regalia. Their identity is indicated in English.

The names given in the Lakota note belong to other subofficers of this particular Independence celebration.

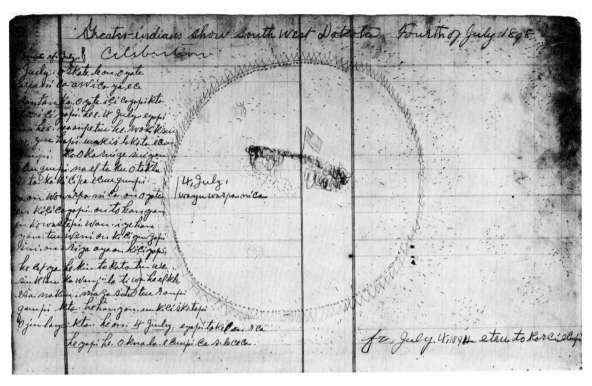

No. 327

NO. 327. "GREATER INDIAN SHOWS," JULY 4, 1898 AND 1903

A title in English: "Greater Indians Show, Southwest Dakota, Fourth of July, 1898, Celebration."

A note in Lakota in red ink, representing the artist's thoughtful criticism of a traditional practice of his people, the give-away (cf. Nos. 329 to 340). Translation:

> Someone has made himself poor helping the poor and needy [i.e., he has spared nothing]. From this kind of Fourth of July celebration the people are getting poorer. Independence Day will keep on getting greater; it will be a thing to remember. But with misunderstanding we Indians celebrate and give away many useful articles unnecessarily. On that account the Indians will get poorer. And no one can be blamed but the tribe itself. If it could be that the people would be

discreetly regulated, it would be all right, but there is no one to indicate the right limit in the give-away. For that reason, if this is kept up, the Indian will give away his last horse; he will go that far to satisfy the demands of a pleasure-seeking people.

Thus Amos indicates his realization of the degeneration of a worthy practice, i.e., care of the poor and needy.[139]

Two short notes in Lakota. Translation: 1. "Poverty maker" (center). 2. "Beginning the celebration of July 4, 1898" (lower right).

The center of the page is occupied by a diagrammatic sketch showing the camp circle with its central dance area, around which is built the green sunshade of pine boughs and in the middle of which is the sacrifice pole, bearing at its top the American flag.

[139] Cf., e.g., Wissler's discussion in "Societies," pp. 64–65, and my article, "Ethical Conceptions of the Dakota," *University of Nebraska Studies*, XXVI, 3–4 (July–October 1926), 58–62.

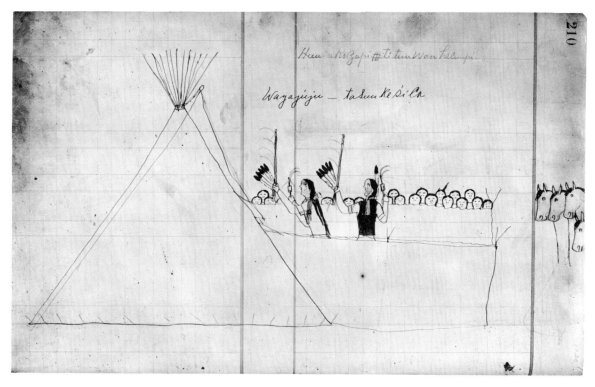

No. 328

NO. 328. "GREATER INDIAN SHOWS," JULY 4, 1898 AND 1903

A note in Lakota. Translation: "Tetons do this, swinging the medicine cane at a ceremony."

A representation of the *Hunka* ceremony of the Dakotas.

Hunka and its agnate *Hunkapi* are words rather difficult to translate. *Hunka* designates a relationship between two people, a relationship stronger than that of ordinary friendship or of blood.[140] "It binds each [person] to his *Hunka*," says J. R. Walker, "by ties of fidelity stronger than friendship, brotherhood, or family."[141] "*Hunkapi*," John Colhoff says, "is a ceremony. I cannot find a word to use for it in English. The nearest is 'making relations' or 'making a name.'"[142]

Walker's comprehensive discussion of the ceremony and its significance[143] indicates that this, in its underlying conceptions and implications and its effects, is one of the Dakotas' most truly ethical practices.[144]

Bad Heart Bull represents in this drawing the prominent rite in the *Hunka*, the rite by which the ceremony is frequently designated, i.e., "waving horsetails over each other." Each candidate was addressed individually. As the officiating shaman waved the *Hunka* wands over the young man seeking the relationship, he spoke to him thus:

"I sought a vision and the Bear God spoke to me.... 'The young man should have the horsetails waved over him; he will provide for his women and children; he will be *brave and truthful and people will listen to him*; he will have plenty and give freely.'"[145]

This was a prophecy. A warning followed:

"If you are lazy or a coward you will sleep with the coyotes. You should not cut your woman's nose. No woman will give her flesh for you. The buffalo will laugh at you. If you tell lies, Iktomi will trick you. Anog Ite will show you both her faces."[146]

---

[140] A relationship found among some other peoples. For a poetic portrayal, see Rudyard Kipling's "The Ballad of East and West."

[141] Walker, "Sun Dance," p. 122.

[142] John Colhoff, letter of February 22, 1929.

[143] Walker, "Sun Dance," pp. 122–140.

[144] Cf. also my own article, "Ethical Conceptions," pp. 44–50.

[145] Walker, "Sun Dance," p. 134.

[146] *Ibid.*

To explain a few vague allusions in this warning, let me say this: sleeping with the coyotes simply meant that one was impoverished in the extreme; cutting off a wife's nose was allowed only if she were unfaithful to her husband; the giving of flesh by a wife refers to the mourning custom according to which a wife gashed her legs till the blood flowed, in proof of the sincerity of her grief; the tricking by Iktomi and the showing of her two faces by Anog Ite meant that misfortune, shame, and despair followed the one who was so treated, that is, the coward and liar.

A later phase of the ceremony symbolized the willingness of the candidate to give all that he had for one in need, even to the food from his mouth and the clothes that he wore.

The final act was a secret ceremony at whose conclusion the conductor again addressed the candidate:

"You are bound to your *Hunka,* and he is as your-

self. . . . What you have is his. What he has he will give you if you wish it. You must help him in time of need. If one harms him you should take revenge, for it is as if you had been harmed. . . . His children will be as your children and your children shall be as his. If he is killed in war you should not be satisfied until you have provided a companion for his spirit. If he . . . seeks a vision, you should aid him."[147]

Of all the prominent rituals of the Dakotas, this is the least closely related to war; its central conceptions and implications are much more closely related to peace and an increasingly moral and spiritual social order and personal life.

The two shamans officiating on the occasion portrayed by Bad Heart Bull are Wrecker (*Wayajuju*) and Bad Horse (*Tasunke Sica*; cf. No. 326).

[147] *Ibid.,* p. 139.

No. 329

No. 329. "Greater Indian Shows," July 4, 1898 and 1903

Large-scale drawing introducing the give-away series (Nos. 330, 331, 333, 334, 335, 336, 337, 339, and 340).

According to custom, different persons are requested by the people to "give away." Costly and magnificent gifts are thus sometimes made; usually the "chiefs" of the occasion give away all of the beautiful beaded and quill-worked garments and trappings which they have worn as officers of the celebration. The whole Fourth of July celebration is

brought to an end by a parade led by the "give-away people," with the "chiefs" of the occasion (Iron Buffalo and Bad Heart Bull in this case) leading.

In the drawings of this series, the people shown riding are those who have made the feast and are "giving away." It is noticeable that the give-away horses are generously ornamented and that they bear valuable equipment of various kinds: beaded garments, saddle blankets, pipes, etc.

No. 330

Give-away.

NO. 330.   "GREATER INDIAN SHOWS," JULY 4, 1898 AND 1903

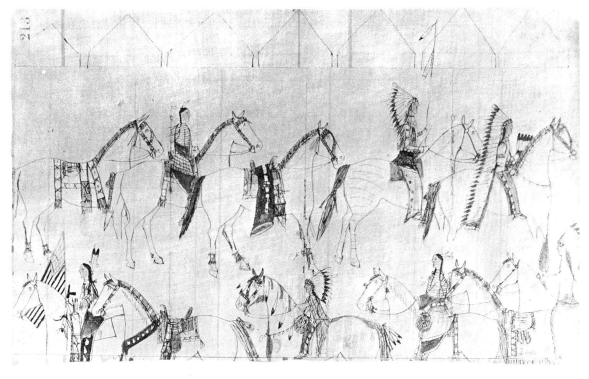

No. 331

Give-away.

NO. 331.   "GREATER INDIAN SHOWS," JULY 4, 1898 AND 1903

No. 332

No. 332. "Greater Indian Shows," July 4, 1898 and 1903

An interruption in the give-away series. A cowboy
bringing in some horses.

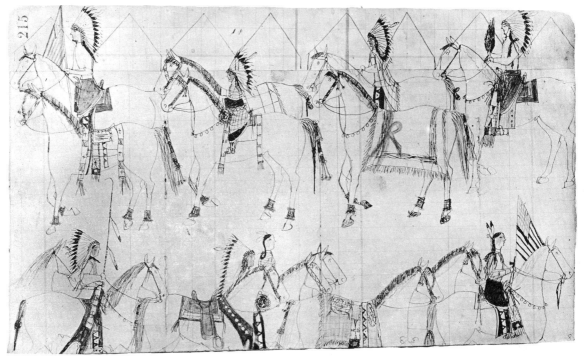

No. 333

No. 333. "Greater Indian Shows," July 4, 1898 and 1903

Give-away.

No. 334

NO. 334.   "GREATER INDIAN SHOWS," JULY 4, 1898 AND 1903

Give-away.

The great variety of possessions given away is suggested. There are tipis, horses, warbonnets, trunks, dishes, cloth (the last three showing that this is late in the history of the Dakotas), blankets, lances, parfleche and embroidered boxes and bags, leggings, moccasins, pipe bags, etc.

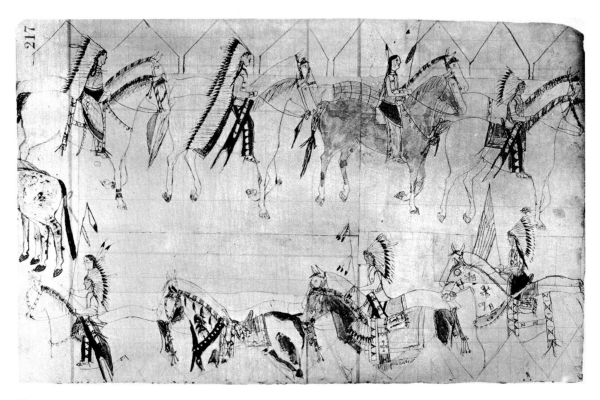

No. 335

No. 335. "Greater Indian Shows," July 4, 1898 and 1903

Give-away.

No. 336

NO. 336. "GREATER INDIAN SHOWS," JULY 4, 1898 AND 1903

Give-away.

A strange mixture of the old and the new. Team, buggy, feathered and beaded work—all are given to someone. "Oglalas have been known to give away things as valuable as this," says the artist's sister Dollie. Similar extravagance is still sometimes practiced at the Fourth of July celebrations.

No. 337

No. 337. "Greater Indian Shows," July 4, 1898 and 1903

Give-away.*

No. 338

No. 338. "Greater Indian Shows," July 4, 1898 and 1903

The *heyoka* performers. Another interruption in the give-away series.

The *heyoka*, or clowns, have come out to perform their wild antics as an appeal for good weather. Only when the sky looks threatening do they perform during such a season as the one being depicted.

The main facts concerning the *heyoka* are that everything with which they are concerned is anti-natural, and that they are somehow related to the lightning and thunder, having dreamed dreams of thunder and lightning.[148]

[148] For discussions of *heyoka*, see Wissler, "Societies," pp. 82–85, and Lowie, "Dance Associations," pp. 113–117.

No. 339

Give-away.

NO. 339. "GREATER INDIAN SHOWS," JULY 4, 1898 AND 1903

No. 340

Give-away.

NO. 340. "GREATER INDIAN SHOWS," JULY 4, 1898 AND 1903

No. 341

No. 341. "Greater Indian Shows," July 4, 1898 and 1903

Large-scale drawing of a mixed parade.

This marks the beginning of that part of the parade which follows the give-away group. The "give-away people" lead the parade, as Dollie Bad Heart Bull and John Colhoff point out.

In these parades, the riders (men and women) appear in their finest regalia.

Amos, in his role of marshal of the day, is riding hurriedly back along the line of march to attend to some detail or other (see background.)

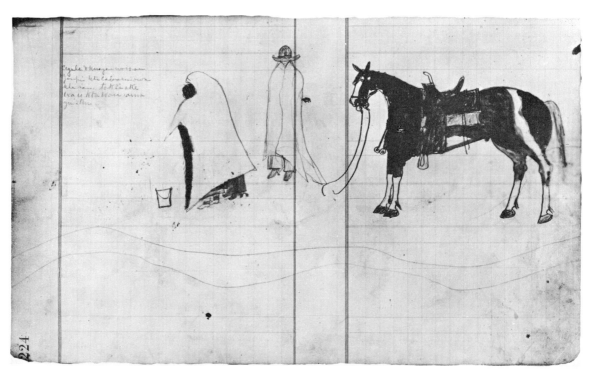

No. 342

NO. 342. "GREATER INDIAN SHOWS," JULY 4, 1898 AND 1903

A note in Lakota. Translation: "This concerns a woman who is carrying water for the preparation of the final feast. A man has stopped her. She rebukes him, telling him that she is in a hurry and that if there is any business to be talked over, it can be done later."

It is very likely that Amos is riding back in such a hurry (see No. 341) to send off the man who is interfering with the preparation of the feast.

The man has waylaid the woman and is attempting to draw her into his embrace within his blanket. A second man, his face muffled in his blanket in the usual courting manner, is looking on, while the horse of the first man stands waiting.

No. 343

No. 343. "Greater Indian Shows," July 4, 1898 and 1903

Mounted warriors riding in the parade.

The leading rider is a member of the Omaha Society, as can be seen by the headdress and the feather bustle (cf. drawing No. 31). Numerous other members of this organization are identifiable in the drawings that follow.

No. 344

NO. 344. "GREATER INDIAN SHOWS," JULY 4, 1898 AND 1903

Indian men in the garb of cowboys, riding in the
parade.

No. 345

NO. 345.   "GREATER INDIAN SHOWS," JULY 4, 1898 AND 1903

Warriors riding in the parade; two of them are
Omaha Society members.

No. 346

NO. 346.   "GREATER INDIAN SHOWS," JULY 4, 1898 AND 1903

Cowboys in the parade.

No. 347

No. 347. "Greater Indian Shows," July 4, 1898 and 1903

Warriors riding in the parade.

The leading rider in this section of the parade is wearing what is called a "leaf shield" (*warpe wahacanka*). It is made of vines and is worn on gala occasions such as this in place of the regular battle shield.

The thunder symbolism is clearly shown in the painting of this man's horse. The wavy, forked line down shoulder, hip, and legs is the lightning symbol. The small circles on neck and flank represent hailstones, which also are associated with thunder.

No. 348

No. 348. "Greater Indian Shows," July 4, 1898 and 1903

Cowboys riding in the parade. The leader is
labeled "Amos B. H. Bull."

No. 349

No. 349. "Greater Indian Shows," July 4, 1898 and 1903

Warriors in the parade.

No. 350

NO. 350. "GREATER INDIAN SHOWS," JULY 4, 1898 AND 1903

A note in Lakota. Translation: "All the Oglalas are becoming aroused [to their opportunities in the new life] and enthusiastic."

Cowboys riding in the parade.

No. 351

Warriors in the parade. The first one is an Omaha
Society member. The second wears a leaf shield (cf.
No. 347).

No. 352

NO. 352.   "GREATER INDIAN SHOWS," JULY 4, 1898 AND 1903

Cowboys in the parade.

No. 353

NO. 353.   "GREATER INDIAN SHOWS," JULY 4, 1898 AND 1903

Warriors and cowboys in the parade.

No. 354

No. 354. "Greater Indian Shows," July 4, 1898 and 1903

A Lakota note giving the words of a Kit Fox Society song. Translation:

> I am the swift fox.
> I am ready to give my life.
> [Then follows a nonsense refrain.]

A group of Kit Fox, or Tokala, Society members ride together singing this song, which is sung in honor of the artist. The import of it is that Bad Heart Bull has his orders from higher powers, that he has not long to live, that he must be ready to die at any moment. One man leads; four men abreast follow him; the two virgin singers bring up the rear.

This drawing shows clearly one of Bad Heart Bull's conventional affectations. When he is portraying more than two horses abreast, he almost invariably draws in the hind legs and feet of only the first two. The deception is thoroughly effective.

This concludes the series depicting the Fourth of July celebration of 1898.

No. 355

NO. 355. EARLY SOCIAL LIFE AND ITS REORGANIZATION

Two Indian cowboys (hats, boots, and spurs proclaim their occupation) pay their respects to two young women.

The red banner floating from a pole at the end of the house (a log cabin, with mud-chinked cracks, characteristic of the Oglalas after their settling upon the reservation) would seem to indicate that a dance

is taking place at this home (the more modern, social dance). Ordinarily, this is a symbolic appeal to the Spirit of the Dance.

The horse here presented is one of Bad Heart Bull's most realistic close-up drawings of a horse. There is fine detail in the tooling of the leather of the saddle.

No. 356

No. 356. Early Social Life and Its Reorganization

Another courting scene (cf. also Nos. 86, 87, 210, 342, and 355).

The only note is the single Lakota word *wiokuwa*, literally, "chasing," a frank suggestion of one aspect of the Sioux conception of courting.

The setting for this scene is rather more primitive than the one immediately preceding, but the subject is the same. Four couples are seen in the foreground. Two mounted young men await their turns or simply look on as interested observers. The typical belted blanket of young men is plainly pictured.

In the background is a miniature portrayal, in pencil, of a portion of the camp circle, with its tipis, where activities similar to those in the foreground are going on. The whole is realistic, and the suggestion of perspective is very convincing. At the same time there is something distinctly decorative in the panel effect of the background.

My informants explain that the figures in the foreground represent couples whose attachments are settled.

No. 357

No. 357. Early Social Life and Its Reorganization

Two cowboys with their horses.

The opening of a series (Nos. 357 to 367, inclusive) depicting roundup and farm scenes.

At the spring roundup there was a representative from each neighborhood to identify stock and attend to the various other details of the occasion. Amos (left) is the representative of his community at this roundup.

No. 358

NO. 358. EARLY SOCIAL LIFE AND ITS REORGANIZATION

A note in Lakota. Translation: "This is done when the Oglalas make roundup."

An Oglala cowboy is driving in his string of mounts in preparation for the roundup. The chuck wagon (extreme left), cook tent, etc., can be seen in the background (left). The rider will use these horses, in turn, during the roundup, which will require hard riding for the next several days.

The last horse on the cowboy's right bears the man's bedroll and such equipment.

The odd lines extending at angles from the wagon (upper left) represent a temporary rope corral or catching pen. Lariats are fastened to the wheels of the wagon and then to the joining of two crossed posts which are held in place by guy ropes. Into this three-sided pen the riding horses are driven to be caught.

No. 359

NO. 359.   EARLY SOCIAL LIFE AND ITS REORGANIZATION

A note in Lakota. Translation: "These are dancing men."

This is the home of someone who is giving a dance —again a more modern, social dance (the pole bears the offering to the Spirit of the Dance). A load of wood has just been brought in, in preparation for the festivities. The suspicious-looking men lying near the woodpile or standing at the corners of the house are simply people waiting for the dance to begin.

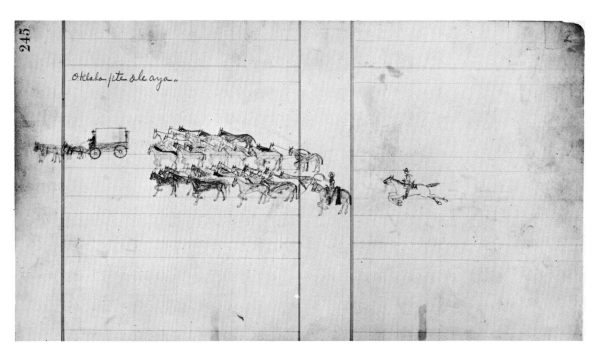

No. 360

NO. 360. EARLY SOCIAL LIFE AND ITS REORGANIZATION

A note in Lakota. Translation: "When the Oglalas went on roundup for cattle."

A miniature showing the chuck wagon, followed by a herd of riding horses attended by two cowboys. The outfit is moving to the next camp.

No. 361

No. 361. Early Social Life and Its Reorganization

Another courting scene (cf. No. 356, etc.).

The apparent interruption in the roundup series may seem more real than it actually is; the boots and spurs of the young men may but indicate that this episode is in reality incident to the roundup and its frequent change of headquarters.

It is noticeable that there are but three young women to ten young men; this also might bear out the suspicion that this courting episode is incident to the roundup. As usual, some of the men sit or lie about, awaiting their turns.

No. 362

No. 362. Early Social Life and Its Reorganization

Two notes in Lakota. Translation: 1. "The home of a man who is thoughtful." 2. "I am contented."

The drawing is a semiminiature of a modern farmplace, to show the ideal result of the proper attitude on the part of the Indian. Here Bad Heart Bull reflects his own progressive attitude toward the new order.

Land, stock, farm equipment, etc., have been furnished, and the owner of this place is making the most of his opportunities.

The sketchy green and brown border in the background represents the line of the trees along a creek.

No. 363

No. 363. Early Social Life and Its Reorganization

A note in Lakota. Translation: "They rode these horses in rounding up the cattle."

The drawing represents the artist himself with the horses which he will use during the roundup (cf. No. 358). The middle horse in the foreground carries the bedroll and similar equipment. Amos' brand, X6, is seen on the right shoulder of the four horses in the foreground.

No. 364

No. 364.   Early Social Life and Its Reorganization

An Indian bringing in a load of hay to be used at the roundup camp for the riding horses.

The camp (similar to the one in No. 358) is shown in miniature in the background (left).

The drawing in this case appears quite stiff. The horses do not "move," although in proportions they are fairly realistic. The hayrack is not altogether convincing either; only two wheels are visible (one front and one back), and the illusion of a fully equipped wagon is not secured.

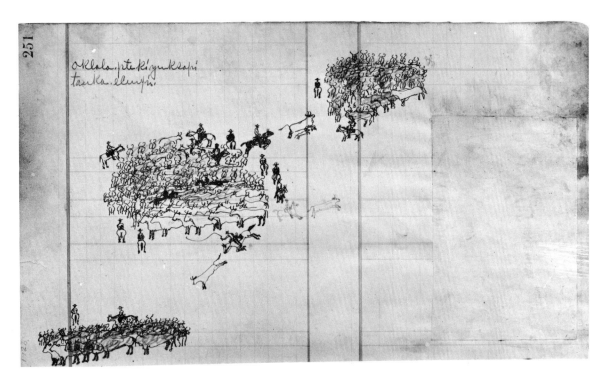

No. 365

No. 365. Early Social Life and Its Reorganization

A note in Lakota. Translation: "The Oglalas had a big job cutting out cattle."

A miniature of the roundup proper; one of Bad Heart Bull's conventionalized but realistic studies.[149] His highly conventionalized cow as seen from the rear and his equally conventionalized horse and rider as seen from the rear are the outstanding features of

[149] Cf. my discussion in Part One, Chapter IV, pp. 51 and 54.

detail. Individual animals in profile view among the cattle are in most cases disproportionately long, but the effectiveness of the whole is not appreciably lessened by this technical defect. The naturalistic movement at certain points (the animals breaking from one herd to the other) and the three-part rhythm of the drawing are significant elements, not only in the securing of the effect of realism, but no less in the building of the composition as such.

No. 366

No. 366. Early Social Life and Its Reorganization

A note in Lakota. Translation: "An Oglala looking for his brand" (evidently Amos, for his horse bears the X6 brand).

Another close-up scene from the roundup.

A steer has been thrown in order that the brand, which is not clear, may be closely examined.

No. 367

NO. 367.   EARLY SOCIAL LIFE AND ITS REORGANIZATION

Another close-up of a bit of the roundup.

The tribal brand of the Oglalas is seen on the steer's left side.

No. 368

No. 368. Early Social Life and Its Reorganization

The next five pages show close-up views of various riders in the roundup; some are in native dress, some in the traditional cowboy costume.

The drawings on this page are representative of the finer, more naturalistic technique of the original ledger pages or of insert series No. 1.

No. 369

NO. 369.   EARLY SOCIAL LIFE AND ITS REORGANIZATION

Two riders in the roundup.

Representative drawings of the poorer type belonging to insert series No. 2.

No. 370

NO. 370. EARLY SOCIAL LIFE AND ITS REORGANIZATION

Two more riders in the roundup.

Both horses are among the less convincing drawings of the original-ledger-page type. The first, however, has undergone a late revision; a patch has been
placed over the rear half of the animal, and the hind
quarters have been redrawn for some reason. The
result is that the front part "moves" while the hind
part does not.

No. 371

No. 371.   Early Social Life and Its Reorganization

Two riders in the roundup.

No. 372

No. 372.   Early Social Life and Its Reorganization

Three more riders in the roundup.

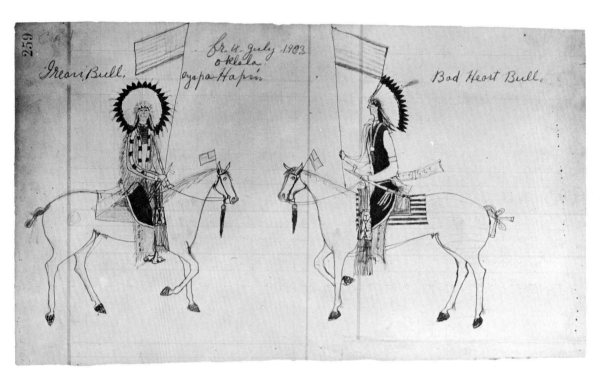

No. 373

NO. 373. "GREATER INDIAN SHOWS," JULY 4, 1898 AND 1903

A brief note in Lakota. Translation: "The Oglalas are still celebrating the Fourth of July in the old way" (in spite of Bad Heart Bull's criticism; see No. 327).

Another close-up drawing of two mounted men in full regalia, which introduces a second Fourth of July celebration—that of 1903.

Again Iron Bull is one of the "chiefs," but this time the *younger* Bad Heart Bull, i.e., the artist, is the other "chief."

A person chosen by the people to do a certain thing for the band (such as acting as "chief" of a celebration such as this and consequently giving most of his possessions to the poor—presumably) was disgraced if he refused, even if he disapproved of the thing. So Amos finds himself involved in a performance with which he is out of sympathy.

No. 374

No. 374. "Greater Indian Shows," July 4, 1898 and 1903

A note in Lakota. Translation: "This is the way the chief committeeman was pictured coming."

A note in English gives the place as White Clay District, the date as July 4, 1903, and Amos B. H. Bull as the committeeman coming (his badge of office is the red, white, and blue band across his right shoulder and chest).

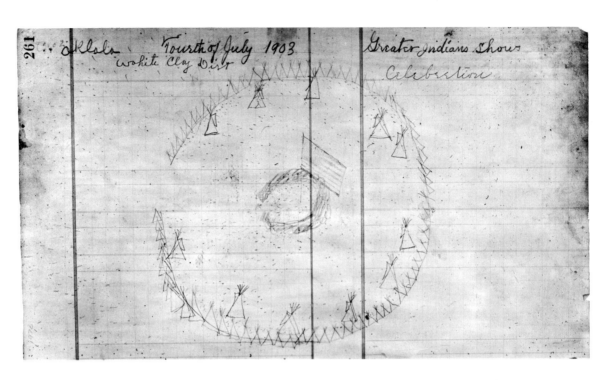

No. 375

No. 375. "Greater Indian Shows," July 4, 1898 and 1903

The note is simply a titular designation, in English except for the spelling of the first word.

"Oklala. Fourth of July 1903. Greater Indians Shows Celebration. White Clay Dist."

Diagrammatic representation of the camp circle and dance area (cf. No. 327).

The inside lodges belong to those who have been chosen to "give away." The tipis and all they contain will be given to the poor.

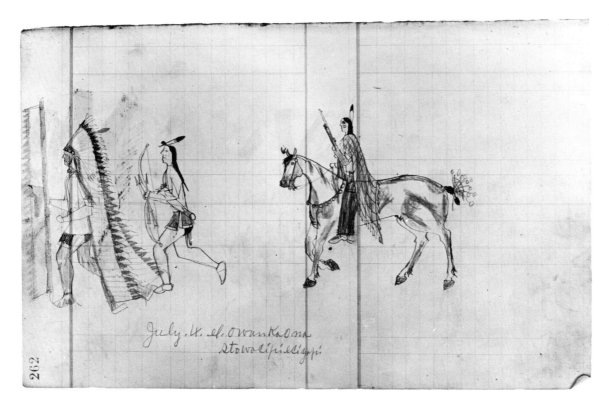

No. 376

No. 376. "Greater Indian Shows," July 4, 1898 and 1903

A brief note in Lakota and the date July 4. Translation: "This is called 'where smoothing-the-place is danced.'"

Introducing a series (Nos. 376 to 391) showing warriors on their way to the "smoothing-the-place-dance." This dance was originally a part of the Sun Dance ritual but has since been introduced as a preliminary gesture in other ceremonies, as here for instance (cf. Nos. 12 and 407).

No. 377

No. 377. "Greater Indian Shows," July 4, 1898 and 1903

Warriors on their way to the "smoothing-the-place-dance."

No. 378

No. 378. "Greater Indian Shows," July 4, 1898 and 1903

Dancers on their way to the "smoothing-the-place-dance."

No. 379

No. 379. "Greater Indian Shows," July 4, 1898 and 1903

Warriors on their way to the "smoothing-the-place-dance."

No. 380

NO. 380. "GREATER INDIAN SHOWS," JULY 4, 1898 AND 1903

Warriors on their way to the "smoothing-the-place-dance."

No. 381

No. 381. "Greater Indian Shows," July 4, 1898 and 1903

Warriors on their way to the "smoothing-the-
place-dance."

No. 382

No. 382.   "Greater Indian Shows," July 4, 1898 and 1903

Warriors on their way to the "smoothing-the-place-dance."

No. 383

No. 383. "Greater Indian Shows," July 4, 1898 and 1903

Warriors on their way to the "smoothing-the-place-dance."★

No. 384

No. 384. "Greater Indian Shows," July 4, 1898 and 1903

Warriors on their way to the "smoothing-the-place-dance."

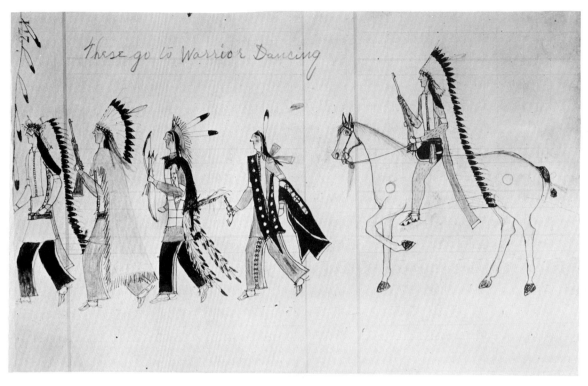

No. 385

No. 385. "Greater Indian Shows," July 4, 1898 and 1903

A note in English: "These go to warrior dancing," i.e., to the "smoothing-the-place-dance."

The fur charm worn by the fourth warrior is the skin of an otter decorated with a double row of small, round mirrors. Similar pieces of apparel are to be seen among the costumes shown in succeeding drawings (e.g., Nos. 388, 389, 394, 396, 399, 403, and 404).★

No. 386

NO. 386. "GREATER INDIAN SHOWS," JULY 4, 1898 AND 1903

Warriors on their way to the "smoothing-the-place–dance."

No. 387

No. 387. "Greater Indian Shows," July 4, 1898 and 1903

Warriors on their way to the "smoothing-the-place-dance."

The second man wears an eagle-bone whistle hung from a cord around his neck.

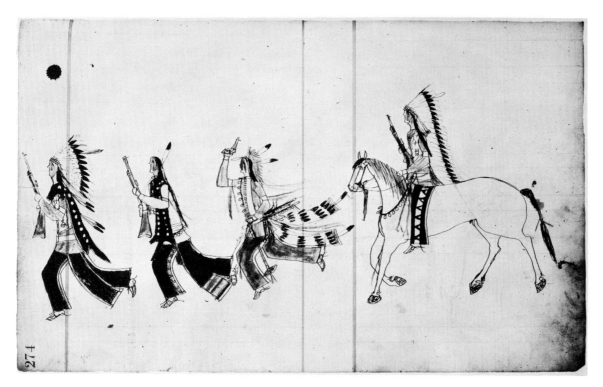

No. 388

No. 388. "Greater Indian Shows," July 4, 1898 and 1903

Warriors on their way to the "smoothing-the-
place-dance."

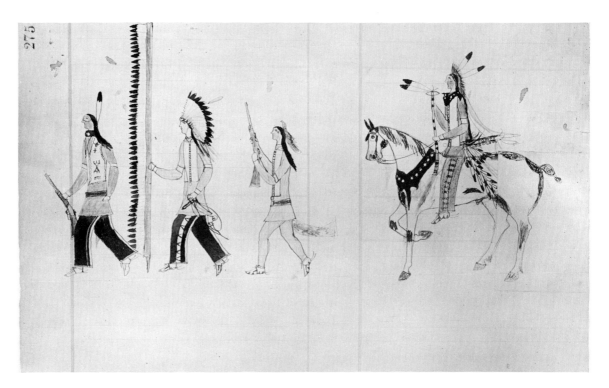

No. 389

NO. 389. "GREATER INDIAN SHOWS," JULY 4, 1898 AND 1903

Warriors on their way to the "smoothing-the-
place-dance."

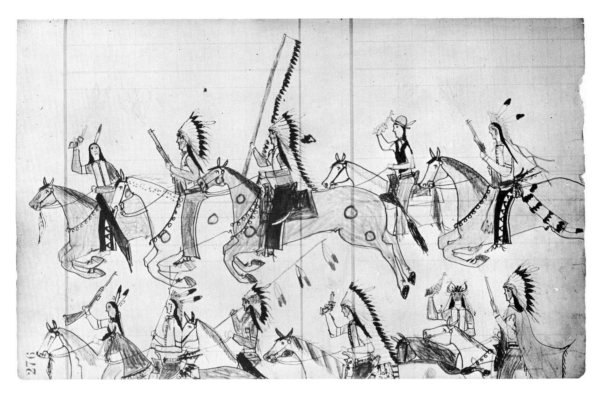

No. 390

No. 390. "Greater Indian Shows," July 4, 1898 and 1903

Mounted warriors charging toward the dance ground, firing guns as they go.

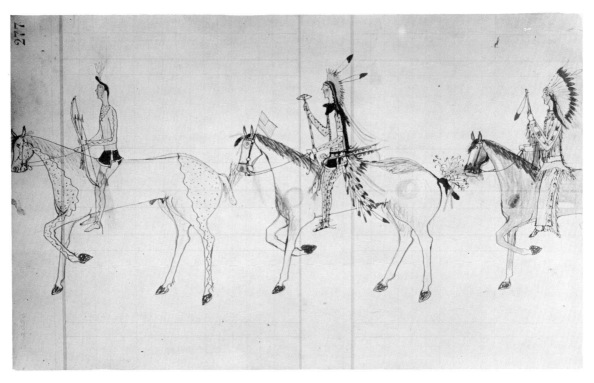

No. 391

No. 391. "Greater Indian Shows," July 4, 1898 and 1903

The beginning of a "charge without firing of guns" (*uci tapi hecaśni*), i.e., a parade of mounted warriors in full regalia.

No. 392

NO. 392. "GREATER INDIAN SHOWS," JULY 4, 1898 AND 1903

A note in Lakota with the date. Translation: "July 1, 2, 3, 4. Continuation of parade. A charge without firing of guns."

The warrior at the left wears a leaf shield (*warpe wahacanka*; cf. Nos. 347 and 351).

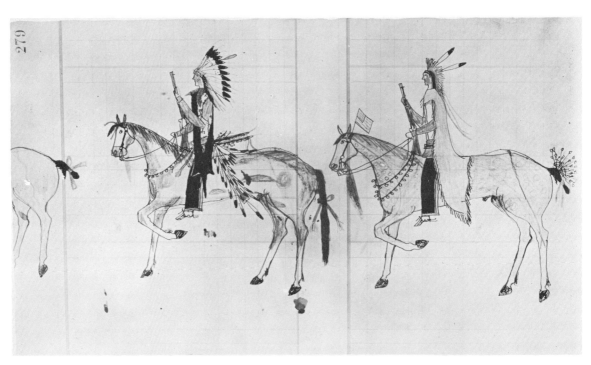

No. 393

NO. 393.   "GREATER INDIAN SHOWS," JULY 4, 1898 AND 1903

Warriors in the charge.

No. 394

NO. 394.   "GREATER INDIAN SHOWS," JULY 4, 1898 AND 1903

Warriors in the charge.

No. 395

No. 395. "Greater Indian Shows," July 4, 1898 and 1903

Warriors in the charge.

No. 396

NO. 396. "GREATER INDIAN SHOWS," JULY 4, 1898 AND 1903

A note in Lakota above the leaf shield at the left.
Translation: "Packs leaves on his back" (cf. No. 347).

No. 397

NO. 397. "GREATER INDIAN SHOWS," JULY 4, 1898 AND 1903

Warriors in the charge.

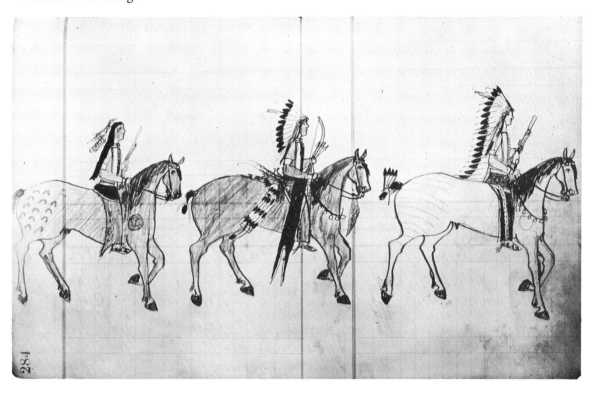

No. 398

NO. 398. "GREATER INDIAN SHOWS," JULY 4, 1898 AND 1903

Warriors in the charge.

No. 399

NO. 399.   "GREATER INDIAN SHOWS," JULY 4, 1898 AND 1903

Warriors in the charge.

No. 400

NO. 400.   "GREATER INDIAN SHOWS," JULY 4, 1898 AND 1903

Warriors in the charge.

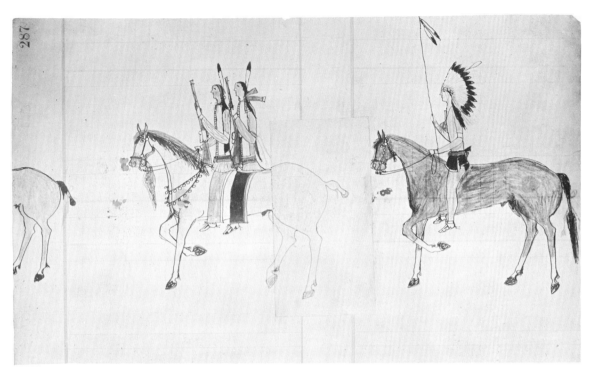

No. 401

NO. 401. "GREATER INDIAN SHOWS," JULY 4, 1898 AND 1903

Warriors in the charge.

No. 402

NO. 402. "GREATER INDIAN SHOWS," JULY 4, 1898 AND 1903

Warriors in the charge.

No. 403

NO. 403. "GREATER INDIAN SHOWS," JULY 4, 1898 AND 1903

Warriors in the charge.

No. 404

NO. 404. "GREATER INDIAN SHOWS," JULY 4, 1898 AND 1903

Warriors in the charge.

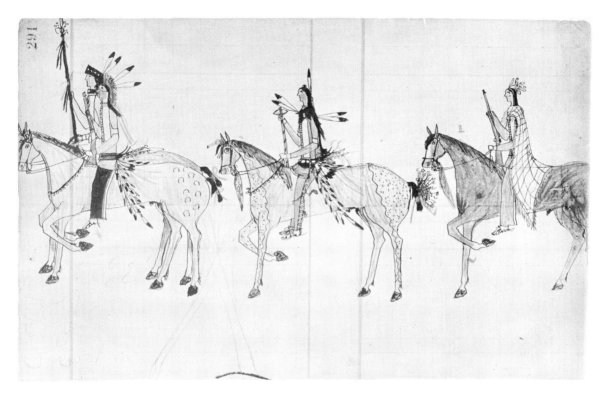

No. 405

NO. 405. "GREATER INDIAN SHOWS," JULY 4, 1898 AND 1903

Warriors in the charge.

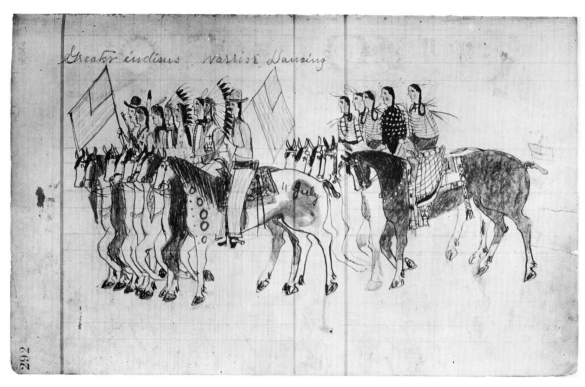

No. 406

No. 406. "Greater Indian Shows," July 4, 1898 and 1903

People preparing to take part in the "smoothing-the-place-dance," in which mounted men perform.★

No. 407

NO. 407. "GREATER INDIAN SHOWS," JULY 4, 1898 AND 1903

A note in Lakota. Translation: "This is the smoothing-the-place-dance."

Warriors on foot form a ring around the dance area (the green encircling the dancers represents the pine-bough shade that surrounds the dance ground). Led by an unmounted shaman (left) bearing a scalp stick, the chosen warriors (it is said that these were picked men who had rescued fellow warriors under fire) on their horses enter the dance ground in regular formation and go through the measured steps of the movement. This is preliminary to other ceremonies and dances.

From the point of view of composition, the drawing is quite well balanced and effective. One of the most interesting elements technically and artistically is the row of warriors' heads as seen from the rear (immediate foreground). At least eight different types of head decoration are depicted.★

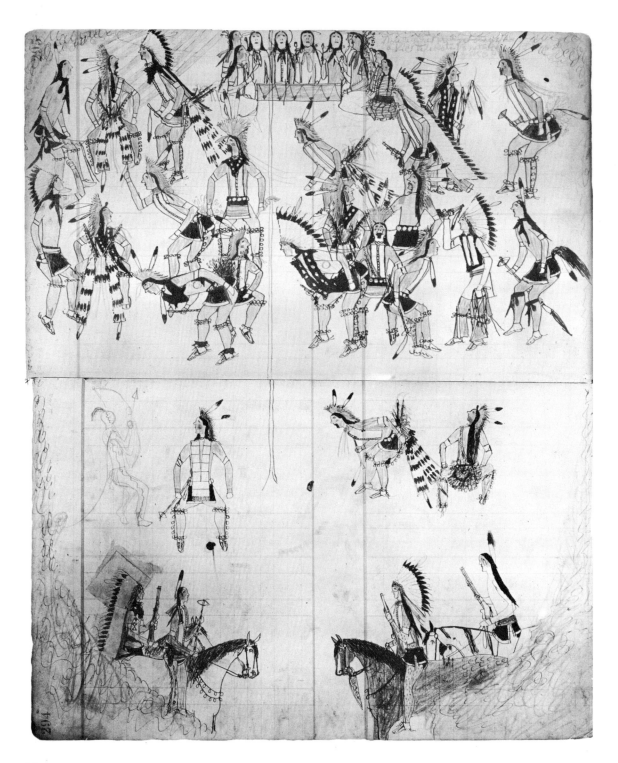

No. 408

NO. 408. "GREATER INDIAN SHOWS," JULY 4, 1898 AND 1903

A note in Lakota giving the words of an Omaha
song. Translation:

    He was their friend,

They were his friends,
Everyone failed him,
Even his own people.

This song was sung in honor of He Dog and in commemoration of the fight on Powder River, March 17, 1876, when a part of Crook's command under Colonel J. J. Reynolds attacked and burned the Sioux-Cheyenne village (cf. No. 297). The composition and the singing of songs of this nature on special occasions was quite customary with the Omaha Society. The ceremony here portrayed is the social Omaha Dance, the public and social portion of the Grass Dance, which originally was truly and entirely ritualistic.

The circle of pine shade around the dance area is suggested by the vague masses of green at the four corners of the page. The varying but typical postures and costumes of the Omaha dancers are clearly in evidence. At one side, opposite the entrance, sit the drummers and singers. At each side of the entrance stand the mounted officials of the day.★

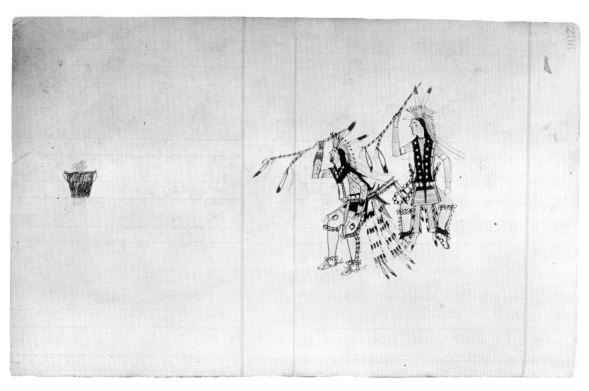

No. 409

No. 409.   "Greater Indian Shows," July 4, 1898 and 1903

The dance of the two forked-spear bearers, from the Grass Dance of the Omaha Society (see also No. 410).

The two men are pictured charging the pot of stewed dog (left).

This was the most spectacular and exciting dance act of the ceremony. Probably this fact accounts for the artist's portraying it in preference to one of the other acts of few performers.

No. 410

NO. 410.   "GREATER INDIAN SHOWS," JULY 4, 1898 AND 1903

The opening portion of the Grass Dance (*Pejin Miknaka Wacipi*, "Grass Tucked in the Belt"). All eight of these chosen dancers of the ritual are "charging the dog."

Wissler summarizes the ritualistic Grass Dance thus:

> Of the more fundamental concepts and procedures of the ceremony may be mentioned the serving of dog flesh. In this there are several distinct performances:—
>
> 1. The scouting of the food kettle after it has been carried into the dance house and the counting of coup upon it as if it were an enemy [cf. No. 410].
> 2. The serving of small bits of dog flesh to a few distinguished men by the bearers of the pointed stick [the "dog fork"] or ceremonial spoon [cf. No. 409].
> 3. Presenting the dog heads to the most distinguished men present and counting of coups by them over the skulls at the end of the feast.
> 4. Gathering all the other bones and passing them around to be prayed over; finally secreting them in some secure place.[150]

My informants do not mention acts 3 and 4 as given by Wissler, but they give in detail the other steps, as well as the subsequent feeding of the crowd and the dismissal ceremony.

The Omaha Dance ceremony (cf. No. 408) is more or less social up to this point; with the Grass Dance, however, it becomes ritualistic, as I suggest above.★

[150] Clark Wissler, "A General Discussion of Shamanistic and Dancing Societies," *APAMNH*, XI, Part 12 (1916), 864. See also Densmore, "Chippewa Music. II," pp. 471–472; Chittenden and Richardson, *Father Pierre Jean DeSmet*, III, 1059–1060; Fletcher and LaFlesche, "The Omaha Tribe," p. 459; Lowie, "Dance Associations," p. 130; and Wissler, "Societies," pp. 48–52, and "Societies and Dance Associations," pp. 451–456.

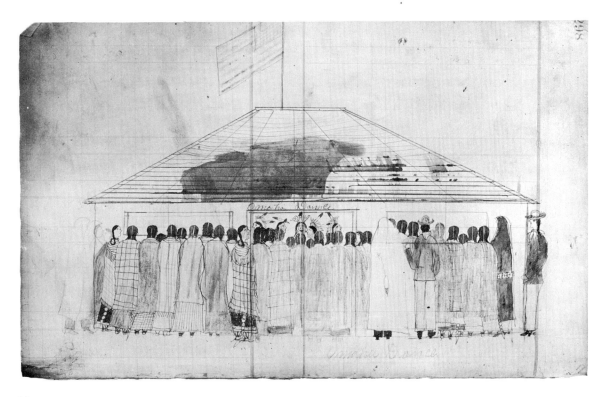

No. 411

No. 411. "Greater Indian Shows," July 4, 1898 and 1903

The modern Omaha Dance house.

No. 412

No. 412.   Early Social Life and Its Reorganization

A note in Lakota. Translation: "Oglalas from White Clay District herding their cattle."

In a large-scale drawing, the artist presents himself in the role of a cowboy. The scene is dated December 3, 1900, but I have discovered no special significance attaching to the date.

To the left, strangely out of perspective, is another of Bad Heart Bull's highly conventionalized portrayals of a herd of cattle (cf. No. 365).

The miniature sketch (upper right) represents the ranchplace of a large cattle outfit in the early days.

The label attached to it reads: "Chenney River, S. Dak. Squn Hamper Creek." The first is a misspelling of "Cheyenne," of course. The second is a misspelling of the nickname "Squaw Humper," given by early-day cowboys to a dry creek which has no real name, either in English or Indian. This creek empties into Cheyenne River at the northwest corner of the Pine Ridge Reservation. It was from this point that the White Clay District roundup wagon used to start. So this drawing belongs to the roundup series.

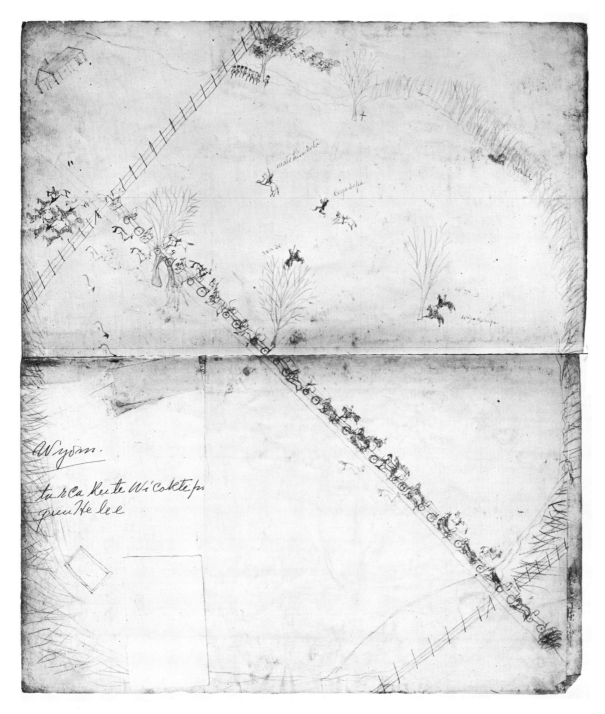

No. 413

No. 413. Early Social Life and Its Reorganization

A note in Lakota. Translation: "Wyoming. When the deer hunters were killed."

A sketchy miniature showing a long wagon train and accompanying mounted men fired upon by a group of men sheltered by the creek bank (top).

The story, according to the Dakotas, is that in the fall of 1903 a group of about twenty-five Oglalas traveled into Wyoming to hunt deer. Because of a misunderstanding, they did not make application to the state of Wyoming for a hunting permit; they had the permission of the government superintendent of the Indian reservation to go, and they thought this was enough.

The Wyoming sheriff, however, was intent on maintaining "law and order." He and his posse hid on Lightning Creek, known to the Indians as *Can Icoga Ota Wakpa* (i.e., Many Driftwood Creek), to await the Indians' approach on their return. As the Dakotas, unconscious of any danger, drew near, the posse opened fire without warning of any kind. A young man familiarly known as Charlie Smith, a Carlisle student, who was riding in the lead, fell at the first volley, fatally wounded. Naturally, as soon as they could, the Indians returned the fire.

In the skirmish that followed, Roan Bear (*Mato Hinrota*) and Black Kettle (*Cega Sapa*) (top center) were the real heroes. The sheriff was killed; so also was Roan Bear. Paint (*Wase*) (center and extreme right) was so hard pressed that he was forced to seek the shelter of the creek (hoofprints show the path that he followed). The artist makes the extreme right figure of Paint a mere smudge in order to indicate that it is half-hidden by the brush. Black Feather (*Wiyanka Sapa*) and a mixed-blood by the name of William Brown (figures at right) are also designated

as prominent in the fighting.

The Oglala name of Charlie Smith, the first casualty, was *A-i-yanke* (Runs at It or Runs for It) or *Akna Inyanke* (Runs by It or Runs Beside). It is by this latter name (in its eastern form, *Agna Inyanke*) that Natalie Curtis Burlin speaks of him when she quotes his song in *The Indians' Book*.[151] His fortitude is still celebrated by this song, which has been incorporated into the Tokala Society music, since he was a Tokala, but which is always called his song.[152] Though mortally wounded, he retained consciousness long enough to sing his own death chant—a song whose melody is very old but whose words are *Akna Inyanke*'s own.

> Lo, the Fox, the Fox am I!
> Still the Fox a moment yet,
> Then the Fox shall be no more.

The song is a brave one and is typical of death songs of warriors. Even in very recent times, when brave warriors who have fallen in battle were to be praised, this song was sung; and when tribute was to be paid to Tokalas, the name of *Akna Inyanke* was always used in special honor to him.

---

[151] Burlin, *The Indians' Book*, p. 51.

[152] For the significance of the name Tokala, see No. 30.

No. 414

NO. 414. EARLY SOCIAL LIFE AND ITS REORGANIZATION

A blurred close-up of the fighting of the preceding drawing. The three main Indian characters in the episode are named: *Cega Sapa* (Black Kettle), upper right; *Mato Hinrota* (Roan Bear), upper center; and Charles Smith, lower center.

The technique used here is that of the insert series No. 2.

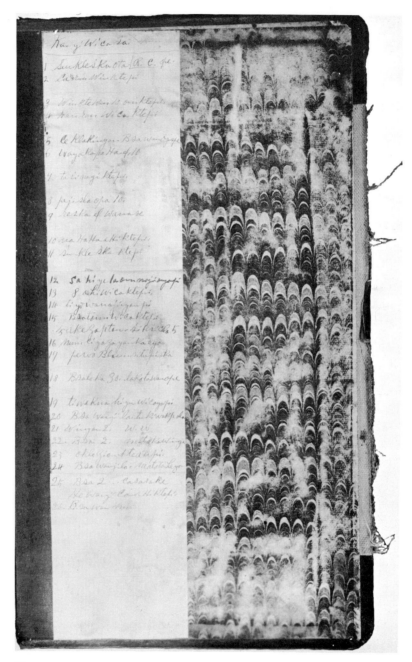

No. 415

NO. 415. INSIDE OF BACK COVER

There is, on the inside of the back cover of the old book, a list of twenty-six brief notations in Lakota which appear to form part of an intended table of contents. It includes notes regarding some events not pictured by Bad Heart Bull and some regarding several that are shown in considerable detail in the record. Several events listed here cannot be clearly identified as to time and place.

I give the notes with translations and brief comments:

1. Note in Lakota. Translation: "Many spotted horses. Red Cloud in the party." An event recalled by the Dakotas as *sunk manupi tanka*, "large horse-stealing expedition." The Crows were the victims. Not only did they lose many horses but also one of their noted chiefs, Spotted Eagle.

2. Note in Lakota. Translation: "A wood donator was killed." I cannot definitely identify the incident. Evidently a man who had been called upon to furnish wood for certain purposes in the camp was killed while fulfilling his duty, but whether he was a Sioux or a Crow is not clear from the note.

3. Note in Lakota. Translation: "A party of Crow Indians afflicted with smallpox were killed." The Dakotas, it seems, attacked the Crows, thinking they were well. After the killing, however, they discovered the condition of the Crows and promptly fled, for "they know the seriousness of the disease," says my informant.

4. Note in Lakota. Translation: "In a party of ten Crows, one hermaphrodite was killed." This corresponds to an entry found in several Dakota Winter Counts for 1848.[153] For reference to hermaphrodites, see not only Mallery's note but also Wissler's brief remarks in his discussion of Oglala societies.[154]

5. Note in Lakota. Translation: "Iron White Man [designated here by a lewd nickname] catches a Crow Indian." A case of an accidental meeting between a lone Crow and a lone Dakota.

6. Note in Lakota. Translation: "Ten Crows were killed on Captive Hill." With this notation we come to the earliest incident that falls definitely within Bad Heart Bull's picture record. The reference here is to the incident treated in No. 32. These last two notes (5 and 6) indicate two of the four very important happenings of the season of 1856–1857.

7. Note in Lakota. Translation: "Yellow Robe was killed." This refers to the killing of the Crow, Yellow Robe, and his son (No. 35).

8. Note in Lakota. Translation: "Along the Greasy Grass River [the Little Big Horn], ten Crow Indians were killed." I do not identify the incident.

9. Note in Lakota. Translation: "A buffalo chase near the Rocky Mountains." Crow hunters were attacked and killed by Dakotas.

10. Note in Lakota. Translation: "Walks Light was killed by the Crows." Walks Light was a Dakota who never carried a weapon—a unique personality among the Sioux of the old days!

11. Note in Lakota. Translation: "Spotted Horse was killed." Spotted Horse, a Crow Indian, greatly impressed the Dakotas by his coolness and courage. Though severely wounded and handicapped by a broken leg, he shot down a mounted enemy who was trying to count coup upon him, and then tried to drag himself within stabbing distance of the fallen foe. Other Dakotas flew to the rescue of their tribesman, however.

12. Note in Lakota. Though not very clear in litera-

tion here and there, the meaning appears to be: "We, with the Cheyennes, were surrounded." This obviously would refer to the episode described in No. 36 and would be rightly placed here for chronological sequence.

13. Note in Lakota. Translation: "Eight Loafer camp Indians [Oglalas] were killed by the Crows." This event is not yet fully identified.

14. Note in Lakota. Translation: "Surrounded the camp." This refers to the first Arrow Creek fight, sometimes called "Defending the Tent." Bad Heart Bull describes it in Nos. 41 to 48 and in No. 218.

15. Note in Lakota. Translation: "Four Crow Indians were killed." A fight which occurred in Montana in 1864 (according to both Bad Heart Bull and the Short Man winter count; see Nos. 49, 50, 51, and 52).

16. Note in Lakota. Translation: "The double riders." A case of two Crows trying to escape on one horse. This is probably a bit from the episode above, but it is not shown in the drawings.

17. Note in Lakota. Translation: "Plume on Head. White Tail Feathers." Names of two Dakotas who figure prominently in a Sioux-Crow episode (see Nos. 53 to 56). Plume on Head is the nickname of a Miniconjou by the name of Buffalo Man, who was chiefly responsible for the routing of the Crows on this particular occasion. White Tail Feathers was a Miniconjou chief who, in a moment of bravado, needlessly lost his life in attempting to count coup upon a Crow warrior.

18. Note in Lakota. Translation: "A Crow war party where a Sioux was with them." This is a reference to the fight in which the traitorous Sioux, Fast Horse, and his Crow confederates were all killed (see Nos. 100, 101, and 102).

19. Note in Lakota. Translation: "The Crows ran the Sioux into camp." This evidently refers to the first part of that long and strenuous engagement in which first the Crows drove the Dakotas to their very doors and then, with a sudden turn in the tide of battle, were themselves sent in full retreat to their own lodges (see Nos. 219 to 284).

20. Note in Lakota. Translation: "A lone Crow Indian at Shell Creek." One of the exploits of the famous Young Man Afraid of His Horses (for others, see, e.g., Nos. 37 to 39).

21. Note in Lakota. Translation: "Two Sioux women were killed." Two added initials are unexplainable, and there is nothing further to identify the note.

22. Note in Lakota. Translation: "Two Crow Indians. Turning Bear." This refers to an occasion on

[153] For example, see the notation in the Battiste Good winter count for 1848–1849 in Garrick Mallery, "Picture-Writing of the American Indians," *ARBAE*, X (1888–1889), 323.

[154] Wissler, "Societies," p. 92.

which a Dakota, Turning Bear, killed two Crows.

23. Note in Lakota. Translation: "Crows counted coup on a man wearing a yellow shirt." The "yellow shirt" identifies the famous warrior Runs Fearless. The incident indicated is his feat of killing three Crows who beset him—one after the other in rapid succession—and of escaping unscathed himself (see Nos. 287 to 293 in the second Arrow Creek fight series).

24. Note in Lakota. Translation: "A lone Crow Indian. Bear Louse." This would seem to refer to the same event as that briefly commemorated in No. 298:

a Dakota, Bear Louse, killed a Crow Indian—in Montana in 1874.

25. Two notes in Lakota. Translation: 1. "Two Crows. Hump." 2. "One Horn was killed." In a Sioux-Crow encounter, a Dakota, Hump, killed two Crows. But in the same fight, a Sioux named One Horn was also killed. I cannot now identify the occasion more definitely.

26. The last note seems to mean nothing. There is the word "Crow," but beyond that I cannot identify anything.

Bibliography

BOOKS

BAESSLER, ARTHUR. *Ancient Peruvian Art.* 4 vols. New York: Dodd, Mead and Co., 1902–1903.

BASLER, ADOLPHE, AND ERNEST BRUMMER. *L'Art precolumbien.* Paris: Libraire de France, 1928.

BOAS, FRANZ, ROLAND B. DIXON, *et al. Anthropology in North America.* New York: G. E. Stechert and Co., 1915.

BOURKE, JOHN G. *On the Border with Crook.* New York: Charles Scribner's Sons, 1892.

BRACKENRIDGE, H. M. *Journal of a Voyage up the River Missouri, in 1811.* Vol. VI in R. G. Thwaites, ed., *Early Western Travels, 1748–1846.* Cleveland: A. H. Clark Co., 1904.

BRININSTOOL, E. A. *Fighting Red Cloud's Warriors.* Columbus: Hunter-Trader-Trapper Co., 1926.

BRINTON, DANIEL G. *The Lenape and Their Legends.* Vol. V in Daniel G. Brinton, ed., *Library of Aboriginal American Literature.* Philadelphia: D. G. Brinton, 1885.

———. *Essays of an Americanist.* Philadelphia: Porter and Coates, 1890.

BRONSON, EDGAR BEECHER. *Cowboy Life on the Western Plains: The Reminiscences of a Rancher.* New York: Grosset and Dunlap, 1910.

BURLIN, NATALIE CURTIS, ED. *The Indians' Book.* New York and London: Harper and Bros., 1923.

BYRNE, PATRICK E. *Soldiers of the Plains.* New York: Minton, Balch and Co., 1926.

CATLIN, GEORGE. *The North American Indians.* 2 vols. London: Published by the Author, Egyptian Hall, Piccadilly, 1841.

CHITTENDEN, H. M., AND A. T. RICHARDSON, EDS. *The Life, Letters, and Travels of Father Pierre Jean DeSmet, S.J., 1801–1873.* 4 vols. New York: Francis P. Harper, 1905.

CLARK, W. P. *The Indian Sign Language.* Philadelphia: L. R. Hamersly and Co., 1885.

COOK, JAMES H. *Fifty Years on the Old Frontier.* New Haven: Yale University Press, 1923.

CUSTER, ELIZABETH B. *Boots and Saddles.* New York: Harper and Bros., 1885.

DAWKINS, WILLIAM BOYD. *Early Man in Britain and His Place in the Tertiary Period.* London: Macmillan Co., 1880.

DEBARTHE, JOE. *Life and Adventures of Frank Grouard.* St. Louis: Combe Printing Co., 1894.

DENSMORE, FRANCES. *The American Indians and Their Music.* New York: The Woman's Press, 1926.

DODGE, RICHARD I. *Our Wild Indians.* Hartford: A. D. Worthington and Co., 1882.

DOMENECH, L'ABBÉ EM. *Manuscrit Pictographique Americain.* 4 vols. Paris: Gide, Libraire-Editeur, 1860.

EASTMAN, CHARLES A. *The Soul of the Indian.* New York and Boston: Houghton Mifflin Co., 1911.

———. *Old Indian Days.* New York: McClure's, 1917.

FINERTY, JOHN F. *War-Path and Bivouac.* Chicago: *Chicago Times,* 1890.

FLETCHER, ALICE C. *Indian Story and Song.* Boston: Small, Maynard and Co., 1900.

———. *Indian Games and Dances, with Native Songs.* Boston: C. C. Birchard and Co., 1915.

FRAZER, J. G. *The Golden Bough: A Study in Magic and Religion.* New York and London: Macmillan Co., 1900.

FRY, ROGER. *Vision and Design.* New York: Brentano's, 1920.

GILMORE, MELVIN R. *Prairie Smoke: A Collection of Lore of the Prairies.* Bismarck, N.D.: Privately published, 1922.

GRINNELL, GEORGE BIRD. *The Indians of Today.* Chicago and New York: Herbert S. Stone and Co., 1900.

———. *The Fighting Cheyennes.* New York: Charles Scribner's Sons, 1915.

———. *The Cheyenne Indians.* 2 vols. New Haven: Yale University Press, 1923.

HANS, FRED M. *The Great Sioux Nation.* Chicago: M. A. Donahue and Co., 1907.

HARRISON, JANE ELLEN. *Prolegomena to the Study of Greek Religion.* London: C. J. Clay and Sons, Cambridge University Press, 1903. New York: Macmillan Co., 1903.

———. *Ancient Art and Ritual.* New York: Henry Holt and Co., 1913.

———. *Themis: A Study of the Social Origins of Greek Religion.* 2d ed., rev. London: Cambridge University Press, 1927.

HEBARD, GRACE RAYMOND, AND E. A. BRININSTOOL. *The Bozeman Trail.* 2 vols. Cleveland: A. H. Clark Co., 1922.

HODGE, FREDERICK W., ED. *Handbook of American Indians North of Mexico.* 2 vols. Bureau of American Ethnology, Bulletin 30. Washington: Government Printing Office, 1907.

HOFFMAN, W. J. *The Beginnings of Writing.* New York and London: Macmillan Co., 1895.

HOWARD, O. O. *My Life and Experiences Among Our Hostile Indians.* Hartford: A. D. Worthington and Co., 1907.

KAPPLER, CHARLES J., COMP. AND ED. *Indian Affairs, Laws and Treaties.* 2 vols. Washington: Government Printing Office, 1904.

KINGSBOROUGH, EDWARD KING. *Antiquities of Mexico.* 9 vols. London, 1831–1848.

LOWIE, ROBERT H. *Primitive Society.* New York: Horace Liveright, 1920.

———. *Primitive Religion.* New York: Boni and Liveright, 1924.

McCLINTOCK, WALTER. *Old Indian Trails.* New York and Boston: Houghton Mifflin Co., 1923.

McLAUGHLIN, JAMES. *My Friend the Indian.* New York and Boston: Houghton Mifflin Co., 1910.

MAXIMILIAN, PRINCE OF WIED. *Travels in the Interior of North America.* Vols. XXII–XXIV in R. G. Thwaites, ed., *Early Western Travels, 1748–1846.* Cleveland: A. H. Clark Co., 1906.

MILES, NELSON A. *Serving the Republic.* New York: Harper and Bros., 1911.

MORTON, J. STERLING, ED. *Illustrated History of Nebraska.* Lincoln: Jacob North and Co., 1907.

NEIHARDT, JOHN G. *The Song of the Indian Wars.* New York: Macmillan Co., 1925.

OLDEN, SARAH EMILIA. *The People of Tipi Sapa.* Milwaukee: Morehouse Publishing Co., 1918.

PARKMAN, FRANCIS. *The Oregon Trail.* Boston: Little, Brown and Co., 1904.

PARKYN, E. A. *Prehistoric Art.* London and New York: Longmans Green and Co., 1915.

PARSONS, ELSIE CLEWS, ED. *American Indian Life.* New York: B. W. Huebsch, Inc., 1922.

RAFN, C. C. *Antiquitates Americanae.* Editit Societas Regia Antiquariorum Septentrionalium. Studio et opera Charles Christian Rafn. Copenhagen, 1845.

ROE, CHARLES FRANCIS. *Custer's Last Battle on the Little Big Horn.* New York: R. Bruce, 1927.

SCHOOLCRAFT, HENRY R. *Historical and Statistical Information Respecting the History, Condition, and Prospects of the Indian Tribes of the United States.* Collected and prepared under the direction of the Bureau of Indian Affairs, per act of Congress of March 3, 1847. Illustrated by S. Eastman, Capt. U.S. Army. 6 vols. Philadelphia, 1851–1857.

STANDING BEAR, LUTHER. *My People, the Sioux.* Boston: Houghton Mifflin Co., 1928.

TONGUE, HELEN. *Bushman Paintings.* Oxford: Clarendon Press, 1909.

WEBSTER, HUTTON. *Primitive Secret Societies.* New York: Macmillan Co., 1908.

WESTERMARCK, EDWARD. *The Origin and Development of Moral Ideas.* 2 vols. New York and London: Macmillan Co., 1906.

WHEELER, HOMER W. *Buffalo Days.* Indianapolis: Bobbs, Merrill, 1925.

WIENER, LEO. *Mayan and Mexican Origins.* Cambridge: Privately published, 1926.

WISSLER, CLARK. *The American Indian.* New York: Oxford University Press, 1922.

———. *The Relation of Nature to Man in Aboriginal America.* New York: Oxford University Press, 1926.

WOODBRIDGE, F. J. E. *The Purpose of History.* New York: Columbia University Press, 1916.

ARTICLES, PAPERS, AND OTHER SOURCES

ALEXANDER, H. B. "Religious Spirit of the American Indian." Reprint from *The Open Court,* January–February 1910. Chicago: Open Court Publishing Co., 1910.

———. "The Ritual Dances of the Pueblo Indians." In *Cooke-Daniels Lectures,* pp. 7–18. Denver: Denver Art Museum, 1927.

———. "Pictorial and Pictographic Art of the Indians of North America." In *Cooke-Daniels Lectures,* pp. 19–30. Denver: Denver Art Museum, 1927.

BATES, COLONEL CHARLES FRANCIS. "Lost and Won." Reprinted from the *New York Times* of June 20, 1926, in *Fifty Years After the Little Big Horn Battle,* a pamphlet of reprints prepared for the anniversary of 1926 by the National Custer Memorial Association.

BECKWITH, PAUL. "Notes on Customs of the Dakotahs," *Annual Report of the Bureau of American Ethnology,* VIII (1886–1887), Part I. Washington, 1889.

BENEDICT, RUTH FULTON. "The Concept of the Guardian Spirit in North America," *Memoirs of the American Anthropological Association,* No. 29. Menasha, Wis.: Collegiate Press, George Banta Publishing Co., 1923.

BLACKBURN, WILLIAM M. "History of Dakota," *South Dakota Historical Collections,* I (1902).

BLISH, HELEN H. "Ethical Conceptions of the Dakota," *University of Nebraska Studies,* XXVI, 3–4. (July–October, 1926).

BRININSTOOL, E. A., ED. "Chief Crazy Horse, His Career and Death," *Nebraska History,* XII, I (January–March, 1929).

BROWN, EDWARD. "The Pictured Cave of La Crosse Valley, near West Salem, Wisconsin," *Wisconsin Historical Collections,* VIII (1877–1879), 174–183.

CADZOW, DONALD A. "Bark Records of the Bungi Midewin Society," *Indian Notes,* III, 2 (April 1926), 123–234. New York: Museum of the American Indian, Heye Foundation, 1926.

CHAMBERLAIN, A. F. "Kootenay Group Drawings," *American Anthropologist*, III (NS), 2 (1901), 248–256.

CULIN, STEWART. "Games of the North American Indians," *Annual Report of the Bureau of American Ethnology*, XXIV (1902–1903). Washington, 1907.

DENSMORE, FRANCES. "Chippewa Music. I," Bureau of American Ethnology, Bulletin 45. Washington, 1910.

———. "Chippewa Music. II," Bureau of American Ethnology, Bulletin 53. Washington, 1913.

———. "Teton Sioux Music," Bureau of American Ethnology, Bulletin 61. Washington, 1918.

DORSEY, GEORGE A. "The Sun Dance of the Ogalalla Sioux," *Proceedings of the American Association for the Advancement of Science*, XXXI (1882), 580–584.

———. "The Cheyenne. I. Ceremonial Organization," *Anthropological Series*, IX, 1 (March 1905). Publication 99, Field Columbian Museum, Chicago.

———. "The Cheyenne. II. The Sun Dance," *Anthropological Series*, IX, 2 (May 1905). Publication 103, Field Columbian Museum, Chicago.

DORSEY, J. O. "Omaha Sociology," *Annual Report of the Bureau of American Ethnology*, III (1881–1882). Washington, 1884.

———. "Games of Teton Dakota Children," *American Anthropologist*, IV, 4 (1891).

———. "A Study of Siouan Cults," *Annual Report of the Bureau of American Ethnology*, XI (1889–1890). Washington, 1894.

DORSEY, J. O., AND CYRUS THOMAS. "Mandan," Bureau of American Ethnology, Bulletin 30, Part 1. 2 vols. Washington, 1907.

FLETCHER, ALICE C. "A Study of Omaha Indian Music," *Papers of the Peabody Museum of American Archaeology and Ethnology*, I, 5 (June 1893). Cambridge: Harvard University, The Museum, 1893. Reprinted in J. O. Dorsey, "A Study of Siouan Cults," *Annual Report of the Bureau of American Ethnology*, XI (1889–1890). Washington, 1894.

———. "Arikara," Bureau of American Ethnology, Bulletin 30, Part 1. 2 vols. Washington, 1907.

FLETCHER, ALICE C., AND FRANCIS LAFLESCHE. "The Omaha Tribe," *Annual Report of the Bureau of American Ethnology*, XXVII (1905–1906). Washington, 1911.

GAMIO, MANUEL. *La Población del Valle de Teotihuacán*. Secretario de Agricultura y Fomenta, La Dirección de Antropología, Tomo I, Volumenes I y II. México, 1922.

GARLAND, HAMLIN. "General Custer's Last Fight as Seen by Two Moon," *McClure's Magazine*, II (September 1898), 443–448.

GODFREY, EDWARD S. "Custer's Last Battle," *Century Magazine*, XLIII, 3 (January 1892), 358–384.

GRINNELL, GEORGE BIRD. "Lodges of the Blackfeet," *American Anthropologist*, III (NS), 4 (1901), 650–668.

HALL, COLONEL HENRY. "Reminiscences." In *The Teepee Book*. Sheridan, Wyo.: Mills Co., 1926. Official Publication, Fiftieth Anniversary, Custer Battle, National Custer Memorial Association. Reprinted from *The Teepee Book*, II, 6 (June 1916), published by Herbert Coffeen of Sheridan, Wyoming.

HARTLEY, MARSDEN. "Red Man Ceremonials," *Art and Archaeology*, IX, 1 (January 1920), 7–14.

HOFFMAN, W. J. "The Mide-wiwin or 'Grand Medicine Society' of the Ojibway," *Annual Report of the Bureau of American Ethnology*, VII (1885–1886), 143–300. Washington, 1891.

———. "Pictography and Shamanistic Rites of the Ojibway," *American Anthropologist*, I–II (1888–1889), 209–229.

———. "The Memominee Indians," *Annual Report of the Bureau of American Ethnology*, XIV (1892–1893), 11–315. Washington, 1896.

———. "Graphic Art of the Eskimos," *Report of the United States National Museum, 1895*, pp. 739–968.

HOUSER, NELL GREEN. "Rare Pictograph in Resources Museum," *Missouri*, August 1929, p. 8.

KROEBER, A. L. "Decorative Symbolism of the Arapaho," *American Anthropologist*, III (NS), 3 (1901), 308–336.

LOEB, E. M. "The Blood Sacrifice Complex," *Memoirs of the American Anthropological Association*, No. 30. Menasha, Wis.: Collegiate Press, George Banta Publishing Co., 1923.

LOWIE, ROBERT H. "Dance Associations of the Eastern Dakota," *Anthropological Papers of the American Museum of Natural History*, XI, Part 2 (1913).

———. "Societies of the Crow, Hidatsa, and Mandan Indians," *Anthropological Papers of the American Museum of Natural History*, XI, Part 3 (1913).

———. "Crow Indian Art," *Anthropological Papers of the American Museum of Natural History*, XXI, Part 4 (1922).

LYND, JAMES W. "Religion of the Dakotas," *Collections of the Historical Society of Minnesota*, II, 2 (1865), 78–79.

MALLERY, GARRICK. "A Calendar of the Dakota Nation," United States Geological and Geographical Survey, Bulletin III, No. 1 (April 1877). Washington, 1877.

———. "The Sign Language Among North American Indians," *Annual Report of the Bureau of American Ethnology*, I (1879–1880), 263–552. Washington, 1880.

———. "Pictographs of the North American Indians: A Preliminary Paper," *Annual Report of the Bureau of American Ethnology*, IV (1882–1883), 3–256. Washington, 1886.

———. "Picture-Writing of the American Indians," *Annual Report of the Bureau of American Ethnology*, X (1888–1889), 25–776. Washington, 1893.

MEEKER, LOUIS L. "Ogalala Games," *Bulletin of the Free Museum of Science and Art*, III (1901). Philadelphia: University of Pennsylvania, 1901.

MOONEY, JAMES. "The Ghost Dance Religion and the Sioux Outbreak of 1890," *Annual Report of the Bureau of American Ethnology*, XIV (1892–1893), Part 2, 653–1111. Washington, 1896.

———. "A Calendar History of the Kiowa Indians," *Annual Report of the Bureau of American Ethnology*, XVII (1895–1896), Part 1, 129–445. Washington, 1898.

———. "The Cheyenne Indians," *Memoirs of the American Anthropological Association*, I, Part 6 (1907).

———. "Heraldry," Bureau of American Ethnology, Bulletin 30, Part 1. 2 vols. Washington, 1907.

MORLEY, SYLVANUS G. "Inscriptions at Copan," Publication 219, Carnegie Institution. Washington, 1920.

ORCHARD, WILLIAM C. "Porcupine Quill Ornamentation," *Indian Notes*, III, 2 (April 1926), 59–68. New York: Museum of the American Indian, Heye Foundation, 1926.

PARSONS, ELSIE CLEWS. "A Pueblo Indian Journal," *Memoirs of the American Anthropological Association*, No. 32. Menasha, Wis.: Collegiate Press, George Banta Publishing Co., 1925.

POND, G. H. "Dakota Superstitions," *Collections of the Historical Society of Minnesota*, II, 3 (1867), 46–49.

RICE, JOHN A. "Additional Notes on the Pictured Cave," *Wisconsin Historical Collections*, VIII (1877–1879), 183–187.

RIGGS, THOMAS L. "A Buffalo Hunt," *South Dakota Historical Collections*, V (OS) (1880–1881), 95–97.

ROBINSON, DOANE. "A History of the Dakota or Sioux Indians," *South Dakota Historical Collections*, II, 2 (1904), 1–523.

SCOTT, HUGH LENOX. "Early History and Names of the Arapaho," *American Anthropologist*, IX (NS), 3 (1907).

SKINNER, A. B. "War Customs of the Menomini Indians," *American Anthropologist*, XIII (NS), 2 (1911).

———. "The Medicine Ceremony of the Menomini, Iowa, and Wahpeton Dakota," *Indian Notes and Monographs*, IV (1920). New York: Museum of the American Indian, Heye Foundation, 1920.

SMITH, HARLAN I. "Archaeology of the Gulf of George and Puget Sound," *Memoirs of the American Museum of Natural History*, IV, 6 (1907), 303–441. Reprint from Vol. II, Part 6, *Jesup North Pacific Expedition*. Leiden: E. J. Brill, Ltd., 1907. New York: G. E. Stechert and Co., 1907.

———. "An Album of Prehistoric Canadian Art," *Anthropological Series*, No. 8 (June 1923). Bulletin 37, Victoria Memorial Museum. Ottawa: Canada Department of Mines, F. A. Acland, 1923.

SMITH, MAURICE GREER. "Political Organization of the Plains Indians, with Special Reference to the Council," *University of Nebraska Studies*, XXIV, 1–2 (January–April 1924).

SPIER, LESLIE. "Sun Dance of the Plains Indians: Its Development and Diffusion," *Anthropological Papers of the American Museum of Natural History*, XVI, Part 7 (1921), 451–548.

SPINDEN, H. T. "Petroglyphs and Pictographs of the Nez Percé," *Memoirs of the American Anthropological Association*, II (1907–1915), Part 3 (1908), 231–233. Lancaster, Pa., 1908.

STRONG, W. D., AND W. E. SCHENCK. "Petroglyphs near the Dalles of the Columbia River," *American Anthropologist*, XXVII (NS), 1 (January–March 1925), 76–90.

STRONG, W. D., W. E. SCHENCK, AND J. H. STEWARD. "Archaeology of the Dalles-Deschutes Region," *University of California Publications in American Archaeology and Ethnology*, XXIX, 1 (1930), 1–154. Berkeley: University of California Press, 1930.

The Teepee Book, Sheridan, Wyo.: Mills Co., 1926. Official Publication, Fiftieth Anniversary, Custer Battle, National Custer Memorial Association. Reprinted from *The Teepee Book*, II, 6 (June 1916), published by Herbert Coffeen of Sheridan, Wyoming.

TEIT, JAMES. "A Rock Painting of the Thompson River Indians, British Columbia," *Bulletin of the American Museum of Natural History*, VIII, 12 (1896), 227–230.

———. "The Lillooet Indians," *Memoirs of the American Museum of Natural History*, IV, 5 (1906), 193–300. Reprint from Vol. II, Part 5, *Jesup North Pacific Expedition*. Leiden: E. J. Brill, Ltd., 1906. New York: G. E. Stechert and Co., 1906.

TOZZER, ALFRED MARSTON. "Animal Figures in the Maya Codices," *Papers of the Peabody Museum of American Archaeology and Ethnology*, IV, 3 (1910). Cambridge: Harvard University, The Museum, 1910.

WALKER, J. R. "Sioux Games. I," *Journal of American Folk-Lore*, XVIII, 61 (1905), 277–290.

———. "Sioux Games. II," *Journal of American Folk-Lore*, XIX, 75 (1906), 29–36.

———. "The Sun Dance and Other Ceremonies of the Oglala Division of the Teton Dakota," *Anthropological Papers of the American Museum of Natural History*, XVI, Part 2 (1917).

WARREN, W. W. "A Memoir of W. W. Warren: A History of the Ojibway," *Collections of the Minnesota State Historical Society*, V (1885).

WILDSCHUT, WILLIAM. "A Crow Pictographic Robe," *Indian Notes*, III, 1 (January 1926), 28–32. New York: Museum of the American Indian, Heye Foundation, 1926.

———. "A Cheyenne Medicine Blanket," *Indian Notes*, III, 1 (January 1926), 33–36. New York: Museum of the American Indian, Heye Foundation, 1926.

WISSLER, CLARK. "The Whirlwind and the Elk in the Mythology of the Dakota," *Journal of American Folk-Lore*, XVIII, 71 (October–December 1905).

———. "Some Protective Designs of the Dakota," *Anthropological Papers of the American Museum of Natural History*, I, Part 2 (1907).

———. "North American Indians of the Plains," Handbook Series No. 1, American Museum of Natural History. New York, 1912.

———. "Societies and Ceremonial Associations in the Oglala Division of the Teton Dakota," *Anthropological Papers of the American Museum of Natural History*, XI, Part 1 (1912).

———. "Societies and Dance Associations of the Blackfoot Indians," *Anthropological Papers of the American Museum of Natural History*, XI, Part 4 (1913).

———. "Riding Gear of the North American Indians," *Anthropological Papers of the American Museum of Natural History*, XVII, Part 1 (1915).

———. "Costumes of the Plains Indians," *Anthropological Papers of the American Museum of Natural History*, XVII, Part 2 (1915).

———. "A General Discussion of Shamanistic and Dancing Societies," *Anthropological Papers of the American Museum of Natural History*, XI, Part 12 (1916).

———. "Structural Basis of the Decoration of Costumes Among the Plains Indians," *Anthropological Papers of the American Museum of Natural History*, XVII, Part 3 (1916).

———. "Indian Beadwork," Guide Leaflet No. 50, American Museum of Natural History. New York, 1922.

———, ED. "Plains Indian Societies," *Anthropological Papers of the American Museum of Natural History*, XI (1916).

———. "Sun Dance of the Plains Indians," *Anthropological Papers of the American Museum of Natural History*, XVI (1921).

Appendix

and

A Note on the Editing

APPENDIX

Descriptive Listing of the Drawings

FOR the sake of convenience, the drawings in this volume have been renumbered consecutively. Both Helen Blish's and the new numbers are given below. Miss Blish explains her original numbering system as follows:

> In order to have a consistent and complete paging for use in critical study of the manuscript, I have adopted a system that entirely disregards the numbering of those pages of the book which bore numbers, which makes possible a ready and definite reference to any page of any size in the book. A single number with *a* and *b* index has been used for left and right pages which face each other. The first drawing in the book is on the left (the inside cover of the book) and is marked *1a*; the page opposite is *1b*, etc. This makes it possible to indicate small insert pages without confusion or too great complexity of pagination, for I simply indicate

these by a numerical addition to the preceding *a* page with which the insert is in contact. Thus, following No. 1a, there are two small insert sheets bearing script; these are numbered *1a-1*, *1a-2* (blank), *1a-3*, and *1a-4* (blank). According to this plan, small inserts are always connected with *a* pages and bear *a* numbers; further, by means of this numbering, one can always tell by a glance at the number which pages are small inserts—a point which is frequently of real assistance.

The information about the colors and techniques used in the drawings was not included in Miss Blish's manuscript but was taken from her color notes, which she compiled in the course of her work on the pictographic history. Wherever it has been possible to determine, from the data given in Chapter VI, the exact sizes of the drawings in the ledger book, they are listed below.

NUMBER	ORIGINAL NUMBER	SIZE	COLORS
1	1a		Black and red ink; gray wash from diluted ink; red and brown (both light) crayon; four colors.
2	1a-1		Black ink.
3	1a-3		Black ink.
4	1b		Black and red ink; gray wash with slight purple cast, in buffalo skin (gray from diluted ink; purple touches from indelible pencil); four colors.
5	2a-b		Black and gray (ink); brown crayon; yellow crayon here and there; one spot of blue crayon; five colors.
6	3a		Black ink; brown water-color paint wash (one horse); indelible pencil; blue paint (water color); brown, red, yellow (all light) crayon; seven colors.
7	3b		Black and red ink; brown, red, blue, green, yellow, purple crayon; seven colors.
8	4a		Black and red ink; brown water color; yellow and blue crayon; indelible pencil; six colors.
9	4b		Black ink; red crayon (in banner); light touch of green and brown crayon (in dance shade and top of pole); four colors.
10	5a-1		Gray lead pencil (outlines and heads); blue, red, green, purple, orange crayon; seven colors.
11	5a-2		Black and red ink; blue water color; orange crayon; gray lead pencil; five colors.
12	5b		Black and red ink; red, yellow, green, purple, blue crayon; six colors.
13	6a		Black and red ink; gray lead pencil; red, yellow, green, blue, brown (light) crayon; seven colors.

NUMBER	ORIGINAL NUMBER	SIZE	COLORS
14	6b		Black and red ink; green, black, red, blue, yellow crayon; five colors.
15	7b		Black ink; green, red, blue, purple, yellow, brown crayon; seven colors.
16	8a		Black and red ink; blue crayon; touch of yellow crayon in black crayon of buffalo hump; purple of indelible pencil here and there; five colors.
17	8b		Black and red ink; gray (diluted ink); red, yellow, brown, blue, green crayon; seven colors.
18	9a		Black ink; gray (diluted ink); two colors.
19	9b		Black ink; gray of diluted ink; black with gray of lead pencil; one touch of purple (indelible pencil); one touch of light yellow crayon; small touch of red crayon; gray of lead pencil dominant; five colors.
20	10a		Black and red ink; gray of ink and lead pencil; three colors.
21	10b		Black ink; gray of diluted ink; red (light), blue, brown crayon; five colors.
22	11a		Black ink; red, yellow, purple, blue, brown crayon; six colors.
23	11b		Black ink; gray of diluted ink; red, blue, yellow, green, black crayon; touch of purple crayon; seven colors.
24	12a		Not given.
25	12b		Not given.
26	13a		Black and red ink; red, yellow, blue, brown crayon; touch of green from overlapping yellow and blue crayon; six colors.
27	13a-1		Black ink; gray lead pencil; two colors.
28	13a-2		Black ink; gray lead pencil (dominant); light red crayon (in bag); light yellow crayon (in streamers); four colors.
29	13b		Black and red ink; gray of diluted ink; red, blue, brown, yellow, orange crayon; touch of purple (from crayon and indelible pencil) in tipi; eight colors.
30	14a		Black and red ink; red, yellow, blue crayon; gray of diluted ink and lead pencil; purple (very little) of indelible pencil; six colors.
31	14b		Black and red ink; red, yellow, blue, brown, green crayon; gray of diluted ink; seven colors.
32	15a		Black ink and crayon; red ink and crayon; blue, brown, green, purple, yellow crayon; seven colors.
33	15b		Chiefly black and gray; black ink; gray of diluted ink; purple (pale) of indelible pencil; brown crayon; two or three touches of yellow crayon; five colors.
34	16a		Chiefly black and dark gray; black ink; dark gray of diluted ink; brown crayon; three colors.
35	16a-2		Black ink; dark blue-gray of diluted ink; blue, brown, red crayon; five colors.
36	16b		Chiefly blue-gray; black ink; dark blue-gray of diluted ink; a few light lines of brown crayon; three colors.
37	17a		Black ink; dark blue-gray of diluted ink; black, blue, orange, red, yellow crayon; six colors.
38	17a-1		Black ink; dark blue-gray of diluted ink; touch of red ink; blue, orange, purple, red, yellow crayon; seven colors.
39	17a-2		Black ink; dark blue-gray of diluted ink; blue, brown, orange, red, yellow crayon; six colors.
40	17b		Not given.
41	18a		Chiefly black outlines (miniature figures); black ink; faint brown of crayon; one note in red ink; three colors.
42	18a-1		Chiefly black and brown; black ink; dark blue-gray of diluted ink; red and brown crayon; touches of blue, green, and yellow crayon; light gray of lead pencil in one horse; seven colors.
43	18b		Chiefly outline picture; black ink; dark blue-gray of diluted ink; brown, purple, red crayon; touch of yellow crayon; six colors.
44	19a		Black ink; dark blue-gray of diluted ink; black, brown, green, orange, purple (light), red, yellow crayon; touch of blue crayon; eight colors.
45	19b		Miniature picture chiefly in black and gray ink outline; brown crayon for blocking in some horses; three colors.

NUMBER	ORIGINAL NUMBER	SIZE	COLORS
46	20a		Similar to preceding picture but with a touch of yellow crayon added; four colors.
47	20a-1		Black ink; dark blue-gray of diluted ink; orange crayon; a bit of red crayon; one short note in red ink; four colors.
48	20a-2		Black ink; dark blue-gray of diluted ink; black crayon; bits of brown, red, yellow crayon; five colors.
49	22a		Black ink; dark blue-gray of diluted ink; bright blue water color; bits of blue, brown, red, yellow crayon; touch of red ink; six colors.
50	22a-1		Chiefly ink outline picture; black ink; bit of gray of lead pencil; touches of purple, red, yellow crayon; five colors.
51	22a-2		Chiefly ink outline picture; black ink; bit of gray of lead pencil; bits of blue, red, yellow crayon; five colors.
52	22a-3		Miniature picture chiefly in black and gray ink outline; some horses blocked in in brown crayon; suggestion of purple-gray of light indelible-pencil marks in miniature tipi portrayal; three colors.
53	22a-4		Black and red ink; dark blue-gray of diluted ink; brown crayon; touches of yellow crayon and purple of indelible pencil; six colors.
54	22a-5		Black ink; dark blue-gray of diluted ink; blue, brown, yellow-orange, red crayon; touch of purple of indelible pencil; seven colors.
55	22a-6		Black and red ink; dark blue-gray of diluted ink; green crayon; touches of blue, red, yellow crayon and one of purple of indelible pencil; seven colors.
56	22b		Black and red ink; touches of red and yellow crayon and of purple of indelible ink; four colors.
57	23b	7 × 12	Black and red ink; dark blue-gray of diluted ink; black, brown, green, purple crayon; almost infinitesimal touch of yellow crayon; seven colors.
58	24a	7 × 12	Black and red ink; dark blue-gray of diluted ink and also some gray-brown of another diluted ink; blue, green, purple, red (so light as to be pink), yellow crayon; eight colors.
59	24b	7 × 12	Black, brown, and red ink; a bit of blue-gray of diluted ink; brown, green, purple, and a bit of red crayon; some purple of indelible pencil; six colors.
60	25a	7 × 12	Chiefly an outline picture in gray and black; black ink (diluted to dark gray in many instances); a bit of green and red crayon; spots of purple indelible pencil; five colors.
61	26a		Black and red ink; blue-gray of diluted ink in a few strokes; brown crayon; four colors.
62	26b	7 × 12	Black and brown ink; gray of lead pencil in a few bits of outline; blue-gray of diluted ink in a few spots; brown, purple, red crayon, with a few spots of blue and yellow; seven colors.
63	27a	7 × 12	Chiefly outline picture in black and dark gray ink; red ink; spots of brown, purple, red crayon; five colors.
64	27b		Again chiefly outline; black and gray of ink, and gray of lead pencil in one instance; black and red crayon; three colors.
65	28a		Again chiefly outline; black and red ink; gray of diluted ink; three colors.
66	28b	7 × 12	Again chiefly outline but almost entirely the dark blue-gray of diluted ink; bit of red ink; very small, light touches of brown, purple, and yellow crayon (the last hardly discernible); five colors.
67	29a	7 × 12	Similar picture, chiefly outline, in black and gray ink; touch of red ink; a few spots of red and purple crayon; four colors.
68	29b		Black ink; blue, brown, green, orange, and spots of red and yellow crayon; purple of indelible pencil; all dull; eight colors.
69	30a		Black ink and touch of red; dark blue-gray of diluted ink; brown, blue, green, purple, and bits of red and yellow crayon; some purple of indelible pencil.
70	30b	7 × 12	Almost entirely outline picture in black and gray ink; dark blue-gray of diluted ink; bits of red ink; small spots of brown, red, yellow crayon.
71	31a	7 × 12	Again chiefly outline—in black and brown ink; dark blue-gray of diluted ink;

NUMBER	ORIGINAL NUMBER	SIZE	COLORS
			very small spot of red ink; small spots of blue, brown, red, yellow crayon; spotting with purple of indelible pencil; color very unobtrusive in this picture; seven colors.
72	31b		Quite in character with No. 71 but without blue crayon and brown ink; six colors.
73	32a		Of same character as two preceding pictures; black and dark gray ink with spotting of red ink; touch of brown and yellow crayon; color purely for spotting; five colors.
74	32b		See No. 73; five colors.
75	33a		Exactly like No. 74 in coloring except for small spots of red crayon added; five colors.
76	33b	7 × 12	Much more prominent color; black, brown, red, and purple (probably from dissolved filling of indelible pencil) ink; very dark blue-gray of diluted black ink; green, red, yellow crayon, with only a small touch of purple; brown, almost entirely that of ink, used to outline and as a wash to block in horses' bodies; seven colors.
77	34a	7 × 12	Color again prominent; black, brown, and purple ink, with very small spots of red; dark blue-gray of diluted ink; blue, brown, green, purple, red crayon, with small spots of yellow; light purple of indelible pencil; eight colors.
78	34b	7 × 12	Similar to No. 77 but without green and with red ink used only as a wash so pale as to be really a pink; seven colors.
79	35a-2 and 35a-3		Chiefly outline in black and gray ink; small spots of purple, red, and yellow crayon and red ink; color hardly noticeable; just a few tipi outlines and terrain indications in dark gray ink in top half of picture; five colors.
80	35a-4 and 35b		Black and red ink; dark blue-gray of diluted ink; a few very small spots of red and purple crayon; touches of brownish-yellow water color; lower half of picture is like upper half of No. 79; five colors.
81	36a	7 × 12	Black and a bit of red ink; dark blue-gray of diluted ink; black and orange crayon, with spot of red and one of yellow; yellow water color; dark gray of lead-pencil marks in a few lines and a Lakota note; dull; five colors.
82	37b	7 × 12	Brown ink prominent in outlining and in spotting picture with emphasized forelocks and tails of horses; almost no outlining in black ink; a bit of spotting with red ink; some purple and very light blue crayon—and one small touch each of red and yellow; one spot of gray of lead pencil; brown, purple, and red only are obtrusive; rather an exceptional picture (as the record goes) in the prominent spotting of tails and forelocks; seven colors.
83	38a	7 × 12	Black ink; a bit of gray of diluted ink; most prominent color is the dark purple of dissolved indelible "lead"; brown wash of diluted ink; spots of blue, brown, green, red, yellow crayon; a bit of the light purple of indelible pencil; gray of lead pencil; eight colors.
84	38b	7 × 12	More colors obtrusive here; black, brown, red ink—brown most plentiful; dark blue-gray of diluted ink; green, purple, and red (usually pink) crayon, with spots of blue; yellow water color; some small spots of purple of indelible pencil; considerable gray of lead pencil; eight colors.
85	39b	7 × 12	Considerable color but all pale except the black; black ink; blue, green, purple, red, yellow crayon; small spots of purple of indelible pencil; gray of lead pencil in tipi outlines and in several faces; seven colors.
86	40a	7 × 12	Yellow and red prominent; some lines and spots in black and red ink; brownish-gray of diluted ink (used as a wash to block in two figures); red, black, yellow crayon, with a small spot each of blue and yellow; red, apparently water color; gray of lead pencil in some outlining and in Lakota note; five colors.
87	40b	7 × 12	Similar to No. 86, but most ink wash lacks brownish cast; a bit of deep purple (dissolved indelible "lead") is added; brown crayon also used; a very little bit of brown ink outlining also added; seven colors.
88	41a	7 × 12	Almost entirely outline in black ink; spots of yellow, brown, red crayon, with barely discernible touch of blue.

APPENDIX

NUMBER	ORIGINAL NUMBER	SIZE	COLORS
89	41a-1		Almost entirely soft colors (smudge effect) in crayon; black ink and some gray of lead pencil and light purple of indelible pencil in outlines; blue, brown, green (always touched with yellow), orange, red crayon—all pale; softer tone effect than in most of the compositions; eight colors.
90	41b	7 × 12	Black and brown ink; blue, brown, green, purple, red, yellow crayon; dark purple of dissolved indelible "lead"; gray of lead pencil; eight colors.
91	42a	7 × 12	Pencil sketch; gray of lead pencil; brown crayon; two colors.
92	42b	7 × 12	Black and brown ink; gray of lead pencil; a few lines in light purple of indelible pencil; blue, brown, green, red crayon; smudge of yellow wash, apparently water color; all colors light and very unobtrusive—in keeping with scouting scene portrayed; eight colors.
93	43a	7 × 12	Black ink; gray of lead pencil; bright red, rose-brown, and yellow-brown of water color; less crayon coloring—blue, brown, green, light red, yellow; eight colors.
94	43b	7 × 12	Black and brown ink; gray of lead pencil; a purple spot of dissolved indelible "lead"; blue, brown, green, red, yellow crayon, all rather light; eight colors.
95	44a	7 × 12	Chiefly outline picture; black ink; green and red crayon, with touch of brown; apparently a touch of red ink wash with red crayon; four colors.
96	44b	7 × 12	Similar to No. 96 but with more color; outlining chiefly in brown ink, with a bit in black; similar combination of red crayon and red ink; blue, brown, green, purple, yellow crayon; seven colors.
97	45b	7 × 12	Two preceding pictures continued; similar color use but with two spots of dark purple of dissolved indelible "lead"; seven colors.
98	46a	7 × 12	Chiefly outline; medium miniature; black ink; gray pencil; spots of blue, green, red, yellow crayon.
99	46a-1		Black ink; gray of lead pencil; light purple of indelible pencil; red and yellow crayon; five colors.
100	46a-2 and 46a-3		Medium miniature outline sketch; red and black ink; dark blue-gray of diluted ink; pale purple of indelible pencil in some outlining; spots of blue crayon; color unobtrusive; five colors.
101	46a-4		Medium miniature outline sketch; red and black ink; dark gray of diluted ink; a bit of light purple of indelible pencil; blue and brown crayon; color very unobtrusive; six colors.
102	46b	7 × 12	Black and red ink; dark blue-gray of diluted ink; bright blue water color; blue-green wash, apparently water color; small, light spots of blue, brown, purple, yellow crayon; colors dull and confused except bright blue water color and a few spots of red ink.
103	47a	7 × 12	Very small miniature sketch, wholly outline; black and red ink; light purple line of indelible pencil; touch of brown crayon; color very unobtrusive; four colors.
104	47a-1	6¼ × 7¼	Black and red ink; light red crayon and touch of pale yellow; light purple of indelible pencil lines; spotting of red ink prominent; four colors.
105	47a-2	6¼ × 7¼	Black ink; dark blue-gray of diluted ink; gray of lead pencil; red crayon, with one small spot of yellow; four colors.
106	47a-3	6¼ × 7¼	Same as No. 105; four colors.
107	47a-4	6¼ × 7¼	Black ink and spot of red; dark blue-gray of diluted ink; gray of lead pencil; red crayon, with spot of yellow; four colors.
108	47a-5	6¼ × 7¼	Black ink; dark blue-gray of diluted ink; gray of lead pencil; red crayon; three colors.
109	47a-7	6¼ × 7¼	Black ink and small spots of red; dark blue-gray of diluted ink; red crayon, with one spot of yellow; four colors.
110	47a-8 and 47a-9	7¼ × 12½	Black ink, with small spots of red; blue-gray of diluted ink; gray of lead pencil; purple and red crayon; four colors.
111	47a-10	6¼ × 7¼	Black ink; blue-gray of diluted ink; red and yellow crayon; crayon red the only prominent color in Nos. 105 to 111.

NUMBER	ORIGINAL NUMBER	SIZE	COLORS
112	47b		Black ink; much dark blue-gray of diluted ink; blue and red crayon (both light); subdued colors; four colors.
113	48a		Dark gray of ink and lead pencil in outlines; light blue crayon, with one small spot of red and a few light lines of brown; some light purple of indelible pencil; all colors very pale; five colors.
114	48a-1		Black ink; gray of lead pencil; blue and red crayon; four colors.
115	48b	7 × 12	Black, brown, and red ink; gray of lead pencil; blue, green, and red crayon, with small spot of yellow; spots of deep purple of dissolved indelible "lead"; color prominent.
116	49a	7 × 12	Black and red ink; gray of diluted black ink; blue and yellow crayon; a few lines in light purple of indelible pencil; strong color contrast; six colors.
117	49b	7 × 12	Black, brown, and red ink; blue and yellow crayon; spots of dark purple of dissolved indelible "lead"; strong color contrast; six colors.
118	50a	7 × 12	Black ink; medium gray of diluted black ink; gray of lead pencil; dull red wash, apparently water color, perhaps a mixture of brown and red ink; touches of light blue, brown, and yellow crayon; six colors.
119	50b	7 × 12	Black, brown, and red ink; dark and light blue-gray of diluted ink; purple and yellow crayon, with small spots of blue; color prominent; seven colors.
120	51a	7 × 12	Black ink, with touches of red; dark gray of diluted ink; dull red wash again, water color or mixture of red and brown ink; blue, green, yellow crayon; spotting of dark purple of dissolved indelible "lead"; color prominent; seven colors.
121	51b	7 × 12	Black and brown ink and pink wash of thinned red ink; dark blue-gray of diluted black ink; blue crayon, with small spots of yellow and orange; lines of deep purple of dissolved indelible "lead"; rather sharp color contrast; eight colors.
122	52a	7 × 12	Black and red ink; gray of diluted black ink; a touch of gray of lead pencil; a bit of the dark red wash; yellow crayon and touch of green; six colors.
123	52b	7 × 12	Black, brown, and thinned wash of red ink; dark blue-gray of diluted ink; blue, blue-green, yellow crayon, with spot of red; touches of very light purple of indelible pencil; color prominent; eight colors.
124	53a	7 × 12	Black ink; dark gray of diluted black ink; dull red wash again, water color or mixture of brown and red ink; spots of blue, brown, yellow-green crayon; dark purple spotting with dissolved indelible "lead"; a few lines of gray of lead pencil; seven colors.
125	53b	7 × 12	Black and brown ink, with light wash of thinned red ink; gray of diluted black ink; blue, blue-green, and yellow crayon; lines of dark purple of dissolved indelible "lead"; gray of lead pencil lines; a few light purple lines of indelible pencil; color prominent; eight colors.
126	54a	7 × 12	Black and brown ink, with spots of red; blue and green crayon, with touch of red; light purple of indelible pencil.
127	54a-2		Black ink.
128	54b	7 × 12	Black, brown, and red ink; black used as outline in some cases, and all three inks used as washes in blocking in figures; blue, brown, red (dots only), yellow crayon; gray of lead pencil; six colors.
129	55b	7 × 12	Miniature (very small) topographical sketch, entirely in single-line outline except for smudges of green crayon to mark line of creek; black and red ink; gray of lead pencil; four colors.
130	56a	7 × 12	Black and brown ink, with small spots of red; dark gray and light brown washes from diluted black and brown inks; blue, brown, green, red, yellow crayon; gray of lead pencil; dull colors; six colors.
131	56b		Black ink, with small spots of red and with brown ink used as a wash in combination with brown crayon; light blue-gray of diluted black ink; brown and green crayon, with spots of blue and yellow; brown, green, and gray dominant; dull coloring except for green; seven colors.
132	57a-b		Black ink; light blue-gray of diluted ink; black, blue, brown, red, yellow crayon; black and brown dominant; coloring dull; six colors.

NUMBER	ORIGINAL NUMBER	SIZE	COLORS
133	58a		Same as No. 132; six colors.
134	58b		Same as No. 132 but with spots of orange and purple crayon and gray of lead pencil; eight colors.
135	59a		Black ink and small spot of red; light blue-gray of diluted ink; black, blue, brown, orange, purple, red, yellow crayon; red dominant; eight colors.
136	59b		Black ink and small spot of red; black, blue, brown, green, orange, purple, red, yellow crayon; deep purple of dissolved indelible "lead"; subdued colors except for purple spotting; seven colors.
137	60a		Black and brown ink, with tiny spots of red; dull red of water color or mixture of brown and red ink; brownish-gray water color (?); gray of lead pencil here and there; spots of blue, brown, and yellow crayon; dull red dominant; six colors.
138	60b		Black and brown ink, with small spots of red; dull red of water color or combined inks; dark blue-gray of diluted ink; dun-gray water color; blue, brown, yellow crayon; a drab picture; six colors.
139	61a		Black and brown ink; a few short lines in red; the same dull-red horses; brownish-gray of diluted ink; blue and brown crayon, with a few spots of yellow and purple; dull red dominant; six colors.
140	61b	7 × 12	Black and brown ink, with small spots of red; brownish-gray of diluted ink; dun-gray water color; blue, brown, red crayon; spots of dark purple of dissolved indelible "lead"; drab in tone; six colors.
141	62a	7 × 12	Black ink and small spots of red; dark gray (intended for black?) of water color (?); blue, brown, green, red, purple crayon; seven colors.
142	62b	7 × 12	Black and brown ink, with spot of red; dark gray wash of water color (?); gray of lead pencil; blue, brown, red, yellow crayon, with touch of green; dark purple of dissolved indelible "lead"; eight colors.
143	63a	7 × 12	Similar to No. 142 but without purple; seven colors.
144	63b	7 × 12	Similar to No. 142 but with *light* purple of indelible pencil; eight colors.
145	64a	7 × 12	Black ink, with touch of red; blue-gray of diluted ink; blue, brown, green, red (very pale), yellow crayon; gray of lead pencil; touch of light purple of indelible pencil; eight colors.
146	64b	7 × 12	Similar to No. 145 but with a bit of brown ink.
147	65a	7 × 12	Black and brown ink, with small spots of red; dark blue-gray of diluted ink; gray wash of water color; blue, brown, green, red crayon, with spots of purple and yellow; gray of lead pencil; seven colors.
148	65b	7 × 12	Black, brown, and red ink; gray of lead pencil; blue, brown, green, red crayon; color more prominent here; six colors.
149	66a	7 × 12	Black and red ink; blue-gray of water color or diluted ink; blue, brown, purple, red crayon, with a heavy line of green; drab in tone except red ink to portray spilled blood; seven colors.
150	66b	7 × 12	Black and brown ink and a spot of red; blue-gray of diluted ink; blue, brown, green, red, yellow crayon; seven colors.
151	67a	7 × 12	Black and red ink, the red in some cases used as a wash; gray of water color; brown, purple, red crayon, with spotting of blue and line of green; some lines in lavender of indelible pencil; more colorful again; eight colors.
152	67b	7 × 12	Similar to No. 151 but with brown ink also and without indelible pencil; eight colors.
153	68a	7 × 12	Black ink and touch of red; gray of diluted ink; blue water color; brown crayon, with spots of blue, green, red, and yellow; seven colors.
154	68b	7 × 12	Black and brown ink; gray of diluted ink; gray of lead pencil; blue, brown, red, yellow crayon, with line of green; dark purple of indelible pencil; eight colors.
155	69a	7 × 12	Black and red ink; gray of diluted ink; blue, brown, red crayon, with line of green and spots of purple and yellow; eight colors.
156	69b	7 × 12	Black and brown ink, with spots of red; gray of diluted ink; gray of lead pencil; blue, brown, green, red crayon, with spots of yellow; seven colors.
157	70a	7 × 12	Black ink; gray of diluted ink; blue, brown, green, red, yellow crayon (all light); a touch of the light purple of indelible pencil; a drab picture; eight colors.

NUMBER	ORIGINAL NUMBER	SIZE	COLORS
158	70b	7 × 12	Similar to No. 157 but with gray of lead pencil and a touch of red ink; eight colors.
159	71a	7 × 12	Black ink and a bit of red; gray of diluted ink; blue, brown, green, red, yellow crayon; a bit of light purple of indelible pencil; colors not prominent; eight colors.
160	71b		Black ink, with touch of red; gray of diluted ink; black, orange, yellow crayon and a bit of blue and brown; one spot of blue water color (?); one spot of purple of indelible pencil; six colors.
161	72a		Ink dominant; colors, but not prominent; seven colors.
162	73b	7 × 12	Ink dominant; crayon and lead pencil prominent also; pale coloring—not prominent; six colors.
163	74a-b	12 × 14	Ink and crayon dominant; colors not prominent; six colors.
164	75a	7 × 12	Chiefly ink and crayon; seven colors.
165	75b	7 × 12	Chiefly ink and crayon; six colors.
166	76a	7 × 12	Black ink and crayon colors; eight colors.
167	76b	7 × 12	Ink and crayon; colors pale; five colors.
168	77a	7 × 12	Colors not prominent; seven colors.
169	79b	7 × 12	Eight colors.
170	80a-b	12 × 14	Semitopographical; ink, crayon, pencil; seven colors.
171	81a	7 × 12	Miniature panoramic; chiefly indelible pencil; considerable crayon; a bit each of lead pencil and black ink outlining; color adds to total effect; six colors.
172	81a-1		Same as No. 171; six colors.
173	81a-2		Same as two preceding pictures; six colors.
174	81b		Like preceding pictures; six colors.
175	82a-82a-1		Like preceding pictures; six colors.
176	82a-2-82b		Similar to five preceding pictures in execution but only black, brown, gray, and purple here; somber; four colors.
177	83a-b	12 × 14	Very sketchy topographical miniature, apparently discarded; almost entirely pencil.
178	84a	7 × 12	Chiefly black ink, sometimes diluted to gray; five colors.
179	84b		Almost entirely ink, chiefly gray of diluted ink; five colors.
180	85a		Almost entirely gray of diluted ink; five colors.
181	86b		Miniature; almost entirely black ink for heavy outlining, sometimes diluted to gray; four colors.
182	87a		Like No. 181; four colors.
183	87b	7 × 12	Chiefly black ink and lead pencil; five colors.
184	88a-b	12 × 14	Chiefly black ink and crayon color; eight colors.
185	89b	7 × 12	Ink and crayon; seven colors.
186	90a	7 × 12	Chiefly crayon; red dominant; five colors.
187	90b	7 × 12	Black ink and crayon coloring prominent; color prominent and *significant*; seven colors.
188	91a	7 × 12	Crayon coloring dominant; color significant; six colors.
189	91b	7 × 12	Black ink for outline and blocking; lead-pencil outline; ink and pencil dominant; five colors.
190	92a	7 × 12	Black ink and crayon color dominant; colors significant—red, black, yellow; four colors.
191	92b		Water color dominant; colors chiefly pale but prominent; five colors.
192	93a		Chiefly black ink; two colors.
193	93a-1		Black ink.
194	93a-2 and 93a-3		Black ink.
195	93a-4		Black ink.
196	93b		Crayon and lead pencil dominant; almost entirely black and gray; four colors.
197	94a-b		Miniature topographical; almost entirely black ink, occasionally diluted to gray; a little crayon coloring; six colors.

NUMBER	ORIGINAL NUMBER	SIZE	COLORS
198	95a–95a-1		Semisymbolic topographical; chiefly black ink and indelible pencil; some crayon; black and purple dominant; five colors.
199	95b	7 × 12	Ink and crayon; eight colors.
200	96a	7 × 12	Black ink dominant; bits of crayon color; six colors.
201	96b	7 × 12	Black ink dominant; considerable crayon coloring; eight colors.
202	97a	7 × 12	Black ink and red water color dominant; four colors.
203	97b	7 × 12	Black ink dominant; crayon coloring; some lead-pencil outlining and blocking; eight colors.
204	98a	7 × 12	Ink and water color dominant (black and red); five colors.
205	98b	7 × 12	Black ink dominant; crayon coloring; seven colors.
206	99a	7 × 12	Gray-brown of diluted ink prominent; bits of crayon and indelible and lead pencil; four colors.
207	99b	7 × 12	Black ink (sometimes diluted to gray), red ink, and water color; color significant; five colors.
208	100a	7 × 12	Black ink dominant; some crayon color; chiefly outline; color not particularly significant; four colors.
209	100b	7 × 12	Ink and pencil outlines dominant; some coloring in crayon; color not significant; seven colors.
210	101a	7 × 12	Black ink and pencil outlines; ink and crayon coloring; gray and red dominant; colors important; six colors.
211	101b	7 × 12	Chiefly outline; black ink dominant; some color in crayon and indelible pencil (dissolved "lead"); color not especially important; five colors.
212	102a	7 × 12	Chiefly outline in black ink; some red and orange crayon coloring; color not significant; three colors.
213	102b	7 × 12	Black and red ink; chiefly crayon coloring; five colors.
214	103a	7 × 12	Black and red ink and indelible pencil dominant; some lead-pencil outlining; colors subdued but significant; five colors.
215	103b	7 × 12	Lead-pencil outlining dominant; color chiefly crayon and dissolved indelible "lead"; six colors.
216	104a	7 × 12	Black ink and blue crayon dominant; colors subdued but important; six colors.
217	104b	7 × 12	Black ink outlining; crayon coloring; five colors.
218	105a	7 × 12	Topographical; lead- and indelible-pencil outlines dominant; green crayon lines; green only significant color; five colors.
219	105b	7 × 12	Black ink, sometimes diluted to gray, dominant; bits of crayon coloring; color not especially important; seven colors.
220	106a	7 × 12	Black ink and crayon coloring dominant; chief colors are black and brown; seven colors.
221	106a-1		Black ink dominant; crayon coloring, chiefly blue, brown, and yellow; six colors.
222	106a-2		Chiefly outline in black ink; bits of color in crayon; six colors.
223	106a-3		Black ink (outlining and blocking) and crayon coloring (brown, blue, green) dominant; seven colors.
224	106b	7 × 12	Black ink prominent in outlining and blocking; coloring in crayon; seven colors.
225	107a	7 × 12	Black ink for outlining and blocking; crayon coloring; six colors.
266	107b		Black ink in outlining and a bit of blocking, and diluted to gray for considerable blocking; coloring chiefly in crayon, with orange dominant; eight colors.
227	108a		Similar to No. 226 in technique but red dominant in crayon coloring; eight colors.
228	108b	7 × 12	Black ink dominant for outlining and blocking; coloring chiefly in crayon, with blue prominent; five colors.
229	109a	7 × 12	Black ink for outlining and blocking (diluted to gray for considerable blocking) and a touch of red; coloring in crayon; seven colors.
230	109b		Similar to No. 229; seven colors.
231	110a-1		Almost entirely black ink, diluted to gray for blocking; touches of red and yellow crayon; four colors.
232	110a-2		Like No. 231 but without yellow; three colors.

NUMBER	ORIGINAL NUMBER	SIZE	COLORS
233	110b	7 × 12	Black ink dominant in outlining and blocking; crayon coloring; touch of gray of lead pencil; colorful; seven colors.
234	111a	7 × 12	Like No. 233 but with touch of green; colorful; eight colors.
235	111b		Black ink, chiefly diluted to gray in blocking; crayon coloring, with brown and blue dominant; dull; six colors.
236	112a		Black ink, diluted to gray for most blocking; red and brown crayon coloring; dull; four colors.
237	112b		Miniature; chiefly outline; black of ink, gray of lead pencil, and purple of dry indelible pencil; three colors.
238	113a-b		*Lower half*: black ink, chiefly diluted to gray in blocking; crayon coloring, with touch of gray of lead pencil; five colors. *Upper half*: black ink, in some cases diluted to gray; black and brown crayon, with touch of red; four colors.
239	116a		Chiefly black ink—outline and blocking; gray of lead pencil; touches of crayon coloring; five colors.
240	116a-1		Notation and very sketchy beginning of panoramic miniature; black ink (diluted to gray in some cases) and a bit of lead pencil; black and white.
241	116a-2		Almost entirely outlining in black ink; touch of red crayon; two colors.
242	116a-3		Black ink, diluted to gray in most blocking; gray of lead pencil; some crayon coloring; six colors.
243	116a-4		Black ink (chiefly diluted to gray in blocking) and some red; mere touches of crayon coloring; five colors.
244	116b		Black ink, occasionally diluted to gray, and some red; black and brown crayon, with touches of yellow and blue; six colors.
245	117a		Miniature panorama, chiefly in outline; black ink; lead pencil; indelible pencil; three colors.
246	119a	7 × 12	Black ink, diluted to gray in all blocking; spots of red; coloring almost entirely in crayon, with brown dominant; six colors.
247	119b	7 × 12	Black ink, diluted to gray in nearly all blocking; some red; coloring chiefly in crayon; seven colors.
248	120a	7 × 12	Black ink, sometimes diluted to gray in blocking; bit of red; coloring in crayon; eight colors.
249	120b	7¼ × 12½	Black ink, diluted to gray in some cases of blocking; coloring in crayon, chiefly brown; eight colors.
250	121a	7¼ × 12½	Black ink (usually diluted to gray in blocking) and bits of red; coloring in crayon; seven colors.
251	121b		Chiefly outline; black ink, diluted to gray for most blocking; one case of blocking in brown ink; touches of crayon color; five colors.
252	122a		Black ink, usually diluted to gray in blocking, and touches of red; coloring in crayon; eight colors.
253	122a-1		Black ink and a bit of red; crayon coloring; five colors.
254	122b	7 × 12	Black ink, usually diluted to gray in blocking; crayon coloring in red and brown, with touch of pale yellow; five colors.
255	123a	7 × 12	Chiefly in inks and dissolved indelible pencil; some crayon coloring; experimenting in either ink washes or water color; rather messy; nine colors.
256	123b		Black and brown ink, both sometimes diluted; chiefly crayon coloring; five colors.
257	124a		More experimenting in water color or mixed ink; crayon coloring also; eight colors.
258	124b	7 × 12	Black ink and some brown and red; color chiefly in crayon; seven colors.
259	125a	7 × 12	Black ink (some diluted to gray) and some brown and red; color chiefly in crayon; eight colors.
260	125b		Black ink, sometimes diluted to gray, and some brown and red; chiefly crayon coloring; seven colors.
261	126a		Black and brown ink; both sometimes diluted; chiefly crayon coloring; six colors.
262	126a-1		Black ink, frequently diluted to gray, and a bit of red; coloring chiefly in crayon; a bit of purple indelible pencil; six colors.

NUMBER	ORIGINAL NUMBER	SIZE	COLORS
263	126a-2		Similar to No. 262 in technique but without indelible pencil; six colors.
264	126b	7 × 12	Black ink and touch of red; crayon coloring; six colors.
265	127a	7 × 12	Black ink, diluted to gray for most blocking; a bit of red; crayon coloring; eight colors.
266	127b		Black ink, with much gray in blocking; crayon coloring; dull; six colors.
267	128a		Similar to No. 266 but with much more crayon coloring and considerable red ink; nine colors.
268	128b	7 × 12	Black ink, with some red and brown; considerable crayon coloring; some lead pencil and touch of indelible; eight colors.
269	129a	7 × 12	Black ink, chiefly diluted to gray in blocking, and touch of red; coloring almost entirely in crayon; seven colors.
270	129a-1		Black ink (diluted in some cases to gray) and touch of red; crayon coloring; seven colors.
271	129a-2		Black ink; considerable blocking in gray; crayon coloring; bit of lead pencil; eight colors.
272	129b		Black ink, in most cases diluted to gray for blocking; considerable outlining in indelible pencil and a bit in lead pencil; otherwise coloring in crayon; rather dull; five colors.
273	130a		Black ink, diluted to gray in blocking, and a touch of red; crayon coloring; some outlining in indelible pencil; rather dull; six colors.
274	130b	7 × 12	Black ink, usually diluted to gray for blocking; bit of red ink; some indelible pencil; chiefly crayon coloring; eight colors.
275	131a	7 × 12	Same technique as No. 274 but less color; six colors.
276	132a		Black ink, chiefly diluted to gray in blocking, and some red; a little crayon coloring; dull; five colors.
277	132b		Miniature panorama; outlining in black ink; some blocking in diluted gray; brown crayon, with touches of red and yellow; five colors.
278	133a-b		*Lower half:* diluted black ink and touch of red; chiefly crayon coloring; color not important; five colors. *Upper half:* black ink, in some cases diluted to gray in blocking; crayon coloring; six colors.
279	135a		Black ink (diluted to gray in almost all cases) and a bit of red; crayon coloring, chiefly brown; dull; seven colors.
280	135b	7 × 12	Black and brown ink; crayon coloring; more colorful than No. 279; six colors.
281	136a	7 × 12	Black ink, diluted to gray in several instances, and red; crayon coloring; a bit of lead pencil; eight colors.
282	136b		Black and brown ink and a touch of red; crayon coloring; six colors.
283	137a		Brown ink and black diluted to gray, and a bit of red; a little crayon coloring, chiefly brown; chiefly outline in effect; dull; six colors.
284	137a-1		Miniature panorama in black and white; black ink, often diluted to gray.
285	138b		Outline sketch; black ink; small spots of crayon coloring; four colors.
286	139b		Black ink; lead pencil; crayon; dull in color but effective; four colors.
287	140a		Black ink, mainly diluted to gray, and a touch of red; brown crayon and a bit of yellow; brown and gray dominant; five colors.
288	140b		Black and white panoramic miniature; outline drawing; black ink, often diluted to gray.
289	141a		Miniature in black ink outline (sometimes diluted to gray); note in red ink; some crayon coloring; a bit of lead pencil; effective; eight colors.
290	142b		Black ink and touch of red; crayon coloring, chiefly brown; four colors.
291	143a		Black ink, some diluted to gray; a bit of crayon coloring; five colors.
292	143b		Like No. 291; five colors.
293	144a		Like preceding two pictures.
294	145a		Black ink; crayon coloring; lead pencil; six colors.
295	145b		Black ink; some crayon coloring (pale); lead pencil; dull; five colors.
296	146b		Black ink; crayon coloring; lead pencil; dull; six colors.
297	149a-b		Panoramic miniature; black ink, often diluted to gray, and some brown; crayon coloring; a bit of indelible pencil; six colors.

NUMBER	ORIGINAL NUMBER	SIZE	COLORS
298	150b		Black ink, sometimes diluted to gray; crayon coloring; touch of lead pencil; six colors.
299	152a		Black ink and some brown and red; crayon coloring; four colors.
300	152b		Black ink; crayon; lead pencil; four colors.
301	153a-b		Panoramic miniature; some outlining in black ink, much in indelible pencil; crayon coloring; very effective; six colors.
302	154a-b		Black ink, chiefly diluted to gray, and red; crayon coloring; some outlining in indelible and lead pencil; seven colors.
303	155a		Black ink, often diluted to gray, and red; a touch of green crayon; lead pencil and some indelible; five colors.
304	156a-b		Black and brown ink and touch of red; a bit of crayon coloring; some lead and indelible pencil; five colors.
305	157a		Black ink, chiefly diluted to gray, and red; brown crayon; lead pencil; four colors.
306	157b		Panoramic miniature; black ink, sometimes diluted to gray; purple crayon spotting; three colors.
307	158a		Like No. 306 in style and technique but with considerable brown crayon added and a touch of red also; four colors.
308	158b		Black ink, largely diluted to gray; brown crayon, with touches of purple, red, and yellow; six colors.
309	159a		Black ink, sometimes diluted to gray; crayon coloring; six colors.
310	160a-b		*Lower half*: outline sketch in black ink; touch of purple and red crayon; three colors. *Upper half*: black ink, chiefly diluted to gray; some crayon coloring; four colors.
311	162a		Black ink; some crayon coloring, chiefly brown; a spot of blue water color; lead pencil; five colors.
312	163a		Lead pencil; crayon coloring; four colors.
313	163a-1		Black (chiefly diluted to gray) and brown ink and a touch of red; four colors.
314	163b	7 × 12	A little black ink; lead and indelible pencil; some crayon coloring; pale coloring; six colors.
315	164a	7 × 12	Black ink, sometimes diluted to gray; a bit of crayon coloring in blue, brown, purple, red, and yellow; color inconspicuous; seven colors.
316	164b		Black ink, often diluted to gray, and indelible pencil; black and white effect; three colors.
317	165a-b		Sketchy miniature panorama in black ink (often gray) and indelible pencil; black and white effect; three colors.
318	166a-b		Black ink outlining; lead pencil; crayon coloring, chiefly black and red; four colors.
319	167a	7 × 12	Black and red ink; lead pencil; crayon coloring; five colors.
320	167b		Black ink; a bit of indelible and lead pencil; crayon coloring; seven colors.
321	168a-b		Chiefly outline; black ink, diluted to gray for most blocking; some lead pencil; some crayon coloring; six colors.
322	169a-b		Like No. 321; six colors.
323	170a	7 × 12	Black (sometimes diluted to gray) and brown ink, with one small spot of red; crayon coloring; five colors.
324	170b		Black and brown ink; red and brown crayon; three colors.
325	171a		Lead and indelible pencil; some blue and black crayon; color insignificant; four colors.
326	172a	7 × 12	Black (often diluted to gray) and red ink; touches of crayon coloring; eight colors.
327	172b	7 × 12	Red ink; lead pencil; a bit of crayon coloring; four colors.
328	173a	7 × 12	Chiefly outline; black ink; short lines of crayon coloring; four colors.
329	173b	7 × 12	Black (sometimes diluted to gray) and red ink; a bit of crayon coloring; seven colors.
330	174a	7 × 12	Black, green, and red ink; indelible pencil; a very little bit of crayon coloring; seven colors.
331	174b	7 × 12	Black (sometimes diluted to gray) and red ink; some crayon coloring; eight colors.

NUMBER	ORIGINAL NUMBER	SIZE	COLORS
332	175a	7 × 12	Black and brown ink; lead pencil; some crayon coloring, particularly red; four colors.
333	175b	7 × 12	Black (frequently diluted to gray) and red ink; some crayon coloring; seven colors.
334	176a	7 × 12	Some black ink in outlining and bits of red; more lead-pencil outlining and some blocking; some coloring in what appears to be water color; crayon coloring; very colorful; six colors.
335	176b	7 × 12	Black (sometimes diluted), brown, and red ink; green ink or water color wash; bits of crayon coloring; seven colors.
336	177a	7 × 12	Much indelible pencil in outlining and blocking; a bit of lead pencil; some crayon coloring; touch of brown ink; eight colors.
337	177b	7 × 12	Black (often diluted), brown, red, and green ink; small bits of crayon coloring; eight colors.
338	178a	7 × 12	A bit of outlining in black ink; much lead pencil; some crayon (brown and black); three colors.
339	178b	7 × 12	Black (sometimes diluted), brown, and red ink; crayon coloring; bit of indelible pencil; eight colors.
340	179a	7 × 12	A little outlining in black ink; some blocking in diluted gray and also brown ink; some spots of red and green ink; considerable indelible pencil; five colors.
341	179b	7 × 12	Black and brown ink and a touch of red; some crayon coloring; a bit of lead pencil; eight colors.
342	180a	7 × 12	Black ink for some outlining; lead pencil; bits of crayon coloring; what appears to be red water color; five colors.
343	180b	7 × 12	Black ink; some lead-pencil outlining; crayon coloring; seven colors.
344	181a	7 × 12	Black (sometimes diluted to gray), brown, green, and red ink; lead pencil; crayon coloring; six colors.
345	181b	7 × 12	Black ink; lead pencil; crayon coloring; seven colors.
346	182a	7 × 12	Black ink, sometimes diluted; a red and a green blocking that may be "muddied" ink or perhaps water color; a bit of crayon coloring; pleasing tones; six colors.
347	182b	7 × 12	Black ink; lead pencil; some indelible pencil (dissolved); crayon coloring; effectively colorful; eight colors.
348	183a	7 × 12	Very similar to No. 346 but with some yellow water color added and purple indelible-pencil touch lacking; six colors.
349	183b	7 × 12	Black ink, sometimes diluted to gray; some lead-pencil outlining; crayon coloring; eight colors.
350	184a	7 × 12	Black ink, frequently diluted; some lead pencil; what appears to be definitely water color in green, red, and yellow; a touch of crayon; six colors.
351	184b	7 × 12	Black ink (outlining and prominent spotting); some lead-pencil outlining; touches of indelible pencil; coloring almost entirely crayon; eight colors.
352	185a	7 × 12	Black ink (diluted to gray) and brown ink; lead pencil; some water color; a fine bit of blue crayon; five colors.
353	185b	7 × 12	Black ink; lead pencil; touch of indelible pencil (sometimes dissolved); coloring chiefly crayon; eight colors.
354	186a	7 × 12	Black (frequently gray), brown, and red ink; red-brown water-color wash; crayon coloring; seven colors.
355	187a	7 × 12	A bit of black ink and some brown; blue and yellow-orange water color; lead pencil; a bit of crayon coloring; seven colors.
356	187b	7 × 12	Black ink; considerable lead pencil; crayon coloring; very effective color contrast; eight colors.
357	188a	7 × 12	Chiefly black ink and lead pencil; a bit of brown, blue, and purple crayon; five colors.
358	188b	7 × 12	Black ink and lead pencil for outlining and blocking; crayon coloring; six colors.
359	189a	7 × 12	Chiefly lead pencil; a bit of indelible pencil (dissolved); some crayon coloring; color not important; six colors.
360	189b	7 × 12	Effect almost that of black and white; a miniature, done chiefly with lead pencil—for outlining and blocking; spots of crayon color used lightly; four colors.

NUMBER	ORIGINAL NUMBER	SIZE	COLORS
361	190a	7 × 12	Black ink (for outlining and blocking), and red; some lead pencil; a bit of indelible pencil; some crayon coloring; eight colors.
362	190b	7 × 12	Almost entirely lead pencil—for outlining and blocking; a bit of black ink for outlining; some green and brown crayon coloring; four colors.
363	191a	7 × 12	Black ink (sometimes diluted to gray), and red; red water color; lead pencil; crayon coloring; six colors.
364	191b	7 × 12	Lead pencil and green crayon; three colors.
365	192b	7 × 12	Panoramic miniature; chiefly in black ink; a bit of lead pencil; occasional light crayon blocking in brown; black and white effect; three colors.
366	193a	7 × 12	Black ink; lead pencil; brown crayon; three colors.
367	193b	7 × 12	Black ink; crayon coloring; six colors.
368	194a	7 × 12	Black and red ink; crayon coloring; one small touch of blue water color; six colors.
369	194b	7 × 12	Black ink, usually diluted to gray; brown ink or water color; red and brown crayon; four colors.
370	195a	7 × 12	Black ink, sometimes diluted in blocking; blue water color; blue, green, red, and yellow crayon; color relatively unimportant; eight colors.
371	195b	7 × 12	Black ink—prominent in effective color contrast; lead pencil; crayon coloring; color very effective; seven colors.
372	196a	7 × 12	Black ink; lead pencil; crayon coloring; five colors.
373	196b	7 × 12	Again, very effective spotting in black ink; a bit of indelible and lead pencil; some crayon coloring; eight colors.
374	197a	7 × 12	Black ink; lead pencil; a bit of water color; a bit of crayon coloring; four colors.
375	197b	7 × 12	Almost entirely lead-pencil outlining; slight touches of crayon coloring; four colors.
376	198a	7 × 12	Black ink; some lead pencil; considerable indelible pencil; some crayon coloring; five colors.
377	198b	7 × 12	Black ink and brown (?); a bit of lead pencil; crayon coloring; a touch of purple ink; eight colors.
378	199a	7 × 12	Black (sometimes diluted to gray), and brown; a bit of lead pencil; crayon coloring; dull in coloring; seven colors.
379	199b	7 × 12	Black and brown ink; a bit of lead and indelible pencil; crayon coloring; eight colors.
380	200a	7 × 12	Black ink, diluted in nearly all cases; a bit of lead and indelible pencil; some crayon coloring; seven colors.
381	200b	7 × 12	Black ink; crayon coloring; color contrast very effective; six colors.
382	201a	7 × 12	Black ink, usually diluted, and a touch of red; some lead pencil and a bit of indelible (dissolved); crayon coloring; seven colors.
383	201b	7 × 12	Black ink; a bit of lead pencil; crayon coloring; nine colors.
384	202a	7 × 12	Black ink, almost entirely diluted; crayon coloring; dull; seven colors.
385	202b	7 × 12	Black ink and a touch of purple; a bit of lead pencil; crayon coloring; effective use of color contrast; eight colors.
386	203a	7 × 12	Like No. 384; seven colors.
387	203b	7 × 12	Like No. 385; eight colors.
388	204a	7 × 12	Like No. 384; seven colors.
389	204b	7 × 12	Like No. 385; eight colors.
390	205a	7 × 12	Black ink, often diluted to gray, and a touch of red; lead pencil and some indelible (dissolved); crayon coloring; eight colors.
391	205b	7 × 12	Black ink; a touch of indelible pencil; crayon coloring; seven colors.
392	206a	7 × 12	Black ink (sometimes diluted) and a touch of red; touch of blue water color; crayon coloring; seven colors.
393	206b	7 × 12	Black ink and a bit of purple; crayon coloring; seven colors.
394	207a	7 × 12	Black ink, usually diluted; some indelible pencil (dissolved); crayon coloring; eight colors.
395	207b	7 × 12	Black ink, some diluted; crayon coloring; six colors.

NUMBER	ORIGINAL NUMBER	SIZE	COLORS
396	208a	7 × 12	Black and brown ink and a touch of red; some crayon coloring; considerable water color; seven colors.
397	208b	7 × 12	Black ink; crayon coloring; green water color; seven colors.
398	209a	7 × 12	Black ink, chiefly diluted; crayon coloring; bit of lead pencil and of indelible (dissolved); eight colors.
399	209b	7 × 12	Black ink and small spot of purple; crayon coloring; eight colors.
400	210a	7 × 12	Black ink, sometimes diluted, and a touch of red; lead pencil; crayon coloring; seven colors.
401	210b	7 × 12	Black ink; a bit of lead pencil; crayon coloring; eight colors.
402	211a	7 × 12	Black ink, usually diluted, and a bit of red; some lead pencil; crayon coloring; eight colors.
403	211b	7 × 12	Black ink and a touch of purple; crayon coloring; eight colors.
404	212a	7 × 12	Black ink, usually diluted, and a touch of red; lead pencil; crayon coloring; seven colors.
405	212b	7 × 12	Black ink; a bit of lead-pencil outlining; crayon coloring; eight colors.
406	213a	7 × 12	Black ink, sometimes diluted, and a bit of red; a bit of lead and indelible pencil (some of the latter dissolved); crayon coloring; eight colors.
407	213b	7 × 12	Black ink (sometimes diluted to gray), and a touch of red; a touch of indelible pencil (dissolved); crayon coloring; effective color contrast; eight colors.
408	214a-b	12 × 14	Black ink and a touch of purple; a bit of lead pencil, also of indelible (dissolved); crayon coloring; eight colors.
409	215a	7 × 12	Like No. 408 but without purple ink; eight colors.
410	215b	7 × 12	Like No. 408; eight colors.
411	216a	7 × 12	Black ink, usually diluted to gray; some lead pencil and a bit of indelible; crayon coloring; eight colors.
412	216b		Black and brown ink; brown and red crayon; three colors.
413	217a-b		Panoramic miniature; chiefly black ink, often diluted to gray; a bit of lead pencil; a little brown and blue crayon; four colors.
414	218a-b		Black ink, usually diluted to gray; extensive muddy gray-brown smear (water color or diluted ink?); lead pencil; some crayon coloring; five colors.
415	Inside of Back Cover		Black ink.

A Note on the Editing

THE primary goal in the editing of Helen Blish's manuscript has been to present the author's material as nearly as possible in its original form. Copy editing has been minimal, restricted to correction of obvious typographical errors and regularization of spelling, capitalization, and punctuation. In no instances have alterations been made which could change the author's meaning. The few editorial explanations that have been made in the text (for example, in the descriptions to drawings No. 77 and 171) are bracketed and designated *ed. note.*

We have followed Miss Blish's spelling of words taken from the Oglala dialect. However, the artist's name, which Miss Blish translates "Bad Heart Buffalo," has been changed herein to "Bad Heart Bull," to conform with the translation carried on government rolls, and because that is the name by which the family is commonly known. The name "Short Buffalo" has likewise been changed to "Short Bull."

A straightforward consecutive numbering system for the drawings has been substituted for Miss Blish's original numbering system, which is explained in the Appendix (p. 513); the pictures and their descriptions are presented in the same sequence as in her manuscript. In a very few instances, for the convenience of readers of this book, direction indications (right, left, top, bottom) in the picture descriptions have been clarified.

Because none of the people who were closely associated with Miss Blish's work on the Bad Heart Bull manuscript—the artist's sister, Dollie Pretty Cloud; Miss Blish's informants, Short Bull and He Dog; her faculty advisor, Professor Hartley Burr Alexander; and Mari Sandoz—are still living, we have been unable to resolve certain inconsistencies in matters of fact. For example, while in Chapter III the author says that the *Ite Sica* (Bad Faces) and the *Canku Ran* (Sore Backs) were two separate Oglala bands, she indicates elsewhere, in her descriptions to drawings No. 305 and 326, that they were the same band. Likewise, in the descriptions of the series of drawings depicting the battle in which Yellow Robe was killed (Nos. 33–35), there is a contradiction concerning the year in which the Crow warrior died. And in Chapter I the year of Bad Heart Bull's birth is given as 1869, whereas in the description to drawing No. 101 we are told that the artist was born in 1867. In the absence of an authority familiar with the Bad Heart Bull pictographic history and Helen Blish's work, and because of the virtual impossibility of verifying events of which there is no reliable written record, we have not attempted to reconcile such inconsistencies, but have inserted a bracketed *sic* where we realize they exist.

The résumé in Chapter VI of the make-up of the artist's drawing book presents a special problem. Although there are apparently some discrepancies in Miss Blish's figures for the number of original ledger and insert pages in the book, a check is not possible, since the ledger book is no longer extant. But where Miss Blish says (p. 73) that 240 of the original ledger pages are available for drawings, a count of the pages listed, minus those that are mentioned as missing, gives a total of 238. Moreover, she says that page 205/206 is missing entirely, but the page number *206* can be clearly seen in drawing No. 323; however, this might perhaps be an insert page from another ledger, although it falls in the sequence of original ledger pages. The author indicates (p. 73) that there are 246 insert pages, but enumerates only 230; possibly this was not intended as a complete listing, but was meant only to show the various *kinds* of inserts. Likewise, the enumeration of minute panoramic drawings on p. 76 lists only 26 of 30 battle scenes in that style; here again, perhaps this is meant as a representative rather than an exhaustive listing. A count of the drawings in the first series depicting the Battle of the Little Big Horn yields 44 rather than 46 (p. 78), and we find 68 rather than 72 drawings of "Greater Indian Shows" (p. 79). The answer may lie in the fact that Miss Blish may have counted certain two-part, double-page drawings as two separate drawings rather than one, as we have counted them;

this explanation would also account for the fact that she gives the total number of drawings in the book as 417 (418, including the inside of the back cover), whereas we have only 415, including the inside back cover. Miss Blish's figures have been allowed to stand throughout; the important consideration—the drawings themselves and her descriptions of them—remains unchanged.